Robotic Vision and Virtual Interfacings

Robotic Vision and Virtual Interfacings

Seeing, Sensing, Shaping

Edited by Luci Eldridge and Nina Trivedi

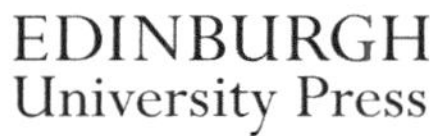

EDINBURGH
University Press

Edinburgh University Press is one of the leading university presses in the UK. We publish academic books and journals in our selected subject areas across the humanities and social sciences, combining cutting-edge scholarship with high editorial and production values to produce academic works of lasting importance. For more information visit our website: edinburghuniversitypress.com

Cover image: Kate Fahey, *I could feel that my eyes were open...* installed at ZK/U, 2019. Courtesy of the artist
Cover design: Stuart Dalziel

Edinburgh University Press Ltd
13 Infirmary Street,
Edinburgh, EH1 1LT

Typeset in Constantia and Avenir Next
by R. J. Footring Ltd, Derby, UK, and
printed and bound in Poland

A CIP record for this book is available from the British Library

ISBN 978 1 3995 2342 4 (hardback)
ISBN 978-1-3995-2343-1 (paperback)
ISBN 978 1 3995 2344 8 (webready PDF)
ISBN 978 1 3995 2345 5 (epub)

EU Authorised Representative:
Easy Access System Europe
Mustamäe tee 50, 10621 Tallinn, Estonia
gpsr.requests@easproject.com

Contents

Shaping

Figures

Contributors

Brian Black
Brian Black is an American designer focused on brand and strategic design for Volvo Cars in Gothenburg, Sweden. His early experiences working as part of a human-centric design team made up of NASA architects and designers at TAXA Outdoors thoroughly shaped his views on design, and the power of shaping products through a true understanding of customer needs and desires. After returning to academia to pursue a masters in Vehicle Design in 2015, Brian focused his efforts on implementing human-centric design processes at Geely Design in Sweden, bringing together UX, interior design and brand to produce products which are more holistic and humanistic for the Lynk & Co. and Zeekr brands. Brian now works at the intersection between brand, strategy and design for Volvo Cars. He conducts and synthesises qualitative research into actionable strategies and design properties for teams, and formulates early-phase product direction for Volvo's future vehicle portfolio.

Ian Dawson
Ian Dawson is an artist, sculptor, lecturer and researcher. He is co-director of the Critical Practices Research Group and Co-Convener of the Materials Lab at Winchester School of Art, University of Southampton. From a background in sculpture Ian works at the intersection between 3D printing and new imaging technologies. He often works as part of a transdisciplinary collaborative team to develop new ways of exploring how material and immaterial practices can be part of knowledge transfer processes. He co-edited *Diffracting Digital Images: Archaeology, Art Practice and Cultural Heritage* (Routledge, 2021), which explores the ontology of digital images and the differing practices that diffraction brings to light.

Luci Eldridge
Luci Eldridge is an artist, writer and Lecturer in Fine Art at Winchester School of Art, University of Southampton, where she specialises in printmaking, critical image theory and cross-disciplinary practice. Her personal practice and research are concerned with the scientific visioning of landscape as seen from satellites or through the cameras

on spacecraft and rovers on other worlds. Her work combines tradi-tional printmaking techniques, lens-based media and collage, with fictional visualisations constructed in 3D software, 3D printing, and projection. She is co-director of Robot Futures, a research group exploring the practices and implications of robotic seeing and sensing. Luci has a PhD in Critical and Historical Studies and an MA in Printmaking, both from the Royal College of Art.

Stephen R. Ellis

Stephen R. Ellis retired from NASA in 2016. He briefly worked in the Oculus division of Facebook (now Meta) on VR–user interface design but quit when it became obvious that the performance of the eye-tracking-enhanced interface could allow the system to know more about its users than they knew about themselves. He has become interested in how the extension of new user interface technology may be ethically controlled and continues to be professionally active, serving on PhD committees, publishing research and occasionally lecturing internationally. The complexity of the design of the VR–user interface has led to his further interest in the nature and management of complexity itself.

Kate Fahey

Kate Fahey is an artist and researcher working with print, sculpture, moving image, sound, text and installation. Her research concerns embodied feminist methodologies and draws on feminist science and technology studies, new materialism and post-humanism. She has exhibited her work widely at institutions, including the ICA, London, the Bluecoat, Liverpool, Arti et Amicitiae, Amsterdam, and VISUAL, Carlow. In 2020 she completed a practice-based PhD at the University of the Arts London with the support of an AHRC Techne studentship. She is a lecturer in Fine Art at Oxford Brookes University and Falmouth University.

Adham Faramawy

Adham Faramawy is an artist based in London. Their work spans media including moving image, sculptural installation and print, thinking through issues of materiality, touch and toxic embodiment to question ideas of the natural in relation to marginalised communities. They lecture at both Goldsmiths University, London, and Ruskin School of Art, Oxford. In 2018 they presented a show on the body and VR for BBC Radio 4, in 2019 they premiered their video piece 'Skin Flick' at a screening at Tate Britain dedicated to their work. They were shortlisted for the Jarman Award in both 2017 and

2021. Their work has been exhibited in solo shows at the Bluecoat, Liverpool, Niru Ratnam Gallery, London, and in group shows at Whitechapel Gallery, Somerset House and Serpentine Gallery. In 2022 they performed their first live work as part of the Serpentine Ecologies programme 'Back to Earth' and screened their work at Tate Modern, London, and Guggenheim, New York.

Joey Holder
Joey Holder is a visual artist, producer and mentor. She has exhibited widely in the UK and internationally, including at the Harvard Museum of Natural History, Athens Biennale, Design Museum, Moscow Biennale, Transmediale and Venice Biennale. Her artwork is fuelled by continued dialogue and collaborations with researchers and practitioners from varied fields, creating fictional worlds and constructed environments that respond directly to contemporary, real-world events. Each artwork is considered a 'set', with filmic, narrative, architectural, visuals and sound elements created uniquely for the conceptual underpinning of the project. Joey has worked with computational geneticists, marine biologists, behavioural psychologists and investigative journalists where the artwork has addressed themes including future farming, synthetic biology and deep-sea ecosystems.

Pearl John
Pearl John is a visiting arts researcher in the Modern Holography research group at De Montfort University, Leicester, where she obtained a doctorate in 2018, and the Public Engagement Leader in Physics and Astronomy at the University of Southampton. Pearl is a practising artist working with holography and lenticular images, seeking to humanise technology; she has an art studio/lab in the Physics and Astronomy department at Southampton, where she makes her holograms. She has an interest in multidisciplinary approaches and research topics and has designed an undergraduate teaching module in Art and Physics soon to be launched at Southampton. She is also a keen drone pilot.

Esther Leslie
Esther Leslie is Professor of Political Aesthetics at Birkbeck, University of London. Her interests lie in the poetics of science and imbrications of politics and technologies, with a particular focus on the work of Walter Benjamin and Theodor Adorno, as well as the poetics of science, European literary and visual modernism and avant gardes, animation and colour. Current work focuses on turbid media

and the aesthetics of turbulence. Her books include various studies and translations of Walter Benjamin, as well as *Hollywood Flatlands: Animation, Critical Theory and the Avant Garde* (Verso, 2002); *Synthetic Worlds: Nature, Art and the Chemical Industry* (Reaktion, 2005); *Derelicts: Thought Worms from the Wreckage* (Unkant, 2014); *Liquid Crystals: The Science and Art of a Fluid Form* (Reaktion, 2016); *Deeper in the Pyramid* (with Melanie Jackson) (Banner Repeater, 2018) and (with Jackson) *The Inextinguishable* (Limerick, 2021).

Gregory Minissale

Gregory Minissale is Professor of Art History, specialising in global modern and contemporary art and critical theory, at the University of Auckland. His research interests are in the psychology of art, mental health, multicultural phenomenologies and queer theory. His books *Rhythm in Art, Psychology and New Materialism* (2021) and *The Psychology of Contemporary Art* (2013, paperback, 2015) are both published by Cambridge University Press.

maya rae oppenheimer

maya rae oppenheimer (PhD) is the founder and co-director of OK Stamp Press. She is also a daughter, sister, aunt and plant-mother of Icelandic and Canary Islander descent who receives joy and financial remuneration as an arts writer/researcher/educator. She was born in Treaty 1 territory and spent over a decade living in London, UK. maya is now an uninvited guest on Kanien'kehá:ka territory, where she preoccupies herself with writing as a social practice and the tangles of narratives that inform our worldviews. Experimental writing, performance, radical pedagogy, open-access publishing, DIY tactics and rogue archival gestures make up her tool kit. maya joined the Faculty of Fine Arts at Concordia University in September 2017 as Assistant Professor in Art History and is now active in the Department of Studio Arts.

Nicola Plant

Nicola Plant is an artist, researcher and lecturer with an academic and artistic practice that spans embodiment, technology and movement-based interactive art. Nicola creates digital interactive artworks, installations and performances, specialising in real-time graphics and movement-based interactivity using motion capture, sensors and depth cameras. Notably her practice develops interactive virtual reality artworks that explore expressive movement and empathy. Her practice more broadly addresses the question of how technology can augment or deconstruct the experience of embodiment. Her work has been exhibited at venues such as the Barbican Centre, the V&A Museum and internationally. She has a PhD in Media and Arts Technology from Queen Mary University of London and her research to date has involved embodied communication, developing machine learning for movement design in virtual reality, and immersive technologies for dance practice. She also lectures in creative computing and machine learning, immersive technologies and interaction design.

Meg Rahaim

Meg Rahaim is an artist and researcher concerned with the ethical implications of digital, networked ubiquity. Her writing uses a critical, speculative approach to interrogate everyday digital image platforms, anchoring artistic invention in shared, contemporary, visual vernacular. In studio practice, she performs a human-scale, digital materiality, translating screen-based ephemera into tangible prints, drawings and textile artworks. Both strands of her creative research are challenged and enriched by comparative exploration of scientific epistemologies. She has been artist in residence at the Wellcome Centre for Human Genetics, Oxford, and conducted textile workshops for understanding genetic inheritance with King's College researchers at Science Gallery London. She is Tutor in Print at the Royal College of Art, London.

Paul Reilly

Paul Reilly has published widely in the field of digital archaeology, particularly in the area of visualisation, virtual archaeology and art/archaeology. He is currently a Senior Visiting Research Fellow in the Faculty of Humanities at the University of Southampton. He is also a practising freelance field archaeologist. Formerly, he worked and consulted extensively in the IT and communications industry as a Global Knowledge Broker at IBM. His primary research interests today revolve around the philosophical and social impacts of digital technology on our understanding of the nature of archaeology and how that knowledge is represented in the digital. His most recent works explore the possibilities and implications of additive manufacturing to and imaging to virtual art/archaeological theory and practice.

Nina Trivedi

Nina Trivedi is a Lecturer in Design: Race and Intercultural Studies at Central Saint Martins. She was resident in critical practice at Royal Academy Schools in 2022–3 and in 2021–2 completed an archives residency with the Decolonising Arts Institute, UAL. Nina completed a PhD at the Royal College of Art in Critical and Historical Studies. She has an MFA from Goldsmiths, University of London, and a BFA from Parsons School of Design.

Bianca Westermann
Bianca Westermann received a doctor's degree in media studies in 2010. Her dissertation on anthropomorphic machinery was published in 2012. She worked as a Lecturer and Research Assistant (Wissenschaftliche Mitarbeiterin) at the department of media studies at the Ruhr-Universität Bochum (Germany) till 2016. Her research interests are centred on mobile media, social robotics and the medial constitution of prostheses, robots and cyborgs as well as the body as a medium. Other areas of interest include the medial construction of postmodern identity in digital media and sound studies.

Series Editors' Preface

Technological transformation has profound and frequently unforeseen influences on art, design and media. At times technology emancipates art and enriches the quality of design. Occasionally it causes acute individual and collective problems of mediated perception. Time after time technological change accomplishes both simultaneously. This new book series explores and reflects philosophically on what new and emerging *technicities* do to our everyday lives and increasingly immaterial technocultural conditions. Moving beyond traditional conceptions of the philosophy of technology and of techne, the series presents new philosophical thinking on how technology constantly alters the essential conditions of beauty, invention and communication. From novel understandings of the world of technicity to new interpretations of aesthetic value, graphics and information, Technicities focuses on the relationships between critical theory and representation, the arts, broadcasting, print, technological genealogies/histories, material culture and digital technologies and our philosophical views of the world of art, design and media.

The series foregrounds contemporary work in art, design and media whilst remaining inclusive, in terms of both philosophical perspectives on technology and interdisciplinary contributions. For a philosophy of technicities is crucial to extant debates over the artistic, inventive and informational aspects of technology. The books in the Technicities series concentrate on present-day and evolving technological advances but visual, design-led and mass mediated questions are emphasised to further our knowledge of their often-combined means of digital transformation.

The editors of Technicities welcome proposals for monographs and well-considered edited collections that establish new paths of investigation.

Ryan Bishop and Jussi Parikka

Acknowledgements

This book started life as a symposium at the Science Museum in 2017. Entitled 'Robot Futures: Vision and Touch in Robotics', it corresponded with the Museum's *Robots* exhibition. We are therefore indebted to the Science Museum – to Tim Boon, Adam Boal and Ben Russell – for facilitating the symposium and for conversations that developed this project in its early days. We are grateful to the Royal College of Art's Research Office for helping to fund the symposium, and to Martina Margetts and Marq Smith for their input. We are grateful to the Royal College of Art and to Chantal Faust in particular for helping us to coordinate several workshops that led up to the symposium which helped us to solidify our ideas. We thank all the participants of both the workshops and the symposium and for presentations and other conversations in the initial stages of the project: Helen Hester, Ryan Bishop, Nea Ehrlich, Gregory Minissale, Joey Holder, Brian Black, Nicola Plant, Stephen R. Ellis, Bianca Westermann, maya rae oppenheimer, Yuri Pattison, James Bridle, Harry Burke, Meg Rahaim, Petar Kormushev, Ruairi Glynn, Simon Julier, Jeremiah Ambrose, Hans-Jörg Pochmann, Rebecca Bligh, James Hedges, James Auger and Tony Dunne.

We extend our gratitude and appreciation to all our contributing authors, artists and designers for their engagement, perseverance and commitment to this book, many of whom have been with us from the very start of this project. We are truly inspired by all of them.

Our deepest thanks go to Technicities editors Ryan Bishop and Jussi Parikka for their critical and intellectual guidance, questions, comprehensive knowledge and insightful observations which have helped to shape and refine this project. We are especially indebted to Ryan for chairing one of the symposium's panels, for seeing the potential in the project in its early stages and for the generosity with his time in helping to see this project through to fruition. Thanks go to Carol Macdonald, Judith Mackenzie and others at Edinburgh University Press and to the reviewers of the manuscript, whose suggestions helped to develop and sharpen both the ideas and the research. Thanks also to Ralph Footring for his wonderful design of the book. It has been a pleasure working with EUP on this.

We are thankful for institutional support for the book from Winchester School of Art (University of Southampton), where Luci works, and Central Saint Martins, where Nina works. We wish to thank Ryan Bishop, Jussi Parikka, Debi Kenny, Nick Rhodes and Rathna Ramanthan from these institutions where we have the pleasure of working. In terms of financial support thanks go to the University of Southampton's Early Career Research and Faculty of Arts and Humanities funds and to Research at Central Saint Martins, UAL.

We wish to thank our friends and family for their support in helping to bring this book to life. Special thanks go to our partners, Alistair Pett and Harry Craze, and to our sons Rowan and Jesse Eldridge-Pett and Indra Trivedi-Craze, who are too little to understand even what an acknowledgement means, but whose futures will likely be affected to one degree or another by many of the ideas – both foreboding and inspiring – addressed in the following pages. We dedicate this book to them.

Introduction. Vision Reshaped

Luci Eldridge and Nina Trivedi

We are already well accustomed to seeing and experiencing the world through screen-based images and on a broader scale the field of robotics and virtual reality is enabling us to see from greater distances, in more detail and with ever more convincing levels of immersion. The marked shift towards remote working and communication in the context of the Covid-19 pandemic highlighted this. 'Robotic vision' is a broad term, used intentionally here to encompass extensive and constantly evolving modes of non-biological and non-human sensing. Standing at odds with how we see, and how we have learnt to interpret images and video feeds, some robotic visions are far from anything we could ever comprehend. From telesurgery, through remote-controlled vehicles, to composite images combining numerous telescope optics constructed through algorithmic intelligence, the meaning of the term 'vision' has transformed. In this context, how must our conceptions of seeing and our embodied relationship to these evolving modes of robotic sensing be reshaped? Can we think towards a new relationship with vision, one that is post-human, post-phenomenological? Towards one that relies upon voices and frameworks from interdisciplinary perspectives that lend fresh 'eyes' (if we may still call them that) to the debate of what, how and why our experiencing and internal processing of the world are not now purely biological?

Robotic vision is multifaceted and deeply layered, encompassing sensing technologies that surpass visual and lens-based apparatus. This importance of being able to see in a multitude of different ways in an ever expanding technologically driven and mediated world is a key focus of this collection, with core ideas stemming from predictions laid out in Jonathan Crary's 1990 book *Techniques of the Observer*:

> Most of the historically important functions of the human eye are being supplanted by the practices in which visual images no longer have any reference to the position of an observer in a 'real', optically perceived world. If these images can be said to refer to anything, it is to millions of bits of electronic mathematical data. Increasingly, visuality will be situated on a cybernetic and electromagnetic terrain where abstract visual and linguistic elements coincide and are consumed, circulated, and exchanged globally. (Crary 1990: p. 1)

Over thirty years on from Crary's prediction, the stereoscopic nature of human vision is being exploited far beyond the dreams of the likes of the nineteenth-century stereoscope inventions of Sir David Brewster and Charles Wheatstone. With the well-established importance of stereoscopic vision being used to capture three-dimensional data through the 'eyes' of robots on other worlds and with virtual and augmented reality technologies becoming mainstream – enabling users to escape to imaginary spaces or explore this world in unprecedented ways – Crary's statement remains relevant. AR is being used to experience and explore data that is gathered by robots on other worlds; an example is the collaboration between NASA and Microsoft on *OnSight*, an augmented reality experience that uses Microsoft's HoloLens headset to enable scientists to 'walk on Mars'. And the development of VR is extending to fields beyond science, computing and military applications; consumer headsets are now available for home gaming with examples including Samsung Gear and Sony PlayStation VR. While robotic vision is key to establishing new knowledge, datasets and new connections, we rely on virtual interfaces – which are becoming more and more expansive – to begin to understand and foster relationships with our robotic technologies. As we witness an increasing ramp-up of technological modes of seeing, it is vital that we explore the contexts from which such technologies stem.

It is intuitive to want to understand the unknown by way of our own experience but the necessity of 'seeing' from another perspective is just as vital. Within science, military and entertainment the ways in which robotic visions are captured (through cameras and sensors) and the ways in which these visions are relayed to our eyes via interfaces (head-mounted displays or computer screens) are often interrelated. For example, drone operators don VR headsets to 'see' as the unmanned aerial vehicle and AR headsets used in *OnSight* enable users to 'see' from the Mars rover's perspective. The intentionality or working objective of the robotic vision (such as that captured on board the drone) and the virtual interface (the head-mounted display) are distinctive in that the robotic device is designed to circulate within a given (real) environment while the virtual space constructed for the viewer via the head-mounted display is artificially simulated. Here there is a shift from real (as captured by the robotic) to artificial (as experienced by the human viewer). Flipping this real–virtual paradigm around, vision technologies capture data from the perspective of the robot and virtual reality technologies reconstruct this data so it may be experienced from a human standpoint. There is a layer of complexity here; whereas data is being captured *in reality*, the robotic device senses from a uniquely technological perspective, through invisible wavelengths of light or sensors that detect chemical or biological qualities. Virtual interfaces then become the connecting space between these visions and how they are understood from a human perspective, whether by placing the human body at the centre of the visual experience, as is the case in head-mounted displays, or manipulating datasets to draw out information to make them comprehensible for the human operator. What is true to both the robotic vision and how it is re-presented within a virtual interface is that each presents a vision that the human operator or user cannot witness with their own two eyes, be it because of distance in time and space, or because it is simulated.

In order to understand the intricacies and distinctions between 'robotic vision' and 'virtual interfacings' as delineated and intertwined within this collection, it is helpful to look at the difference between 'telepresence' – a term coined in 1989 by Marvin Minsky – and 'virtual reality' – coined in 1987 by Jaron Lanier (Virtual Reality Society 2009). In *The Robot in the Garden: Telerobotics and Telepistemology in the Age of the Internet* Ken Goldberg defines telepresence in opposition to virtual reality. He states that 'although [William] Gibson's term "cyberspace" encompasses both, the distinction is vital: VR is simulacral, TR is distal' (Goldberg 2000: p. 5). Influential technologies like the telescope, telephone and television were developed 'to provide knowledge at a distance' and telerobotic systems were developed in the 1950s 'to facilitate *action* at a distance', with systems used for the remote handling of radioactive materials dating back to the 1940s (Goldberg 2000: pp. 3, 7). Now being used in undersea and outer-space exploration, bomb disposal, military surveillance and surgery, telerobotics facilitates action and knowledge acquisition at a distance, formulating 'mediated perception[s] of a distant reality', to cite Martin Jay (2000: p. 158). 'Reality', then, is arguably experienced as imaginary because it does not take place for the operator on the ground through their own two eyes.

In this way, robotic visions are intrinsically linked to definitions of virtual reality in that they relay visions that are not often present *physically*. 'Virtual' means both 'not really existing' and 'almost the same' and so *virtual reality* is a contranym combining two words with opposing meanings (Bryant & Pollock 2010: p. 11). The term also has a history within computing, coming from software engineering to 'connote any type of computer phenomenon' that forms its basis in reality, and replicates physical realities within a digital space, virtual mail and libraries being examples (Heim 1992: p. 29). It is in this sense that metaphors are virtual as, although they refer to the material world, they 'reside in the immateriality of language', remaining only as substitutes for something literal (Friedberg 2006: p. 12). The image may also be considered a virtual manifestation of an object and virtual reality technologies like head-mounted displays push this concept further in an attempt to simulate an experience of this data for the human viewer. This is explored further by Anthony Bryant and Griselda Pollock in their introduction to *Digital and Other Virtualities: Renegotiating the Image*: 'There is similarity with the actual thing; but it is not the thing itself. It is not the real; yet it is not false'; in a non-technological sense, virtuality must also be considered in relation to imagination and phantasy (Bryant & Pollock 2010: p. 14). Taking these definitions into account, then, the meaning of the term 'virtual reality' in this collection is twofold. It encompasses spaces of illusion like HMDs and computer interfaces which also represent objects that, not being physically present, exist for the viewer as virtual – visions captured and relayed by robotic and telerobotic devices.

While telepresence (through drones, satellites and microscopic cameras) seeks to place our perspective elsewhere, be it through visible light and photographic perspective or though invisible wavelengths of light and at invisible scales, virtual reality technologies attempt to reconstruct this information for the human viewer or operator. The virtual interfacings surveyed within this collection – which range from the post-processing of images of Mars through to the construction of imaginative and immersive worlds in head-mounted displays – recapitulate robotic forms of vision for the human operator in which technological and optical modes of seeing become combined.

Vision plays a large part in these technologies, in how we see and how machines are designed to see photographically, stereoscopically, but also in other non-human ways that reveal aspects of this world and others that are invisible to human vision. These technologies enable us to see the world from a multitude of perspectives, be it in science and engineering or within a visual arts context. By new ways of seeing the world enabled through machine vision, we become aware of our own limitations, but we must also be cautious of how and why these technologies mediate what we see. It is already well established by media and technology theorists such as Joanna Zylinska, James Bridle, Michael Lynch, N. Katherine Hayles, Sarah Kember and Donna Haraway, among others, that we should be very wary of what we are looking at when it comes to robotic vision and how automation – visual and otherwise – could have lasting impacts on the nature of humankind. Technological advances in the field of robotics are progressing rapidly. We are witnessing an unprecedented surge in the field of drones, the exploration of the depths of our oceans and the surfaces of other planets, and the development of computer intelligence, both in terms of our domestic lives, the software we use on a day-to-day basis, and on a more global scale. And while such technological modes of seeing have been designed by humans for humans, the resulting 'visions' have surpassed anything within the realm of human comprehension as algorithmic intelligence and data processing speeds black-box these tools. As the artist and writer Trevor Paglen writes: 'What does it mean that "seeing" no longer requires a human "seer" in the loop?' (quoted in Strecker n.d.).

In 'Undigital Photography: Image-Making beyond Computation and AI' Joanna Zylinska draws connections between her 2017 definition of 'nonhuman photography' – 'photographs that are not of, by or for the human' (Zylinska 2017: p. 5) – and Paglen's expansive definition of photography as 'seeing machines' (Zylinska 2021). Both 'nonhuman photography' and 'seeing machines' encompass a broad array of images and imaging practices like satellite images, infra-red, QR codes, automated licence recognition, facial recognition and Google Street View cars, as well as the systems in which such images are stored and circulated, with political, social and geographical consequences (Paglen 2014). These images, as both authors maintain, are barely viewed by people and instead are used for machine interpolation and machine learning. As machine learning techniques stemmed from online advertising and searches that were low risk, with minimal effect to human lives, there emerged a belief that accurate models used in computer vision must be overly complicated and uninterpretable. Joanna Radin and Cynthia Rudin explain that in machine learning, 'black box models are created directly from data by an algorithm, meaning that humans, even those who design them, cannot understand how variables are being combined to make predictions', even if 'one has a list of input variables' (Radin & Rudin 2019). Embedded within the definition of a black box, then, is that there is no way to completely understand how and why the algorithm comes to a particular decision. As machine learning depends on providing a bank of data to the machine so that it can develop algorithms that can then be applied to other data that the machine has not yet encountered, much of what the algorithm does depends on the input variables. If this data is inaccurate or biased, so too will the algorithm be biased.

In a 2016 text 'Intimate Pressure' Nora Khan writes presciently about forms of immersion that are experienced via and through online virtual encounters and new forms of vision and visuality based on the attention to the screen, the literal time spent looking and its retinal impact. In line with Paglen and Zylinska, she elsewhere writes of the underlying intentions and ramifications of many of these systems:

> How we see or unsee is the primary ethical question in a culture and computational regime that privileges vision. And how we see, name, and know the world is increasingly influenced and shaped by how machines see, name, and know.... The logic and illogic of how we are seen, named, and known, is at the heart of contemporary political deadlocks: who is seen, considered innocent in intention by default, then protected? Who is unseen, then: considered unruly, uncivilized, better placed in solitary confinement, pending a trial for likely crime? And of all the developments in AI, machine vision most clearly helps create mapped determinations of who we are and what we are capable of: our employability, our loan eligibility, and our trustworthiness. (Khan 2019)

The ways in which algorithms are exacerbating gender and racial biases are highlighted powerfully in the 2020 documentary *Coded Bias*. The documentary explains that through the use of non-diverse datasets – images predominantly of white men – machine learning processes are writing inherently biased algorithms. *Coded Bias* brought further to the mainstream the research of MIT Media Lab's Joy Buolamwini exploring the role of racism in coding and algorithms. In the documentary Buolamwini describes how certain AI systems could not 'read' faces with variations of skin tones, specifically Black faces. Buolamwini and Timnit Gebru researched facial analysis systems that matched faces from a large dataset of photographs and assessed characterises such as gender, age and mood. Significantly, they noted that with the systems, people were misgendered or gender more often was on the binary and there was bias in facial tracking in the systems. This led them to examine how to establish ways to work with nuanced variations of skin tones, by increasing images in large datasets used in the systems. Buolamwini and Gebru's platform for their research, Gender Shades, offers a detailed archive of their work (see Buolamwini 2018) and the pair argue that 'since computer vision technology is being utilized in high-stakes sectors such as health-care and law enforcement, more work needs to be done in benchmarking vision algorithms for various demographic and phenotypic groups' (Buolamwini and Gebru 2018: p. 2). As Safiya Noble writes in *Algorithms of Oppression: How Search Engines Reinforce Racism*, 'data and computing have become so profoundly their own "truth"' that it is a struggle to hold companies accountable for errors which are increasingly leading to 'racial and gender profiling, misrepresentation, and even economic redlining' (Noble 2018: pp. 27–8). Such concerns around inherent bias within machine learning and its wider implications has led the European Commission to examine the need for transparency in algorithmic AI systems and how systems reproduce bias without the awareness of designers (European Commission 2020). Research such as this – whether related to the realm of health-care, mortgage lenders or criminal justice – highlights the need for clarity in the logic of these systems. These are instances where images and data are captured and read not by humans but by machines. As we learn to depend upon technologies we radically do not understand, our choices increasingly being led by algorithms and AI, we should ask, as Zylinska does, 'Whose vision is AI promoting? Who is doing the looking, in what way and to what purpose?' (Zylinska 2021: p. 235).

On a wider scale, workforce automation and warfare have brought with them sinister concerns around the evolution of some kind of super-intelligence that will one day outsmart humankind. But while the threat of a superior intelligence is currently deemed low risk, the impact of automated technologies, how these are being developed, and along what social, political and economic grounds, are very real causes for concern. Such questions are at the forefront of much of the recent research from thinktanks such as MIT's Media Lab and the Algorithmic Justice League as well as the Centre for Study of Existential Risk affiliated with the University of Cambridge and the Ida B. Wells Just Data Lab based at Princeton University. Also important to note is the crucial and timely Pandemic Portal, run by Ruha Benjamin. This project was created by researchers and students from Princeton University and aims to examine the ways in which data can be utilised to understand structural and institutional racism, poverty and care, which were impacted or exacerbated by the conditions of the Covid-19 pandemic. What, then, does it mean to put faith in machines that hold no sense of responsibility and in turn what are the political, ethical and legal consequences from the fallout of drone strikes, driverless car manoeuvres and algorithms that log your social media perusals and online shopping? We have become accustomed to the benefits these tools have to offer, redirecting our route through rush-hour traffic, assessing the development of a foetus in the womb, enabling some form of socialising to continue despite government-enforced lockdowns. But as robots learn to 'think' for themselves, that is, to make algorithmically informed decisions determined by the data they have captured, the role of the human as programmer and processor diminishes and our reliance on robotics and what it enables for human progress intensifies.

While much might be said about the criticalities of robotic vision and machine learning, it must be also noted that the new ways of seeing and sensing the world enabled through robotic vision make us aware of our own limitations as physical beings bound by space, time and the human brain, with robotic technologies of course eliciting positive and productive relationships and uses. This stance will indeed come through in a number of chapters in this collection and it is important to highlight that our critique is not always one of pessimism and fear. Not being bound by the human body has huge benefits, and artificial computer-driven machine vision can be helpful with anything from brain surgery to disaster relief, with aid distribution and evacuations during hurricanes, tornados and floods, for example. The team behind the Noble Intelligence initiative is working with satellite and weather datasets in order to organise how to analyse disaster relief and to help with reconstruction efforts (McKinsey & Company 2021). The datasets and algorithms can be used to determine how many people will be displaced from their homes during disasters, aiding relief efforts and helping to determine medical care needs. AI algorithms can identify flooding or damage in areas with satellite images and weather forecasts, allowing rescuers to distribute emergency aid more efficiently. The advancing field of neurosurgical AI-based robotics is another example of a positive and productive outcome, and is helping to improve diagnosis as well as pre- and postoperative oncological care for patients with brain tumours. The authors of the article 'Artificial Intelligence in Brain Tumour Surgery – An Emerging Paradigm' advocate for the development of databases that can 'train further AI and [for] algorithms [to] become open access [to] encourage wider technological advancement' (Williams et al. 2021). There are various levels of automation within surgery: partial, conditional, high and full. Partial automation uses robotic aids, with the human making all decisions within the process. Conditional automation sees some aspects of surgery become automated, with the human overseeing the process. High automation uses surgical robots to perform operations; another example is the CyberKnife system, which provides non-invasive radiation therapy (Cyberknife 2021). Full automation is seen in instances where no human analysis or help is required at all. It has been proven that using robotics can help to maintain guidelines in such fields (Williams et al. 2021).

Robotic Vision and Virtual Interfacings will address how and why vision is key to permitting, establishing and sustaining meaningful relationships between the robotic device and human operator and the perception of the world beyond the limits and narrow viewpoints of the human body or user while also raising pertinent issues around the problems associated with the black-boxing of these alternative modes of seeing. From a range of perspectives and through the analysis of specific examples within the broad scope of what might be defined as robotic vision and virtual interfacing, this collection interrogates the distinctions and intersections between robotic and human modes of seeing, sensing and shaping our experiences of the world. Authors in this collection probe the construction and use of images that are the products of remotely operated devices, algorithmic intelligence and machine interpolation. Such images are moving us away from the perspectival 'window', beyond the limits and narrow viewpoints of the human body, and into a new visual arena that requires specialist knowledge for interpretation. Broadly, this collection reflects upon how vision is being simulated in robotics and virtual and augmented realities as well as highlighting the role vision is playing in establishing new forms of human–machine interaction. In doing this we aim not only to highlight the successes and limitations of such technologies but also to identify potential risks for the future of vision, visuality and virtuality.

Embodied Vision

The chapters in *Robotic Vision and Virtual Interfacings. Seeing, Sensing, Shaping* survey these issues in light of the current and projected future state of robotics specifically in regard to machine vision, virtual and augmented reality applications and the need, or perceived need, for endowing the robot with human characteristics, be it superficially how the robot 'looks' or technically how the robot records and interacts with the world around it.

Recent exhibitions exploring the history of robots such as *Robots* at the Science Museum (February 2017 – September 2017) and *AI: More Than Human* at the Barbican (May – August 2019) have explored how robots are an archetype of science fiction, ethical and social considerations and how science fiction is often used as a lens to explore wider issues pertinent to the day. The portrayal of robots and android forms in films has, of course, a long history, but more recent, real-world examples of humanoid robots such as Hanson Robotics' Sophia robot (the first robot to become a citizen of a country, in October 2017) and Japan's Kodomoroid TV Presenter are made to look, speak and feel uniquely human. While the embodiment of the human in, for example, Amazon's Echo may appear to appeal to our desire for friendly robotic companions whom we may empathise with, endowing robots with anthropomorphic qualities that enable them to capture and sense their surroundings in ways analogous with our own perception is a necessity for seeing and understanding the world from our own narrow human perspective.

This edited collection stems from the proceedings of a conference we convened at the Science Museum, London, on 8 July 2017, titled *Robot Futures: Vision and Touch in Robotics*. The conference explored how humans are embodied in robotics more widely and from a range of perspectives: scientific, engineering, art, design and cultural theory. Robots are given 'eyes' and 'hands' in order to relate perceptions and experiences of places and objects physically unavailable to us. Although such robots might not 'look' human, it is the desire to see stereoscopically, and to feel through all the senses, that endows robots with anthropomorphic qualities. The conference explored how we see and feel *through* the robot and how robots enable a more embodied experience, which is nonetheless mediated. Furthering this notion of seeing and feeling through robots, the conference also explored the development of virtual reality technologies that are increasingly enabling us to see and feel *as* the robot in order to get us closer to a more immersive experience. These concepts expanded into the ideas surrounding vision and virtual interfacings, and the themes of seeing, sensing and shaping within this collection.

The way humans and robots perceive their surroundings and in turn make decisions based upon this data relies in large part on what they can see, and there are key ways in which these modes of seeing converge and differ. In the section on Seeing, in his chapter 'Will Robots Daydream?' Gregory Minissale unpacks the difference between analytical vision, a highly efficient form of vision often used by robotic technologies, and 'mind wandering' vision, that is, a kind of 'inefficient' vision more in tune with how humans visually percept the world. Minissale speculates that in order to make robots in our own image, we must endow them with the ability to utilise *both* forms of vision. Thereby, what must be achieved is a transformative synthesis of robotic and human vision. Throughout this book we will ask how and why embodiment – that is, how the robotic device forges its relationship with its environment and human interactor through distinctly human characteristics and senses – is key to enabling meaningful relationships between emerging technologies in the field of robotics and virtual reality. Pearl John furthers this in her chapter 'When Robots Ignore Us: The Affective Impact of Robotic Artwork and Development of Drone Art', which is also in the section on Seeing. Through a post-human and post-phenomenological perspective she maintains that a human–robot synthesis (in both the making and experiencing of robotic artworks) is key to maintaining some kind of illusion of control and empowerment. Similarly, the body of the user is crucial to establishing human–machine synthesis in virtual reality technology artworks, which is an important aspect within the chapters on Sensing. The role of the user's body is unpacked by Nicola Plant in her chapter, 'Embodiment and the Perception of Nonhuman Sentience in Virtual Reality Interactive Art', in which the artist asks how technology can augment or embody the experience of embodiment, that is, the role of the body in the virtual world shaping what the user sees through their physical movement and gestures. Her VR artwork *Sentient Flux* highlights the movement of the body as being key to visual perception and the importance of emulating this within convincing virtual environments. And from a science and technology studies perspective, former head of the Advanced Displays and Spatial Perception Laboratory at the NASA Ames Research Center Stephen R. Ellis explores how the mechanics of vision have been utilised throughout history in order to develop forms of what we now call 'virtual' or 'augmented' reality using head-mounted displays. In 'On the Meaning of Virtual Environments and the Evolution of Life' Ellis argues that the development of virtual reality tools may represent an inflection point within human history, radically altering and extending how we see the world and in turn how we interact with it. Pearl John sets the groundwork for much of these debates in her detailed analysis of specifically how robotic vision works; this is tied to examples from science fiction and the role of fiction in fuelling certain misconceptions of how robots 'see', as well as the more ominous readings of such technologies.

Wider Impacts of Robotic Vision

The promise of a robotic future as portrayed in films and the media might seem alluring to some, enabling higher levels of scientific analysis, possible companionships and more precise modes of construction but as well we know there are also deeper and darker concerns of the consequences of technological progress that get to the heart of everyday reality. Though arising from a perspective that is principally linked to vision and the visual, this collection also touches upon some of the ethical implications and social ramifications of how robots are designed, the implicit or explicit gendering and racial stereotyping of robots, and what impact this has on interactions between robots and humans. There are germane questions surrounding race, gender and the ethical-political quandaries such as how different economies and workforces are impacted by increasing digitisation and technological change, and what disproportionate impact will this have on people, and more specifically on African, Caribbean, Asian, Middle Eastern, First Nations and Indigenous communities.

Replacing humans with robots in various sectors may offer preventive strategies for harm. Yet the increasing threat of automation to those in precarious socioeconomic situations and the question of whether automation will keep people in cycles of long-term unemployment has come to the forefront of recent debates surrounding this issue. What are the potential impacts on workforces? The efficiency and productivity of automation are things that designers and theorists have been critiquing and the ability to assign to robots jobs that pose risk or danger or that could harm the health of humans is being debated as workers will be required to develop various digital skills in order to engage in the future workforce. In the section on Shaping, Bianca Westermann and maya rae oppenheimer question some of these ideas in their chapters. oppenheimer's 'The Robotics Division of the Dramaco Instrument Company Introduces the Ensocellorator Reliance Pro 2' is an ongoing art project and piece of creative fiction in the form of a speculative business pitch which poses ethical questions and debates social dynamics while using historical archives, psychology and sociology of technology methods to critically explore the domestication of robots. Questions about the anthropomorphism of robots and arising socio-ethical issues stem from design considerations about racialisation as well as the perceived gendering of robots (Bartneck et al. 2018). And questions of consent arise in the genre of sex robots as well. Responses to humanoid robots used for social purposes and the interpretation of responses have been the focus of research for fields exploring the ethical implications and social ramifications of how robots are designed as distinctly 'white' (Bartneck et al. 2018; Sparrow 2019). In 'Encounters with Artificial Social Companionship and Embodied Representation' Bianca Westermann examines the robot as both a tool and a companion, but we are reminded that there is still a long way to go before these animated objects can be anything but 'other' from us as humans.

Artificial intelligence and robots have been used for digital surveillance and forms of warfare, including with cybercrimes, cyber-warfare and drones. This brings about questions of state power and biopolitics. We need to rethink our relationship with robots, how we build these relationships based on human interaction and how these interactions can in turn affect our own ethical outlooks. *How* such relationships are formed is in large part based on how robots and images are designed and perceived by their interactors and this is a theme that traverses all the sections of the book. In 'Discrete Accidents of Photogrammetry: Re-presenting Pure Surface in Google Earth', which appears in the section on Seeing, Meg Rahaim analyses the traces of deliberate obfuscation in the construction of algorithmically produced Google Earth scenes. Rahaim aims to see through and past the robotic interface, eliciting a framework for understanding the role of networked, surveillant, robotic images in the corporate acquisition and control of human behaviour.

As such, notions of private and public encounters with data, information and the lived experience will be unpacked. Curator and writer Legacy Russell suggests how we may begin to push back on surveillance capitalism and the interfaces with which we have become so accustomed in her 2020 book *Glitch Feminism*. Within this line of thinking Russell also offers critical reflections on inherent bias in apps and the collection of data, highlighting some similar examples to Ruha Benjamin's in the book *Race After Technology* (2019). Both authors cite and refer to levels of bias and racism in Google's image recognition coding in 2015 and Google's Arts & Culture app in 2018. In Benjamin's *Race After Technology* the author defines – stemming from the history of Jim Crow Laws that enforced racial segregation – 'The New Jim Code' as 'the employment of new technologies that reflect and reproduce existing inequalities but that are promoted and perceived as more objective or progressive than the discriminatory systems of a previous era' (Benjamin 2019: p. 5). Benjamin researches discriminatory design and racism in coding and apps, and considers the ways technologies and data can hinder or help social progress and justice. She writes: 'Codes, in short, operate within powerful systems of meaning that render some things visible, others invisible, and create a vast array of distortions and dangers' (Benjamin 2019: p. 7).

An example of the ways in which lens-based imaging enters these debates is early Kodak film stock's privileging of lighter skin tones, reflecting a mode of adjustment to a certain kind of idealised (and biased) 'normal' (Zhang 2015). Film photography tended to have a bias towards 'whiteness', contradicting prior assumptions that photography was impartial. 'Shirley' cards were used as industry-standard colour reference cards between the 1940s and 1970s and the accuracy of colour balance in photographs was based on the skin tones of white women and colourful surroundings. Lighter-coloured skin tones photographed very well, but photographs of darker skin tones, especially in images that depicted both light and dark, showed subjects with little or no visible facial features due to differences in required exposure levels. It was not until the 1990s, when Kodak developed a new film (Kodak Gold Max), that film photography was able to capture different skin tones (Zhang 2015). In her chapter 'Sweeping Away the Dust: Mars as Reconstructed Image', Luci Eldridge highlights the preference for 'white-balancing' images of the planet Mars and our desire to see that which we cannot physically comprehend through an Earthly lens, as images are edited in post-processing to filter the Martian landscape through lighting more representative of that on Earth. The question of both colour-balancing images of Mars and early film photography's inability to accurately represent darker skin tones is that the subject represented is not necessarily invisible, it is just not able to be seen through a particular kind of lens.

In terms of these debates circulating around equality and diversity, at the forefront of the field of social robotics (Sparrow 2019) are propositions on how to, and whether to, attribute racial identities to robots (Howard & Borenstein 2018). This raises ethical and political issues with the design process. Key to note here is the lack of diversity in engineers and companies that design programs such as FaceApp or HP computers and some of these ideas are explored in Meg Rahaim's chapter, 'Discrete Accidents of Photogrammetry'. Questions surrounding the gendering of robots adds to the problematic dialogues about how robots are to be designed. Moreover, questions revolve around the implicit or explicit gendering of robots, how robots are categorised and what impact this has on interactions between robots and humans. Can the gendering of robots be a marker of likeability or trustability? What responses are evoked from humans, whether it be aggressive responses or responses of affection? In turn, how can the human–robot relationship impact the user's perceptions of gender and stereotypes of behaviour of gender (Bartneck et al. 2018)?

Glitching Bodies/Glitching Vision

Written in the format of a manifesto, *Glitch Feminism* considers some of these pertinent roles of race and gender as impacted by the internet. The performance of the self and selfhood as formed online within internet structures and platforms, bodily concerns and non-binary identities is also explored. The liberatory potentialities for non-binary identity and for race and gender more broadly are considered, as Legacy Russell writes:

> A body that pushes back at the application of pronouns, or remains
> indecipherable within binary assignment, is a body that refuses to

perform the score. The non performance is a glitch. This glitch is a form of refusal. (Russell 2020: p. 8)

In line with this thinking, Rosa Menkman's *The Glitch Moment(um)* (2011) is a study of the theory, practice and social context of 'Glitch Art', in which the digital glitch is discussed both as a break in the transparent portrayal of information and as an aesthetic. Menkman proposes that the glitch manifests itself through any break in the medium's transparency, representing 'a loss of control' in which 'the "world" or the interface does the unexpected' (Menkman 2011: pp. 14, 41). It might seem 'unexpected', 'irrational', enabling us to see past the glossy interface of the screen and into the construction of the image, into the mechanism of the device used to construct it (Menkman 2011: p.41). It is the break in illusion that unveils the real thing, the presence of the image rather than the thing that the image represents. The 'digital break' throws the viewer into a 'more risky realm of image and non-image, meaning and non-meaning, truth and interpretation' whereby the viewer is consciously aware of the act of looking (Menkman 2011: p. 31).

Further defining the idea of the glitch, Russell continues:

> The glitch acknowledges that gendered bodies are far from absolute but rather an imaginary manufactured and commodified for capital. The glitch is an activist prayer, a call to action, as we work towards a fantastic failure, breaking free of an understanding of gender as something stationary. (Russell 2020: p. 9)

Both Kate Fahey in her chapter 'Blinking Eyes: The Embodied Registers of Military Drone Camera Footage on YouTube' and Luci Eldridge in her chapter 'Sweeping Away the Dust: Mars as Reconstructed Image' – which both appear in the section on Sensing – consider the glitch in manners that take the definition away from 'glitch' as a break or disruption in a transparent interface and in manners that align with Russell's thinking on the glitch as being progressive. For Simon O'Sullivan in his 2009 essay 'From Stuttering and Stammering to the Diagram: Deleuze, Bacon and Contemporary Art Practice', the glitch

> names two moments or movements. To break a world and to make a world [...]. The glitch is then a moment of critique, a moment of negation – but also a moment of creation and of affirmation. Indeed, the glitch – in whichever regime it operates and ruptures – is the 'sound' of this something else, this something *different* attempting to get through. (O'Sullivan 2009: p. 251)

Both Fahey and Eldridge maintain that although the glitch brings to the fore the materiality of networked, surveillant and coded images, the devices used to capture and translate them, and the interfaces through which they are experienced, it does so in ways that enliven the images, enabling viewers to have a different kind of experience that is both immersive and productive. As Eldridge argues, the glitch has the potential to reconfigure the surface of the image in such a way as to construct a new form of seeing and sensing beyond the visual, as it appears directly to the robotic device.

Theoretical frameworks surrounding human and non-human relations can be elicited from New Materialist and Feminist New Materialist perspectives, which are interested in the relationship between things, objects, bodies, humans, materialities and these interconnected relationships. As can be seen in the writings of Rosi Braidotti, Karen Barad, Jane Bennett and Donna Haraway, for example, Feminist New Materialists are theorising about matter and forging a pathway for ethico-political questions and post-anthropocentric subjects and subjectivities, as well as post-human ones. They are also considering a materialist position to broach issues of agency. Bodies and matter and technological interfaces and mediations are integral to their philosophical approach. These interdisciplinary philosophies approach materiality and matter and their connection to human and non-human worlds and are drawn upon by authors in this collection, including Meg Rahaim, Kate Fahey and artist/archaeologist collaborators Ian Dawson and Paul Reilly. Within the field of New Materialisms these authors address non-human modes of perception of the physical world and also of social processes, post-human feminisms, post-human subjectivity, the re-othering of bodies and encounters and (non-)encounters with other bodies. In 'Blinking Eyes' Fahey focuses on UK and US military drone footage available online. The artist and writer explores the absence of bodies, redacted information and propagandistic notions of this readily available footage and questions how and why an embodied encounter between humans and non-humans can occur. The loops of perception that can be seen in Fahey's artworks and writing are further explored through Ian Dawson and Paul Reilly's diffractive approach to interrogating and repurposing a Mesolithic flint pick. Appearing in the section on Shaping, their chapter details their collaborative practice of photogrammetry, 3D modelling and 3D printing, all carried out virtually and remote from one another during the Covid-19 lockdowns. Through it the authors provoke a New Materialist framing of images and data that has been and continues to be produced through human–robotic intra-actions.

Human vision is being productively and proactively disrupted by robotic vision. The glitch is employed to reconfigure, the looping perceptions of image-capturing devices eliciting a back and forth of data and knowledge through virtual encounters and remote, mediated experiencing. What is achieved is a reshaping of perceptions, of the visions captured by the robotic devices which are made distinctly human, and human visions which are made distinctly robotic in order to see and sense beyond the body. As the human and robotic become ever more enmeshed within this encircling synthesis, we are clearly on the cusp of new ways of seeing.

Seeing, Sensing, Shaping

In addressing the distinctions and intersections between robotic and human modes of visualising, *Robotic Vision and Virtual Interfacings: Seeing, Sensing, Shaping* interrogates the construction and use of technologically produced images and their makers. The authors in this collection consider how past and present robotic devices effect how we perceive the world and see things; how principally image-making practices enable us to reframe our experiencing of the world.

Robotic Vision and Virtual Interfacings is structured around three key sections ('Seeing', 'Sensing' and 'Shaping'), each of which includes chapters by scholars working at the forefront of these issues and aims to take the reader on a journey through how vision is constructed and images are captured, how such devices and images are being used in accordance with virtual interfaces to consider notions of embodiment and human-centred perspectives, how robotic tools are being used to facilitate and reconstruct our perceptions of presence, being present, and in turn how we may begin to navigate the vacillating loops of human–robotic modes of sensing through multifaceted modes of vision. Within this collection, authors working in the fields of art history, critical image theory, the history of design, sociology and science and technology studies converge on the nexus of New Materialism, Media Studies and Cultural Theory. Alongside more traditional academic research, the contributions include more speculative approaches combining creative writing; this is true of the chapters written by Meg Rahaim, Kate Fahey, Luci Eldridge and maya rae oppenheimer. Interwoven between the three main sections are image-based interludes from artists Joey Holder and Adham Faramawy and designer Brian Black. The ideas in the book as a whole are explored implicitly or speculatively via these chapters that aim to critique, use ideas from, or speculate on the future of robotic vision and virtual interfacing. In bringing together academic research and artistic reflections, we aim for a conversation to be created among the texts and images in order to explore an interdisciplinary perspective from the arts, humanities and sciences.

The first section of the book, titled 'Seeing', explores the differences between machine and human vision in the perception of how images are being constructed or analysed through algorithmic processing. This section will also examine how robots and humans interact with the visual world and have a physical and virtual presence within it, considering how human and robotic forms of vision are being synthesised. In 'When Robots Ignore Us: The Affective Impact of Robotic Artwork and Development of Drone Art' Pearl John offers insight into the workings of robotic vision and focuses on the emotional impact of robotic artworks that are eliciting interactive experiences between users and robots. She considers forms of robotic vision – specifically drones – that are expanding the visual artist's aesthetic and conceptual vocabulary. In 'Will Robots Daydream?' Gregory Minissale debates the importance of both analytical and mind-wandering vision within robotics, arguing that if we ever desire to make robots in our own image, an image that requires feeling that one is a being in the world, robots will need to oscillate between these different modes of vision in the same way humans do. In 'Discrete Accidents of Photogrammetry: Re-presenting Pure Surface in Google Earth' Meg Rahaim presents traces found within Google Earth, a familiar robotic vision of everyday life, that point to the depresentation, or deliberate obfuscation, of their role as algorithmically composed aesthetic objects. Observations from exploring the virtual reconstruction of a London park on screen in Google Earth combined with those witnessed by her own two eyes raise questions around surface, friction and embodiment that point to the disembodied flows of personal information back to the surveillance capitalism giant Google.

In the second part of the book, titled 'Sensing', a consideration of the body of the viewer becomes integral in the examination of images captured remotely and advanced uses of virtual reality, in terms of both virtual screen-based images and more immersive head-mounted displays. In 'Blinking Eyes: The Embodied Registers of Military Drone Camera Footage on YouTube' Kate Fahey analyses her own artistic practice and installation *I could feel that my eyes were open...*, two films exploring the restaging of operative images in a practice of image-making that draws to the fore the occlusion and reconfiguration of encounters with bodies living and dying under drones. Artist Nicola Plant discusses the motivation behind her artwork *Sentient Flux,* a virtual reality experience that invites movement with interactive particles. The piece questions whether moving with interactive particles can give a sense of an intersubjective connection between the nonhuman particle form and the human user. The artwork extends the artist's research in human interaction, asking what interactions give the perception of intersubjectivity in a computer-generated experience; the sense that something is alive and sympathetic to the audience. In 'On the Meaning of Virtual Environments and the Evolution of Life' Stephen R. Ellis argues that the required control and filtering by human users of the hardware and software elements within virtual reality systems resemble analogous structures that have evolved within living organisms to similarly manage complex interactions. For Ellis, this analogy suggests that the advent of virtual environment simulation may represent a new phase of organic evolution on earth, phases of which in the past have been associated with diffusion of life to ever expanding spatial environments. Consequently, he argues, the advent of virtual environments may be seen as an event leading to the beginning of life's further expansion into the physical as well as virtual universe. In 'Sweeping Away the Dust: Mars as Reconstructed Image' Luci Eldridge interrogates the use of post-processing and colour-balancing images of Mars. Within scientific representational practices, images become malleable entities, active reconstructions that enable geologists to reveal chemical compositions and stratigraphic structures of remote landscapes. She argues that the robotic visions of the Mars rovers are reconfigured in manners that fracture the relationship between vision and representation but elicit a new form of seeing and sensing this virtual landscape-as-image. In this section, seeing as the robotic and seeing as the human become combined as a kind of practice that must be undertaken in order to form a meaningful human–machine synthesis.

In the final section, titled 'Shaping', we witness a different kind of human–machine interaction, whereby the robot becomes a tool for social purpose and enables us to reshape our interactions with the world. Here the notion of embodiment has cultural and political ramifications that ask us to question and rethink our own concept of presence and perception. In 'Robotic Presences: Encounters with Artificial Social Companionship and Embodied Representation' Bianca Westermann examines how social robots – those built to be interacted with by the general public as social companions – can shape our own human perceptions of being present. maya rae oppenheimer's 'The Robotics Division of the Dramaco Instrument Company Introduces the Ensocellorator Reliance Pro 2' is a script for a performance-lecture delivered at the 'Robot Futures' conference in 2017 at the Science Museum, London. It is part of an ongoing work that adds to the activities of a fictive and plausible technology manufacturing company that has, in the past ten years, branched into the consumer and business-to-business surveillance and AI markets. It details the launch of the Ensocellorator Reliance Pro 2, a device designed to read and process coded messages by cross-referencing data gathered by previous models; it is proffered to be a digital truth serum running on deep data analysis which is then actionable by the host robot carcass. Ian Dawson and Paul Reilly's 'Metalithic Postcards During the Pandemic' elicits a rethinking and reshaping of ancient archaeological technologies – flint picks – re-imagining these artefacts through reflectance transformation imaging and 3D printing and placing them back into the landscape to gain their own life and new relationships with passers-by. This practice foregrounds the contrast between human and nonhuman perception and the project presents a transdisciplinary perspective addressing the multimodal and cross-modal haptic/sculptural sensing ways of knowing multi-temporal (Ancient and modern) technologies. In this final section, the robot is a tool or companion, and vision traverses back and forth between human and device, the interconnecting relationship facilitating a constantly evolving shaping and reshaping of a multitude of perceptions, to frame and generate new perspectives that are themselves multifaceted, layered and processual.

Image-based chapters by Joey Holder, Brian Black and Adham Faramawy provide interludes between the sections to reflect upon technological vision, virtuality and human–robot synthesis within speculative design and artistic practices, contributing to the multifaceted exploration of the new ways in which robotic vision is expanding the human sensorial. These chapters are not meant to be explicit or illustrative of the ideas explored throughout the book nor are they 'real' or working models, but practices that seek to engage critically, projecting possible future worlds, scenarios and technologies where vision is re-imagined to elicit new perspectives. Joey Holder's art installation *Ophiux* appears after the section 'Seeing'. In this piece, imagined biological imaging machines visualise how current digital technologies are used to extract data from DNA. Combined with a film incorporating footage from remotely operated underwater vehicles, the installation plays with different modes of robotic seeing and digital data gathering. It converges two modes of remotely acquired invisible vision, bringing them together in a speculative installation that causes viewers to rethink their own experience with technological modes of seeing. Brian Black's *The*

Overview Effect project – which comes after the section 'Sensing' – is an experience concept designed to increase users' understanding of unmanned space exploration through a virtual reality interface allowing them to drive a rover across an extraterrestrial surface. It offers a speculative insight into the potential use of virtual reality tools in remote planetary exploration, a visual sensorial experience that positions the viewer's body and mind at the heart of the experience. Adham Faramawy's *Hi! I'm happy you're here!* was an augmented reality sculpture, launched in 2015. It existed as an app users could download from the App Store and Google Play, to view on their smart-phone or tablet device. By taking a photo of a target image the app allowed users to view and circumnavigate the sculpture in real time. The sculpture was a continually morphing screen-like object embedded with a video of people continually smiling, waving and greeting users. The app also allowed users to take pictures of the sculpture in situ and share the images on social media, which appeared on the artist's website as a means to track the movement of the piece through virtual space. It considers its integration within the interface and how it is inseparable from the virtual experiencing of bodies between different time zones and places ultimately oscillating between the virtual body and robotic body. This contribution comes after the section 'Shaping'. In conjunction with these visual pieces, Meg Rahaim, Kate Fahey, Nicola Plant, and Ian Dawson and Paul Reilly all incorporate their own practice-led research into their chapters. Together, these contributions provide a new lens through which to consider and speculate upon the new ways of seeing being elicited by robotic vision and virtual interfaces and the crucial role artists and designers play in helping us think critically about the social, political and ethical ramifications of our technologically driven and mediated world.

Esther Leslie's Afterword 'Concluding Perception' utilises critical image theory to offer a speculative contemplation of how artists and media users are thinking about the issues presented in the collection, while considering trajectories for directions of the research field. Her Afterword is a space in which the author explores representation and the interaction and reactions of robots in different parts of our lives, weaving in theoretical underpinnings of ethics surrounding machine learning and deep learning systems. In her concluding remarks, she offers ways to think about critical image theory as she includes examples of lab-grown eyes, xenobots and deepfakes and their ramifications in medical, biological and aesthetic fields.

Through bringing together these contributions we aim to inspire an interdisciplinary perspective, thinking critically about humanity's desire to explore through robotic devices, what robots can offer us in terms of visual perception and analysis, the synthesis of human–machine seeing, and how fictional narratives and artistic practices are raising questions about such forms of mediated seeing. The terms 'robotic vision' and 'virtual interfacings' might indeed be interpreted and looked at from face value in terms of what the robot 'sees' and how this form of seeing is relayed to both human and other robotic devices in the form of on-screen images and data. But the terms might also be considered on a deeper level, inherently tied up with human experience and serving as a basis for understanding – or at least attempting to understand – the human–robot relationship. As post-humanist and post-phenomenological debates have highlighted, we must move towards a rethinking of what it means to be human and to see things through, as and with the robotic.

Robotic vision and virtual interfacings are just some aspects in a vastly complex web of issues, but they can be used as a lens through which to explore the wider political, social and ethical technological landscape. As the symbiotic relationship between human and machine continues to unfold, robotic vision facilitates not only an enabling, but a reshaping of our perception of the world.

References

Bartneck, C., Yogesswaran, K., Ser, Q. M. and Woodward, G. (2018) 'Robots and Racism', in *Proceedings of the 2018 ACM/IEEE International Conference on Human–Robot Interaction*. Available at https://dl.acm.org/doi/10.1145/3171221.3171260 (accessed 3 May 2019).

Benjamin, R. (2019) *Race After Technology*. Cambridge: Polity.

Bryant, A. and Pollock, G. (eds) (2010) *Digital and Other Virtualities: Renegotiating the Image*. London: I. B. Taurus.

Buolamwini, J. (2018) Algorithmic Justice League, MIT Media Lab. Available at http://gendershades.org. (accessed 3 May 2022).

Buolamwini, J. and Gebru, T. (2018) 'Gender Shades: Intersectional Accuracy Disparities in Commercial Gender Classification', *Proceedings of Machine Learning Research* 81: 1–15.

Crary, J. (1990) *Techniques of the Observer*. Cambridge, MA: MIT Press.

Cyberknife (2021) 'How It Works'. Available at https://cyberknife.com/cyberknife-how-it-works/ (accessed 10 January 2022).

European Commission (2020) *White Paper on Artificial Intelligence: A European Approach to Excellence and Trust*. Available at https://ec.europ.eu/info/sites/default/files/commission-white-paper-artificial-intelligence-feb2020_en.pdf (accessed 3 May 2022).

Friedberg, A. (2006) *The Virtual Window: From Alberti to Microsoft*. Cambridge, MA: MIT Press.

Goldberg, K. (ed.) (2000) *The Robot in the Garden: Telerobotics and Telepistemology in the Age of the Internet*. Cambridge, MA: MIT Press.

Heim, M. (1991) 'The Metaphysics of Virtual Reality', in Helsel, S. K. and Roth, J. P.

(eds), *Virtual Reality: Theory, Practice and Promise*. Westport, WA: Meckler, pp. 27–34.

Howard, A. and Borenstein, J. (2018) 'The Ugly Truth About Ourselves and Our Robot Creations: The Problem of Bias and Social Inequity', in *Science and Engineering Ethics*. Available at https://pubmed.ncbi.nlm.nih.gov/28936795 (accessed 3 May 2019).

Jay, M. (2000) 'The Speed of Light and the Virtualisation of Reality', in Goldberg, K. (ed.), *The Robot in the Garden: Telerobotics and Telepistemology in the Age of the Internet*. Cambridge, MA: MIT Press, pp.158–9.

Khan, N. (2016) 'Intimate Pressure.' Available at https://noranahidkhan.com/2016/04/24/intimate-pressure (accessed 24 November 2020).

Khan, N. (2019) 'Seeing, Naming, Knowing', *The Brooklyn Rail*. Available at https://brooklynrail.org/2019/03/art/Seeing-Naming-Knowing (accessed 24 November 2020).

Menkman, R. (2011) *The Glitch Moment(um)*. Amsterdam: Institute of Network Cultures.

McKinsey & Company (2021) 'Harnessing Artificial Intelligence and Other Advanced Technologies to Address Social and Humanitarian Crises'. Available at: https://www.mckinsey.com/business-functions/mckinsey-analytics/how-we-help-clients/noble-intelligence (accessed 12 April 2022).

Noble, S. (2018) *Algorithms of Oppression: How Search Engines Reinforce Racism*. New York: New York University Press.

Paglen, T. (2014) 'Is Photography Over?', Available at https://www.fotomuseum.ch/en/series/is-photography-over (accessed 19 May 2022).

O'Sullivan, S. (2009) 'From Stuttering and Stammering to the Diagram: Deleuze, Bacon and Contemporary Art Practice', *Deleuze Studies* 3(2): pp. 247–58. Available at http://dx.doi.org/10.3366/E1750224109000622 (accessed 2 September 2019).

Radin, J. and Rudin, C. (2019) 'Why Are We Using Black Box Models in AI When We Don't Need To? A Lesson from an Explainable AI Competition', *Harvard Data Science Review* 1(2). Available at https://hdsr.mitpress.mit.edu/pub/f9kuyi8/release/7 (accessed 19 May 2022).

Russell, L. (2020) *Glitch Feminism*. London: Verso.

Sparrow, R. (2019) 'Robots Has a Race Problem', *Science, Technology and Human Values*. Available at https://journals.sagepub.com/doi/abs/10.1177/0162243919862862 (accessed 30 July 2019).

Strecker, A. (n.d.) 'An Urgent Look at How Artificial Intelligence Will See the World'. Available at https://www.lensculture.com/articles/trevor-paglen-an-urgent-look-at-how-artificial-intelligence-will-see-the-world (accessed 19 May 2022).

Virtual Reality Society (2009) 'Who Coined the Term "Virtual Reality?"' Available at http://www.vrs.org.uk/virtual-reality/who-coined-the-term.html (accessed 10 May 2022).

Williams, S., Layard Horsfall, H., Funnell, J. P., Hanrahan, J. G., Khan, D. Z., Muirhead, W., Stoyanov, D. and Marcus, H. J.(2021) 'Artificial Intelligence in Brain Tumour Surgery – An Emerging Paradigm', *Cancers (Basel)* 13(19): 5010.

Zhang, M. (2015) 'Here's a Look at How Colour Film Was Originally Biased Toward White People'. Available at https://petapixel.com/2015/09/19/heres-a-look-at-how-color-film-was-originally-biased-toward-white-people (accessed 30 July 2016).

Zylinska, J. (2017) *Nonhuman Photography*. Cambridge, MA: MIT Press.

Zylinska, J. (2021) 'Undigital Photography: Image-Making beyond Computation and AI', in Dvorák, T. and Parikka, J. (eds), *Photography Off the Scale: Technologies and Theories of the Mass Image*. Edinburgh: Edinburgh University Press, pp. 231–52.

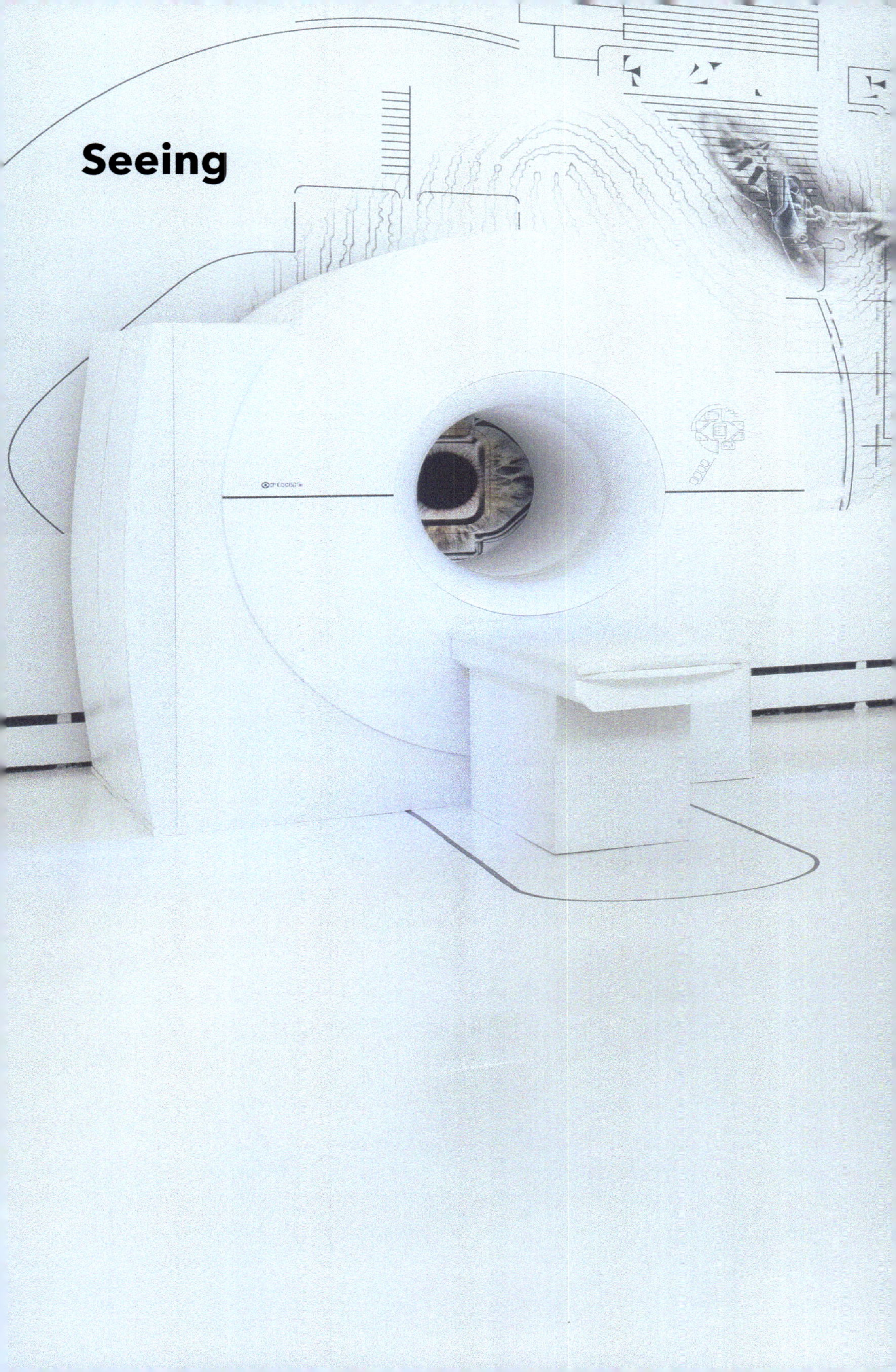
Seeing

1 When Robots Ignore Us: The Affective Impact of Robotic Artwork and Development of Drone Art

Pearl John

Development in robotic technology expands our vision, both practically and philosophically, providing artists with a new creative vocabulary and novel perspective. The term 'robot' was introduced by Czech playwright Karel Capek in his 1920 play *RUR – Rossum's Universal Robots* (1920), which referenced forced labour by slaves. Artists and historians argue that the robot is hard to define because the technological creature itself is so enmeshed with mythological figures, automata and science fiction (Devlin 2018; Kac 1997; Reichardt 1978). For the purposes of this chapter, I use a broad definition too, encompassing science fiction and science fact. Artist and writer Eduardo Kac described a framework for the understanding and analysis of robotic art as including automated machines which are remote controlled, cybernetic and have an element of autonomous behaviour (Kac 1997). Kac claims that the fascination robots exert on the population at large has unexplored emotional implications (as well as social and political), and that these implications must be coupled with the new aesthetic dimension of robotic behaviour in which the object 'perceives' the viewer and the environment. Considering Kac's claims, this chapter seeks to answer two questions: How have artists explored the emotional implications of robots? And, how have technical advances in robotic vision enhanced our own vision practically and philosophically?

First, the discussion touches on the long-held culture of fear of robots and their apparent sentience. The fear is evident in the work of filmmakers such as Lang (1927), Wise (1951) and the more contemporary work of Garland (2014) and Joy and Nolan (2016–21). The fear stems from robots having weaponised robotic vision and their lacking in empathy or emotion (Szollosy 2016). Secondly, I argue that the birth of robotic art by Nicolas Schöffer (1960) and Nam June Paik (1960) was dependent on robotic sight – with use of sensors enabling interactivity between robot and viewer (Handhardt 2000). Thirdly, I argue that the emotional response of the viewer/participant to the artwork is an essential element to the interactive/cybernetic system because participants' feelings lead to their physical movement (Bech 2014; Mrongovius 2011). In order to create social robots, technology seeks to elicit a range of emotions from robot interactions and I explore the exploitation by artists Anna Dumitriu and Alex May of our tendency to anthropomorphise robots (Dumitriu and May 2011), the phenomenon that describes the human tendency to see human-like shapes in the environment (Złotowski et al. 2014). Fourthly, I discuss how drones, the remotely operated vehicles designed for munitions' purposes and surveillance, are zoomorphised, or seen as animal-like rather than human, and how artists such as Flanders and Sawatzky (2013) and Heather Philipson (2020) have used the emotional impact of the technology for its threatening connotations. However, other artists, such as filmmaker Abelardo Gil-Fourner (working with academic Jussi Parikka) and holographer Vaughan Wozniak-O'Connor (2018), expand the emotional vocabulary of the medium of drone art by referencing new applications beyond the production of the operational image (Paglen 2014). Their artwork explores emotional and physiological responses to the landscape using the drone as a tool rather than a spectacle. Lastly, the discussion focuses on the emotional impact of drone swarms on audiences, the latest development of robotic technology. Swarms are being used by lighting companies to entertain large audiences, who respond with awe. The robot's gaze is turning away from the viewer/participant and towards other robots, and artists such as Boredom Research are exploring the drone's simulated feelings while they provide us with new perspectives.

A Culture of Fear

The history of robots is a rich area of ancient myth, technological development for science and industry, and entertainment – including science fiction (Devlin 2018; Kac 1997; Reichardt 1978). People's emotional responses to robots appears always to have included fascination and fear. This fear seems to have three roots: (1) robots are superior in terms of their ability to work and may replace us, (2) robots have been weaponised so are seen as a physical threat, and (3) we anthropomorphise or zoomorphise robots and perceive them as sentient creatures without feelings.

The fears that robots are weaponised and may replace humans at work were evident in early filmmaking, for example in *Metropolis*

(Lang 1927) and two decades later in *The Day the Earth Stood Still* (Wise 1951). Both early films feature robots in dystopian futures. In *Metropolis* the central character, a gynoid, transforms to replace the heroine during a threatening period of industrialisation, and in *The Day the Earth Stood Still* the cyborg character threatens to destroy humans to save the planet. Clips from the films have been watched by over one and two million viewers respectively on YouTube, indicating a public fascination with the historical creative representation of robots. While there has been a wealth of depictions of robots in science fiction since the 1950s, a fascination with and fear of robots are still culturally evident in contemporary filmmaking. Two recent representations of robots in film and television, *Ex Machina* (Garland 2014) and *Westworld* (Joy and Nolan 2016–21), again present dystopian worlds with gynoids and androids replacing humans by outperforming them, and then destroying them. Advancements in technology over the decades have led to a change in science fiction robots being mechanical in appearance to hyperreal and almost indistinguishable from humans, but the emotional impact on audiences is still the same (fear).

The fear of being replaced at work by robots stems from the changing nature of work and is illustrated by news headlines such as: 'Up to 20 million manufacturing jobs around the world could be replaced by robots by 2030...' (Celan-Jones 2019). This news article cited a survey by Oxford Economics which also claimed that approximately 1.7 million manufacturing jobs had been lost to robots since 2000. Robots outperform humans in manufacturing work, not just because they can perform repetitive actions tirelessly, but also because of their superior sight; they are able to see flaws which are undetectable to the human eye and are thus useful in quality control functions.

Not only is there fear about being replaced by robots but there is a concern that in employing robots we are treating them badly and they will at some point become sentient and retaliate. Robots are often anthropomorphised. In *Robots: Fact, Fiction and Prediction* (1978) Jasia Reichardt describes a project in which she surveyed children in a London school about the gender of robots:

> To boys they were 'it', to the girls they were 'he', or 'she' if the robot served a man ... man has turned the robot into 'an underprivileged sort of person'. And, indeed, in literature the robot has become a metaphor for a second-class citizen. (Reichardt 1978: p. 7)

She also claims that, as subjugated beings, robots are threatening: 'Man, having constructed the robot, has begun to distrust this new image of himself' (Reichardt 1978: p. 7). The robotic characters who reach sentience in *Ex Machina* and *Westworld* are treated appallingly by the humans and their wish to escape is presented somewhat sympathetically by the narrative. Psychology researcher Michael Szollosy describes robots as having been portrayed in the media as monstrous, projections of human anxieties regarding the dehumanising tendencies of science and reason without empathy (Szollosy 2016).

Robotic Vision

An important aspect of the threat of being replaced by robots and the fear of sentience is robot vision, which is generally misunderstood. In science fiction the mechanics of robotic vision itself is often presented as weaponised. For example, the cyborg in *The Day the Earth Stood Still* shoots laser beams from the eyes. The holographer Jon Mitton parodies weaponised sight in his holographic stereogram *You Will Obey* (1992) illustrated in Figure 1.1, which depicts a moving

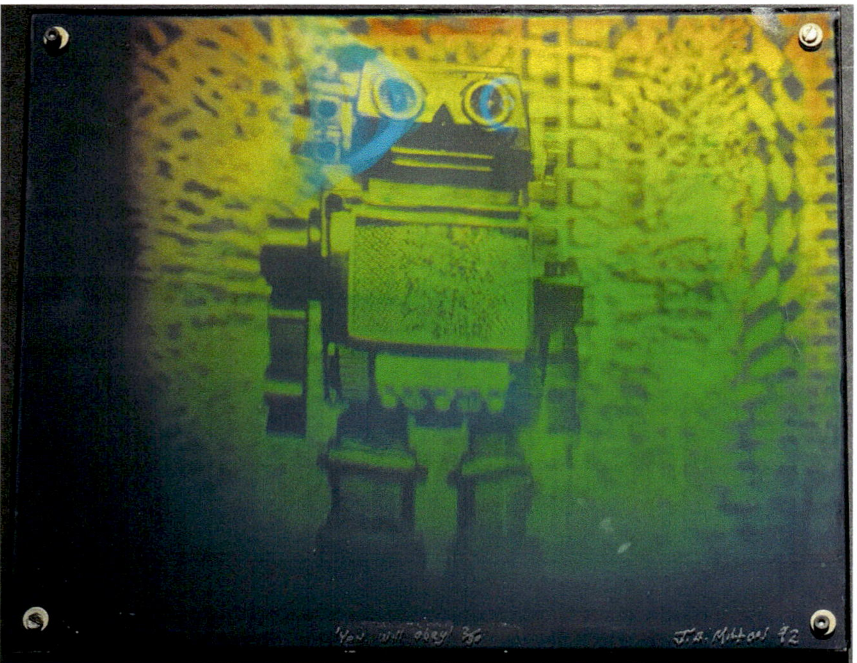

Figure 1.1 Jon Mitton, *You Will Obey.*
10″ x 8″ holographic Stereogram, 1992.

toy robot which totters backwards and forwards shooting hypnotic rays of light from its eyes, animated by the viewer's movement to and fro in front of the hologram. This illustration of threatening robotic vision taps into a Platonic and scientifically inaccurate understanding of how we see: the idea of extromission, in which light is thought to emanate from the eyes to touch an object, and then return to the eye. This erroneous understanding of how humans see was described by writer and educator James Elkins in *The Object Stares Back: On the Nature of Seeing* (1996) and illustrated by researcher John Kevin O'Regan, at the University of Paris, in his internet article Ancient Visions' (n.d.), shown in Figure 1.2.

Elkins describes how powerful the theory of extromission is, despite being incorrect, referring to the psychoanalyst Jacques Lacan's theorising on the subjective gaze:

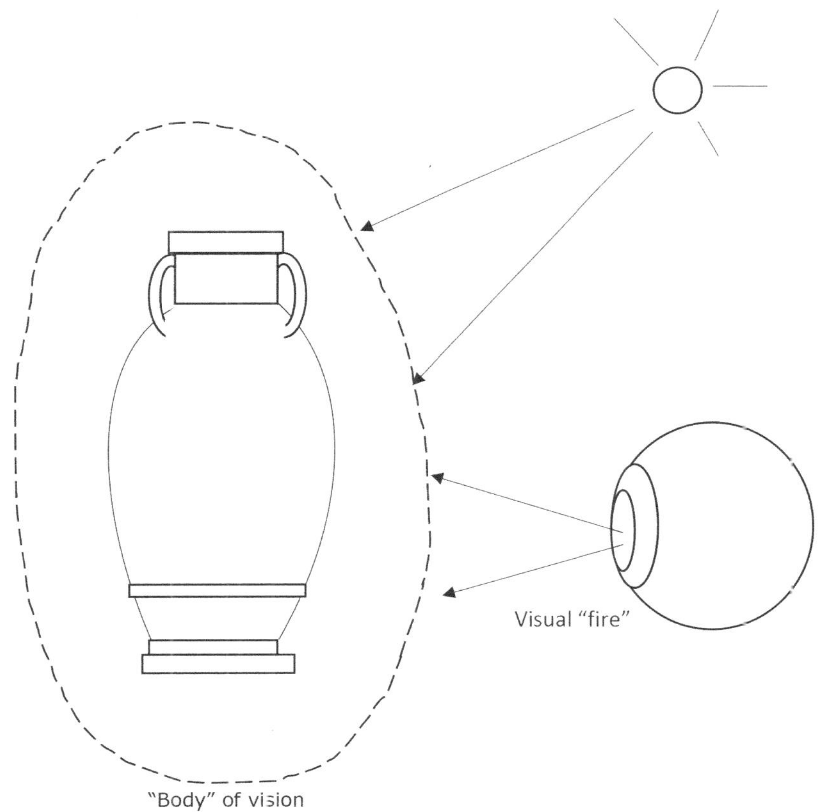

Figure 1.2 John Kevin O'Regan, an illustration of extromission.

> I look at someone or something, it looks back, and our gazes cross
> each other ... if I am looking at an inanimate object it has a certain
> presence – it looks back, and again I can understand that as the echo
> of my gaze. I see and I can see that I am seen ... the whole scene is a
> kind of trap: we are 'caught' ... manipulated, captured in the field of
> vision. (Elkins 1996: p. 70)

The language Elkins uses describes a disconcerting loss of control when we are 'looked back' at by an inanimate object, and this is all the more unnerving when there is a question of whether the robot is sentient, what Donna Haraway describes as the 'Spectre of the Ghost in the Machine' in her 'Cyborg Manifesto' (Haraway 1985: p. 150). Human sight is actually based on photons from external light sources reflected by objects reaching the eye, where electrical signals are transported down the optic nerve and processed in the brain. We imagine that robots have similar sight processes, with their sensors or cameras; however, this is incorrect. They do not have what the post-phenomenologist writer Don Ihde refers to as an embodied relationship with the world – they have a hermeneutic one (see Rosenberger and Verbeek 2017). Robot vision does not rely on three-dimensional images using cameras – it is four dimensional. Its processes are temporal and spatial and based on sensing technologies. Robotic vision is in some ways superior to human vision; for example, it is mostly uniform across all parts of the field of view and it is perfect for periodic tasks, like identifying defects in objects. It is very accurate in such cases and can extract patterns from images that humans cannot even perceive (Pastor 2020). Hence it can be argued that robotic vision expands human vision.

However, robotic vision has its drawbacks. In the article 'Robotics: How Machines See the World', journalist Frank Swain interviewed scientist Peter McOwan, who described some of the current limitations of robotic vision: 'Robots have problems recognising shadows ... computer vision suffers really badly when there are variations in lighting conditions, occlusions and shadows.... Shadows are often considered to be real objects' (Swain 2014). These limitations explain why self-driving cars do not come equipped just with video cameras for seeing but also use ultrasound, radar, sonar, laser and infra-red detectors.

The robotic artwork *HARR1* (Dumitriu and May 2011) (shown in Figure 1.4 below) experienced the problems described above; the robot could see in infra-red, using laser scanning processes, having a view of the world beyond the range of visible sight for humans, but *HARR1* experienced pareidolia (seeing faces where there are none).

The robot said 'I love you' to the wall when dappled sunlight created an optical illusion of a face (Dumitru and May 2014).

Robotic vision expands our own vision practically and philosophically as reaching new spaces enlarges our experience of the world, and in reaching previously inaccessible places robots can make us more humane. Robots can enable a viewer to remotely access areas through telepresence that we cannot physically reach; some areas are inaccessible because they are physically dangerous for a human to do so. For example, robots are used by the police and military to remotely disarm bombs (Department of Homeland Security 2020) and by scientists and engineers to clear up nuclear waste (Cholteeva 2020). Robots were used by hospitals to enable communication between patients and their families unable to visit them during the Covid-19 pandemic. Figure 1.3 depicts a robot named Pepper, built by Softbank Robotics, being used to remotely link family members (Schöpfer 2020).

A telepresence robot was also used by Hastings Contemporary Art Gallery during the first UK national lockdown in the Covid-19 pandemic, to enable visitors (including myself) to tour the building and view the exhibitions. 'The Double', a two-wheeled videoconferencing robot (an iPad attached to a Segway), was built by Bristol

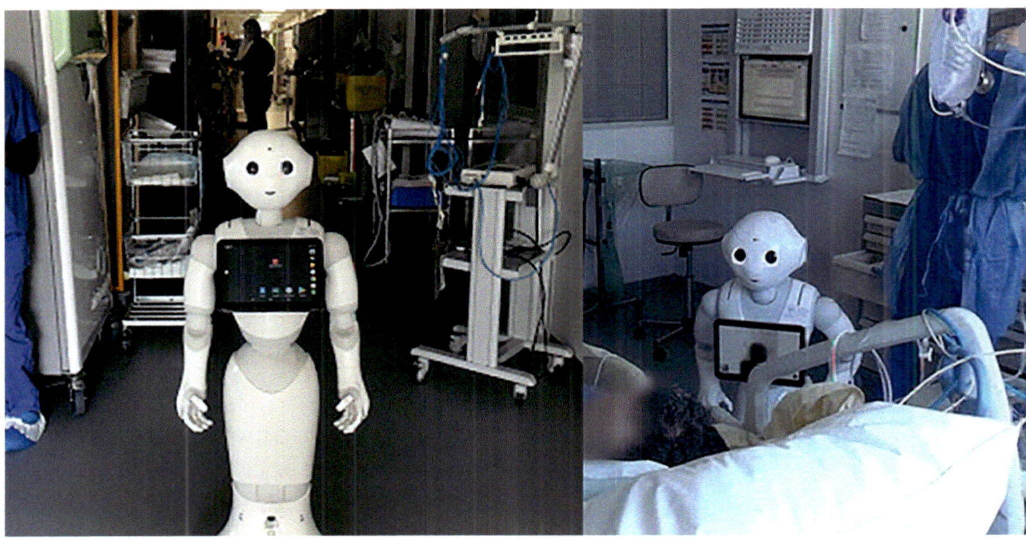

Figure 1.3 Pepper, a social robot supporting hospital patients and their families. Softbank Robotics, 2020.

Robotic Labs and controlled remotely by the Visitor Services Manager Rowan Bunney. The robot allowed people to visit a site virtually which was closed physically. It was a fascinating experience. The robot trundled through the building as the tour guide described the architecture and exhibits via a videoconferencing program similar to Zoom. However, the tour experienced technical problems when the robot stopped working on a couple of occasions. The robot relied on a Wi-Fi connection for its remote control and areas of the building had poor coverage, resulting in a lost signal and a need for the robot to be restarted. Despite the technical problems the tours were successful: Bunney shared that the robot had enabled a new international audience to have virtual access to the gallery, and exhibitions therein, who would not otherwise have travelled in person to visit it.

Robotic art emerged from a culture and public feeling of fascination and fear of robots, a misunderstanding of the technological processes which enable robots to see, and a tendency towards anthropomorphising robots. Advancements in technology are leading to wider applications of robots, beyond weaponisation and towards more humane and useful applications to help solve societal problems. As robotic technology has progressed, artists have engaged with the new vision and perspectives that robotic art has afforded. The next section explores the development of robotic art and how it engages with its audiences.

Robotic Art

Artist and academic Eduardo Kac claimed that the following aspects have been considered central to the development of robotic art: (1) interactivity between the audience/participants and the artist, (2) robot vision and human vision, (3) the emotional engagement of the participant, or audience member and (4) the impact of anthropomorphism (Kac 1997). These aspects have been evident in robotic artwork from its inception.

There is broad agreement that the artist Nicholas Schöffer was the first to produce robotic artwork with the piece *CYSP 1* (Cybernetic Spatiodynamic Sculpture), produced in 1956 (Benthall 1972; Kac 1997; Reichardt 1978). The robot *CYSP 1* incorporated all of the key aspects Kac outlined and marked the transition from kinetic art using electromechanical technology to cybernetic systems artwork using electronic control systems. Cybernetics was theorised by Norbert Wiener in 1948, who described cybernetic systems as 'mechanisms for communication and common control of machines and animals' (Wiener 1948). Schöffer's artwork required a partici-pant to provide feedback as part of the system. The use of sensors in *CYSP1* was critical to the transition to robotic art because they enabled interactivity between the artwork and its environment. The sensors Schöffer employed consisted of a photocell, microphone and homeostat, the last of which provided the electronic control system. The robotic artwork was fixed to a base, moving in response to the intensity of environmental lighting, colour and sound provided by the artist and participant. The artwork relied not only on the sensors of the robot, but also on the feelings of playfulness and movement of the participant in response to the robot in order to create the cyber-netic feedback system.

Artist and play researcher Tine Bech described interactive artworks as those in which audiences physically and visibly interact with the work, with the artwork activating the viewer into playing and con-necting (Bech 2014: pp. 33–4). Practice-based researchers survey audience responses to interactive artworks (Edmonds 2011; John 2018: pp. 74–80) to determine the emotional impact of interactive artworks because the audience is integral to the artwork. Without emotional impact, the viewer will not react physically to cause a two-way interaction:

> It is impossible to understand an interactive artwork by just consider-ing the art object unrelated to its audience and the audience actions, and hence, the artist's focus will be on a combined artificial (artwork) and human (audience) art system. (Edmonds 2011: p. 19)

Bech quotes play researcher Andy Polaine in her PhD dissertation to explain the link between engaged interaction and movement: 'Play with an interactive artwork is usually non-verbal and involves a dance of physical movements' (Bech 2014: p. 33). Schöffer emphasised the aspect of interactivity by presenting his robot as a dancer in the first exhibition of *CYSY 1*. The robot appeared in a choreographed ballet performance with Maurice Béjart, who executed a pas de deux to the accompaniment of a concrete music composition by Pierre Henry.

Ernest Edmonds describes interactive works as art systems rather than artworks, to emphasise the role of the viewer participant in the art (Edmonds 2011). Edmonds created a taxonomy of different levels of interactivity between artwork and participant in new media art which is relevant to robotic art and useful when defining interactiv-ity: level 1 has no interactivity, while level 5 involves interactivity building over time, through automated learning (Edmonds et al. 2004). While the interactive artwork requires a participant, Bech argues that participatory art is distinct from interactive art in that participatory art includes an element of socially engaged art, whereas interactive art need not (Bech 2014: p. 35).

Another important element of robotic art is the emotional impact of anthropomorphism. In *Robot K-456* (1964) Nam June-Paik presented his robot as a female performer who came to a tragic end to illicit emotional responses from his audience. His robot had breasts and defecated beans as it walked along the pavement in New York and was then hit by a car as it crossed the road (Hanhardt 2000: p. 53). The interactivity was between the artist and the artwork, rather than between the audience and the robot, though, as the robot was remote controlled. The performance had a range of emotional impacts on the audience, from amusement to shock. Social robotics researcher Karolina Zawieska argued in her paper 'Social Robots: Fostering Creativity through the Illusion of Life' that the human tendency to anthropomorphise robots leads to creativity: 'anthropomorphisation is a fundamentally interpretive process, where not only people do perceive robots as alive, but they also imagine them as such' (Zawieska 2014).

This creative aspect is exploited by contemporary artists Alex May and Anna Dumitriu, who portray robots as having a range of emotions, including boredom, envy and love. May and Dumitriu have worked together on a range of robotic artworks exploring simulated robot emotions and actual audience emotion. In *HARR1 (Humanoid Artistic Research Robot 1)* (2011) their robot with a childlike appearance was designed to appear to get bored unless the audience kept interacting with it. The robot's attention was focused on a viewer, until the viewer stopped moving, then the robot's attention appeared to wander away. May's marketing of the artwork emphasised its emotional impact, as shown in Figure 1.4. The website reads 'Visitors who stand in front of HARR1 exhibit initial interest as they see HARR1 respond to their movement and expect further interaction. However, HARR1 gets bored resulting in visitors feeling rather rejected.'

My Robot Companion (Dumitriu and May 2014), shown in Figure 1.5, featured a robot head designed by the artists which 'stole' audience members' faces. The robot body was designed by the Adaptive Systems Research Group at the University of Hertfordshire. The head scanned its audience members or viewers and then said 'I like your face' in a manner which suggested that the robot felt envy. It then projected an image of the viewer's face onto its own from inside the facemask. The research project, which partnered May and Dumitriu with the Adaptive Systems Research Group, explored the point at which a robot face entered Mori's 'Uncanny Valley' and

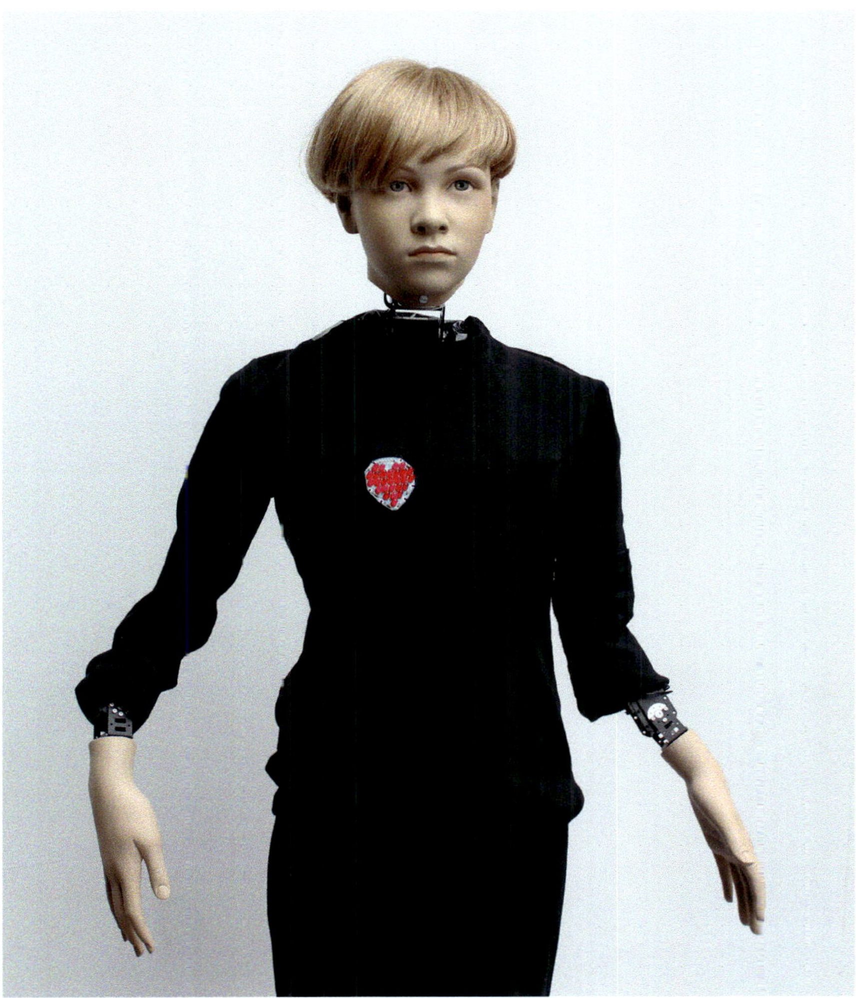

Figure 1.4 Alex May and Anna Dumitriu, HARR1 (Humanoid Artistic Research Robot 1), 2011.

became unnerving for the viewer. *HARR1* and *My Robot Companion* expand the range of our emotional responses to robots, exploring post-human relationships.

Jakub Złotowski et al. (2014) argue that humans anthropomorphise objects where they perceive the object can see in the way that we see and sense, that is, with two eyes and two ears; however, where the robot clearly does not see in the same way that we do, the robot is zoomorphised. The next section discusses how developments in

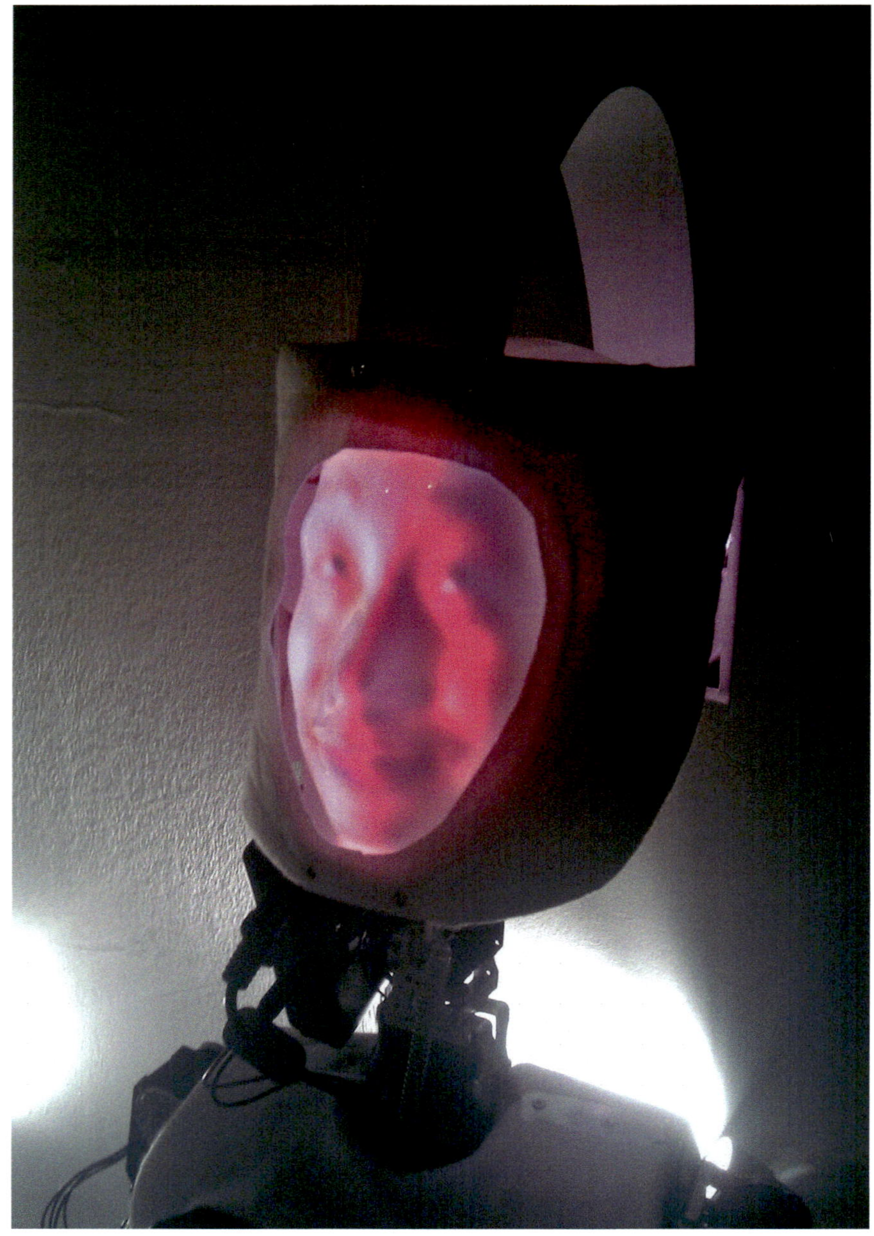

Figure 1.5 Alex May and Anna Dumitriu, *My Robot Companion*, robot with projected face, 2012.

drone technology have expanded our way of seeing and being, and the emotional responses of audiences to drones and drone art.

Beyond Fear: Looking at and Seeing with Drones

Drone technology has expanded the creative vocabulary of robotic art, providing artists with new ways of imaging, making and seeing. Arthur Holland Michel, Director of the Center for the Study of the Drone at Bard College, New York, describes drone art as 'that which includes both works that are created using drone technology and works that in some way address or depict the drone' (Holland 2014). However, I have chosen to focus on art which incorporates the robot itself, rather than artwork that merely represents it. First, I will discuss drone vision, that is, the expansion of human vision through telepresence and the production of the problematic operational image referenced by James Bridle. Secondly, I will describe the work of artists in the Public Studio collective, as well as Heather Phillipson, Vaughan Wozniak-O'Connor, and Abelardo Gil-Fourner, the latter working with new media theorist Jussi Parikka, all of whom zoomorphise the drone while referencing new, more positive applications of drone technology, that is, for wedding photography, agriculture and search and rescue, with a wide range of emotional impacts. I conclude with a discussion of drone swarms, the emerging technology being used by entertainers and simulated by artists as having their own emotions.

Drones, or unmanned aerial vehicles, were developed for militaristic surveillance then munitions purposes, arguably during the First World War, and became widely used by the USA after 9/11/2001 (Imperial War Museums n.d.). Artist Harun Farocki coined the phrase 'operational images' to describe the politics of image making especially in the military industrial context. Operational images track, navigate, oversee, control, visualise and detect (Farocki 2004). The artist Trevor Paglen (2014) describes operational images as 'images made by machines for other machines'. This makes drone vision threatening to the beholder. They actually see in two different ways, through video camera and sensors. The video camera is for the operator, while the drone detects its position in space through the Global Positioning System (GPS), and proximity to other objects with infra-red or radio frequency (RF) sensors, all of which are dependent on the make and model of the drone. All these different elements of sight and sensing make drone vision complex, enabling the operator through telepresence to expand human vision across great distances.

Post-phenomenological writer Kirk Besmer describes this expanded sense of self:

> Robust real-time communicative action in and feedback from a remote environment provide users of these technologies with a sense of presence in the remote environment. Users often feel as if they are there, at the remote site, whether it be a virtual or a real location. (Besmer 2017: p. 55)

Despite drone pilots feeling as though they are present elsewhere, they are not, and the use of drones in war is ethically problematic not least because of the physical distance between opposing sides. Dr Ross Bellaby, Senior Lecturer in Politics at the University of Sheffield, in 'The Aesthetics of Drone Warfare' roundtable discussion in 2020, described warfare with drones as relying on a 'PlayStation mentality' which is psychologically damaging to the operator (Aesthetics of Drone Warfare 2020). In this problematic context artists' responses to drone technology include work with a strong element of fear and anxiety. In *Drone Shadow 001* (2012) James Bridle tapes out a large drone outline on the ground in a car park which references not only the shape of the drone shadow on the ground where the viewer is under a potential threat of attack from above, but also the taping out of a victim of a crime scene on the ground, emphasising the problematic ethical nature of drones used in warfare.

Smaller drones have also been used for military surveillance, which again makes even small-drone vision threatening to those being look at. Computing systems researchers Victoria Chang and Marshini Chetty surveyed people on their responses to small commercial drones and the findings were reflected in their research paper '"Spiders in the Sky": User Perceptions of Drones, Privacy, and Security', that is, the public were found to anthropomorphise and fear drone swarms (Chang and Chetty 2017). However, Chang and Chetty's research did not inform participants of the wealth of new applications for the technology for more positive purposes than munitions and surveillance, such as wedding photography, landscape aerial photography, search and rescue, mapping, agriculture, entertainment and many others. These new applications are expanding the potential for the emotional impact of the robots themselves on audiences and are providing artists with a new tool.

Drone vision provides a novel view from above, previously only briefly available to air balloons and helicopters. Artists are beginning to use drones as a tool for documenting their work. For example, Luke Jerram has used a drone to film his most recent large-scale temporary outdoor installation *In Memoriam* (2020). The artwork is a

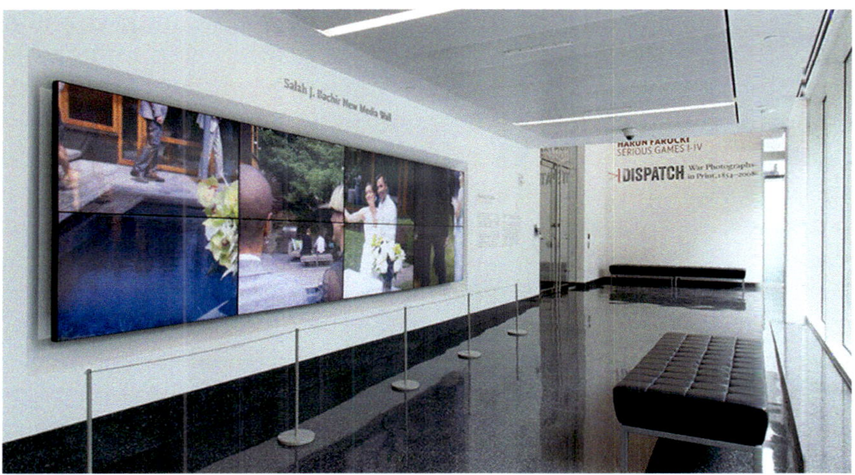

Figure 1.6 Public Studio, *Drone Wedding*, installation shown at the Ryerson Image Centre, 2014.

temporary memorial featuring large flags located on the south coast of England; the shape of the red cross made from red flags positioned within white flags is visible only from above and the drone enables an internet audience to see this view of the work.[1]

The artist collective Public Studio formed by Canadian artists Tamira Kawatzky and Elle Flanders has referenced two aspects of drones at weddings: first, the wedding guests killed by military drone strikes in Afghanistan and Pakistan; and secondly, the relatively new phenomenon of drone wedding photography. Drones are now used to take outdoor aerial shots of large groups of family and friends, by rotating the drone (effectively making it fly 'backwards') and spotlighting the group as the drone climbs upwards and away. The result is a newly clichéd image of the group waving and receding into the distance.[2] Public Studio used a juxtaposition of the historical militaristic drone application with the new wedding photography tool to project an element of discomfort into their eight-channel video installation *Drone Wedding* (Public Studio 2014). The video installation depicted a staged wedding using drone surveillance techniques (Figure 1.6). A highly pixelated black and white image

---

1   In personal correspondence, Jerram was keen to point out that the use of the drone was for documenting the artwork only: he did not consider his drone imagery to be part of his artwork.
2   This is a move taught at the drone school I attended with wedding photographers and videographers.

can be seen on the left-hand-side video channels, simulating film footage taken from many miles away, synonymous with militaristic drone usage. A soundtrack features Chelsea Manning's WikiLeaks exposé of US drone pilots killing innocent Iraqis and journalists. The emotional impact on the viewer is uncomfortable. The guests appear under physical threat of attack and their privacy violated. The drone is an unwanted guest at the wedding, subverting the usual use of wedding photography drones used to capture large groups of people. This application of drone technology relies on interactivity between the artist and the technology, but when the viewer is excluded from any aspect of interactivity the emotional impact is more negative.

Drones tend to be zoomorphised, viewed as more animal-like than human-like because of their shape and sound, and the ways in which they move, see and sense. Social robot researcher Jakob Złotowski describes the work of Carl Di Salvo, who argues that it is the potential manner of interaction between human and robot which determines anthropomorphism: 'it is necessary to build robots with features that enable them to perceive the world similarly to humans, i.e. using two cameras (in place of eyes) and two microphones (ears)' (Złotowski et al. 2014: p. 349).

Heather Phillipson's Fourth Plinth sculpture *The End* (2020) relies on our zoomorphism of the drone which sits on top of an enlarged scoop of whipped cream, along with a giant cherry, and a fly which is a reminder that drones also buzz like insects. The drone is both looked at, as part of the sculpture, and sees, transmitting a live feed of Trafalgar Square via an accompanying website, www.theend.today. The drone camera view offers viewers a 'sculpture's eye perspective' on the surrounding area (Hutchinson 2020) or a God-like and dispassionate view of the tiny people going about their business below which are almost insect-like themselves. Both the drone and the fly are an unpleasant element of the image of the swirl of cream and cherry on top of breeze blocks without a cone; the oversized food is contaminated and unpalatable, both attractive and repulsive. The viewer cannot control the drone and while we observe through the drone, we are powerless to interact; we have become the surveyors.

However, drone technology is moving beyond military surveillance for a multitude of more positive applications (such as seed bombing in agriculture, or for architectural design and urban mapping) and, as a result, the emotional impact of the drone for the artist and audience member is expanding beyond fear and disgust. Media theorist Jussi Parikka and filmmaker Abelardo Gil-Fourner, and holographer Vaughan Wozniak-O'Connor reference these positive new applications for drone technology in their work.

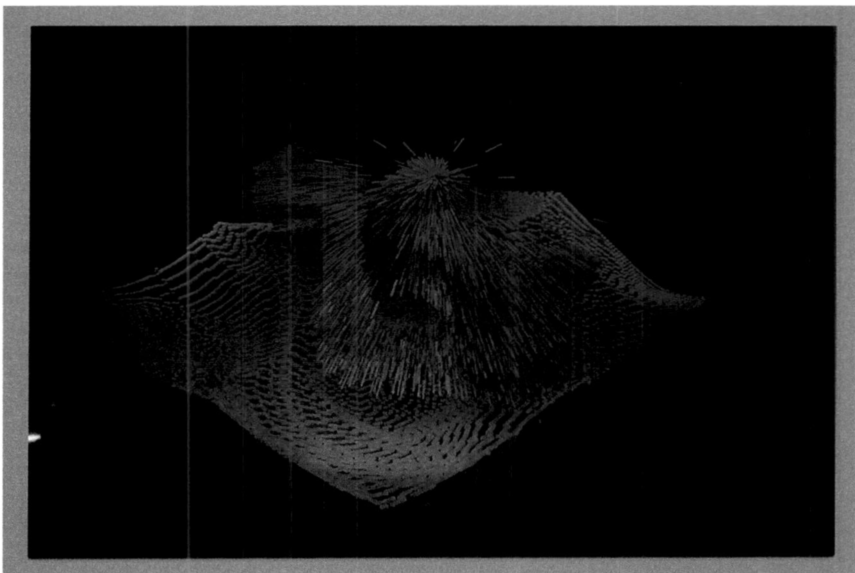

Figure 1.7 Vaughan Wozniak-O'Connor, digital animated hologram, 2013.

Parikka and Gil-Fourner's video essay describes the process of scanning land as transforming the earth's surfaces into data while Wozniak-O'Connor uses the drone in a process of holographic image making, mapping his emotional experience of the land (Figures 1.7 and 1.8). Three-dimensional holography was first produced by physicists Emmett Leith and Juris Upatnieks from the Synthetic Aperture Radar (SAR) imaging lab at Michigan University funded by the US Defense Department in the 1960s (Johnston 2006). Holograms have themselves been used as operational images, providing soldiers with three-dimensional maps to refer to in the field during combat. However, in response to the use of drones for the mapping of environments using LIDAR and the simulation of the maps in virtual reality for architectural design and urban planning purposes, Wozniak-O'Connor extended the concept of transforming the earth's surfaces into data to include mapping psycho-geographical areas and the emotional impact of place. Wozniak-O'Connor took his drone for a walk via a tethering command in his drone app and linked himself with lie-detector technology to record his physical responses and the depth of his emotional response to the landscape. To record the three-dimensional data which was produced during the encounter he printed a four-dimensional digital hologram, preserving the emotional experience of the landscape over time (Wozniak-O'Connor 2018). The four-dimensional hologram captures up to 2,000 images from different viewpoints creating a 3D animated holographic image which includes an element of time. The imaging system can be likened to a printed recording of the way in which a robot sees, combining stereoscopic images from multiple cameras. The drone is a tool which extends the vision of the artist as well as being part of the performative element of the artwork.

While tethered to the drone, Wozniak-O'Conner conceptually became a cyborg. The synthesis of man and drone results in drone art

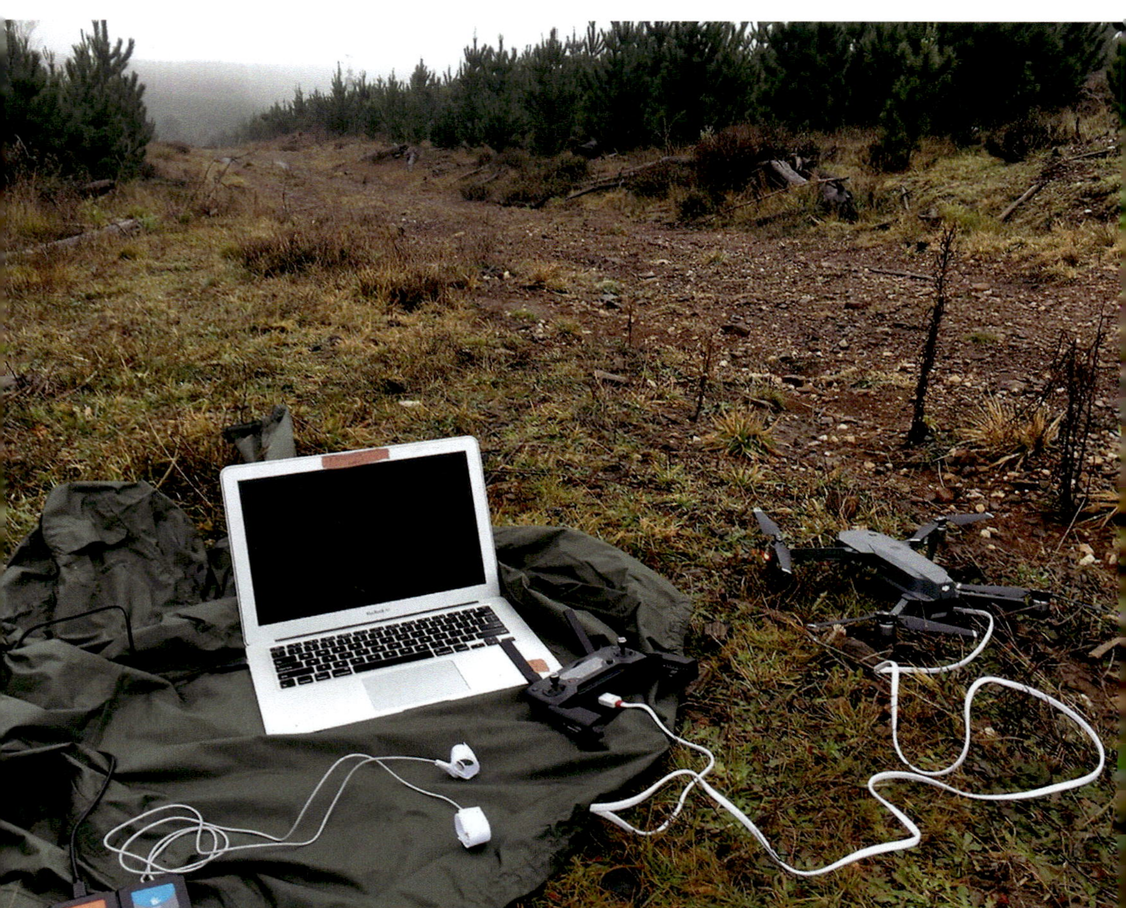

Figure 1.8 Vaughan Wozniak-O'Connor, image of landscape and drone, 2018.

expanding its emotional vocabulary to include the artist's emotions and experiences, with the result that the drone loses its threat. This relationship between robot and human was described by Donna Haraway in 'A Cyborg Manifesto':

> There are several consequences to taking seriously the imagery of cyborgs as other than our enemies. Our bodies, ourselves; bodies are maps of power and identity.... The machine is not an it to be animated, worshipped, and dominated. The machine is us, our processes, an aspect of our embodiment. We can be responsible for machines; they do not dominate or threaten us. We are responsible for boundaries; we are they. (Haraway 1985: p. 180)

Recent developments in drone technology have led to a new robotic medium – the drone swarm. Drone swarms are either pre-programmed, responding to computer control, or are autonomous. Drones can now share with one another their positioning via visual markers – in effect they now look at each other. The impact of drone swarms is on the shared vision and behaviour of the robots (Yong 2014) and as a result the concept of interactivity between robot and participant based on a mutual focus is no longer so important in robotic art. The emotional impact of drone swarms is one of awe when used for entertainment purposes. Intel describes 'dazzling' its audiences with its light shows that use up to 2,066 drones, which fly in formation to create animated 3D images. Each drone has inbuilt LEDs and acts as a kind of pixel in the construction of a larger image (Intel n.d.). This is an exciting form of temporary light sculpture, which is limited by the battery life of drones (Intel limits their performances to fifteen minutes) but has creative potential beyond mere entertainment that is yet to be exploited. However, there is what defence writer James Johnson calls a 'rapid proliferation of a new generation of artificial intelligence (AI)-augmented and -enabled autonomous weapon systems (AWS) most notably drones used in swarming tactics' (Johnson 2020). Drone swarms will be playing an increasing part in warfare and the extent to which they will be acting on their own is uncertain as the ethical nature of AI in munitions is under discussion.

Lastly, artists have expanded audiences' responses to drone swarms beyond awe and fear by projecting emotional lives onto drones. Boredom Research – a partnership between British artists Vicky Isley and Paul Smith – imagined drones' emotional lives in an apparently post-human world in *Robots in Distress* (2017) (Figures 1.9 and 1.10). The piece simulates underwater drones working as an

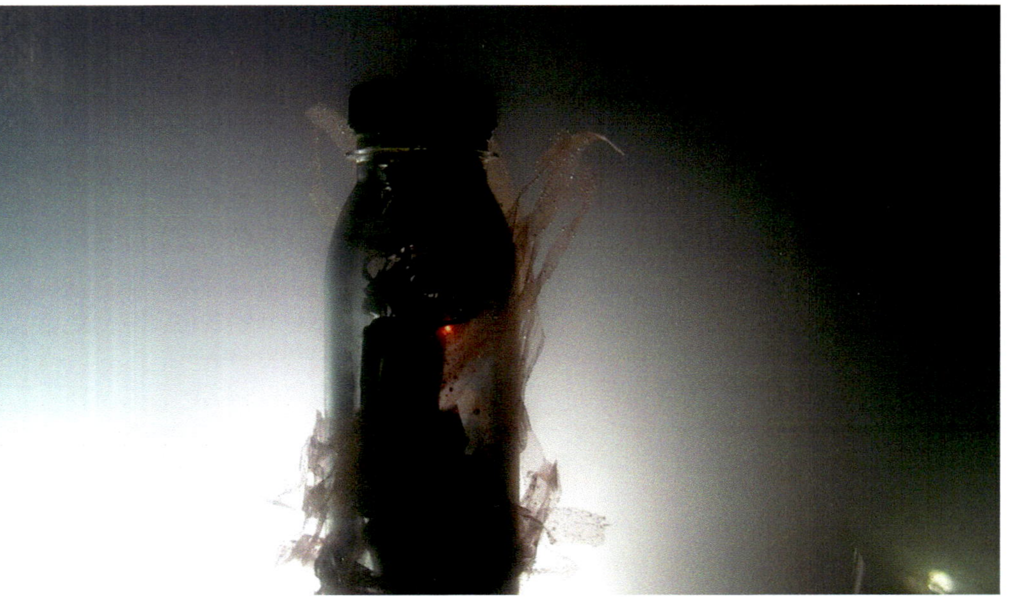

Figure 1.9 Boredom Research, *Robots in Distress*, underwater drone maquette, 2017.

artificial neural network (ANN) enhanced with the incorporation of artificial hormones for increased performance and efficiency. Boredom Research were inspired by working with SubCULTron and researchers at the Artificial Life Lab (Karl Franzens University, Graz, Austria), who are creating the world's largest underwater robot swarm to monitor the heavily human polluted Venice Lagoon. The simulated underwater drones in the artwork bob up and down and flash their lights at one another in a murky, polluted environment of their own. The artwork provokes feelings of sadness and empathy in the viewer, both at the polluted environment the drones are monitoring, and at the apparent emotional state of despondency and hopelessness in the robots who are attempting to clean up our environment.

Drone swarms enable robotic art to move beyond the interactivity that focuses on a robot and participant in an art system. The primary relationship in drone art is the interactivity between drones and the artist, and between drones themselves; the audience no longer has control.

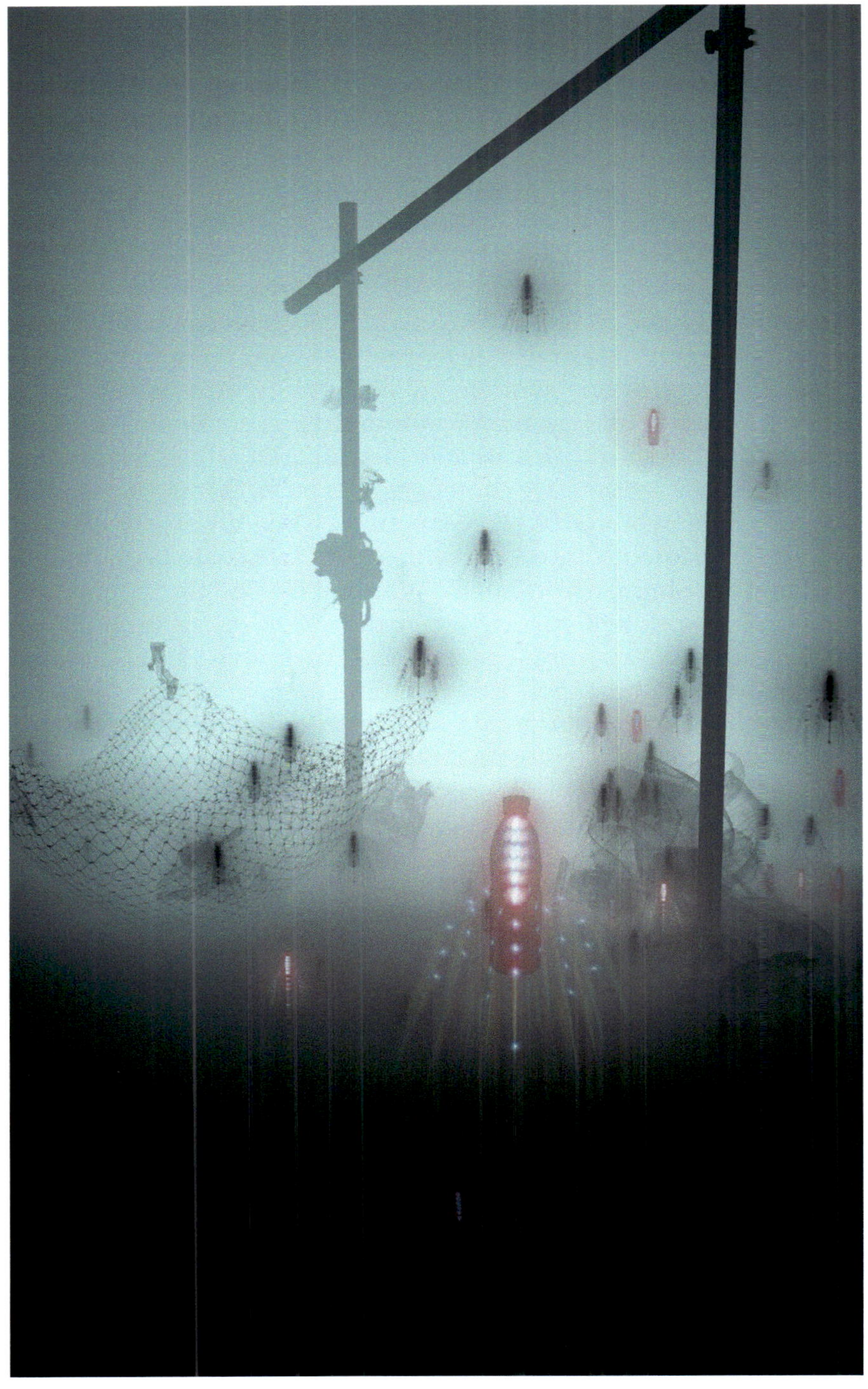

Figure 1.10 Boredom Research, *Robots in Distress*, simulated environment, 2017.

Conclusion

This chapter has outlined how robotic technology expands and extends our vision, enabling us to see differently as robots explore places and spaces previously inaccessible to humans using different methods of seeing and sensing. Development in robot technology has led to applications beyond the militaristic and industrial, enabling artists to use robots to elicit a range of emotions from their audiences beyond just fear from physical threat and fear of robot sentience. Robotic art began with interactivity between a robot and a participant in an art system which depended upon the robot and participant looking at one another and responding with movement. It was also necessary for the participant to have an emotional response to the interactive artwork – usually playfulness – which made them move. In effect, artists have choreographed participants' movements through manipulation of their emotions while giving the participant the illusion of control over the robot. Artists are beginning to explore a post-human world that has moved beyond the interactivity between artwork and participant in the cybernetic system. When tethered to a drone an artist becomes a cyborg, able to map physical and emotional landscapes. With the development of drone swarms and autonomous robots, artists are exploring interactivity between drones and simulated emotional responses to elicit our own. While drones have enabled artists to see from a new perspective, the view through or with a drone swarm seems not to have been utilised yet. As a result of anthropomorphism and zoomorphism, looking with robots appears to be a lot more empowering and less frightening than being looked at or ignored.

References

Aesthetics of Drone Warfare (2020) Festival of Social Science roundtable discussion, University of Sheffield, 8 September 2020.

Bech, T. (2014) *Playful Interactions: A Critical Inquiry into Interactive Art and Play*. Unpublished PhD thesis, UWE.

Benthall, J. (1972) *Science and Technology in Art Today*. London: Thames and Hudson.

Besmer, K. M. (2017) 'What Robotic Re-embodiment Reveals about Virtual Re-embodiment. A Note on the Extension Thesis', in Rosenberger, R. and Verbeek, P. (eds), *Postphenomenological Investigations: Essays on Human–Technology Relations* (Postphenomenology and the Philosophy of Technology). Lexington Books, Kindle version, pp. 55–71.

Boredom Research (2017) *Robots in Distress (Drone Robot and Simulation)*. Available at https://boredomresearch.net/wp/blog/author/boredomresearch (accessed 30 September 2020).

Bridle, J. (with Einar Sneve Martinussen) (2012) *Drone Shadow 001* (installation). Available at https://jamesbridle.com/works/drone-shadow-001 (accessed 10 February 2021).

Celan-Jones, R. (2019) 'Robots "to replace up to 20 million factory jobs" by 2030, BBC News. Available at https://www.bbc.co.uk/news/business-48760799 (accessed 29 September 2020).

Chang, V. and Chetty, M. (2017) '"Spiders in the Sky": User Perceptions of Drones, Privacy, and Security', in *CHI '17: Proceedings of the 2017 CHI Conference on Human Factors in Computing Systems May 2017*, pp. 6765–6. Available at https://cpb-us-w2.wpmucdn.com/voices.uchicago.edu/dist/1/2826/files/2020/12/chang.pdf (accessed 1 May 2021).

Cholteeva, Y. (2020) 'Making Chernobyl Safe: A Timeline'. Available at https://www.power-technology.com/features/making-chernobyl-safe-a-timeline (accessed 2 February 2021).

Devlin, K. (2018) *Turned On: Science, Sex and Robots*. London: Bloomsbury.

Department of Homeland Security (DHS) (2020) 'Snapshot: U.S. – Israeli Robot Accessory Arm Provides Enhanced Capabilities and Precise Manipulation'. Available at https://www.dhs.gov/science-and-technology/news/2020/04/07/snapshot-us-israel-empower-bomb-squad-robots-second-arm (accessed 2 February 2021).

Dumitriu, A. and May, A. (2014) *HARR1: My Robot Companion*, in *Robot House Artist Residency Colloquium 2013*. Available at https://annadumitriu.co.uk/portfolio/harr1-my-robot-companion (accessed 18 September 2020).

Edmonds, E. (2011) 'Interactive Art', in Candy, L. and Edmonds, E. (eds) *Interacting: Art, Research and the Creative Practioner*. Oxfordshire: Libri Publishing.

Edmonds, E., Turner, G. and Candy, L. (2004) 'Approaches to Interactive Art Systems', in *Proceedings of the 2nd International Conference on Computer Graphics and Interactive Techniques in Australasia and South East, Singapore*. New York: AMC, pp. 113–17.

Elkins, J. (1996) *The Object Stares Back: On the Nature of Seeing*. San Diego: Harcourt.

Farocki, H. (2004) 'Controlling Observation', in Elsaesser, T. (ed.), *Harun Farocki: Working on the Sight-Lines*, pp. 289–95. Amsterdam: Amsterdam University Press, pp. 289–95.

Flanders, E. and Sawatzky, T. (2013) 'Drone Wedding', in *Til Drones Do Us Part*. Exhibition at Ryerson Image Centre, Toronto, Canada, 17 September–19 December 2013. Available at https://www.publicstudio.ca/drone-wedding (accessed 16 September 2020).

Hanhardt, J. (2000) *The Worlds of Nam June Paik*. New York: Guggenheim Museum Publications, pp. 53–6.

Haraway, D (1985) 'A Cyborg Manifesto: Science, Technology, and Socialist-Feminism', *The Late Twentieth Century Socialist Review* 80; and in Haraway, D. (1991) *Simians, Cyborgs and Women: The Reinvention of Nature*. New York: Routledge, pp. 149–81.

Haraway, D. (2016) *Staying with the Trouble: Making Kin in the Chthulucene*. Durham: Duke University Press.

Hastings Contemporary Robot Tours (2020) Available at https://www.hastingscontemporary.org/robot-tours/Rowan Bunney (accessed 29 April 2021).

Holland, M. A. (2014) *Rethinking the View from Above* (film). Available at https://apexart.org/media/apexart-rethinking-view.mp4 (accessed 30 August 2020).

Hutchinson, J. (2020) 'Heather Phillipson's Fourth Plinth sculpture unveiled', *Artist's Newsletter*, 31 July. Available at https://www.a-n.co.uk/news/heather-phillipsons-fourth-plinth-sculpture-unveiled (accessed 16 September 2020).

Imperial War Museums (n.d.) *A Brief History of Drones*. Available at http://www.iwm.org.uk (accessed 29 September 2020).

Intel (n.d.) 'Intel Shooting Star Drones Light up the Sky', *Intel News Fact Sheet*.

Available at https://www.intel.co.uk/content/www/uk/en/technology-innova-tion/drone-light-show-fact-sheet.html (accessed 27 September 2020).

Jerram, L. (2020) *In Memoriam*. Available at https://www.lukejerram.com (accessed 29 September 2020).

John, P. (2018) *Temporal and Spatial Coherence: Chronological and Affective Narrative Within Holographic and Lenticular Space*. PhD thesis, De Montfort. Available at https://www.dora.dmu.ac.uk/handle/2086/18127 (accessed 8 September 2023).

Johnson, J. (2020) 'Artificial Intelligence, Drone Swarming and Escalation Risks in Future Warfare', *RUSI Journal* 165(2): 26–36.

Johnston, S. (2006) *Holographic Visions: A History of New Science*. Oxford: Oxford University Press.

Joy, L. and Nolan, J. (2016–21) *Westworld* (TV series). HBO.

Kac, E. (1997) 'Foundation and Development of Robotic Art', *Art Journal* 56(3): 60–7. Available at https://www.ekac.org/roboticart.html (accessed 27 September 2020).

Lang, F. (1927) *Metropolis* (film). Available at https://www.youtube.com/watch?v=K6iF5sINVns (accessed 20 September 2020).

Mitton, J. (1992) *You Will Obey*. Gallery 286, Jonathan Ross Collection. Available at http://www.jrholocollection.com/collection/mitton.html (accessed 16 September 2020).

Mrongovius, M. (2011) 'The Emergent Holographic Scene: Compositions of Movement and Affect Using Multiplexed Holographic Images', unpublished PhD thesis, RMIT University.

O'Regan, J. (2011) *Ancient Visions*. Available at http://nivea.psycho.univ-paris5.fr/FeelingSupplements/AncientVisions.htm (accessed 16 September 2020).

Oxford Economics (2019) 'How Robots Change the World'. Available at https://www.oxfordeconomics.com/recent-releases/how-robots-change-the-world (accessed 28 September 2020).

Paglen, T. (2014) 'Operational Images', in *E-flux Journal* 59 (November). Available at https://www.e-flux.com/journal/59/61130/operational-images (accessed 27 March 2021).

Parikka, J. and Gil-Fourner, A. (2020) *Seed, Image, Ground*. Available at https://www.fotomuseum.ch/de/situations-post/seed-image-ground (accessed 28 March 2021).

Pastor, S. (2020) 'Is Computer Vision Better Than Human Vision?' Available at https://medium.com/neuravisio/is-computer-vision-better-than-human-vision (accessed 29 March 2020).

Phillipson, H. (2020) *The End*. Fourth Plinth, Trafalgar Square Sculpture, with accompanying live feed. Available at http://www.theend.today (accessed 28 September 2020).

Reichardt, J. (1978) *Robots: Fact, Fiction, and Prediction*. New York: Viking Press.

Rosenberger, R. and Verbeek, P. (2017) *Postphenomenological Investigations: Essays on Human–Technology Relations* (Postphenomenology and the Philosophy of Technology). Lexington: Rowman and Littlefield.

Schöffer, N. (1956) '*CYSP 1* (Cybernetic Spatiodynamic Sculpture)', in *Artists and Robots: The Exhibition, Réunion des musées nationaux – Grand Palais, Paris, 5 April–9 July 2018*. Available at https://www.youtube.com/watch?v=AxXESPzSqn4&list=PL9LWAQYUI74shyfQvGf6RPgi6QUGgJ7xO&index=2 (accessed 30 September 2020).

Schöffer, N. (1960) 'Lumino-Dynamics' (film), exhibited at the Institute of Contemporary Arts, London: British Pathe. Available at https://britishpathe.com/video/stills/lumino-dynamics (accessed 19 September 2020).

Schöpfer, T. (2020) 'The Clever Use of Robots During COVID-19', *EHL Insight*. Available at https://hospitalityinsights.ehl.edu/robots-during-covid-19 (accessed 2 February 2021).

Swain, F. (2014) 'Robotics: How Machines See the World', BBC Future. Available at https://www.bbc.com/future/article/20140822-the-odd-way-robots-see-the-world (accessed 9 February 2021).

Szollosy, M. (2016) 'Freud, Frankenstein and Our Fear of Robots: Projection in Our Cultural Perception of Technology', *AI & Society* 32(3): 433–9.

Wiener, N. (1948) *Cybernetics: Or Control and Communication in the Animal and the Machine*. Paris: Hermann & Cie; Cambridge, MA: MIT Press (2nd revised edition 1961).

Wozniak-O'Connor, V. (2018) 'Geoplatial Aesthetics: Mapping Place in Digital Holography', in *Proceedings of the 11th International Symposium on Display Holography* (ISDH2018), University of Aveiro, Portugal, 25–29 June 2018, pp. 105–8. Available at https://www.vaughanwoconnor.com (accessed 9 February 2021).

Yong, E. (2014) 'Autonomous Drones Flock Like Birds: Copters Can Arrange in Formation and Coordinate Flight Patterns Without Central Control', *Nature*, 24 February. Available at https://www.nature.com/news/autonomous-drones-flock-like-birds-1.14776 (accessed 1 May 2021).

Zawieska, K. (2014) 'Social Robots: Fostering Creativity through the Illusion of Life', in *Proceedings of the Workshop on Humanoid Robots and Creativity at the IEEE-RAS International Conference on Humanoid Robots (HUMANOIDS2014)*. Available at https://www.researchgate.net/publication/268505063_Social_Robots_Fostering_Creativity_through_the_Illusion_of_Life (accessed 10 February 2021).

Złotowski, J., et al. (2014) 'Anthropomorphism: Opportunities and Challenges in Human–Robot Interaction', *International Journal of Social Robotics*. Available at https://link.springer.com/article/10.1007/s12369-014-0267-6 (accessed 10 February 2021).

2 Will Robots Daydream?

Gregory Minissale

Ways of Seeing

In this chapter I compare two kinds of vision: analytical vision, which depends on logical inferences, and mind-wandering vision, involved in viewing landscapes and artworks, using involuntary and non-conscious impulses. If we ever desired to make robots in our own image, an image that requires feeling that one is being in the world, robots would also need to oscillate between these different modes of vision. With reference to some generative artworks, I suggest how this oscillation works in aesthetic vision.

In American writer Philip K. Dick's *Do Androids Dream of Electric Sheep?* (1968), a number of ethical problems arise concerning the notion of humans designing robots to be like themselves: a salient example concerns whether it is fair to conceal from robots the fact that their childhood memories, secret desires and dreams were programmed into them in order for them to be convinced that they are human. At the root of this is the notion that processing repressed memories leads to self-discovery and a truly authentic life. It seems that in order for an unconscious life to function, it must be a dark precursor, an invisible companion, subverting and expanding consciousness. If made explicit, its hold over us disappears. This obliviousness drives us to discover things about ourselves, particularly in our engagements with the visual. Vision is often inextricably bound up with desire, the desire to get closer to something, to explore, possess, or become one with the thing seen. How does this sense of discovery through trial and error, a truth we believe is worth living for, compare with a truth predetermined and manufactured in a factory? It could be argued that this point in particular establishes a distinct incommensurability between humans and robots When humans see things, their minds wander through a rich sense of self, but what kind of self will robots explore while gazing at the clouds? And why are any of these important for aesthetic vision?

Mind wandering is usually associated with the brain's resting state, supported by the 'default mode network' (DMN), a group of brain regions involved in daydreaming and reminiscing. This can be contrasted with the focused and analytical executive network that supports searching for clearly distinct objects in the visual field. For example, imagine you are looking after someone's apartment while they are on holiday. You want to make a cup of tea, even though you are not familiar with the house. You will be looking in all the logical places while ignoring aesthetic judgements about the sofa, colour coordination, or whether it feels homely. This sounds generally commonsensical, or even universal, but there are many cultures where apartments, and kitchen cupboards, are not organised in such a manner. The kind of vision associated with this kind of purposeful thought is highly ordered and controlled, often linear, and guided by a plan or model held in the mind. One can imagine that these kinds of visual routines can be eventually uploaded into a robot's searching algorithms.

The executive network promotes intentional behaviour, while the DMN allows for more relaxed, involuntary moments. Fox et al. (2013: p. 1) write that mind wandering can be tinged with fantasy not restricted by a single topic which might demand focused, purposeful attention and planned outcomes. Such thought has been likened to daydreaming and meditation. Various psychological studies suggest that creative insights occur in the 'resting' state, when the mind is decoupled from demanding tasks that require precise attention. It is this mode of dampened attention we see in mind wandering, which 'enhances creativity by increasing unconscious associative processing' (Baird et al. 2012: p. 1121).

During mind wandering, the eyes tend not to analyse visual details even while looking at them. It is often assumed that this is just a case of poor attention. Some traditional approaches to mind wandering assume that it is an obstacle to learning in classrooms (Smallwood et al. 2007), as working memory resources are diverted to the processing of memories or fantasies rather than analysing external details. But viewers enjoy wandering aimlessly over vast landscapes, constellations and the glistening sea or exploring intimate textures, skin and hair. These are perceptions accompanied by a large set of memories and emotions which determine the kind of iterated and rhythmic viewing involved. Outward directed, low-key perception aids introspective journeys. Looking at the sea allows one to get in touch with unconscious, basic feelings and to meditate. The kind of vision associated with this thought is general, often called configural, viewing, and is frequently non-linear, chaotic and improvised. It presents some interesting problems in terms of programming robot vision. Robots would need not only to be attuned to the visual pleasures of landscapes and bodies and the purposelessness in episodes of mind-wandering vision, but also to be highly tolerant of stochastic processes that underpin daydreaming and reverie, but which nevertheless can lead to insights about one's inner life. These episodes can be highly idiosyncratic and self-referential, often guided by a human's cultural, oneiric and emotional resonances and desires, many of them unconscious.

Robotics has undermined traditional, narrow concepts of human intelligence and creativity. Dada artists, writers such as William S. Burroughs, composer John Cage and others used algorithms and machinic processes to embrace chance procedures and 'deprogram' themselves from societal norms and logics. However, this does not mean that the algorithms or machinic processes are themselves 'subconscious'. While algorithms and computer vision may stimulate an optical unconscious in the viewer, it makes no sense to talk, as Celis Bueno and Schultz Abarca do (2020), of an algorithmic unconscious, or computer optical unconscious, on the basis that algorithms and machines are not conscious. Not being conscious is not the same as mind wandering or daydreaming – all located in the human subject, not in the artwork or algorithms that nevertheless might stimulate these in viewers. A cup and saucer or an artwork (and, so far, a robot) are not conscious. It makes no sense to falsely attribute unconsciousness to it. Unconscious activity is not the same as no activity. In artistic practices that use randomised algorithms to create art, viewers can follow the visual patterns, rhythms and cues generated by the machine algorithms to simulate daydreaming and make spontaneous associations, just as we would read certain kinds of poetry.[1] But again, in these cases it makes little sense to call the algorithms that generate the images and cuts conscious or unconscious phenomena.

Of course, there are many arguments about whether AI will ever be conscious – one of the strongest continues to be John Searle's 'Chinese room' argument:

> Searle imagines himself alone in a room following a computer program for responding to Chinese characters slipped under the door. Searle understands nothing of Chinese, and yet, by following the program

---

[1]   There is also the example of computer-generated art that introduces variations in formal artistic styles such as the CAN, the Creative Adversarial Networks group at Rutgers, which can be said to simulate creative processes. However, it seems hasty to call this program 'an algorithmic unconscious'. Similarly, DeepDream is a machine-generated program designed by Google engineer Alexander Mordvintsev that employs an artificial neural network to identify and enhance patterns in images using algorithms, said to produce experiences that are 'similar to' dreamlike hallucinogenic visions.

for manipulating symbols and numerals just as a computer does, he sends appropriate strings of Chinese characters back out under the door, and this leads those outside to mistakenly suppose there is a Chinese speaker in the room. (Cole 2020)

These arguments traditionally centre on whether a robot is or can be conscious. This binary dualism (consciousness or the absence of consciousness) is not to be conflated with the two positive presences I discuss here: a consciousness that is reducible to what it intends, reflects and abstracts, and an unconsciousness that passively – and non-logically – explores and transforms sensorimotor sensations, memories and affects the viewer has experienced, is experiencing and might experience as projections. This represents a complex set of temporalities emerging from contingencies of experience. It seems that in the robot context, intention, reflection and abstraction may be present, while unconsciousness is entirely absent: it is not a part-nership of two positive presences. It is only one presence: a complex set of algorithms meant to simulate sensations, memories and affects and their complex temporalities from a position of intentionality. The purported unconscious element is not entirely free or stochastic but still has its foot strongly planted in the domain of consciousness. The unconscious does not have a 'meant to' aim and purpose. It makes an incursion into any intentionality and even undermines it in order for something 'unprethinkable' to emerge precisely as a rupture. This argument is supported by experts in AI:

Prior to conceptual cognition, successful continued action in and interaction with the surrounding physical and sociocultural world, based on collective intentionality, holistic perception, and immediate experience, are at the core of sensemaking and human intelligence. It expresses itself as tacit 'knowing how' and skillful acting, which allocates pre-representational meaning to things, to dealing with them, and to interactions with others, thus constituting a social practice. Computer systems, even those being enabled to adapt to environmental conditions by sensor data, attain their functional-ity solely through conveniently designed algorithms from outside, based on propositional knowledge about their field of application. They, therefore, lack intentionality and self-determined activity as an indispensable material basis for perception, making sense, and experience. Attributing 'artificial intelligence' to computer systems distracts the awareness from the fact that all intelligence is on the side of the programmer who provides the computer system with func-tions that, as its objectifications, solely mimic or simulate intelligent behaviour in a generally limited way ... more recent efforts on the part of AI and robotics for 'embodying' their systems in order to broaden the range of automatic behaviour do not really change the picture. (Gill 2019)

Another obstacle for robot mind-wandering vision concerns memories, which are often intertwined with present perceptions. Sutton suggests that not only are memories often incomplete and context sensitive, they can arise within the flow of a thinker's present or longstanding desires and needs, as well as her 'forward-looking or anticipatory features and functions' (Sutton 2009: p. 229). And for Sutton, memories are coded within social systems of values and influences, and are made to feel autobiographical although they are publicly shared. This suggests something of a collective unconscious that emerges in long-honed cultural and social traditions and inter-dependencies.

Daydreams allow for unusual 'irrational' narratives and structuring relations between concepts and provide an important resource for artistic practice. Thus, in a Surrealist-inspired painting or in fairy stories and myths, a person can be found in the belly of a whale or the petals of a flower. Many artworks scramble the 'grammar' of logical construction, not only with the hybridity of a single object's features but by juxtaposing objects that we would not logically find together. The 'message' remains ambiguous, enchanting or humorous because it reminds us that we have a rich and abiding relationship to the unknown of the subconscious, and even a cultural unconscious. With Meret Oppenheim's *Déjeuner sur l'herbe* (1936), a cup and saucer are covered in fur. Either as a cup in a lap of fur, or fur in the 'lap' of a saucer, the work has a perverse logic, as many of our dreams do. Artworks such as these remind us that we often enjoy being reminded of the non-logical aspects of dreams, as we would reading *Alice in Wonderland* or watching dream sequences in movies.

Visual Art

As I have suggested, artworks help us to understand why mind-wandering vision is valuable. The art historian Rosalind Krauss is an important critic of the pure opticality of high modernism and its pretensions to being 'the display of reason, of the rationalised, the coded, the abstracted, the law' (Krauss 1993: p. 21), which she believes leads to an increasingly positivist art history. An important corrective to the cognitive understanding of vision, according to which modernist art requires conscious and willed looking, is that this kind of vision represses the 'optical unconscious': barely registered desires, fears and drives that influence the experience of looking at art. When the executive control network and 'mindfulness' of metacognition are not functioning optimally because of exhaustion through physical exercise, the influence of drugs or alcohol, or even through religious rituals of exhausting energy by repeating words or actions, 'surreal' effects and conceptual juxtapositions are common. This principle of 'irrational' association is precisely what happens with the uncanny or uneasy feeling we might have in experiencing Luis Buñuel's *Un Chien Andalou* (1929), for example, and has something to do with how it induces 'irrational' dreamlike non sequiturs. Such works are a reminder of the principles of irrational conceptual combination, which we customarily adopt in dreaming thoughts or which occur with sleep deprivation. Forms of abstract art can work with us to sustain mind wandering as a kind of shape-shifting or sifting through memories. This finds a correspondence with the French critic Jean Paulhan's thoughts about fantasies mapped onto arbitrary surfaces, a wall, or an abstract painting, which can

> transform a mouse into an elephant or pumpkin into a carriage ... the objects metamorphosed belong to two different orders: one to our inner and personal thoughts, the other on the contrary to external objects ... such metamorphosis does not take place in a fairy tale; nor does it exist for credulous children. Serious minds, trained in scientific methods: Langevin, Sartre propose this to us very naturally. As though we were so profoundly mixed up with the world and so merged with it that our most personal thoughts were less thoughts than reality. (Paulhan 2002: p. 186)[2]

This is a kind of visual stream of consciousness in cooperation with suggestive shapes, 'involuntary sculptures', where forms continually bubble up and disperse. In the same vein, Leonardo da Vinci's advice to students was to observe the arbitrary stains and irregularities on the wall. In the scraps of text we have come to know as his *Treatise on Painting* (1270), Leonardo explains:

> Do not despise my advice, which reminds you ... to stop sometimes and look into the stains of walls, or the ashes of a fire, or clouds, or mud, or other like spots, in which, if you consider them well, you will find the most marvellous inventions; for the *ingegno* [imaginative ingenuity] of the painter is roused to new inventions, whether of compositions of battles of animals and men, or of various compositions

2   *Informel* is a period in post-war French painting, exemplified by Jean Fautrier and Jean Dubuffet, that experimented with formless abstract works.

of landscapes and monstrous things ... because the *ingegno* is roused to new inventions by indistinct things [*cose confuse*]. (da Vinci [1270] 1956: p. 37)

Yet this mind wandering while absent-mindedly viewing stains on a wall is not just limited to looking. 'Psychogeography' emerged from Guy Debord's Situationist 'dérive' practice: an unplanned, aimless stroll that walkers cultivate in order to experience the aleatory and incidental where one finds objects in a flea market or alley that trigger affective or uncanny thoughts and memories. This kind of aleatory vision is non-linear, driven by the pleasure derived by chance encounters with smells, noises and faces encountered in the street or urban landscape. This suggests that robotic vision, if it were to duplicate this kind of vision, would also need to suppress efficient processing of visual details in favour of experiencing the pleasure of non-logical and chance connections.

I have suggested that vision occurs in concert with unconscious desires that are non-linear, but it also works with other senses, which can be non-linear. For example, imagine trying to make out the shape of a wooden sculpture in the dark. While one is following the contours, knots and grain of the wood one is also forming reveries, mental images, with the hands following the qualities of materials. This sensuous vision follows unanticipated pleasures of touching and discovering textures, circular iterations over particular areas, smoothing out over flat plans. Bachelard notes that the hand 'also has its dreams and its hypotheses. It helps us to understand matter in its inmost being. Therefore it helps us to dream of it' (Bachelard [1942] 1999: p. 106). Touch is non-linear in that its procedures are not successive; it tarries in circular movements or strikes out on random paths and in random directions, registering the sustained and continuous chaos of texture while forming mental images, yet can be supervised or released by the power of vision. Soothing and repetitive, touch can be serotonergic, and yet it also shares proper-ties with an oneiric duration or automatism. Braun et al. (2015) cite the Futurist Filippo Tommaso Marinetti and his understanding of 'tactilism' as a way to engage with art, a kind of 'blindfolded "journey of the hands" over textured panels ... surface variables, vibrations, temperatures ("thermic sensations") of different materials' (p. 53). I see this as a kind of metastability, where the hands, through muscle memory, bring images to the mind, which dissipate in favour of more chaotic metamorphoses, as the hand discovers ambiguities that escape conceptualisation. By metastability, I mean a process that involves both order and disordered aspects. It is important to remember that this metastability between ordering and shaping images and releasing them into chaotic flows is fully embodied through direct contact with materials, which in themselves can have chaotic as well as relatively ordered features. Will advanced forms of robot intelligence increase or decrease, or even find irrelevant, this haptic wandering between order and disorder?

This embodied aspect is important. Hubert Dreyfus resisted the computationalism of the 1960s and 1970s with such books as *What Computers Can't Do* (1972, 1992). Using Heidegger's *Dasein*, which means that one's body and movement are situated and engaged in an activity that is deeply immersive, Dreyfus showed that a robot cannot move, think and act in the world based on programming alone to anticipate all its contingencies. It needs to move and touch things in the world in order to learn what it feels like to be an embodied actant in particular situations. These ideas were an important influence on the 'actionist' robotics of later years, where robots were modelled as bodies interacting with objects and relying on sensorimotor feedback and adaptation, rather than on preprogrammed instructions, which are not easily adjusted to arbitrary or chaotic things happening in the world.

There are many studies that provide specific and detailed empirical support for the idea that internal neural dynamics produce features of chaos in cooperation with features in the world. One very good example is Freeman and Skarda's experiments on the olfactory bulb of the rabbit. This celebrated research shows that receptors 'allow the nose to capture odorant molecules at very low concentrations but, because the airflow through the nose is turbulent, the inhaled air carries the molecules to a different set of receptors with each sniff' (Freeman 2001: p. 68). The internal neurodynamics are metastable and open to external molecular metastability, described best using principles of chaos theory:

> Odour information was then shown to exist as a pattern of neural activity that could be discriminated whenever there was a change in the odour environment or after training. Furthermore the 'carrier wave' of this information was aperiodic. Further dissection of the experimental data led to the conclusion that the activity of the olfactory bulb is chaotic and switches to any desired perceptual state (or attractor) at any time. (Korn and Faure 2003: p. 789)

Different action potentials, perceptual routines and sets of responses are held in readiness but not committed to until something sparks a phase transition or criticality that will lead to the 'global' phenomenal identification of the odour or the learning of a new odour (plasticity): 'chaos confers the system with a deterministic "I don't know" state within which new activity patterns can emerge' (Korn and Faure 2003: p. 821). Rather than manipulating symbols or indexes of the world and its features, the brain and nervous system are continuously in a state of activity, in real-time contact with the surrounding world. For Freeman, the rabbit's olfactory system provides evidence that the brain's metastable activity allows it to be open to contingency. An external perturbation can be sampled and may trigger larger matching of global patterns, routines and moments of stability or iteration. Thus, in the 'olfactory bulb, neither a neuron, nor a cell assembly, is designed to serve a single purpose. Rather, they can implement several functions depending upon the internal states of the brain and the constraints placed upon it by environmental factors' (Korn and Faure 2003: p. 829). Vision thus is not only multi-sensory, using our sense of rhythm, touch and smell – it requires us to give up the *intention* to see things, because this would pre-empt a serendipitous discovery. Or there could be no discovery at all: this is a kind of daydreaming vision, where we are happy to surf the crest of a wave of arbitrary details in the visual field. A robot would need to be content with this kind of daydreaming vision for its own sake, taking pleasure from the failures of efficient, logically driven, vision.

Chaos in the environment, the motion of particles and other contingencies, comingle with the organism's biology, place, orientation, health, age and neuronal assemblages, together forming an immediate dynamic complexity or criticality, until relative stability is achieved. Examples of this stability might include identification, gestalt processes, memory retrieval, contemplation or contentment. Freeman and Skarda show that the brain accommodates in readiness numerous dynamic systems that engage with the world, clearly illustrating the importance of a dynamic approach to understanding vision, that it co-opts chance and chaos:

> Perception is an interactive process of destabilisation and re-stabilisation via self-organised dynamics. Thus, we come to view the brain as the location where a self-organised process of patterning takes place, a process that reaches back toward the stimuli giving them form at the same time as it creates their biological meaning for the organism ... chaotic activity enables the rapid state transitions essential for information processing. (Skarda and Freeman 1990: p. 279)

While it is true that external perturbations have an effect on internal dynamics, chaotic behaviour can be self-generated by neurons and can help to shift and modulate perceptions, which are not fixed copies of external stimuli but creative interpretations. Such interpretation, arrived at by cooperating with non-logical processes, sets a high bar for AI. While it thus seems that we, as viewers, are in control and intend our actions, that we are the authors of our actions, this understanding of vision as open to the universe of chance and contingency suggests that our reading of visual details is continually influenced by chaotic triggers and associations. This already complex and variable set of events is complicated even further by neurotransmitters, such as serotonin, adrenalin, dopamine and oxytocin, producing reward, pleasure and inspiration, that operate at the same time and 'can switch the activity of the cell from one stable firing pattern to the other' (Korn and Faure 2003: p. 796). Again, it is clear that the inner desire to see – and visualise – the unexpected and the chaotic outside in the world is itself unexpected and chaotic. Could the robot acquire this kind of consonance between internal and external worlds that enhances the pleasures and joys of not being in control?

Aesthetic Vision: Where Mind Wandering and Conscious Monitoring Oscillate

How might we define aesthetic vision? Leder et al. (2004) provide a useful psychological model of aesthetic processes, showing how a great number of mental operations co-occur during the art experience. Their model is as follows: Perceptual analysis → implicit memory integration → explicit classification → cognitive mastering → evaluation → then back to perceptual analysis (in a loop). This model suggests a reciprocity between bottom-up processes (perceptual processes which recognise complexity, contrast, symmetry recognition in the visual field) and top-down processes (conceptual, categorical and attentional organisation from memory areas or areas responsible for reasoning and planning in the brain) which modify or interpret these bottom-up processes. The top-down processes have been further divided into more specific processes the authors have called 'implicit memory integration' (where recognition of forms or situations depicted in art are integrated or compared with examples from previous experience). There are also: explicit classification (the processing of style and content of the artwork); cognitive mastering (the processing of art-specific information where personal taste might intervene); and evaluation (where aesthetic judgements are made in conjunction with feelings of reward or satisfaction). Part of this model also suggests a feedback loop where 'modern art empowers loops of processing in which hypotheses concerning the meaning of an artwork are continuously altered and tested until a satisfactory result is achieved. The processing of these loops can be pleasing itself and essential for aesthetic experiences' (Leder et al. 2004: p. 500). Meanwhile, David Freedberg insists that painting can often show 'how emotion can only be fully expressed through the body itself' (Freedberg 2011: p. 344). This means that encounters with artwork allow the viewer to *feel* embodied, which is part of *Dasein*, being-in-the-world. Yet because each artwork is different, this feeling will be moderated by detachment, formal analysis and categorisation. Situatedness, context, memory, perceptual cues of the artwork and personal taste all affect degrees of self-reference, including feeling embodied.

Aesthetic vision may be seen as a balance between unconscious, or semi-conscious, intuitive feeling and conscious, analytical judgement – but this balance is effected by specific situations, contexts and the lifelong acculturation of taste by the viewing subject. Viewing art requires something of Leonardo da Vinci's openness to abstract shapes and forms that suggest objects or scenes, when one 'surrenders' to the shape-suggesting forms of abstract art by reducing strong premeditated (or programmed) analysis that discounts random variables as 'noise'. But inspiration can emerge from such noise. One needs an evaluative process at some point, involving metacognition, in order to select unusual images or associations for memory and perhaps for later use. While one would expect that robotic vision would not find it difficult to evaluate unusual associations for such a later use, it must be prepared to modify any plan or objective if this too quickly dismisses the aesthetic pleasures emerging from random variables.

This suggests an alternation between involuntary mind wandering and controlled, focused analysis, both supported by the cooperation of different brain networks. In particular, Ellamil et al. (2012) observed co-activation of the executive and default networks during creative interpretations of artworks, suggesting that one slips in and out of self-awareness during creative evaluation. The authors conclude:

> the dichotomy between generation and evaluation appears to be ubiquitous in psychological theories of the creative process, with novel ideas produced during generative phases and their utility assessed during subsequent evaluative phases. This dichotomy is also present in artists' accounts of their own creative process, which they often describe as alternating between rough sketching of ideas and critiquing those ideas to guide the next cycle of sketching and critiquing. (Ellamil et al. 2012: p. 1783)

This suggests the alternation between different networks but, closer to studies of co-occurrence, the authors note that the activity over the two networks is highly correlated throughout the task of creating drawings on a pad in an fMRI scanner. In all likelihood, this switching from executive and evaluative processing to default associative and affective processing is fluid, and probably works in the same way as the coupling, decoupling and recoupling theorised by De Bruin and Kästner (2011), which consists of 'smearing' between states attentive to internal contents and states attentive to external contents. The executive system is useful for checking the relevance of ideas that arise spontaneously in mind-wandering episodes and it may be required in the evaluation of creativity. For this to happen quickly during sketching, drawing or painting, the dynamic coordination of the two networks will be needed. Ellamil et al. cite many studies that demonstrate the role of executive control in various creative endeavours. including:

> piano improvisation, creative story generation, word association, divergent thinking, fluid analogy formation, insight problem solving and visual art design. During these creative tasks, high cognitive control enables a deliberate, analytic mode of information processing that facilitates the evaluation of the utility of novel ideas and allows individuals to focus on the pertinent task details and to select the relevant generated ideas. Therefore, the executive network may contribute specifically to the evaluative mode of creative thought. (Ellamil et al. 2012: p. 1784)

The authors note that while 'evaluating the products of one's own creative activity, creative individuals frequently pay attention to their – largely unconscious – "gut reactions"' (p. 1784). It thus seems that, apart from the point I made earlier about vision being bound up with an existential matter of allowing the robot the freedom to destroy what is expected of it, to be an anarchist or a cyberpunk, a robot must also have the opportunity for the mind to wander chaotically, and even involuntarily, in order for random newness, creativity and discovery to emerge with the world. And this is intimately intertwined with mind-wandering vision, which connects improvised thoughts that arise from arbitrary cues in the visual world that are not following premeditated (or programmed) rules.

Mind wandering and dreaming go beyond well-rehearsed arguments based on the binary dualism of human consciousness versus robot (non-)consciousness. This is because mind wandering can be seen as semi-conscious, drifting away from conscious awareness while often returning to it. And in addition to this, the duplication of the human by the robot may not be the only way to think about AI. Andy Clark (2003) argues because of artificial limbs, sense organs and implants and the ability to connect to complex algorithms, humans will evolve into cyborgs. This opens up the possibility of humans joining with robots – the former piloting the latter through and beyond the binary consciousness and non-consciousness. It could be that AI could enhance artistic vision through robot and human cooperation rather than creating each to be the same as the other. An example of this vision in artistic practice can be found in the way New Zealand artist Simon Ingram's painting machine was augmented in his collaboration with John-Pochin to become *Monadic Device* (Figures 2.1 and 2.2).

The work, first shown at the Sydney Contemporary in 2018 centres on a response to electrical activity in the brain monitored by an EEG headset, processed by computer software and painted on canvas by Ingram's machine. Ingram listened to music, read books and sketched while wearing the headset. The machine was programmed to paint lines that:

> wander around a canvas, avoiding paths previously traced and tun-
> nelling under or glancing off lines it encounters. While connected

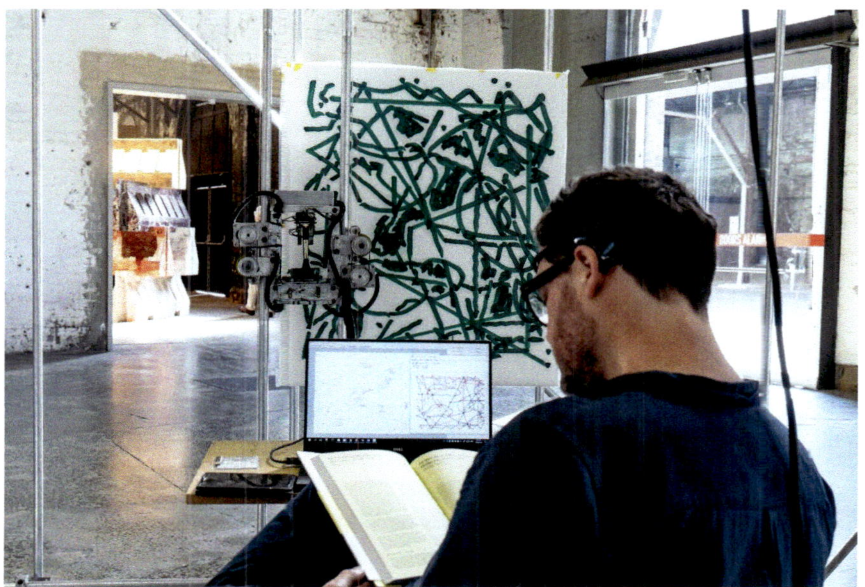

Figure 2.1 Simon Ingram, *Monadic Device*, 2018.
Photo credit: Jacquie Manning.

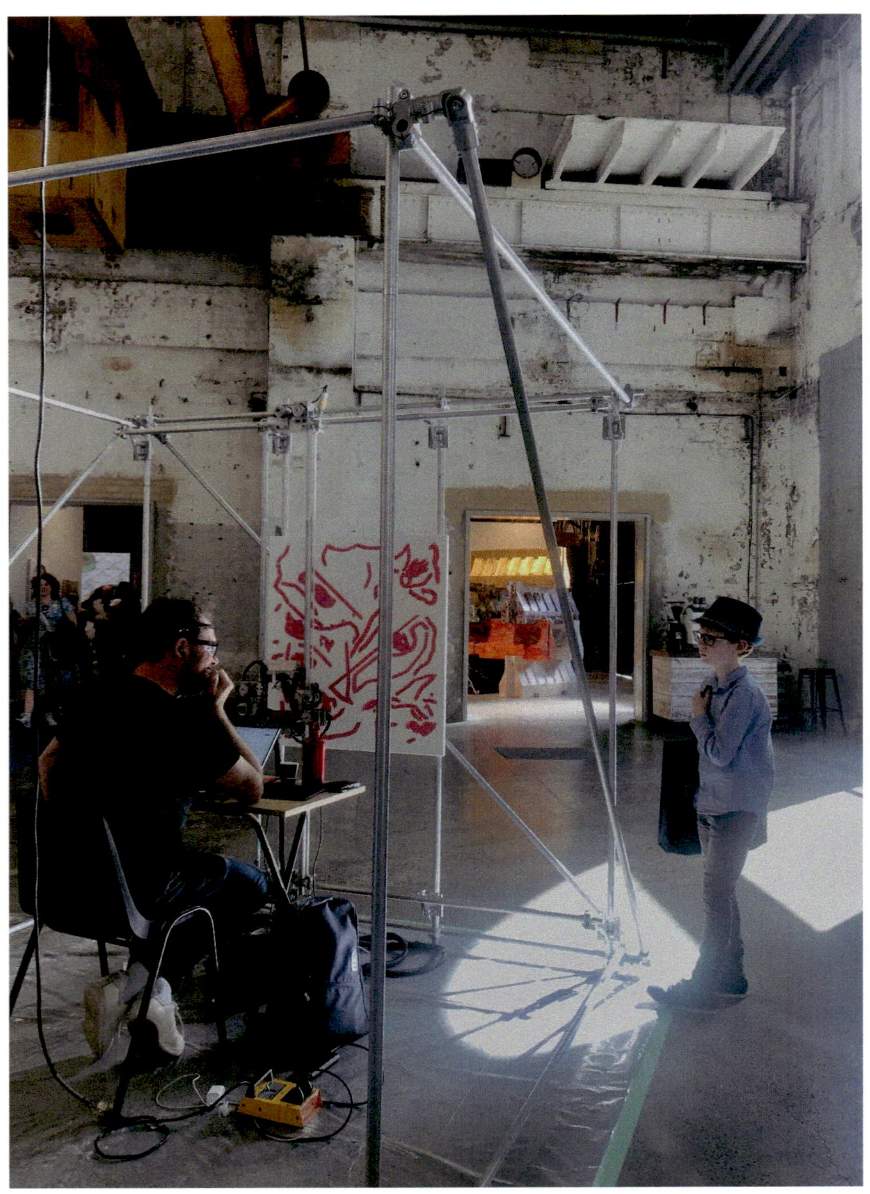

Figure 2.2 Simon Ingram, *Monadic Device*, 2018.
Photo credit: Mikhaela Rodding.

to the painting machine, a person's beta brainwaves determine the length of the line and their alpha brainwaves whether the lines turn left or right. (Ballard and Ingram 2020)

It is interesting that the device translates the alpha waves associated with conscious control and beta waves associated with semi-conscious activity such as mind wandering. Together, they represent the cooperation of these tendencies. In the exhibition 'The Algorithmic Impulse' at the City Gallery, Wellington, in 2020, Ingram opened up the *Monadic Device* to visitors. They were encouraged to engage in activity significant to them. They might read, draw, ride a bicycle, or even crochet while wearing the EEG headset monitoring neural oscillations such as alpha and beta waves that are codified by software to control the movement of a painting machine, as in the earlier Sydney version. However, for *The Algorithmic Impulse* (Figure 2.3), the artist added another level of feedback. The neural oscillations controlling the machine were translated as sound and shared to the mixing desk of the Moniker, a subset of the Wellington band The Phoenix Foundation. Moniker improvised to this 'neural sound', as Ingram wore an EEG headset listening to their music. His brainwaves were 'streamed not just to a painting machine but through a midi application that allows the data to be sonified, becoming a layer in the music', to become a 'kind of duet' (Ballard and Ingram 2020).

Both generative artworks involve a feedback process that demonstrates the principle of Clark's extended mind or cognition. But they avoid having a brain–body–machine assemblage reducible to

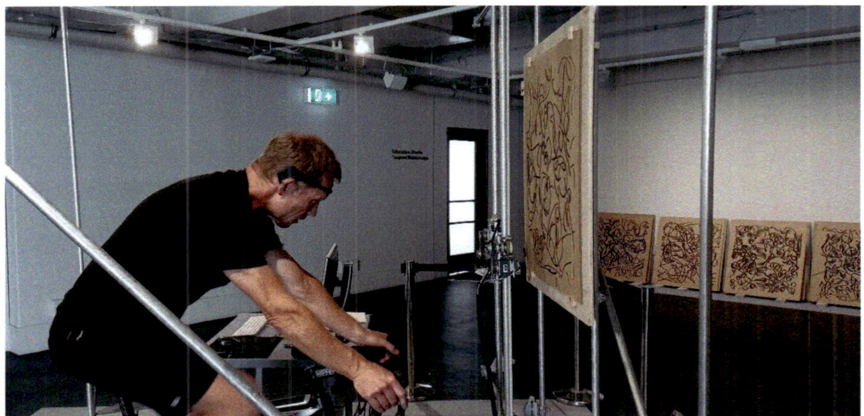

Figure 2.3 Simon Ingram, *The Algorithmic Impulse*, 2021.
Photo credit: Mikhaela Rodding.

the kind of rational control associated with robot vision. Artistic and creative vision, closely aligned to mind wandering (drawing, listening to music), generates neural oscillations picked up by the EEG headset. The painting machine's mark-making is informed by the interplay of these brain frequencies to create abstract paintings that can be studied and analysed aesthetically and rechannelled into further rounds of image-making. The artist draws, his brainwaves are translated and input into a machine which responds with its own drawing. The artist can also respond to this machinic drawing, et cetera. This model bypasses the traditional dualism of human/non-human actants by having them contribute different, symbiotic kinds of image-making, rather than having only one of them solely responsible for the creative process. It also shows how logical and non-logical processes can cooperate in producing images that appeal to an aesthetic vision similarly balanced between the logical and the non-logical.

The Self and the Other

Many studies suggest that different kinds of mind wandering can happen, with varying degrees of self-reference, often with a rich source of 'self' that is being processed while we look at art, landscapes, or gaze at clouds. Christoff et al. view mind wandering as fluctuations in attention to external stimuli, from little or no attention in dream states to spontaneous mind wandering: 'While hiking on a forest trail, a woman's thoughts move from the gravel on the path in front of her to a slug crawling up a stump, and then to a leaf floating in a puddle' (2016: p. 723). In such examples, mind wandering and spontaneous thought occur *with* external objects, as if the objects are players on the stage of mind wandering. This suggests that 'external players' act as a material medium for internally oriented thought.

Vessel and Starr have shown fMRI activation in areas associated with the default mode network in humans viewing paintings, a selection of landscapes, portraits, and still-lifes, that they reported to be beautiful (Vessel et al. 2012, 2013). The authors suggest this is because of the self-referential aspect of the DMN, which requires some self-referential processing and 'self-relevance'. They hold that DMN activation in viewing artworks emphasises the consistency of self-relevance rather than the inconsistencies of mind wandering, as do I. This may indicate a presupposition that art must produce harmony rather than dissonance, in which case my approach, diverging from the emphasis given to the ego or self, is not meant to oppose Vessel and Starr but to insist on the diversity of experiences that artworks are able to encourage.

In any case, there is much debate as to what might be contained in 'self-relevance'. As has been argued elsewhere (Minissale 2013: pp. 233–50), the self is a complex philosophical and psychological problem. It could be understood in a rich sense (a reflective self, involved in metacognition) or as a kind of vague background hum (a pre-reflective self) or, strangely, as a sense of 'losing oneself'. It remains to be seen which kind of self-reference the robot will develop and for what purpose. Vessel and Starr accept that

> [t]rait studies may reflect a set of processes whereby observers don't simply think about themselves, but, more specifically, match traits with self-inspection, as a part of broader social cognition. In a similar manner, release from deactivation during aesthetic experience may reflect observers' matching self-inspection with their perception of an object. (Vessel et al. 2012)

This point complements the idea that internal and external contents can be interwoven with the help of the DMN. What is important in Vessel and Starr's work is the 'intense feeling' evoked by artworks, recruiting aspects of the DMN, and how this might be squared with the mind wandering which also recruits aspects (possibly different ones) of the DMN. This allows us to infer 'self-wandering' or wandering ideas about the self, rather than building complex higher-order cogitations on the self which would reduce the time given to other kinds of engagement with an artwork. Many artworks activate feelings of empathy and ego-dissolution, known in psychoanalysis as the 'oceanic feeling', where the self is projected onto or finds expression through the features of artworks, even if they are abstract and inanimate. This chimes in with Vessel and Starr's statement that 'our brains detect a certain "harmony" between the external world and our internal representation of the self, allowing the two systems to co-activate, interact, influence and reshape each other' (Vessel et al. 2012). This suggests that the encounter with an artwork recruiting the DMN need not involve an explicit self-awareness and may invoke a relatively formless feeling of transcendent or contemplative oneness with the work (often interpreted as the oceanic feeling). This feeling can still activate the markers for 'self-reference'. In other words, contemplation of a Rothko painting may lead to thoughts and feelings which we would cognitively call 'beauty', but these feelings could also involve *Dasein*, immersion, 'abstraction', or being absent in the world and losing one's sense of self in the grander scheme of things, and in all these examples the DMN could be active. It seems rather convoluted that in order to provide robot vision with this rich experiential substrate, from which a deeper sense of self emerges with others, that it should have to be lost in certain ways in order for it to be found again and looked at anew. But this is certainly what happens with aesthetic vision.

Mind wandering in particular seems to support this self-erasure in order to 'become' one with the thing one sees. To some extent this can be understood as chaotic dynamics, cued by the low-level perception of a landscape, that allow rhythmic switching between different mental states. This switching or interweaving between 'internal' and 'external' contents would feel indistinguishable, particularly if accompanied by emotional or affective dimensions: empathy arising from motor imagery modelled by the rhythm of the landscape, the sinuous reach of trees, winding river beds, the arbitrary iridescence of trembling irises that remind us of a lost friend. Balzac reminds us of a character who finds 'a mysterious relationship between his emotions and the ocean's movements ... to guess matter's thoughts' (see Bachelard [1942] 1999: p. 172). Bachelard takes up the outlines of this idea and suggests that 'an *extraordinary* tempest is a tempest seen by someone who is in an *extraordinary* psychological state' (p. 172). He deepens this reverie, noting that 'correspondences are established in rare and solemn moments. Inward meditation provides contemplation in which the innermost recesses of the world are disclosed. Meditation with closed eyes and contemplation with wide-open eyes suddenly have the same life' (p. 173).

Conclusion

I have continually returned to the dualism of conscious, logical, ordered vision versus semi-conscious, non-logical, chaotic vision. Evolution has helped humans to switch between these modes effortlessly in order to relate to the world's own inherent tendencies of order and chaos, suspending simple understandings of the freedom of will. I caution that the emphasis that science places on the first kind of vision as a superior and objective way to evaluate the world misconstrues the second kind of vision as merely subjective. Thus, we are left with the dualism that there is simply the external world of non-self, the world 'out there' and the internal world of self 'in here'. Science is viewed as an objective and rational analysis of external structures 'out there' in the world, while art is often characterised as the domain of inwardness and subjectivity. Will advanced forms of robot intelligence increase or decrease these distinctions? Will robots be well versed only in the first kind of logical vision as part of analysing the world, while finding no use for the second kind of vision, which actually connects us to the world *as it is* in its own non-logical aspects? Maintaining the balance between these different ways of connecting with the world constitutes a fundamental challenge to *Dasein*. Only by exercising our evolved way of switching from logical to non-logical vision does the world appear not simply *for us* but also *for itself*. *Dasein* is not just being-in-the-world, but involves coexisting *with it* from a non-anthropocentric position. This deeper understanding of *Dasein* can be understood as a continuity where 'outward directed perception and inner-directed introspection become indistinguishable' (Ehrenzweig [1967] 1993: p. 273). Thus, consciousness, the mind, and being are not just things that happen in the head. They emerge from the continuous interactions between inner and outer events, a continuity that undermines the notion of a cognitively supreme, detached viewer, robot, human, or god surveying nature, matter and the world beneath it. This is the flow of being-in-the-world in both an extended spatial and an intimately emotional sense. This is fundamental to aesthetic vision and underpins our deepest empathy for others. If indeed we are going on a journey to traverse another dualism – that between the human and the robot – the freedom to daydream with eyes wide open will be of crucial significance.

Acknowledgements

Thanks to Simon Ingram, Nina Trivedi, and Luci Eldridge for valuable feedback on this text.

References

Bachelard, G. [1942] (1999) *Water and Dreams: An Essay on the Imagination of Matter*. Dallas, TX: Dallas Institute of Humanities.

Baird, B., Smallwood, J., Mrazek, J., Kam, W. J., Franklin, M. S. and Schooler, J. W. (2012) 'Inspired by Distraction: Mind Wandering Facilitates Creative Incubation', *Psychological Science* 23(10): 1117–22. Available at https://doi.org/10.1177/0956797612446024 (accessed 27 April 2022).

Ballard, S. and Ingram, S. (2020) 'Simon Ingram and John-Paul Pochin Talk to Su Ballard'. Available at https://citygallery.org.nz/blog/simon-ingram-and-john-paul-pochin-talk-to-su-ballard (accessed 27 April 2022).

Braun, E., Fontanella, M. and Stringari, C. (eds) (2015) *Alberto Burri: The Trauma of Painting*. New York: Guggenheim Museum Publications.

Celis Bueno, C. and Schultz Abarca, M. J. (2020) 'Memo Akten's Learning to See: From Machine Vision to the Machinic Unconscious', *AI & Society*. Available at https://doi.org/10.1007/s00146-020-01071-2 (accessed 27 April 2022).

Christoff, K., Irving, Z. C., Fox, K. C. R. Spreng, N. and Andrews-Hannah, J. (2016) 'Mind-Wandering as Spontaneous Thought: A Dynamic Framework', *Nature Reviews Neuroscience* 17: 718–731. Available at https://doi.org/10.1038/nrn.2016.113 (accessed 19 September 2023).

Clark, A. (2003) *Natural-Born Cyborg.* Oxford: Oxford University Press.

Cole, D. (2020) 'The Chinese Room Argument', in *Stanford Encyclopaedia of Philosophy.* Available at https://plato.stanford.edu/entries/chinese-room (accessed 27 April 2022).

Da Vinci, Leonardo [1270] (1956) *Treatise on Painting* (Codex Urbinas Latinus 1270), trans. P. McMahon. Princeton: Princeton University Press.

De Bruin, L. and Kästner, L. (2011) 'Dynamic Embodied Cognition', *Phenomenology and the Cognitive Sciences* 11(4): 541–63.

Dick, P. K. (1968) *Do Androids Dream of Electric Sheep?* New York: Doubleday.

Dreyfus, H. L. (1972) *What Computers Can't Do.* New York: MIT Press.

Dreyfus, H. L. (1992) *What Computers Still Can't Do.* New York: MIT Press.

Ehrenzweig, A. [1967] (1993) *The Hidden Order of Art: A Study in the Psychology of Artistic Imagination.* London: Weidenfeld and Nicolson.

Ellamil, M., Dobson, C., Beeman, M. and Christoff, K. (2012) 'Evaluative and Generative Modes of Thought During the Creative Process', *NeuroImage* 59(2): 1783–94.

Fox Kieran, C. R., Nijeboer, S., Solomonova, E., Domhoff, G. and Christoff, K. (2013) 'Dreaming as Mind Wandering: Evidence from Functional Neuroimaging and First-Person Content Reports', *Frontiers in Human Neuroscience* 7(412): 1–18.

Freedberg, D. (2011) 'Memory in Art: History and the Neuroscience of Response', in Nalbantian, S., Matthews, P.M. and McClelland, J. L. (eds), *The Memory Process: Neuroscientific and Humanistic Perspectives.* Cambridge, MA: MIT Press, pp. 337–58.

Freeman, W. J. (2001) *How Brains Make Up Their Minds.* New York: University of Columbia Press.

Gill, K. S. (2019) 'From Judgment to Calculation: The Phenomenology of Embodied Skill. Celebrating Memories of Hubert Dreyfus and Joseph Weizenbaum', *AI & Society* 34: 65–175. Available at https://doi.org/10.1007/s00146-019-00884-0 (accessed 27 April 2022).

Korn, H. and Faure, P. (2003) 'Is There Chaos in the Brain? II. Experimental Evidence and Related Models', *Comptes Rendus Biologies* 326(9): 787–840.

Krauss, R. (1993) *The Optical Unconscious.* Cambridge, MA: MIT Press.

Leder, H., Belke, B., Oeberst, A. and Augustin, D. (2004) 'A Model of Aesthetic Appreciation and Aesthetic Judgments', *British Journal of Psychology* 95: 489–508.

Minissale, G. (2013) *The Psychology of Contemporary Art.* Cambridge: Cambridge Press.

Paulhan, J. (2002) 'Fautrier the Enraged', in Carter, C. L., Butler, K. and Bois, Y.-A. (eds), *Jean Fautrier, 1898–1964.* New Haven: Yale University Press, pp. 178–87.

Skarda, C. A. and Freeman, W. J. (1990) 'Chaos and the New Science of the Brain', *Concepts in Neuroscience* 1(2): 275–285.

Smallwood, J., Fishman, D. J. and Schooler, J. W. (2007) 'Counting the Cost of an Absent Mind: Mind Wandering as an Underrecognized Influence on Educational Performance', *Psychonomic Bulletin and Review* 14(2): 230–6.

Sutton, J. (2009) 'Remembering', in Robbins, P. and Aydede, M. (eds), *The Cambridge Handbook of Situated Cognition.* Cambridge: Cambridge University Press, pp. 217–35.

Vessel, E. A., Starr, G. G. and Rubin, N. (2012) 'The Brain on Art: Intense Aesthetic Experience Activates the Default Mode Network', *Frontiers of Human Neuroscience* (6)66. Available at 10.3389/fnhum.2012.00066 (accessed 5 August 2019).

Vessel, E. A., Starr, G. and Rubin, N. (2013) 'Art Reaches Within: Aesthetic Experience, the Self and the Default Mode Network', *Frontiers of Human Neuroscience* 7(258). Available at 10.3389/fnins.2013.00258 (accessed 5 August 2019).

3 Discrete Accidents of Photogrammetry: Re-presenting Pure Surface in Google Earth

Meg Rahaim

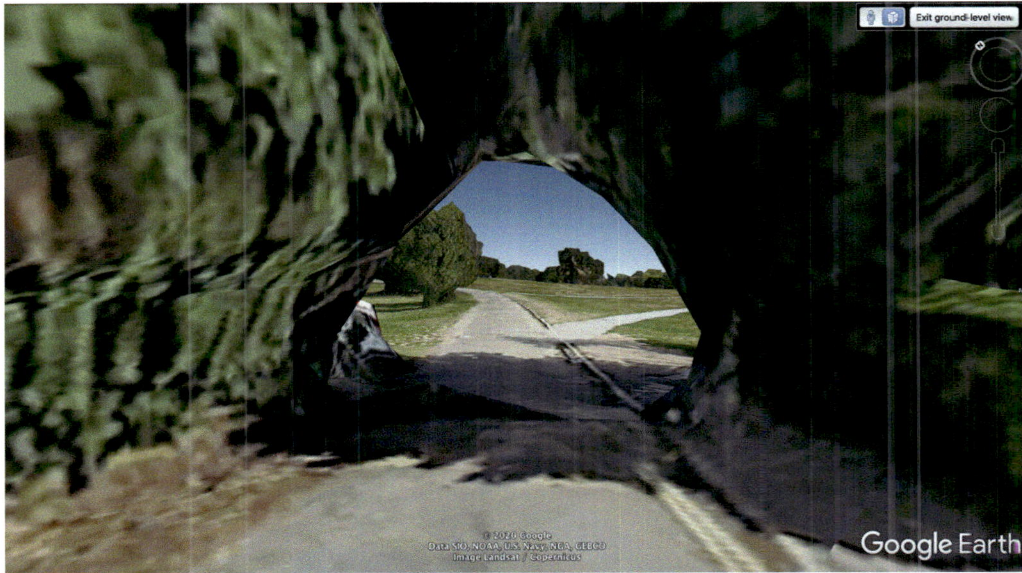

Figure 3.1 Entrance to the park, looking in.

The entrance to the model is a bulbous and faceted canopy of green, its surface composed of the heavily compressed and pixelated textures of leaves.[1] These presumably photographic textures foreshorten dynamically as I press the arrow key to advance toward, beneath and through the threshold, the canopy eventually disappearing in the rectangular periphery of the robotic vision of my local park.

1   Images in this chapter are screenshot documentations of a virtual walk through Google Earth's model of my local park in summer 2020.

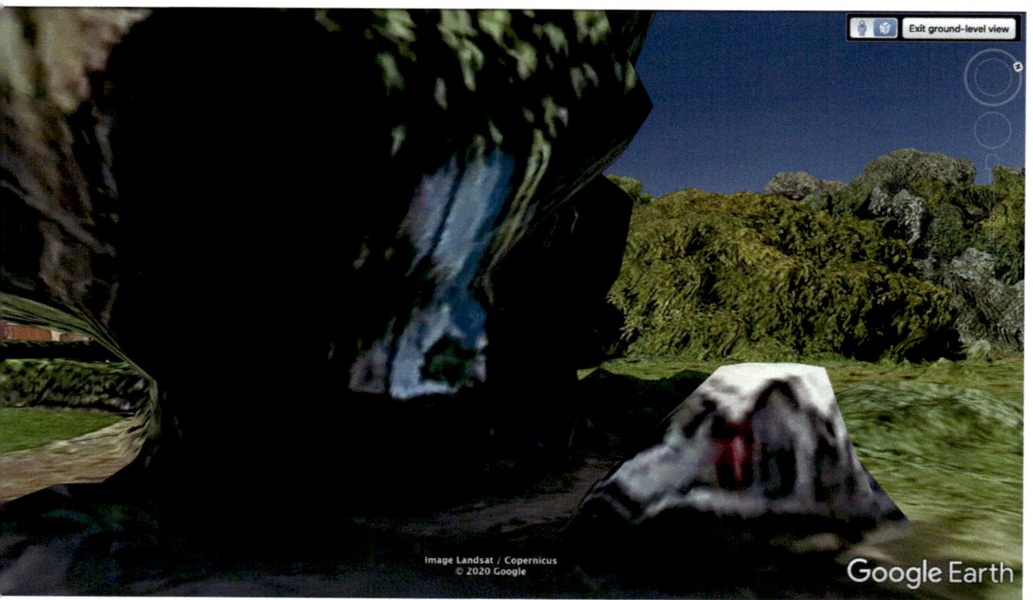

Figure 3.2 Map, subsumed.

To my immediate left appears the suggestion of a small vehicle, a mainten-ance cart used for rubbish collection. Its contours asymmetrically slope and slide as if melting into the ground around it. There is a flash of red where a window might be, but no image of a driver.

Sliding further round to see where I've been, the boughs of the tree-form entrance appear to overlap a signposted welcome map. On closer inspection, I find the sign is not embraced by, but subsumed into the surface of the tree-form, the rough projection of the park a green patch in the lower right-hand corner of a two-tone, cyan smear.

Rotating my view toward the expanse of the park, grey paths diverge into green and brown terrain. The horizon is a frozen phalanx of tree-forms, their upper edges crisp like cut paper against the perfectly curved gradation of the blue dome centred directly above my position. My anticipated centrality is confirmed by a quick upward pivot.

From the moment I open the Google Earth (GE) application, I am presented with a reminder of how images in everyday life habitu-ate injustice. Though racial injustice is not the central focus of this text, it is relevant that an odd, but easily overlooked, design choice suggests the whole world is set forth at my white, right-handed fingertips. With a click-and-drag, the earth shifts and rolls subject to the movement of what appears to be my closed-fisted grasp. Before this spindle-less desktop globe, I might believe myself the seated arbiter of the world.[2]

With each movement of this globe, so slide the stars beyond it, as though fixed in a web and anchored to a point at the very core of the orb. Unseated by their strangely fixed relationship, I become a body tumbling in space, pushing my way around a static framework of heavenly bodies, circling disorientated, pivoting gravity-less off the edge of an unmoving object outside time itself.

That familiar grabbing-hand cursor is also the disembodied, white-gloved hand of a cartoon mouse, himself derived from an abject pageantry of racism and inequality. Though intended to promote user identification and the impression of agency, its cartoonishness, not to mention its coding with respect to race and right-handedness, undercuts its efficacy (Jones 2011).[3] Its bloopy fingertips never quite achieve the illusion of grasping the planet's surface. Clenched fast, they close around nothing. Perhaps this is, after all, not the hand that pulls the world into view, but a disembodied fist that strikes at phantoms in the dark, ineffectively batting away that which it cannot divine or control.

This cursor image embodies the reality and illusion of privilege with respect to the robotic apparatus of vision (GE) and the world it attempts to represent. Its superficial functionality can be interpreted by the user as a graphic projection of personal control and explora-tion – and indeed this projection serves its master (not its user). At the same time, the minstrel glove's persistent appearance in popular culture despite its disturbing history reminds me it is a treachery of images that reinforce privilege and injustice, thus unpicking the comfortable myth of centrality.[4]

The glove is not unique as an example of screen-based representa-tions that compromise the user's appreciation for the complexity and strategic nature of the technology at hand. The term 'depresentation'

---

2   Belisle describes user centralisation: 'When users take up and enact the mode of visibility that a representation offers, they lend themselves to its structural proposition. They invest the kind of coherence and visibility that the repre-sentation offers as if it rearticulates the coherence and visibility of whatever it represents' (2020: p. 121).

3   Jones points out: 'the icon is [...] an indexical sign convincing users of an active synchronicity with her, or his, own hand movement. And yet [...] most people in the world [...] do not possess skin described as "white"; moreover 12 per cent of people are left-handed' (2011: p. 240).

4   Nicholas Sammonds describes the white gloves in relation to the illusion of control, centrality, agency (2015: pp. 25–6).

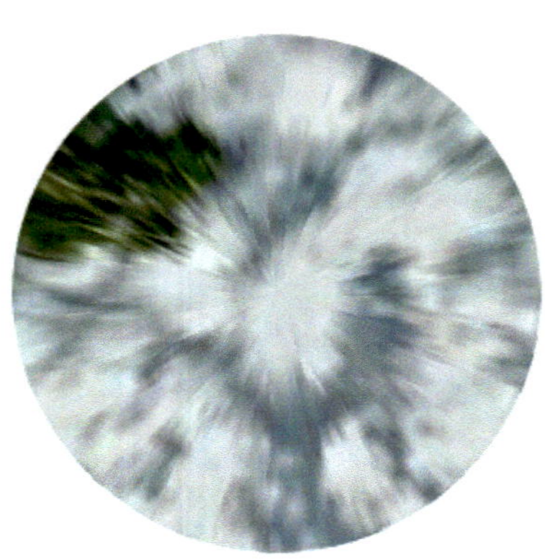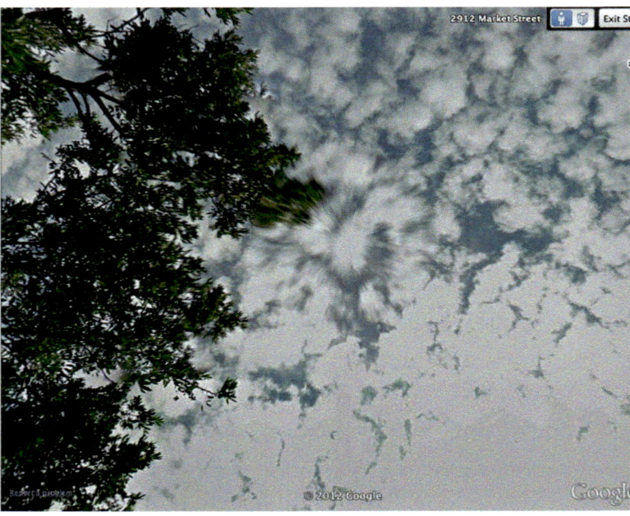

Figure 3.3 Left: Meg Rahaim, *Gods Eye IV*, digital inkjet print, 80 cm x 80 cm, 2014. Right: Source image for the artwork.
Images courtesy of the artist. Source: image screenshot from Google Street View in 2012.

describes such examples of interface design wherein the material reality of a function is obfuscated by the ontologising effect of its graphic signifier (van den Boomen 2009: p. 256). *Re*-presentation is an artistic methodology of identifying and recontextualising instances of depresentation in a way that critiques their obfuscation. For example, in the series of prints *Gods Eyes*, I appropriate via screenshot a visual anomaly of the Google Street View (GSV) sky that resembles the shape and striations of a human iris. Edited onto a white background, the radiating seams of the circular composite relate the digital-material construction of the original to the creeping omniscience of the program that produced it. A number of contemporary practices utilise similar methods, particularly in relation to Google's networked surveillant images, including Clement Valla's *Postcards from Google Earth*, Doug Rickard's *New American Picture* and Mishka Henner's *Dutch Landscapes*.[5]

In this chapter, I attempt the re-presentation of a specific set of networked surveillant images. In written speculation, I present

5   Jon Rafman's *9 Eyes*, Jenny Odell's *Satellite Collections* and *Satellite Landscapes* and James Bridle's *Dronestagram* also recontextualise corporate surveillance images to reveal something of their strategic origins.

traces found within a familiar sort of robotic vision of everyday life that point to two things. The first is the depresentation, or deliberate obfuscation, of their strategic origin. The second is the effect of robotic vision – in other words, the algorithmically composited model meant to mimic human vision – in sustaining and extending the power of the surveillance giant known as Google.

The dispossession cycle, identified by Shoshana Zuboff, describes the process by which tech giants have been able to normalise their continuous extraction of data from human behaviours, enabling the achievement of reliable prediction and control of those behaviours (Zuboff 2019: p. 137). Zuboff illustrates this using the case of unauthorised extraction of personal information from private homes by GSV cars, including Google's subsequent legal actions and technological developments in response to being exposed. The example makes clear the deliberate manner in which networked surveillant images are produced and deployed in the ongoing reification of human experience into products for sale. I look to such images, and my use of them, to understand my place in this process, and to develop methods of resistance within written and image-based creative practice.

Like the gloved hand that invokes both a cheerful fictional character and a culture of racist mockery, the GE images I peruse evoke both reverie and fear. In both cases, they depresent a gluttonous and disorientating standardisation of vision, and insinuate their platform into everyday life and culture through visual spectacle and their appeal to the disinterested passivity of privilege.

I advance into the terrain between the paths, passing over a patchy surface indicating the dried grass of midsummer, scanning left, then right for a place to linger and survey my surroundings. I should not have to compete for a good spot. It appears I am alone.

A row of trees ahead form a continuous object rather than a collection of individuals, the spaces between trunks forming canopied passageways like the one at the entrance. Passing through one, I come upon a leafy mass hovering motionless above a shadowed mound. Beyond it, I find another.

Past these aberrations of physics and photogrammetry, a scattering of shallow, grey shapes like felled timber lead to a large, double tree-form. Circling the conjoined trunks, I notice an oddly yellow patch on their surface. As my viewpoint changes, its shape slides into something like a person: a child with a shock of black hair and a yellow t-shirt, subsumed like the entrance map into surface.

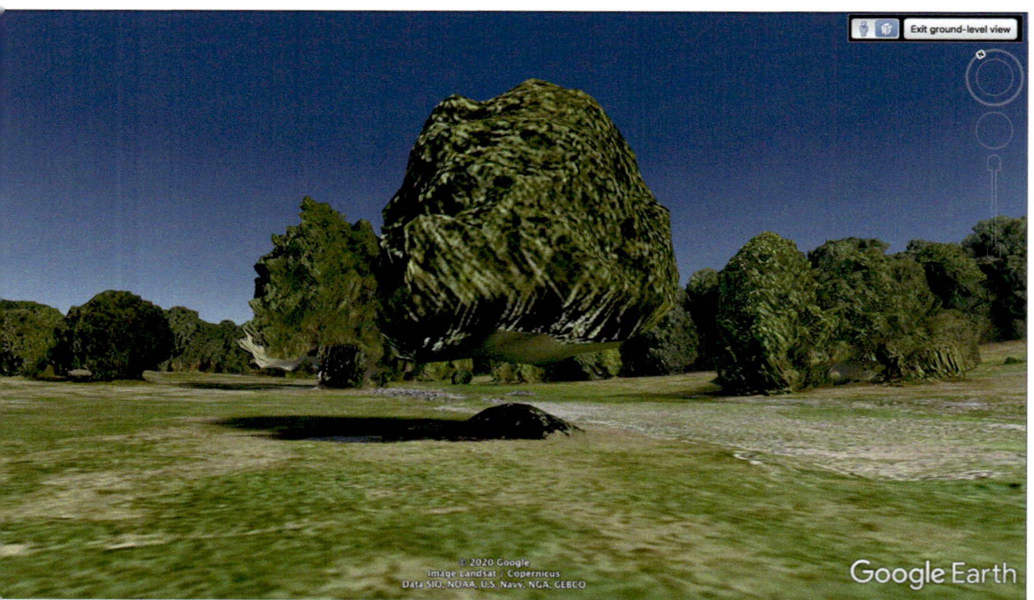

Figure 3.4 A trunkless tree.

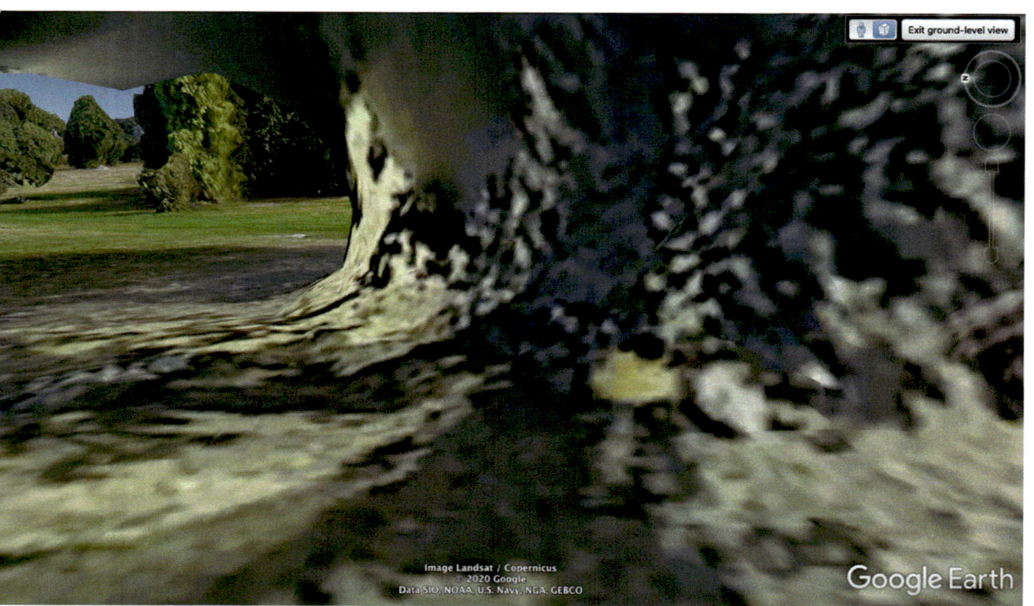

Figure 3.5 The child, subsumed.

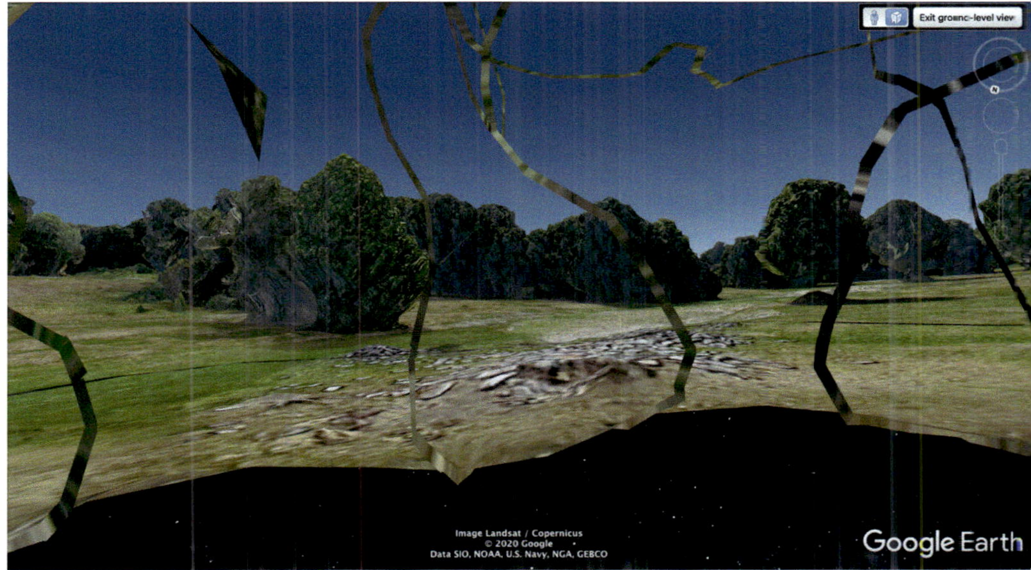

Figure 3.6 Inside the tree.

I advance toward the child's image. Holding the arrow key down a moment too long, I breach its surface to find myself looking at a hole in the ground into outer space, complete with stars and the dusty indication of the Milky Way.

Pivoting my view up and toward the sky dome, I am surrounded by floating ribbons of foliage, a lattice structure indicating the tree's shape.

Another push of a key, I am out the other side and the ground is below me once again.

In the large public park near my home, local people escape the close horizons of city and suburb, their eyes relaxing into a middle-distant gaze across a rolling expanse of green. They sun themselves, find shelter under a tree, or trek off into the shady corridor of a woodland trail. Mobile reception is notoriously poor here.

In GE, the pitch and elevations of this park's open spaces are convincingly rendered. The trees are voluminous and recognisable. Picnickers are flattened into the pixelated texture of the ground or the surface of a nearby 3D structure. A colourful, incongruous pattern of pixels echoes on the underside surface of a balloon-like mass of tree hovering above the ground, like a distorted reflection.

Using GE's 3D buildings feature at ground level, apparently solid forms – whether architecture or vegetation – are revealed to be otherwise. Empty structures, their walls are single-sided and have no depth. They are *pure surface* as can only be achieved by the airless light of the screen. Leaves do not rustle in the wind. Branchless, they do not bend. There is no atmosphere, no breath.

On the other side of the tree, I look uphill toward a forest and advance toward an opening in the tree line. Green spikes like crystals emerge from the ground in irregular pyramids. The onscreen image jumps up and down as I navigate into a corridor of tree-forms.

To the left, I see the image of a shadowy recess. Piercing its surface, I am met with a huge groundlessness. A wavy mesh of green ribbons stops just short of the horizon to meet the far edge of a waterless lake of outer space.

As I cross this expanse, the ribbons undulate smoothly and silently overhead. Pivoting my view downward, my screen is filled with blackness and stars. I hover outside the model, but inside the programme. My position is logged and geospatially specific, but I am also nowhere.

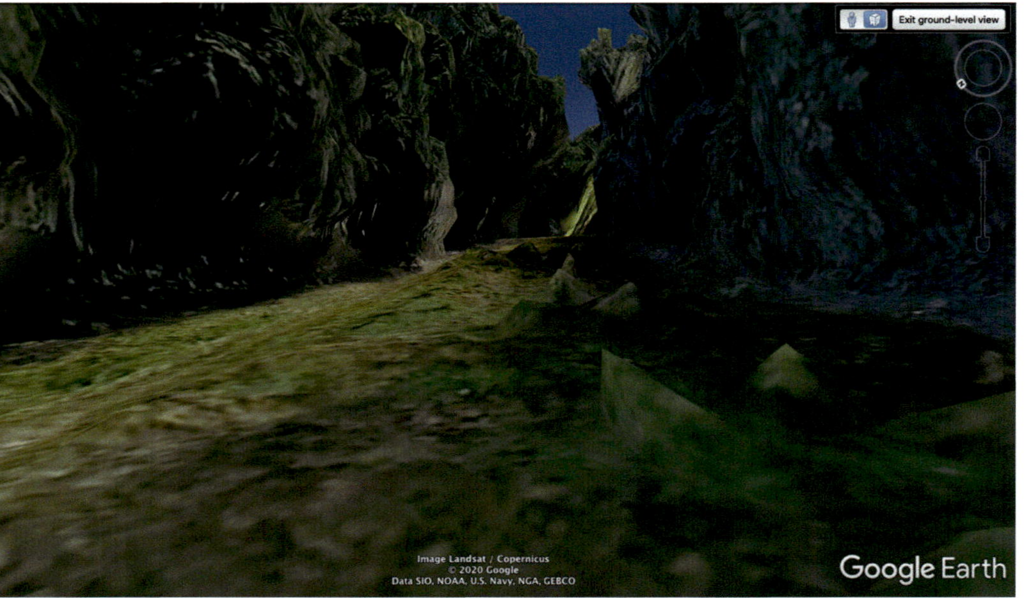

Figure 3.7 Corridor with green spikes.

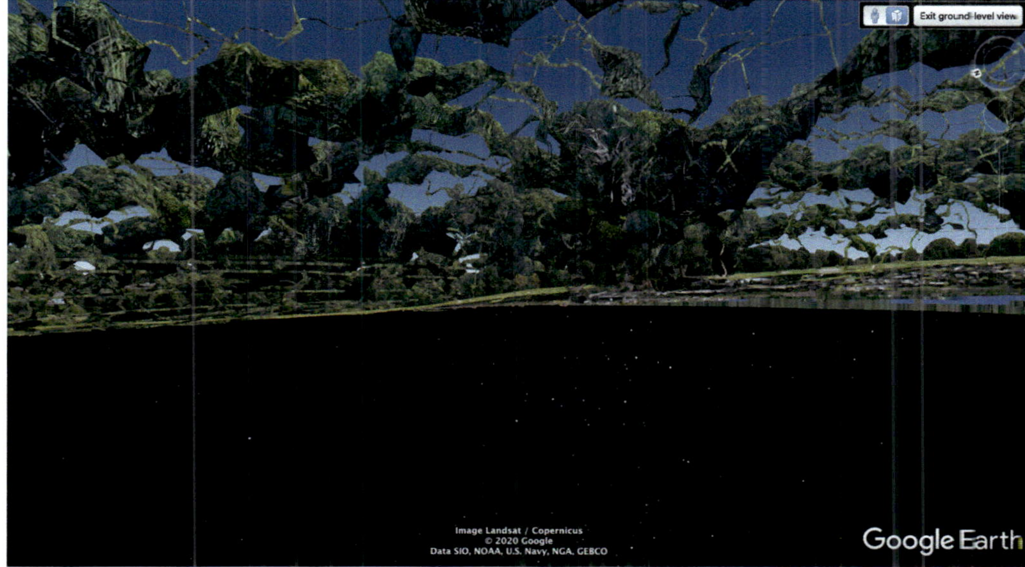

Figure 3.8 The lake.

Surveillance pervades everyday life to differing degrees based on location. Where I live, in a leafy suburb of a heavily surveilled city, it does so in both visible and invisible ways. CCTV screens on public transport and in shops. Personal mobile devices. Speed and traffic cameras. Satellites. Aircraft.

Itself a product of surveillance, GE is neither map nor photograph, strictly speaking, but its use relies on operators' familiarity with both forms insofar as they imply objectivity, record and reference. Like the big picture view of GE at the opening of the app, the continuity and photographic aesthetics of the park model's imagery, including depictions of human activity, produce a sense of simultaneity, suggesting the entirety of the park image was captured in a single moment on a particular day. The reality, of course, is that this is nothing like a snapshot. Neither photographic nor biological, it is a meticulously planned, algorithmically composited model, a data-based reconstruction, a robotic vision. Forced to straddle the objectivity of machine-envisioned landscape and the contingency of photographic capture, the vision suffers something of an identity crisis, and rupture presents itself.

To this point, in framing the space of the park as an objective, observable landscape, it would seem unnecessary to include passing events such as picnicking. A public park, however, profuse in lush foliage and awash in sunlight, yet empty of people awakens the viewer to the sterility of the visual projection. Human presence becomes a rhetorical move, an attempt at establishing pathos, at engendering a sense of familiarity not only with the geographic location, but with the social purpose and anticipated experience of the depicted space.

But nothing can move in this park, so nothing moving is modelled. The process used to produce 3D objects cannot map a moving object, a jogger, say, onto a still projection with any great success. They are not included in the finished projection.[6] The sunbather at rest or the picnic spread beneath a tree are, in their stillness and relative bas relief, apt candidates for inclusion in a unity of pixelated surface. Their lonely occupation of an expanse is a noticeable incongruity. Because they could just as easily be omitted as a jogger or a dog at play, their inclusion smacks of intentionality, of design, of strategy.

While depiction of human activity, insomuch as it signifies photographic capture, might present the model as a unique, time-specific and indexical representation of the lived space of the park, the subsumption of the human figure into the surface of this model alludes to dispossession taking place on a grander scale. What it means to refer to GE as a robotic vision is not simply that it is the composite vision of a process of computing. It is to do with the absence of a kind of interiority that accompanies biological perception. The larger programme of dispossession is one of the subsumption of human bodies and experience into data-based image ensembles that are produced, managed and performed by machines in a way that evades human oversight.

Adrian MacKenzie and Anna Munster propose that the amassing, formatting and processing of astoundingly large image ensembles in deep-learning AI constitutes 'a new mode of perception, and indeed a reformulation of visuality itself ... [called] *platform seeing*' (2019: p. 5). Fundamentally unlike biological perception, this new way of seeing is not attuned to the subject, content or meaning of images, but only to the detectable connections between and among them that might enable prediction in the pursuit of profit.

6   The 3D objects in GE are produced from overlapping, GPS-tagged photographs taken from an aeroplane flying in a grid formation. Time lapses between passes of the aeroplane prevent moving objects from producing coherent forms (Dennis 2017).

Friction is anathema to flow, whether of images or of capital. Platforming is a process whereby standardisation begins not with the image data once collected, but with the means by which people produce that data in their everyday lives. Through personal networked devices, our most private images are born ready to contribute to a dynamic ensemble of data and processing of which we are incapable of having an overview (Mackenzie and Munster 2019: p. 15). This is a tangible example of the role of platformed standardisation in the process of dispossession. The subsumption of the body and the illusion of coherence in Google Earth's depiction of public space are not merely emblematic of this. As it displaces biological vision in the production and interpretation of images, the implied objectivity of invisual standardisation, whether in the psychedelic horror vacuii of Deep Dream-ing[7] or the pure surface of Google Earth, has the capacity to disorientate us from the physical world.

The ground in the park is soft and green from weeks of rain followed by cool, autumn sunshine, and it cushions my feet as I walk across a field and down a hill.

Many trees have lost their leaves, bearing less resemblance to the ample volumetrics of their digital approximations. They are twisted grey networks of twigs and branches now. All of their trunks reach the ground.

I've come to visit a large oak, its own leaves still deeply green and defiantly abundant. Approaching the trunk, I hear the intermittent 'thup' of an acorn hitting the ground. I circle to its western side, where I saw the image of the child in the model. I do not expect to find the impression of a figure in the side of the tree, or dig a hole in the earth to reveal a starry chasm, but I would like to put my hand on some tree bark.

What I find in place of a small child in a yellow shirt is a half dug-up cache of acorns before an opening at the foot of the trunk. The hole at the seam of tree and earth is too small for a fox or rabbit, too low for a squirrel to nest. Its recess turns sharply inward, preventing line-of-sight investigation. I am not brave enough to put my hand in dark places.

I sit on a lonely slice of felled tree, my eyes tracing patterns of stretch and separation in the oak's grey bark. Above me, leaves and branches radiate into space in fractal variation. A magpie hops between the tree and me. I make a tittering sound and she comes curiously close, hoping I brought lunch. I did not.

7   Deep Dream is a visualisation tool by-product of Google's deep-learning AI. The hallucinatory spectacle it produces, including *The Gate to a Deep Dream* (DDG Generator 2020), is a visual incarnation of the invisual standardisation described by Mackenzie and Munster.

Discrete accidents of photogrammetry are fleeting. With each update, the model achieves greater detail and appearance of accuracy. The god's eyes I saw in the sky a few years ago are now gone, their seams screeded-over like wet plaster. But accidents will continue to occur, especially in the attempt to represent a dynamic subject. The flows of capital are intertwined with the improvement of illusion in such a way that the image will wax inexhaustibly toward seamlessness. But it can only wax. While humans may accept a level of visual description that fools the eye, what does an algorithm know of such thresholds if written to amass and improve?

Each rupture I find in that purity of surface is an artefact, an index of the state of the art at one moment in history. The phantom image of a little boy mapped onto the form of a tree trunk is a special kind of artefact. It is the index of the trauma of his subsumption, of his flattening, and of the misfortune of being in a certain place at a moment of image capture.

Trauma, in its modern clinical understanding, is an embodied condition. Bessel van der Kolk makes it clear that

> trauma is not just an event that took place in the past; it is also the imprint left by that experience on mind, brain, and body. This imprint has ongoing consequences for how the human organism manages to survive in the present. (2014: p. 21)

Trauma pins the bearer to the event, so that it remains present for or is carried by them into each unfolding present, despite passage of time or change in location. Christina Sharpe invokes 'the wake' as a framework for understanding a trauma that supersedes ordinary conceptions of traumatic memory by its multiplied, continuous and distributed nature. In the wake of a shared, historic and ongoing trauma, such as Black slavery and its effects on the lives of Black people, 'the past that is not past reappears, always, to rupture the present' (Sharpe 2016: p.15). It is the dynamic experience of trauma as an outward flow, widening indefinitely from a point of occurrence to encapsulate the multitude of subjects caught within it.

To say this child's subsumption is trauma is to point to its widening multiplication of effects. This trauma pins and re-pins him across time and space in a way that chimes with Sharpe's past that is not past, yet trades its biological instantiation for a technological one. By the production of this networked surveillance, the child is captured, flattened, subsumed and made reproducible. His trauma multiplies and recurs indefinitely, alive in the flow to the computed surface on my screen in one moment, and on indeterminable other screens at other times, travelling him at great speed and distance without his knowledge or permission.

It is possible for bearers of trauma to suffer symptoms without conscious memory of the initiating event; however, reclaiming and confronting these memories is key to treatment (Van der Kolk 2015: p. 204). Years from now, when this boy feels discomfort, incompletion, anxiety, despair, he will not know it is because he was spliced in this way, but it will do no good for him to investigate. His image will have been replaced in the model by something more accurate, less accidental. He will remain pinned by his trauma in electrons and silicon in some air-conditioned underground archive of blinking green lights and fibre optic cables, as well as to the bark of a tree beneath my fingertips, his life forever compromised by a series of accidents of photogrammetry committed in support of a programme of capital that will not pay for his therapy.

It's a sunny day for November. At the edge of the tree's shadow the grass is sparse and clumped, the ground littered with twigs and green acorns. Sweeping aside some of nature's debris, I spread a blanket and stake my loosely rectangular claim for the hour.

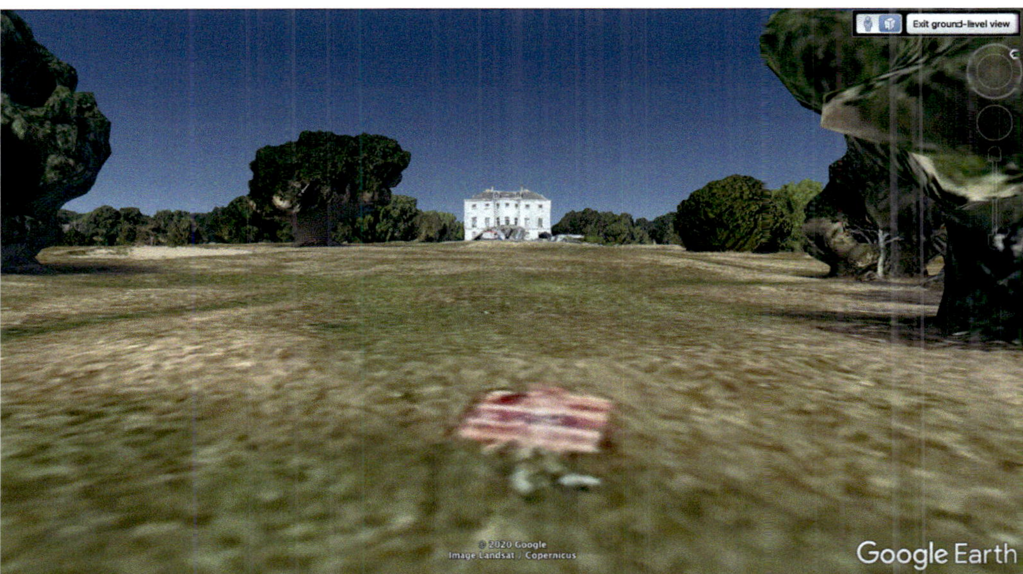

Figure 3.9 Looking north-east up the hill.

Lying here, I am met with the physical shape of the world in eruptions of knobbly roots poking my back, the sharp edge of a leaf stem popping through the fabric to scratch my hand, and the patch of grass giving way beneath my head with a muffled hush.

Overhead a small, white airplane passes, recording something like a photograph of me on my dark blue blanket, my white-sneakered feet protruding from its edge.

In a flurry of pixels, I am flattened, frictionless.

Writing around the GE model of my local park is an attempt to excavate something from the ramping purity of a technologically envisioned surface, from the privatisation of public spaces through data capture and robotic envisioning, by sharing moments of rupture that suggest the human cost.

Visual clues to depresentation are opportunities for intervention, not simply because they signal the obfuscation of the model's histories and operativity. The ontologisation of the model as pure mimesis detached from agenda actually enables the strategic deployment of the surveillant apparatus. The false yet comforting centrality I find in the model replaces my lived orientation in a world of other bodies, encouraging me to linger within it, as well as to disregard its negative effects on those bodies.

Through speculation, re-presentation initiates a process of understanding the role of robotic vision in the programme of surveillance capitalism. The curious presentation of human activities, in particular the stark imbalance between moving bodies and bodies at rest, suggests the deliberateness of their inclusion. As an attempt at establishing pathos, it highlights the need for the programme to appeal to the user, and doubly fulfils this need by distracting from, and therefore obscuring, its historic military origin and contemporary surveillant nature. In addition, accidents of photogrammetry, whether by the omission of a tree trunk or by the subsumption of one body into the surface of another, reveal the material incongruity of the model and the world. Ruptures caused by the misalignment of one form of data-based imaging to another evidence the composite, robotic nature of the vision itself and signal the threat of disembodiment posed by the programme of surveillance that deploys them.

Trauma produces its own geographies, abides by its own physics, orientating victims to a warped world of bodies and experience, anchoring them to distant places and events through deeply embedded memory. Likewise, trauma disorientates its victims to the present moment as its imprint echoes and multiplies across lifetimes, subjects and platforms. The vision of the child in the yellow shirt indicates a novel form of trauma because, rather than rooting itself within the living body, it *disembodies* its victim. It does so not by erasure or liberation, but by theft. Unbeknownst to the victim, it records, copies and stores something of that body within itself. Cleared from public evidence by a regular schedule of updates, and stored inaccessibly in a private digital mauscleum, it eludes approaches to healing that rely on identifying the source of traumatic memory.

This trauma of subsumption makes a living body into raw materials from which it weaves the projection of its own platform. Surveillance capitalism is the travesty of this subsumption at scale, and a distributed, traumatic wake in the making. Any resistance to this naturalised subjugation has to begin with its recognition, something made difficult by the invisuality of the technology itself. The notion of disembodied trauma offers a new framework for understanding how invisual abstraction disorientates individuals from injustices done against them and sustains their subsumption into the depthless landscape of pure surface.

References

Belisle, B. (2020) 'Whole World Within Reach: Google Earth VR', *Journal of Visual Culture* 19(1): 112–36.

Bridle, J. (2021) *James Bridle/Dronestagram*. Available at https://jamesbridle.com/works/dronestagram (accessed 7 April 2021).

DDG Generator (2020) *The Gate to a Deep Dream*. Available at https://www.youtube.com/watch?v=Acst11cFmxE&t=9s (accessed 7 April 2021).

Dennis, N. (2017) *Google Earth's Incredible 3D Imagery, Explained*. Available at https://www.youtube.com/watch?v=suo_aUTUpps (accessed 7 April 2021).

Henner, M. (2011) *Dutch Landscapes – Mishka Henner*. Available at https://mishkahenner.com/dutch-landscapes (accessed 7 April 2021).

Jones, P. (2011) 'A White Right Hand', *Convergence* 17(3): 237–44.

MacKenzie, A., and Munster, A. (2019) 'Platform Seeing: Image Ensembles and Their Invisualities', *Theory Culture and Society* 36(5): 3–22.

Odell, J. (2021) *Jenny Odell. Projects*. Available at https://www.jennyodell.com/projects.html (accessed 7 April 2021).

Rafman, J. (2020) *9-eyes*. Available at https://9-eyes.com (accessed 7 April 2021).

Rickard, D. (2012) *A New American Picture*. Available at https://dougrickard.com/a-new-american-picture (accessed 7 April 2021).

Sammonds, N. (2015) *The Birth of an Industry: Blackface Minstrelsy and the Rise of American Animation*. Durham: Duke University Press.

Sharpe, C. (2016) *In the Wake: On Blackness and Being*. Durham: Duke University Press.

Valla, C. (2012) *Postcards from Google Earth*. Available at http://www.postcards-from-google-earth.com (accessed 7 April 2021).

Van den Boomen, M. (2009) 'Interfacing by Material Metaphors: How Your Mailbox May Fool You', in Van den Boomen, M. (ed.), *Tracing New Media in Everyday Life and Technology*. Amsterdam: Amsterdam University Press, pp. 253–65.
Van der Kolk, B. (2014) *The Body Keeps the Score: Mind, Brain and Body in the Transformation of Trauma*. London: Penguin Random House.
Zuboff, S. (2019) *The Age of Surveillance Capitalism: The Fight for a Human Future at the New Frontier of Power*. London: Profile Books.

4 Ophiux

Joey Holder

Two images following:
Figure 4.1 *Ophiux*, medical room installation at Wysing Arts Centre, Cambridge, 2016.
Image credit: Joey Holder.

Figure 4.2 *Ophiux*, medical room installation at Wysing Arts Centre, Cambridge, 2016.
Image credit: Joey Holder.

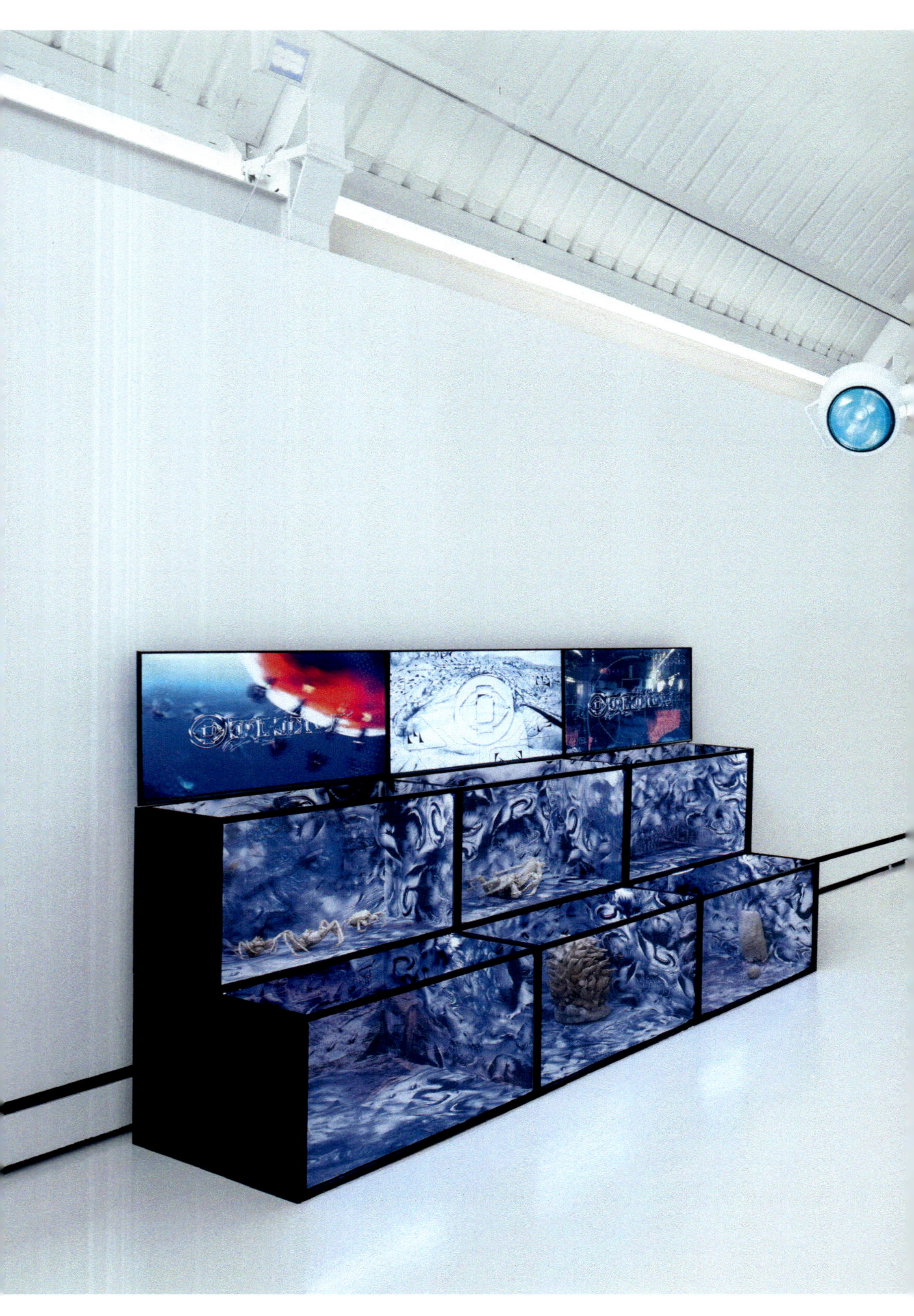

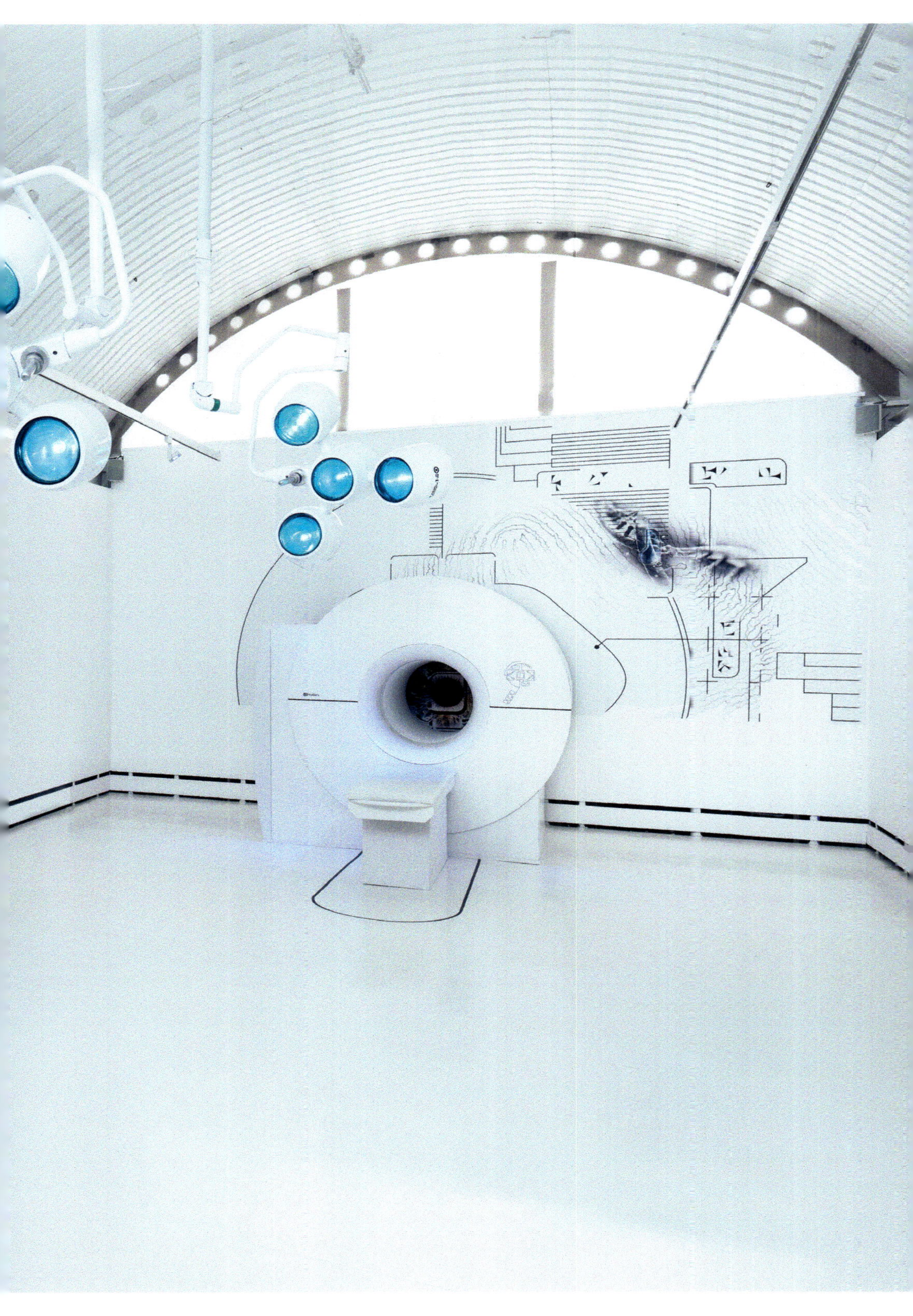

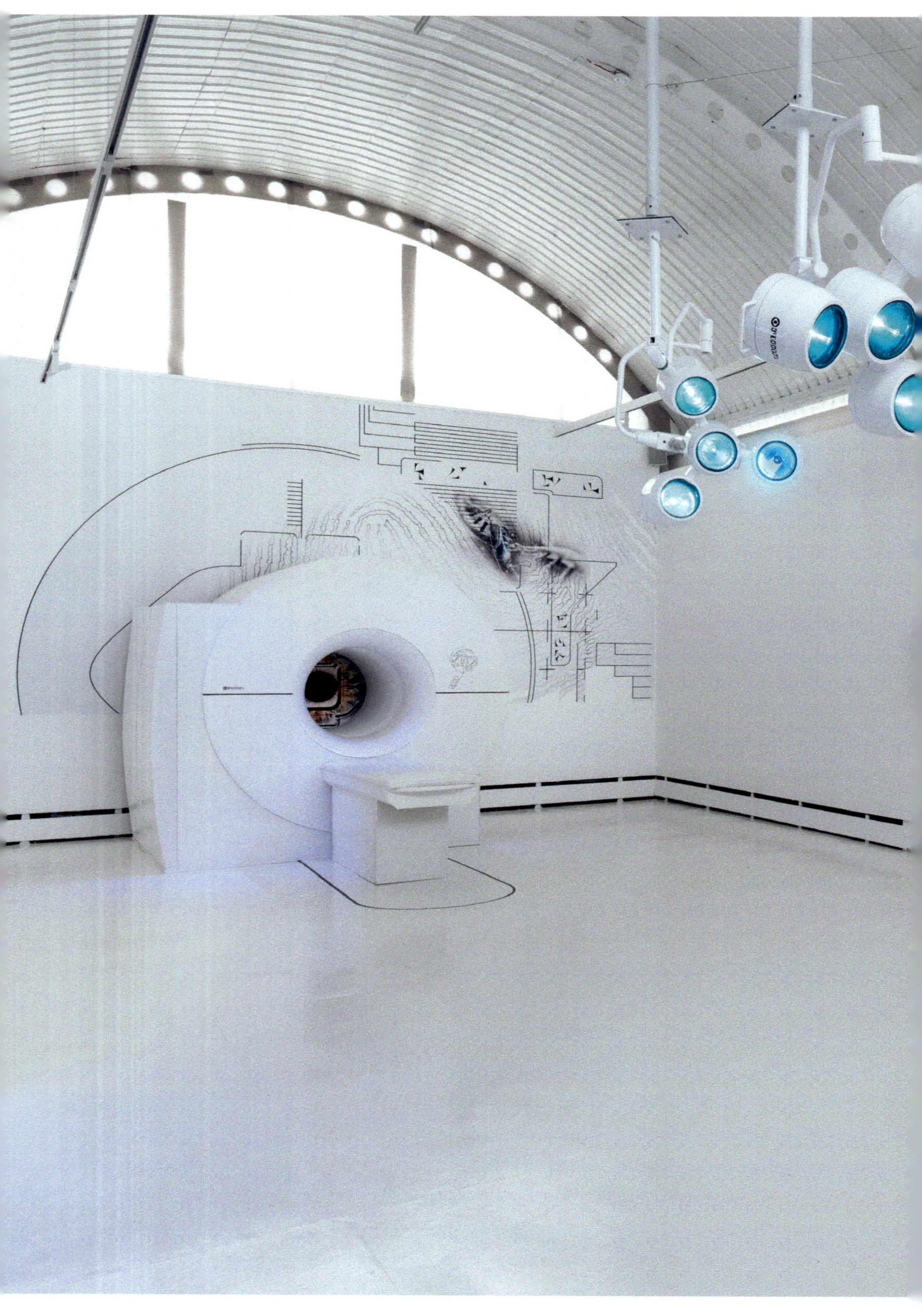

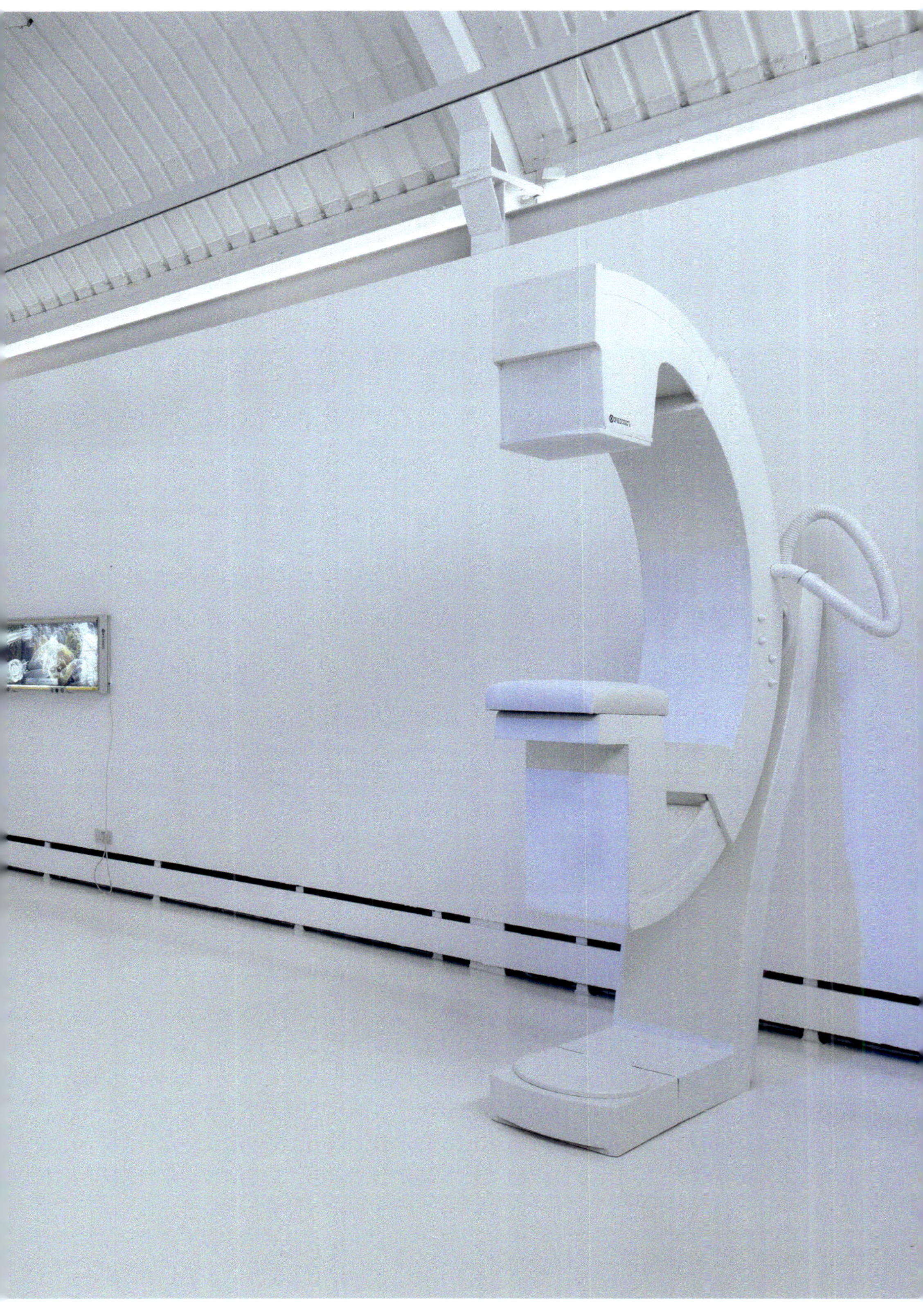

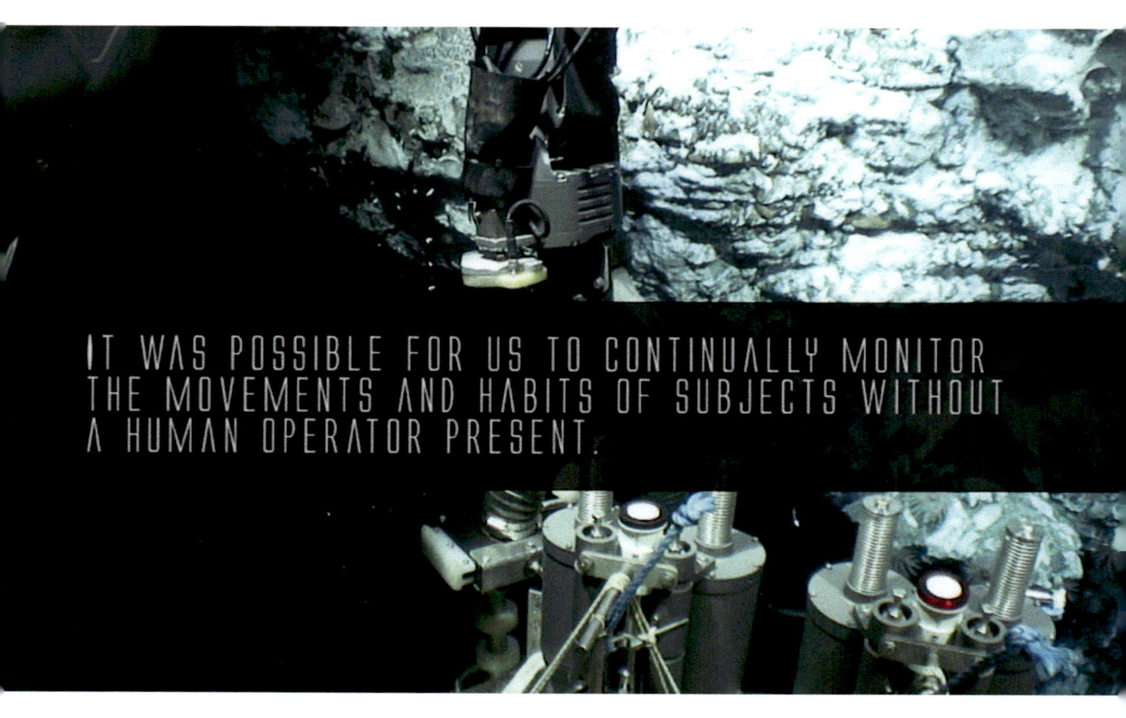

Figure 4.3 *Ophiux*, film still, 2016.
Image credit: Joey Holder.

Our research and development activities are based on profound biological understanding.

From successful deep-sea biodiversity assessments, we have comp etely mapped the marine ecosystem…

Genomic DNA was isolated from the Amphipod Pereopods.

Before the advent of genetic technologies shamans were able to see inside the body at a microscopic level.

Modern science confirmed ancient knowledge.

Genetic information was stored in a data bank above ground….

Sophisticated, self-assembled, bio-processing.

The proofread sequences of the specimens were aligned using ARB software, with molecular characterisation of the species complex.

Data flowed between the aquatic environment and the high-tech medical interior via a complex mesh created by the synthetic mycelium.

Ophiux was able to completely control the gene expression of the subject through precise environmental sensors.

Entirely new genetic sequences, and thus entirely new life-forms.

It was possible for us to continually monitor the movements and habits of subjects without a human operator present.

The technology was combined with other methods of observation to provide a fully comprehensive 24/7 monitoring system.[1]

1   Voice of 'Ophiux', a speculative pharmaceutical company created by Joey Holder.

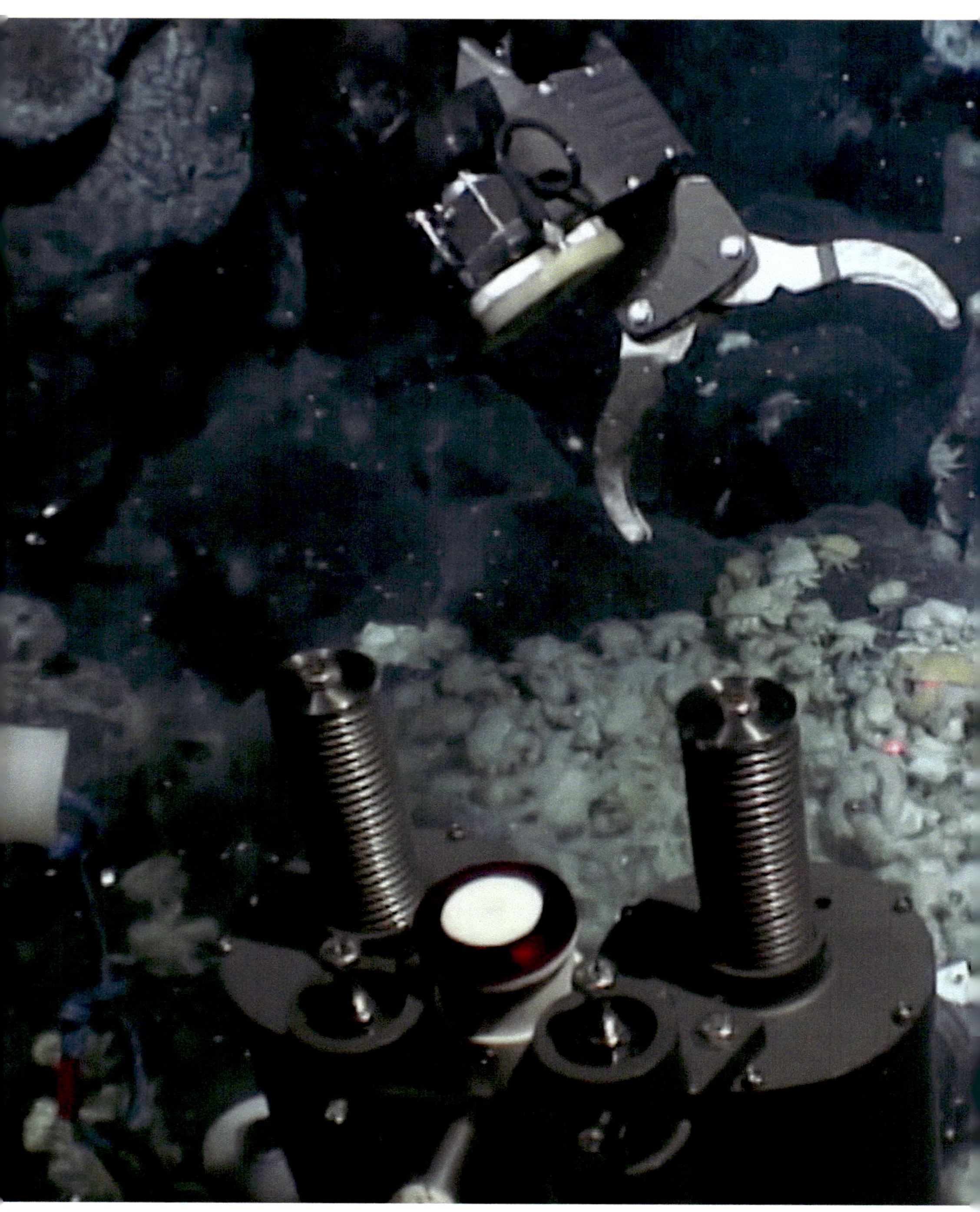

Figure 4.4 *Ophiux*, film still, 2016.
Image credit: Joey Holder.

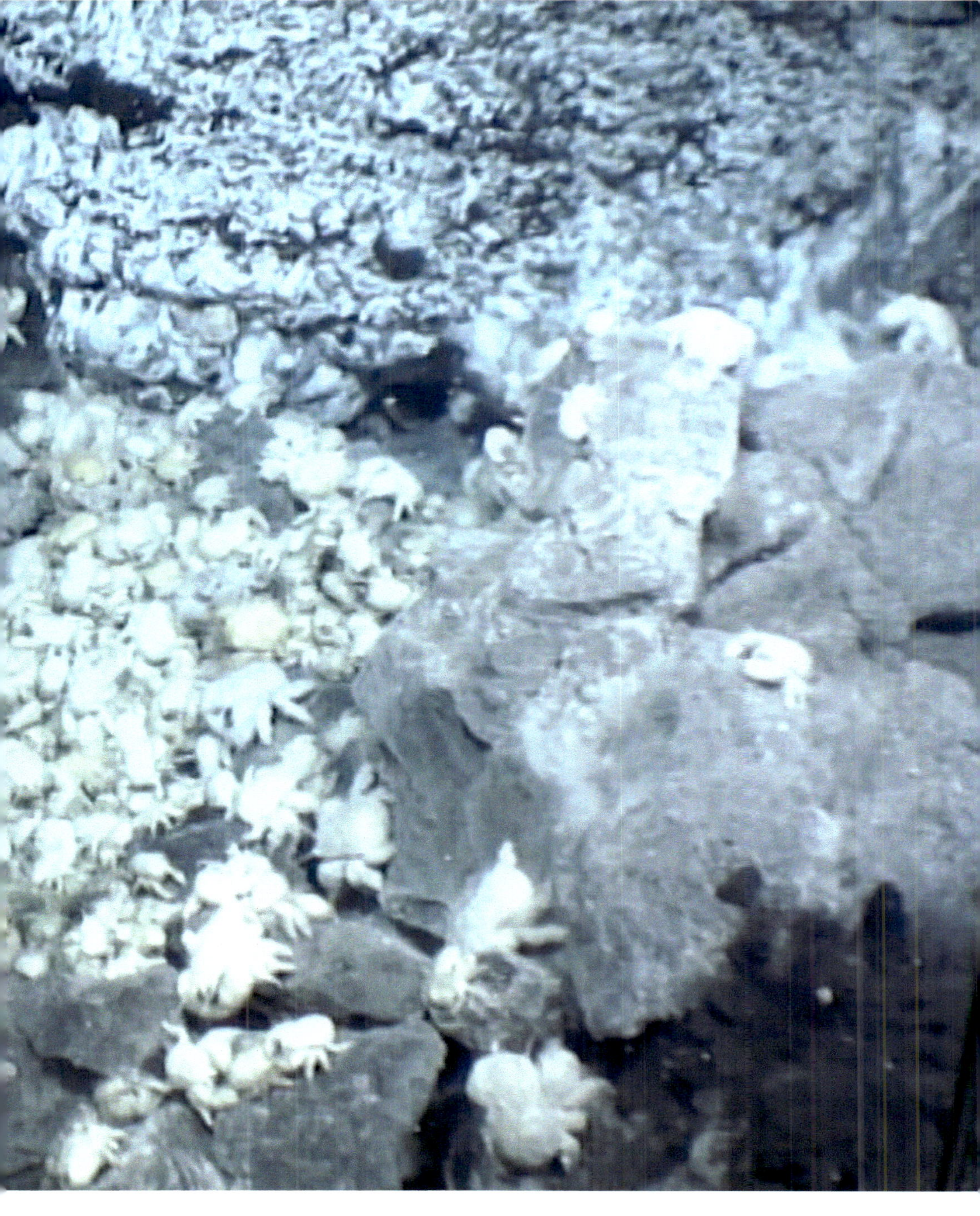

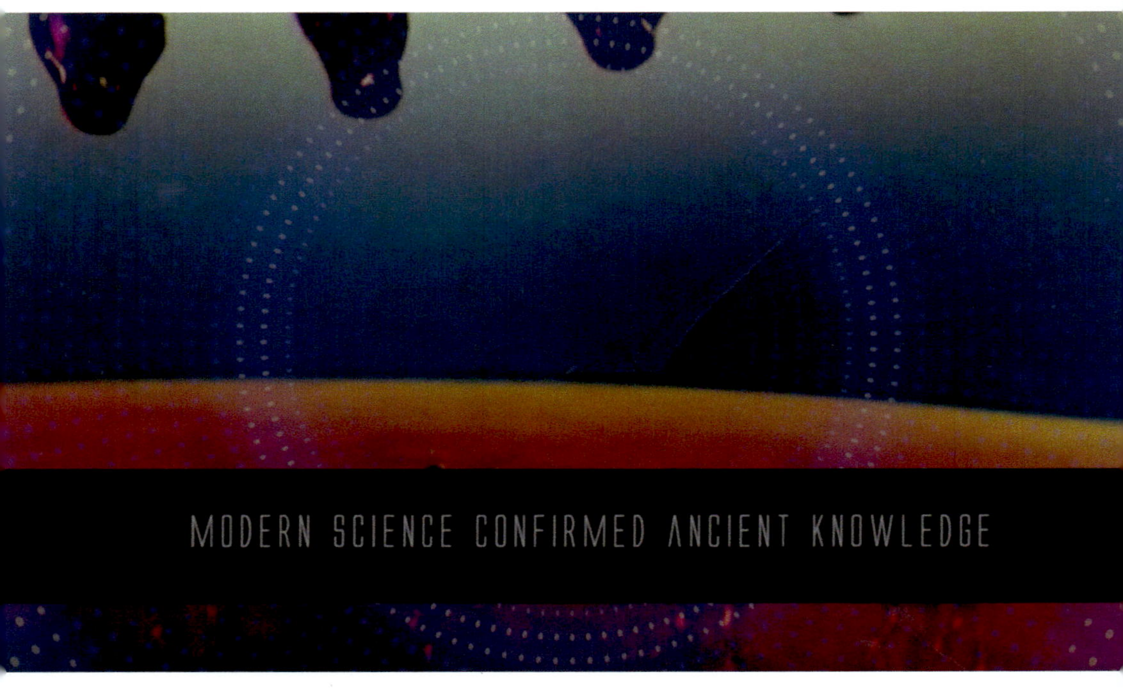

Figure 4.5 *Ophiux*, film still, 2016.
Image credit: Joey Holder.

Ophiux

Joey Holder

Film and medical room installation at Wysing Arts Centre, Cambridge, 2016

The above narration from the artwork *Ophiux* refers to a fictional pharmaceutical company and its desire to map the marine ecosystem as a way to form a sequence capable of benefiting human life expectancy. The installation mimics idealised medical environments, with clinical white sterility, and features large machines evocative of MRI scanners and X-ray lightboxes, with images of magnified microbes and marine specimen tanks. This speculative future-scape of visuals includes images captured from arctic submarines alongside medical and computer-generated imagery.

Founded on current scientific research, *Ophiux* provides a glimpse into an imagined near future in which synthetic biology has been fully realised and applied, both to advance human evolution and to increase life expectancy. The installation envisages larger than life-sized models of biological imaging machines, as well as genetic sequencing equipment, being used by the speculative pharmaceutical company Ophiux to collect and programme data from human bodies and other organisms. The installation visualises how current digital technologies are used to extract data from DNA, reflecting on the reality of today's health-care quandaries where we are witnessing an increase in the mapping and digitisation of our medical profiles.

Alongside the futuristic biological imaging machines, *Ophiux* includes a film incorporating footage from an underwater remotely operated vehicle (ROV) which samples creatures from the deep sea for scientists wishing to study them. These unique ecosystems could provide the key to understanding the beginning of life itself, as the conditions around the deep-sea vents called 'black smokers' are thought to be the same as those when life began. While the imaging machines proposed by Holder are representative of possible forms of robotic vision to interrogate human biology invisible to our eyes, the film draws on current robotic vision being used to 'see' and comprehend that which is equally invisible to human eyes: the depths of the oceans. The ROV can withstand immense pressures at depths of up to 6,500 m, as well as the intense heat and chemicals pumped out from the underwater vents. These kinds of machines allow us to have presence in what would otherwise be completely inhospitable conditions. Disembodied from their human operators they enable telepresence; the cameras on board embody a kind of vision, allowing the robot to relay its visible surroundings of this alien underwater world.

To conceive the exhibition, Holder worked in close collaboration with Dr Marco Galardini, Computational Biologist at the European Bioinformatics Institute at the Wellcome Trust Genome Campus, Cambridge, and Dr Katrin Linse, Senior Biodiversity Biologist at the British Antarctic Survey, Cambridge, to obtain visualisations of complex genetic data and the deep-sea footage seen in the film. Combined, the film and installation play with notions of robotic seeing and digital data gathering, on a level that is both scientific and technological but that has sinister means and commercial gains. What is present in Holder's installation is the importance of robotic vision in extracting data in a whole host of situations, whether it is the medical imaging contraption's ability to infiltrate the microcosmic depths of our skin, cells and DNA, or the ROV's carefully directed video camera penetrating the deep depths of the oceans.

—

Ophiux was originally commissioned by Wysing Arts Centre in 2016 and toured to Sonic Acts, 'The Noise of Being' exhibition in Amsterdam in 2017. The film was co-commissioned by Deptford X and has been screened at various venues in the UK and internationally. The project was made possible with a generous grant from the Arts Council England.

Joey Holder's practice is in collaboration with researchers and practitioners such as marine biologists, technologists, geneticists, behavioural psychologists and journalists. The creation of speculative worlds and fictional spaces or world-building are core to her practice. Holder's multimedia installations are in response to the reality of our lived world and she considers each artwork as an audio and visual space.

Sensing

5 Blinking Eyes: The Embodied Registers of Military Drone Camera Footage on YouTube

Kate Fahey

I am an artist and researcher broadly interested in forms of knowledge production that interrupt scientific and calculative logic. These interests are linked to my previous career in therapeutic radiography and my background in printmaking, both concerning – to a certain extent – the technical aspects of image-making. Furthermore, my practice-based research often explores the complexities of the scanned body's relationship to the technologies of image capture, and the role of images in this relationship.[1] I work across a range of media: moving image, sound, writing, sculpture, print and digitally aided making. In this chapter I will discuss a body of work titled *I could feel that my eyes were open...*, produced and installed at ZK/U Centre for Art and Urbanistics in Berlin in spring 2019. This multi-channel sound and video installation was the culmination of a five-month research residency at the centre, which is situated in a former railway station. There are a number of architectural parasitic interventions attached to the main station building, including a pavilion titled *Ständige Vertretung!* (Permanent Representation). The work was installed in *Ständige Vertretung!* during an OpenHaus weekend event in May 2019. It consisted of two synchronised moving images (one projected onto the ceiling and one shown on a screen mounted to the ceiling) multi-channel sound and a custom-made mattress upon which viewers could lie to experience the installation.

I could feel that my eyes were open... emerged from a long-term research project concerning the US and the UK's representation of drone warfare, specifically their uploading of footage of drone strikes

---

1   By calculative I mean a quantitative, orderable and numerical rationale for understanding the world. This techno-scientific conceptualisation renders bodies as data through a series of mappable, discrete, mathematical points. Drawing on Martin Heidegger, Catherine Waldby relates the calculability of techno-scientific knowledge to an extractive logic. She states: 'The operation of modern technology is to order the world as use value and immediate resource, to make it knowable and accessible ready to hand, through such ordering' (2000: p. 29).

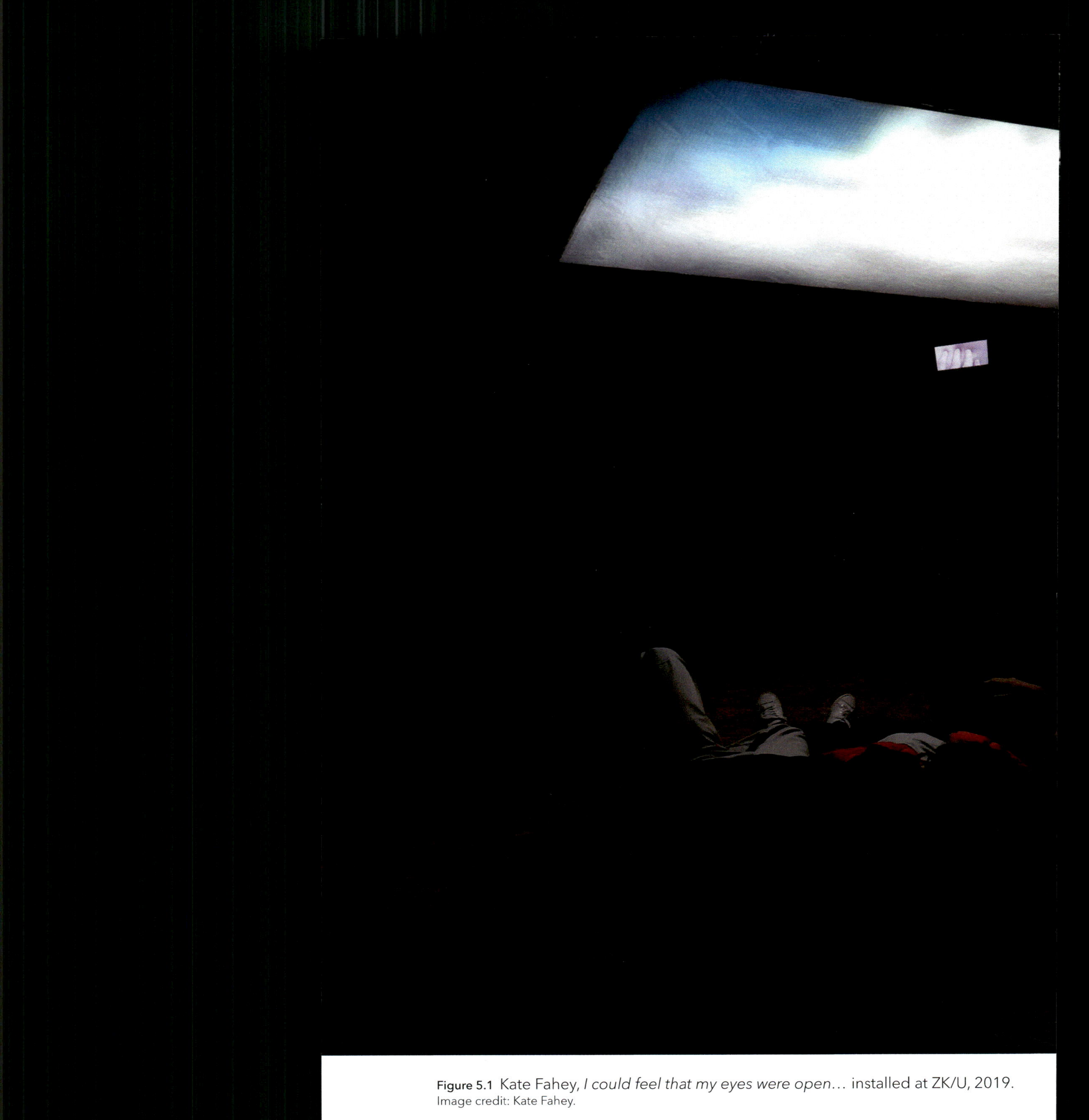

Figure 5.1 Kate Fahey, *I could feel that my eyes were open…* installed at ZK/U, 2019. Image credit: Kate Fahey.

to their official YouTube channels.[2] Drawing on feminist theories of Judith Butler, Donna Haraway, Karen Barad and Rosi Braidotti, among others, I will discuss how my studio practice and the subsequent installation of the work established an embodied feminist approach to these operative images. This embodied feminist position was based upon a relational condition in which nature and culture, interior and exterior, mind and body are entangled, contingent, mutable and productive of each other (Blackman 2008: pp. 34–5). Exploring this feminist praxis could, I speculated, reveal alternative perspectives on, and perceptions of, the interrelation of power, vulnerability, technology and bodies from those conveyed through the techno-scientific presentation of drone warfare on YouTube. Furthermore, I felt that this approach could engender the potential to interrupt and destabilise the perception and understanding of objective and authoritative forms of knowledge purveyed by military institutions. This position drew upon and adapted Donna Haraway's theorisation of a 'feminist objectivity', discussed later in this chapter, constituting a view from a complex and contradictory body as opposed to a simplistic and disembodied view from above (Haraway 1988: p. 583).

The operative content uploaded to YouTube by the US and UK militaries present the promise of an enhanced, calculative and technically mediated mode of seeing. They produce a detached, objective perception of drone warfare as clean, rational and precise. Harun Farocki introduced the term 'operative image' to describe images that have a role in automatic targeting through pattern recognition and pixel matching, such as those utilised in cruise missile strikes. This marked a major change in how aerial images were being used in military operations. In his text, he suggested that operative images went beyond representation to be part of an operation, actively targeting, 'doing things in the world' (Farocki 2004). Operative images are functional in nature rather than solely representative, in this case used for the active targeting of weapons and the destruction of life (Farocki 2004). It is this category of images, generated by the targeting systems of manned and unmanned strike aircraft such as drones, fighter jets and helicopters that were being uploaded to YouTube by

2   This content is still available online. See for example the Ministry of Defence video 'RAF Strike on ISIL Vehicle in Iraq June 26', on its *#DefeatingDaesh* playlist, uploaded on 1 July 2015 to its official YouTube channel, https://www.youtube. com/watch?v=iUEsnBtlvmg (Ministry of Defence 2015b) and US CentCom, 'Airstrike Against an ISIL Military Garrison April 8 near Ar Raqqah, Syria', uploaded on 13 April 2015 to its official YouTube channel, https://www.youtube.com/ watch?v=3uxFUMA4GPY (US CentCom 2015).

the Ministry of Defence (MoD) and United States Central Command (US CentCom) channels from as early as 2009 up until 2017. The edited clips are all less than a minute long and are organised in playlists with titles such as *Operations* and *#DefeatingDaesh*. The uploads contain videos primarily generated through Operation Shader and Operation Inherent Resolve in Iraq and Syria. Operation Inherent Resolve was a US military campaign against Islamic State (ISIS) in coalition with the UK, French and Turkish militaries, among others. Operation Shader was the UK military strand of the Operation Inherent Resolve campaign, and according to the UK government, airstrikes were ongoing in March 2021 (gov.uk 2021). However, the uploading of drone strike footage to YouTube by US CentCom ceased from 2015 onwards and by the MoD from 2017.

Shaping the Perception of War

In this military context, drone vision has been lauded as all seeing, enabling perception beyond the limits of human vision in terms of the geographical distance between the operator and the drone, the thermal imaging techniques used, and notions of persistent presence – *the unblinking eye*. The operative images I was looking at appeared to be a hybrid of both visually interpretative and performative codes, promoting a vision of accurate, bloodless and sanitised warfare. Thus, although they are images that have been instrumental in the destruction of life, they were and continue to be encountered as part of a networked agenda that represents and acts to shape the perception of the so-called war on terror through the ideology of a technically precise and bodiless war.[3] For Judith Butler, these *frames of war* regulate who is recognised as living and therefore grievable. Grievable lives, according to Butler, presuppose lives that matter as they have at first been recognised *as* a life (2010: p. 15). She argues;

> persons use technological instruments, but instruments surely also use persons (position them, endow them with perspective, establish the trajectory of their action); they frame and form anyone who enters into the visual or audible field, and, accordingly, those who do not [...]. (2010: pp. xi–xii)

3   My use of the term 'so-called war on terror' describes the on-going global policing strategies employed by the US and UK militaries, among others, rather than the 'Overseas Contingency Operations', a euphemism devised by the US described by W.J.T. Mitchell as a 'bureaucratic obfuscation' (2011: p. 23).

Framing restricts what can be 'heard, read, seen, felt and known' and therefore works to conduct a 'dehumanising norm' and prevent 'any sensate understanding of war, and the conditions for a sensate opposition to war' (Butler 2009: p. 100). In the context of the footage I was watching on YouTube, framing contributes to the de-realisation of war through the multiple ways the body is absented from the operative moving images. This framing includes not only the optical aspects of operative images, but also the temporal, linguistic, technical and processual ways they are framed specifically on the YouTube platform. For example, unlike real-time military drone camera feeds, the content on YouTube is pixelated. The glossy, reflective and vitreous high-definition surface of my screen also intensifies the feeling of emotional, cultural and physical distance from the bodies and events on the ground along with the human practices and decisions involved in creating the images.

Although resembling grey-scale photographs, the thermal image is a form of remote sensing that detects infra-red radiation emitted from the surfaces of objects and humans with a temperature above absolute zero. It re-describes bodies beneath its gaze as identifiable by the algorithmic computation of their heat signature. This form of visualisation inscribes and de-corporealises bodies in particular algorithmic and cultural ways; bodies are visually coded according to the algorithmic categories of military techno-scientific practice that renders them 'white hot' or 'black hot' depending on the visualisation settings. This practice inscribes the colonial gaze on oppressed and marked bodies living and dying under drones. Throughout this chapter I refer to 'bodies living and dying under drones' where possible to attempt to avoid any inscription of what I understand as *other* as an 'identity marker which signals the dangerous, the deviant, the different' (Clark 2018: p. 614).[4] In this context, the colonial gaze can be defined as a Western ocular-centric gaze based on the promise of the discernment with clarity and accuracy of the 'truth' about particular human bodies through white, racist discursive practices. Its predication on objectivity and science creates the 'theoretical space for a view to develop subjectless bodies for analyses, classification and categorisation' (Yancy 2008: p. 2). This complex technical mediation influences not only drone operators' decision making and actions,

---

4   Although not all viewers of these images are in the West, and not all viewers in the West are detached from the conflict and/or normalised to warfare by the media, 'I' am the body whose life is preserved at 'their' expense. 'They' are bodies marked as *other* or whom I refer to where possible as 'bodies living and dying under drones' throughout this text. My use of italics indicates that when I do use the word 'other', it is not my lexicon or voice.

but also shapes the public perception of war. Thermal imagery is most readily associated with military and hunting practices, and thus bodies visualised through its gaze are overcoded and othered as de-corporeal targets. These processes normalise the subjugation of those marked bodies as targets for 'discriminatory observation and attack' (Wall and Monahan 2011: p. 250). In this cultural sense, the thermal gaze homogenises all bodies in its view, whether human or non-human, as marked. In the MoD and US CentCom uploads to YouTube, the bodies of those living and dying under drones have been absented through various editing procedures, and I do not see thermal bodies. Regardless of these processes, registering images through the thermal view contributes to the images' technical appearance. Thermal vision's algorithmic gaze arguably loses the corporeal, lively and embodied aspects of the operative content. It legitimises a colonial encounter that presents landscape as disembodied, calculative and uninhabited. In the operative content uploaded to YouTube, bodies are not only occluded through the thermal gaze but also pixelation, the removal of sections of the moving image containing this information and arguably the redaction of sensitive content on the screen pertaining to targeting information and timing. What remains are grey-scale thermal images of explosion clouds and landscapes sometimes populated by buildings and infrastructure; they are images that obscure bodies living and dying under drones. The absence of geospatial markers enhances the ideological presentation of the landscape as uninhabited.

Another noticeable characteristic of the military uploads to YouTube is the specific way their linguistic captions focus on objects and events rather than bodies.[5] In the titles and captions, attention is drawn to objects in the landscape, for example 'bridges', 'strongholds', 'bunkers', 'compounds', 'tunnels', 'fighting positions', 'vehicles', 'trucks' and 'armoured tanks'. If the presence of humans is alluded to it is as 'targets', 'fighters', 'ISIL' and 'DAESH'. In many cases, the content is described in such a way that the military's 'only target, or only intended target, or only immediate target, appears to be another weapon: that their effect is to "disarm" rather than to injure' making the actual injuring and injurability of bodies invisible (Scarry 1985:

5   For example, 'RAF strike on ISIL vehicle in Iraq July 9. On Thursday 9 July, an RAF Reaper observed ISIL terrorists carrying out welding on an armoured pick-up truck at a derelict industrial site, most likely converting it for use as a large car-bomb. Despite the target being parked in a roofed bay, the Reaper's crew were able to score a direct hit with a Hellfire missile which destroyed the vehicle' (Ministry of Defence 2015a).

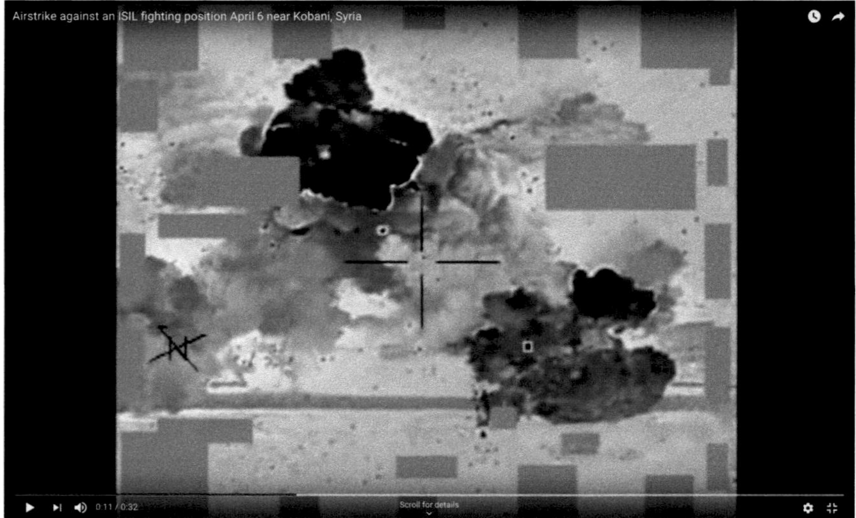

Figure 5.2 Screen grab from the US CentCom YouTube channel.

p. 68).[6] Indeed, on YouTube, attention is drawn to bomb factories, car bombs and weapons storage bunkers. The technical words used by the military conform to the scientific logic of objective reality, contributing to the illusion of control and rationality. Words such as 'neutralised' and 'eliminated' are used to describe destruction of 'targets'. The language also conforms at times to the bombast of military propaganda, employing phrases such as 'scoring a direct hit'. The captions therefore contribute to an ideology of technicality beyond their technical function, relating to power, vision and control. This excess is embedded in terms such as 'hunter-killer' and references to humans as 'prey' in the wealth of sensational literature around military drone technology (Noys 2015: p. 4). These linguistic metaphors also serve to obscure the very human processes involved in the drone assemblage, arguably contributing to an obfuscation of bodies living and dying under drones. This gap between the functional language of the image, both linguistic and technical, and the represented information in the images themselves was one of the reasons I was drawn to them. The content exemplifies how passive and distracted encounters with images can often mean that 'we look at and we see as we are told to' (Guerin 2015: p. 9). Thus, the language

6   Although her text predates the so-called war on terror, Scarry's writing expands upon the multiple ways in which the act of injuring, and therefore the human body, is 'disowned' in accounts of warfare (1985: pp. 60–165).

of the captioning plays a pivotal role in the way these narratives are selected and produced to serve the interests of military powers. Both uses of language, technical and sensational, obscure the lives targeted by the operative images.

Can you hear me?

I can hear you. I can see you now – can you see me?

Encountered through the optical, temporal, linguistic, technical and processual *frames* of YouTube, including those outlined above, uploaded official military operative content enters an attention economy, competing for views, comments, likes and shares, with alternative and unofficial coexisting content. This content includes propaganda, leaked military operative content, soldiers' video-diaries, victim testimony, news reports, videos captured by civilians and witnesses on the ground, with each aiming to reconfigure viewers' perception of conflict. Watching the videos online, my overall sense was one of detachment. I felt distant and separate from the activities they represent. Through the proliferation of this operative content there is a normalising effect that is part of the military's agenda, harnessed through the uploading of a multiplicity of low-resolution videos compressed into bite-sized clips. It is therefore not only the operative footage, but also the screen and the YouTube platform that act to align, frame and calibrate perception with the logic of the military robotic vision that produces and furnishes the content and the ways it is encountered. By 'encounter' I mean broadly the ways people watching these videos on YouTube understand the impact of drone strikes on bodies from a distance through a process of mutual recognition, in Butlerian terms (Butler 2009: pp. 3–4). This encounter, or non-encounter, is between bodies, both individual and multiple, with whom we are intertwined yet whom we may never come into contact with, except perhaps through the media and/or culture.[7] I found it imperative to problematise this content because the capacity to respond and the nature of this response are predicated on these frames that occlude, reconfigure and regulate bodies living

---

7   Building on Butler's theorisation, Caroline Holmqvist argues that the perception of a bodiless war constitutes a non-encounter or 'eschewal of encounter' with bodies of people living and dying under drones, with bodies marked as *other*. It denies 'people/populations their ontological status of being' (Holmqvist 2013: p. 648).

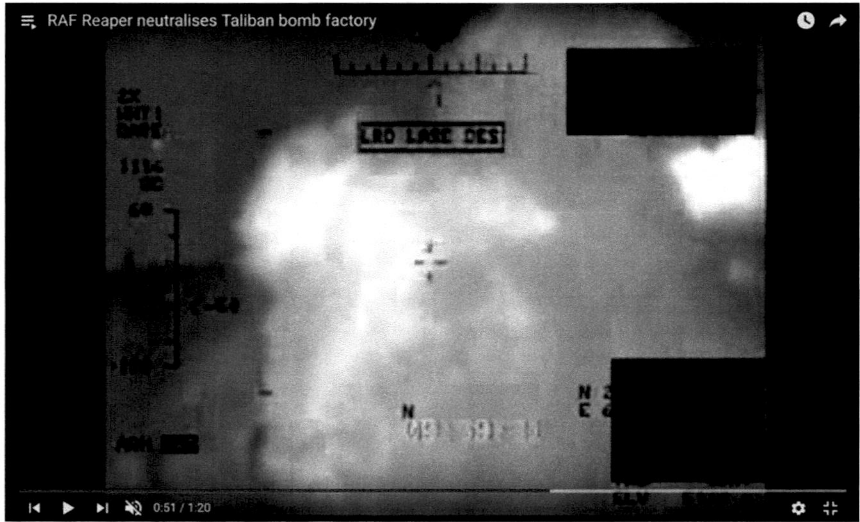

Figure 5.3 Screen grab from the RAF YouTube channel 'Operations'.
This playlist has now been deleted and the content has been absorbed into the MoD's YouTube playlist '#DefeatingDaesh'.

and dying under drones. Presumptions about other bodies shape how we respond to conflict individually and at state level, including responses affected by the media and the military such as indifference and retaliation, but also compassion and hospitality.[8]

Situated Practice

Through *I could feel that my eyes were open...*, I explored the potential of restaging these operative images to create a slower, more contemplative, embodied encounter. Working with moving-image, sound and installation practice, I sought to attend to the ways these images (and how we come into contact with them on YouTube) occlude and

8   Underlying this position is the writing of Judith Butler on precariousness as constituting a social condition in which vulnerability means that our lives are dependent on others. It involves, according to Butler, 'exposure both to those we know and to those we do not know; a dependency on people we know, or barely know, or know not at all' (2009: p. 14). The ontology of the body is the central concern of vulnerability since it is the body that is porous to, and exposes us to the other: to their gaze, their touch, their violence (Butler 2009, cited in Lloyd 2008: p. 94). However, as stated, vulnerability could also expose compassion and hospitality. Vulnerability forms the basis of Butler's ethics of grievability.

reconfigure encounters with bodies living and dying under drones. Undoubtedly, the operative images and the military channels and playlists in which they are found are intended to be read as documentary evidence of a technically precise and bodiless form of war. Any attempt to counter the absenting of bodies with forensic, empirical documentary evidence could, however, run the risk of being associated with how modes of reportage of the truth about remote populations are linked to their domination (Steyerl 2011). This not only includes documentary practice, but even the processes of imaging-making, bearing in mind their historical and contemporary links to military technology. Gayatri Chakravorty Spivak theorises that any attempt to speak for the subaltern is also a muffling of their voice. She argues that it is impossible for us to recover the voice of the subaltern or oppressed colonial subject marked as *other*. She points out that any articulation of the heterogeneous subaltern subject results in them becoming either not subaltern anymore or in fact reinscribed and represented according to Western intellectual logic (Spivak 1988: pp. 271–313).[9] I also therefore attempted not to represent subaltern bodies or those marked as *other*, but to challenge the idea that these images are produced through seamless and objective processes.

During the production of the work, and drawing on Donna Haraway, I progressively adapted a situated and partial approach, acknowledging and exploring the vulnerability of bodies, both human and non-human. By situated, I mean a specific type of vision that challenges the concept of scientific objectivity, one that is embodied rather than transcendent, and takes into account how visual systems work 'technically, socially and psychically' (Haraway 1988: p. 583). By partial, I mean a position that is split and contradictory and locatable in opposition to both relativism and totalisation. Relativism and totalisation are, according Haraway, 'god tricks'. She describes the 'god trick' as a metaphor for how science furnishes a disembodied, objective form of knowledge through technically mediated positions. Robotic vision, for example, promises 'vision from everywhere and nowhere, equally and fully' (1988: pp. 581–3). Aerial and thermal imaging technologies such as the operative drone content I was looking at particularly subscribe to this logic. Through the physical detachment of the human observer, they produce a scientific, rational and impartial view from above. This perspective arguably legitimises a colonial encounter in which 'ground truth vanishes

---

9 Furthermore, I am reminded of Edward Said's critique of how Western academic scholarship marks certain bodies as unable to act for themselves (Said 1979: p. 11).

in the ultimate "God-trick", whose terrible vengeance depends on making its objects visible and its subjects invisible' (Gregory 2004: p. 54). As previously stated, in many of the operative videos online, the landscape appears empty of life and abstract, resembling the surface of the moon, the aerial view evoking a transcendent and omniscient viewpoint. Adapting a more situated and partial approach, I sought to destabilise the ideas of authority, containment, control and binary relations purveyed through these images and open the possibility for them to exist other than as totalising, superior and persistently present.

Haraway argues that in order to challenge scientific objectivity, it is necessary that the 'object of knowledge be pictured as an actor and agent, not as a screen or a ground or a resource' (1988: p. 592). Sensing rather than *picturing* bodies, both human and non-human in terms of their agency, appeared as an important aspect of this work.[10] It was my intention to explore this embodied, new materialist perspective, in its subversion of binary logics such as intimate and distant, and subjective and objective. Through practice I sought to understand the technical image as embodied, lively and unstable rather than abstract, omniscient and totalising. This position emerged with particular concern for the ethical implications of art practice engaging with drone warfare through and from an ongoing critical evaluation of my practice and the practice of others. Rather than replicate the ideology of the *unblinking eye*, I explored how these technically mediated ways of seeing are rife with unruliness – errors, bias and glitches. The potential of artistic production in this context is that it could open momentary disruptions, interrupt or *stutter* the perception of bodiless and technically precise warfare propagated through these images online and potentially create the conditions for a more relational response.[11] Through intimate, self-reflective and imaginative practice, I sought to generate an embodied and relational encounter with the restaged operative image.[12]

10 *Agency* in this context is understood as an attention to the non-passive and the vibratory, resisting disembodied, objective categorisation. My understanding emerges from Karen Barad's agential realist theory, discussed later in this chapter, in which matter becomes an active rather than passive agent and agency is understood as an 'enactment' (Barad 2003: p. 821).
11 I will elaborate on the logic of the stutter later in this text.
12 By relational, I mean to consider the 'virtual links that a body can form with other bodies' (Braidotti 2002: p. 104).

Ok so I just want to check - you would like me to read aloud the text on screen?

Ok

I'm not sure how comfortable I am

I could feel that my eyes were open...

I could feel that my eyes were open... was a multi-channel audio-visual work installed in *Ständige Vertretung!*, a small, single-room pavilion located under the terrace roof of the former railway station at ZK/U. One film was installed as a projection and the other on a screen, juxtaposing the pixelated operative image and close bodily imagery. Elevated above ground level, the pavilion has a distinctive sloping ceiling and is accessed via an exterior staircase. For the purposes of moving-image projection, the interior of the pavilion was completely darkened. Upon entering the space, viewers encountered two synchronised moving images installed on the sloping ceiling, one a large projection and the other a small screen adjacent to the projection. The sonic aspects of the work, a voice-over and low-level bass sounds, emanated from two sets of speakers. One set was positioned at ground level, at either side of the space. Another set was inbuilt into the small screen installed on the ceiling. On the floor lay a large black mattress upon which viewers could lie or sit to watch the moving images above and listen to the sounds emanating from the speakers. Due to the scale of the space and the set-up of the installation, the number of viewers was limited to three or four at a time; they would enter and sit or lie in the space together.

The installation of the work in this assembled nature enabled a multi-sensory, corporeal encounter with restaged operative images. In particular, the sonic, haptic and proprioceptive elements of the installation acted to potentially disrupt the visuality and apparent representational authority of the image-based elements.[13] The

---

13 Haptic perception is defined by Laura U. Marks as the way the body experiences touch, through tactile, kinaesthetic and proprioceptive functions, and haptic visuality then as more embodied sensory experience in which 'the eyes themselves function like organs of touch' (2002: p. 2). Marks suggests that haptic visuality 'enables an embodied perception: the viewer responding to the video as to another body, and to the screen as another skin' (1998: p. 333).

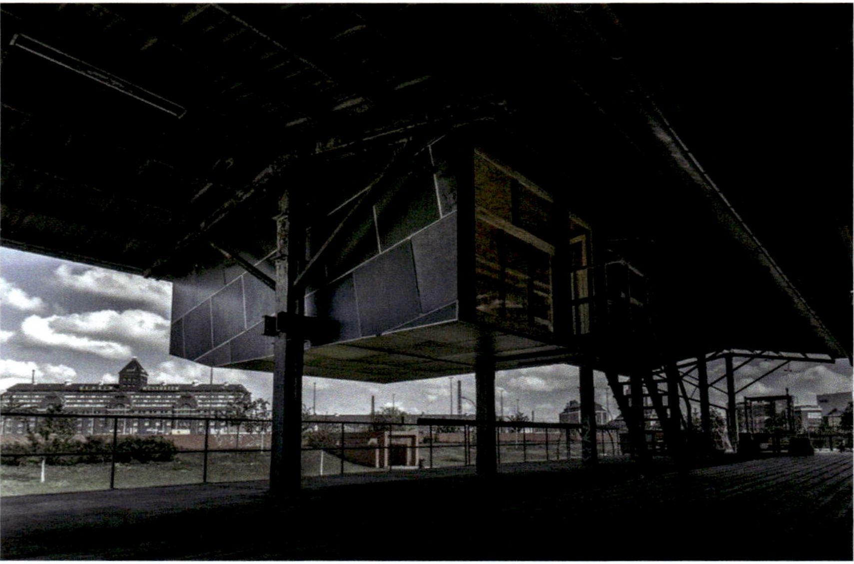

Figure 5.4 Digital photograph of *Ständige Vertretung!*, ZK/U Centre for Art and Urbanistics, Berlin.
Image credit: Ishka Michocka.

operative images published on YouTube by the US and the UK militaries are part of a public relations campaign, in which the image is staged – presented in a mode other than which it was originally created and utilised (to aid in the targeting of weapons) to present drone warfare as clean, bodiless and precise. By restaging, then, I mean the appropriation of this content from YouTube into artistic practice through iterative studio-based processes and their subsequent re-presentation as moving images which were then embedded into an alternative hybrid installation environment. In *Ständige Vertretung!*, both the projected and screen-based moving images were installed on the ceiling of the space. The experimental way through which the body of work was experienced was also orchestrated through practical means of seating and lying arrangements: viewers experienced the installation by lying down on the mattress provided. Installation practice allowed for the specific proprioceptive and spatial aspects to be explored with greater levels of complexity. These arrangements opened the possibilities to subvert our relationship to the visible via the screen to explore and expand hybrid, multi-perspective, multi-scalar and multi-sensory encounters with the restaged operative image. Thus, the encounter with the image on YouTube was restaged to re-present the operative image in a context which could potentially engender a reconsideration of the content, a slower experiential and multi-sensory embodied mode of encountering the images.

You're breaking up a little – can you see me? The screen has gone black – wait I can see you but you're pixelated

                        Can you hear me okay?

What are you searching for?

The video work projected on the ceiling of *Ständige Vertretung!* contained pixelated drone footage produced from one of the few non-thermal moving images available on the MoD's and US military's YouTube channels. In the process of making the work, my selection of full-colour operative drone footage was a gesture against replicating the thermal gaze because of the way it inscribes bodies as targets, generating a colonial encounter both culturally and through calculative, algorithmic processes. Through screen capture, the embodied process of looking at one of these videos was recorded while zooming in, out and panning. The footage was opened in Adobe Photoshop to capture these gestures. The screen recording explored a more intimate perception of the digital materiality of the moving image, albeit technically mediated through the lens of editing software. In the footage encountered online, there is a temporal aspect that is often edited out and overlooked; although drone pilots spend hours watching and following the lives of potential targets, most of the videos the military uploads to YouTube are less than a minute long. The process is presented as fast, efficient and technologically sophisticated through short, impactful clips. They are edited to follow a similar pattern, ending just after the explosion cloud; the consequences are erased from view, apart from the visual assurance of an on-target strike. When editing the recordings of my exploration of the videos in Adobe Photoshop, I slowed down the playback speed; the pixels moved much more slowly across the screen as the mouse panned the image and zoomed in and out. Screen capture therefore created multiple temporalities, that of the slowed-down drone camera footage, that of my jerkier movements in Adobe Photoshop, and that of the temporality of the film itself, which ran to just over five minutes.[14]

Visually, the moving image teetered between abstract blues and white amorphous forms; however, a number of visual artefacts and noise also appeared once the image had been rendered. The file was engrained with these visual embodiments of spontaneous miscommunications in technical processes: glitches. The most obvious visual outcome was a broken line of pixels, different versions of which traversed the screen a number of times. This brightly coloured mosaic interrupted the pixel grid (created by zooming in on the video in Adobe Photoshop), but also the colour palette of the video. This visual experience of pixelation and glitches drew attention to the surface and tactile materiality of the image, the 'electronic texture', rather than its depth or representative capacity, enabling a more embodied perception (Marks 1998: p. 333). Thus, the visible was perceived through haptic and proprioceptive modes, entangled with other senses. These artefacts were raw, unmediated and spontaneous, interrupting the impression of smooth technical processing and the temporal flow of the moving image. Glitches revealed the unprogrammed liveliness of the materials of technology, intervening in the perception of the digital content but also actively interrupting any notion of smooth interaction between humans and machines. Acting as a break in the flow of time, colour and electronic pathways, these visual artefacts not only operated to 'compromise the totality' of technology's grasp, but also revealed the 'material actions of otherwise hidden circuits and software'. Here we find hints of the 'non-human forms of authorship and relational traces created by the digital processes that co-construct the image' (Pasek 2017: pp. 44–5). Rather than conceiving these glitches exclusively as vulnerabilities in the technical process, it is a stance more akin to when 'the animism of computers does not rest in the militaristic command of a user nor in the essence of a file's source code; it is rather the agential assemblage of all these causal forms acting together' (Chun 2008, quoted in Pasek 2017: p. 45). The movements of the film were jumpy and the intermittent glitches appeared as brightly coloured mosaics flashing throughout.

Installed on the ceiling adjacent to the projection was a small screen. Through the screen's inbuilt speakers the voice-over emerged into the space, performing a fictional Skype conversation. Mediated through Auto-Tune, the viewers encountered a trembling female voice

14 Documentation of the installation can be viewed at https://www.youtube.com/watch?v=V9NmxJQyQpM&ab_channel=KateFahey (accessed July 2023).

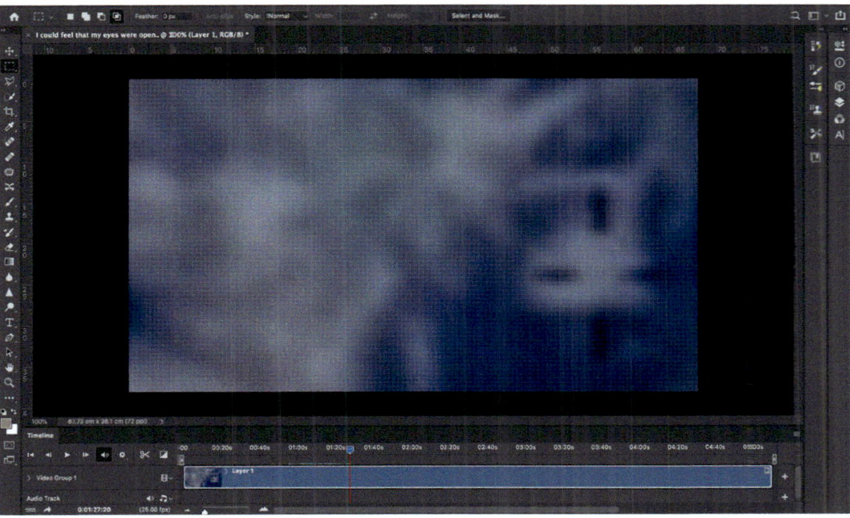

Figure 5.5 Screen grab from Adobe Photoshop showing a work in-progress image. Image credit: Kate Fahey.

conversing through a poor internet connection with an unknown and unheard other. The conversation appeared to be in a permanent state of breaking and making connections. This imagined conversation between myself and an other / another / myself / my other, another version of myself / other embodied an increasingly situated and fictional approach. Furthermore, moving beyond any linear or singular narrative, it entered a more experiential mode where the voice split into multiple others both questioning and responding. The connection was bad, but the trembling voice asked the listener to look at the videos online and to repeat some of their captions. The conversation kept breaking up and they struggled to communicate. The dialogue was direct, emergent and expressed the discomfort of looking at the content on YouTube. Unfolding performatively, it was interrupted by breaks generated by a poor internet connection produced through the editing process; in post-production much of the linguistic content was removed leaving gaps and fissures in the conversation. This exploration embodied the ways language failed and broke down in an attempt to know and articulate the experience of bodies marked as *other*, specifically bodies living and dying under drones. What remained was a stuttering conversation expressing an attempt to connect and communicate. Furthermore, the voice-over pushed against replicating the ways the video captions also imply a technical ideology of exactitude, clarity and an unequivocal

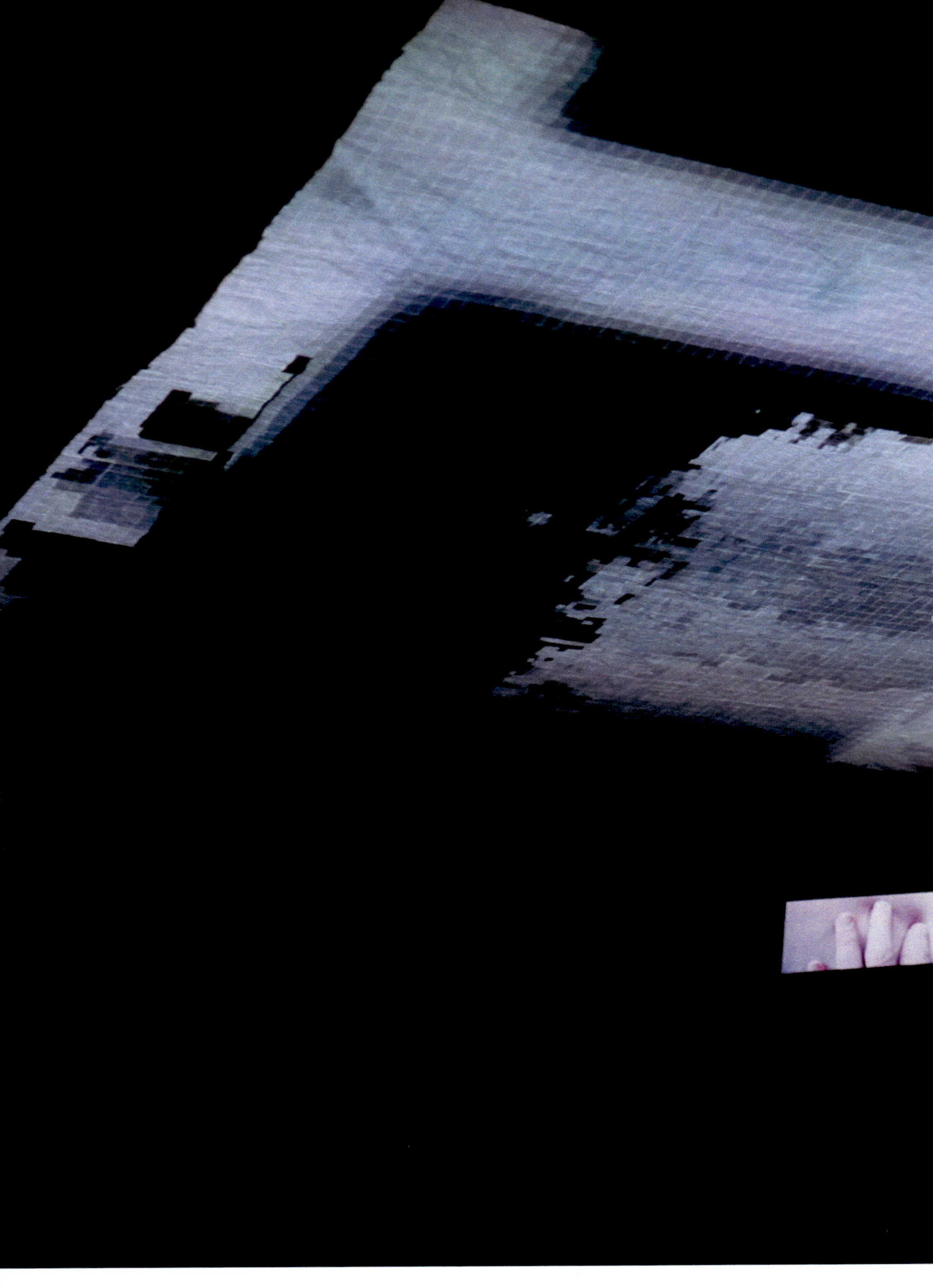

Figure 5.6 Kate Fahey, *I could feel that my eyes were open…* installed at ZK/U, 2019.
Image credit: Kate Fahey.

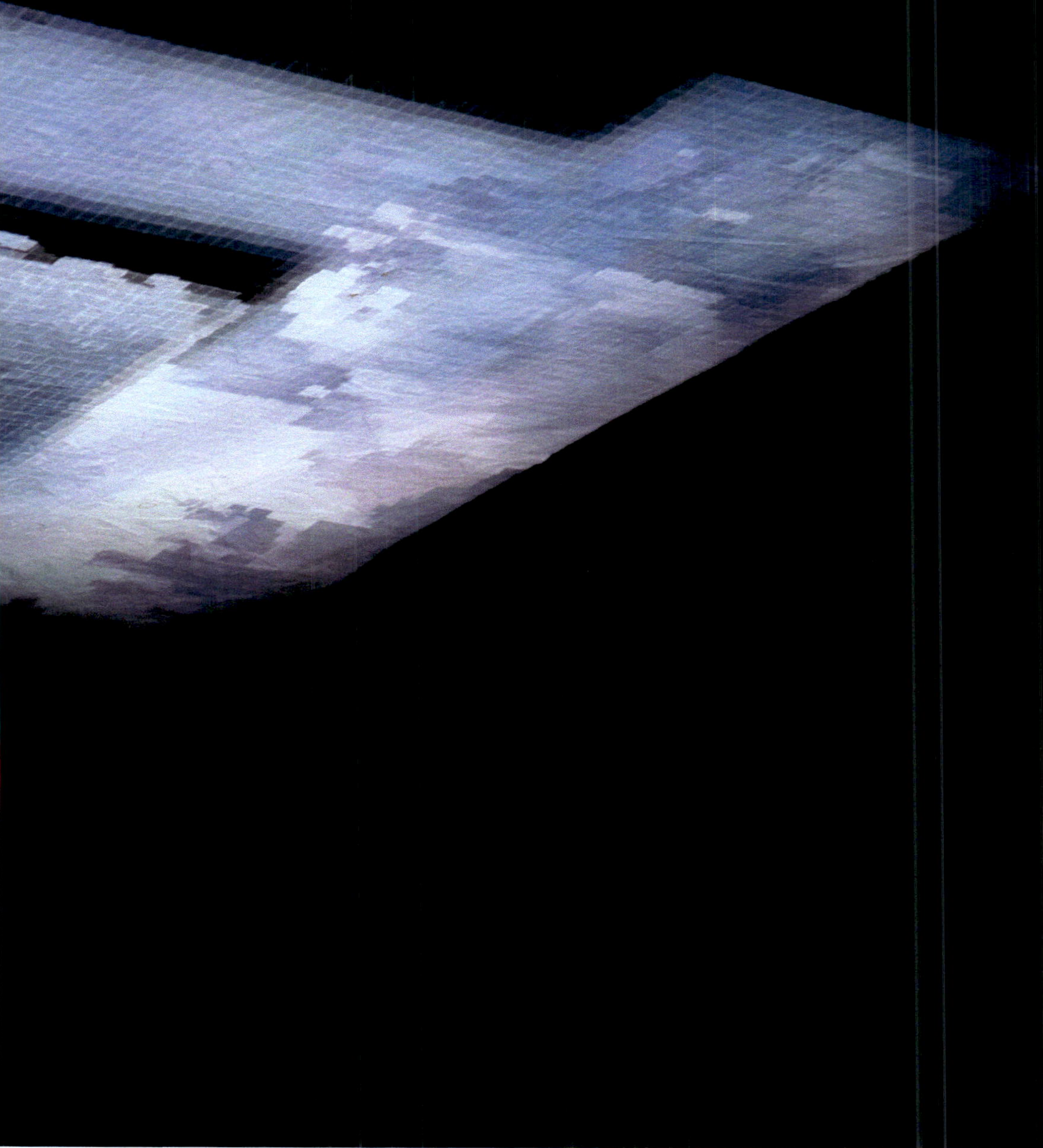

Figure 5.7 Kate Fahey, *I could feel that my eyes were open…* installed at ZK/U, 2019. Image credit: Kate Fahey.

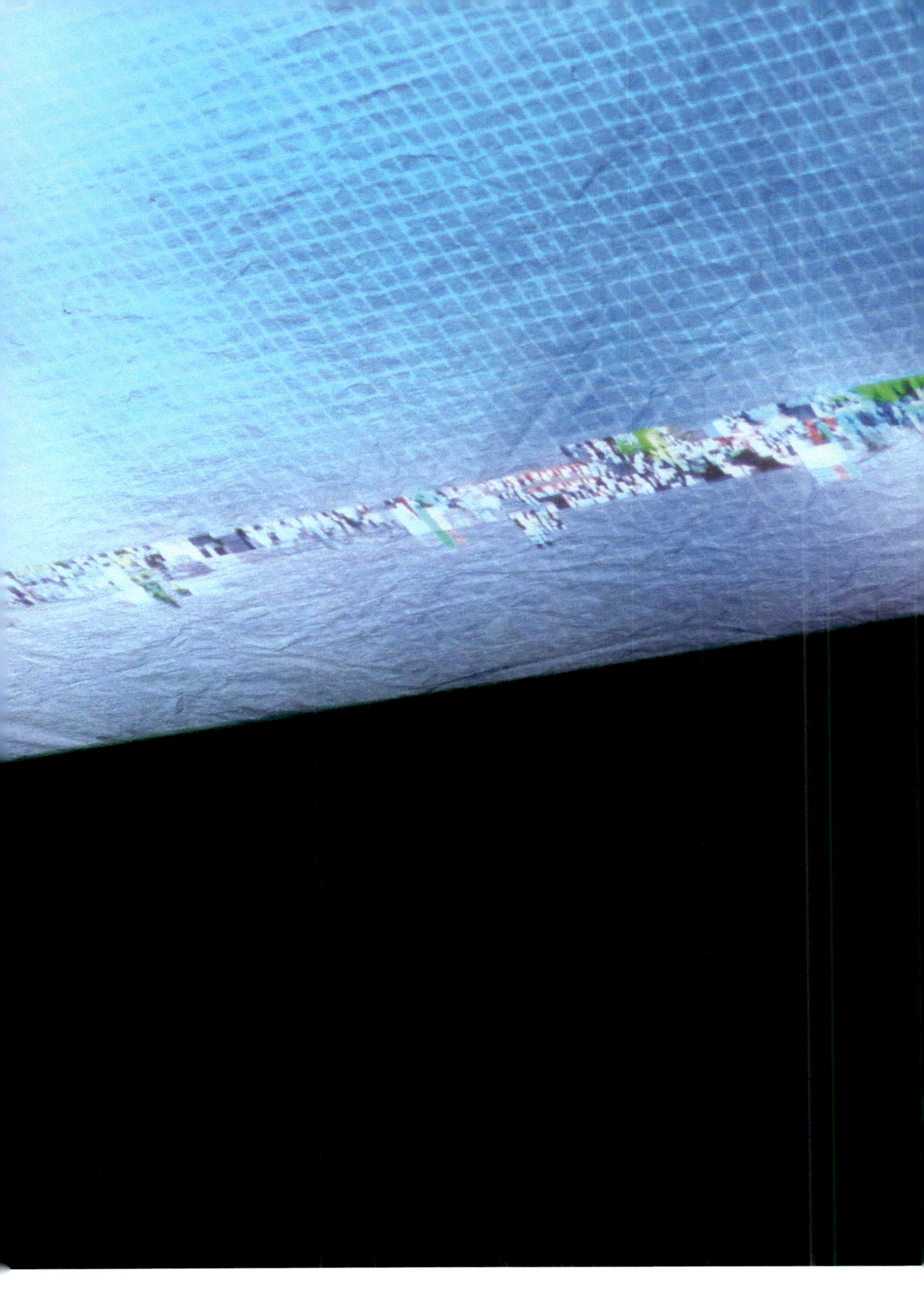

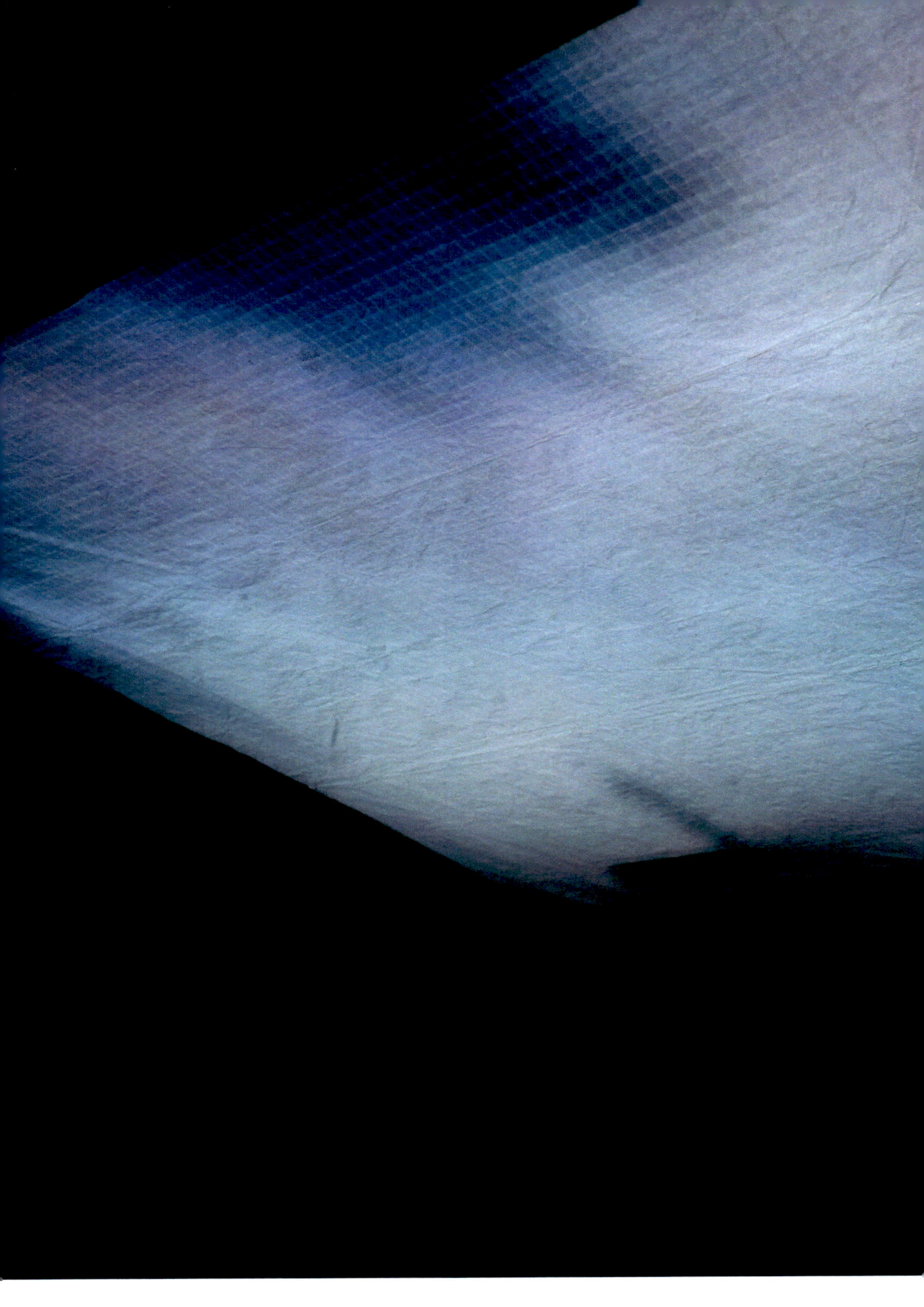

Figure 5.8 Kate Fahey, *I could feel that my eyes were open…* installed at ZK/U, 2019. Image credit: Kate Fahey.

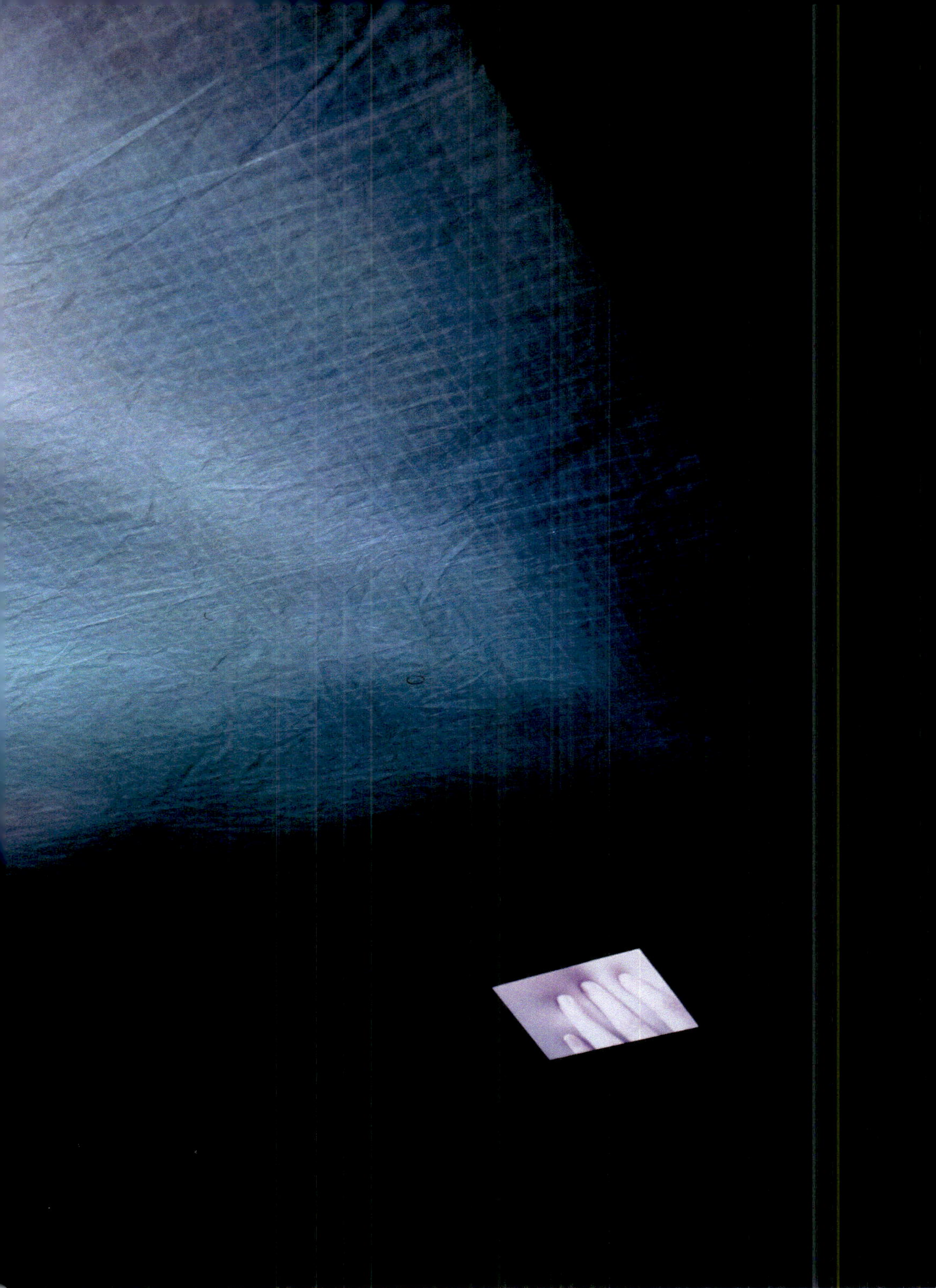

relationship to fact. Drawing on these gaps and holes, the notion of stuttering can be understood as both a porosity and an agitation that pushes against dominant systems of communication. Stuttering (or the logic of the stutter), in this sense, may 'speak back' to this pressure enacted upon it, 'in the form of the unclear, the improper, the tensed and the pressured' (LaBelle 2014: p. 135). Thus, the liveliness and performative gesture of broken-up language and stuttered telling intervened in the military's linguistic representation of these events. Karen Barad states that performativity in this sense 'is precisely a contestation of the excessive power granted to language [...] a contestation of the unexamined habits [...] that grant language and other forms of representation more power in determining our ontologies than they deserve' (2003: p. 802). Her account of performativity embodies a dynamic reading of matter and its agency, along with attending to the relationality of bodies, incorporating non-human and techno-scientific practices.[15]

The small screen from which the voice-over emanated displayed a moving image of a close-up of several pink fingers pressing into pink flesh. Installed on the ceiling adjacent to the projection, viewers could experience it by lying down on the mattress provided. The fingers pressed slowly into the skin, a resistance marked in the surrounding tissue, yet it simultaneously appeared tender and delicate. Further research had led me to a technique used by people who stammer to help control their speech, a gesture where they press their fingers into their bodies, to feel their way through the syllables.[16] As I spoke the voice-over words my gesture of pressing my fingers into my thigh was recorded and in post-production the footage was slowed and softened by blurring it slightly. The frame was cropped closely to the fingers so that it was difficult to tell what part of and whose

15 Drawing on Maurice Merleau-Ponty, Judith Butler argues that the notion of performativity comprises both linguistic and material 'speech acts and bodily acts' (Butler 2009, quoted in Lloyd 2008: p. 198). Through speech acts, she argues, certain social and ideological conventions are performed into reality, the enactment of which has effects on what is perceived of as reality, particularly how these performative, discursive practices materialise the body. Although she argues that language and materiality are embedded in one another, her theorisation of the matter of the body is one that is shaped and shapes primarily through language. For Butler, matter is a 'process of materialisation that stabilises over time to produce the effect of boundary, fixity, and surface', positioning the matter of bodies primarily as subject to processes of regulatory power structures rather than as materially agential (Butler 2011: p. 9).
16 This is an example of a strategy known as hand tapping, a method of speech pacing in which speech is accompanied by a body movement that aims to slow down the rate of speech. Other pacing strategies include tapping a foot or a specially designed pacing or alphabet board (Van Nuffelen et al. 2010).

body I was touching, and who the 'I' was that was deliberately sinking my / their fingers into the pinkish-white flesh. There was a kind of anxiety to this repeated gesture of one body pressing against an other / another / myself / my other, another version of myself / other. In a quantum theoretical approach, Karen Barad suggests that through the movements of particles, touching oneself is always an encounter with the 'infinite alterity of the self', stating that 'all touching entails an infinite alterity', so that touching others is also touching the self, and touching the self is also 'touching the strangers within' (2012: pp. 213–14). We are brought into touch with the incalculable other within which lies, as Barad suggests, the root of 'caring', where caring is not implied in a curative or corrective way, but instead as a 'troubling of the self' (2012: p. 217). In the moving image, bodies were engendered as matter*ing* rather than material and sensing rather than seeing. Out of pace with the voice-over, this embodied perception through the movement of the fingers no longer functioned as a tactile aid for the speaking voice. The voice was destabilised and dislocated by the fingers moving; the movement itself became a stuttering of the temporality of the voice-over and the adjacent projected moving image.

I need to take a break to breathe.

My mouth is dry.

Viewers of *I could feel that my eyes were open…* could lie horizontally and experience the installation of both moving images above them on the ceiling. The moving images were synchronised so that at times either one played alone, and at other times neither image appeared, casting the space into total darkness between intermittent blinks of the screen and projector. The entire work was looped in the installation with no beginning or end, into which viewers could enter or leave at any time. The loop was just over five minutes in total, though many viewers remained lying in the space for longer. The performative nature of the installation, simultaneously grasping materially and sensorially towards communication and a communication break-down, connection and disconnection, suspended many viewers who waited for a revelation that never arrived. The voice-over appeared and disappeared intermittently, yet the bass and static sounds remained constant throughout. The darkness and sonic aspects of the work, which also comprised the architectural and material qualities of the space itself, enveloped and immersed the viewers, interrupting day-to-day reality outside the installation.[17] Even before entering the space, one could hear the low-level bass sounds and feel the vibrations emanating from the floor-based speakers. The sounds, which played consistently throughout the installation, created a deep rumbling that reverberated through the structure. Intermittently a crackling noise emerged from the speakers, markers of sonic artefacts and interference.[18]

Sonically, the voice-over captured not only the conversation, but its intra-actions with the fabric of the recording surroundings and the high-pitched hum of the borrowed microphone used in the recording process. The process embodied a new materialist approach, in which voices 'result from intra-actions among corporeality, sounds, technologies, particular cultural techniques, practices of vocalising, [...] also engender[ing] intra-actions between several feeling, acting, and thinking bodies' (Fast and Tiainen 2018). This understanding emerged from Karen Barad's agential realist theory of mattering, in which agencies and phenomena do not precede but rather emerge through their mutual relations. She argues that phenomena are not understood as individual subjects existing in and experiencing a world which is separate from them, but instead how they progressively 'co-constitute one another' (Barad 2003: p. 815). Through a process of 'intra-action', which Barad defines as the entanglement of matter and agency, matter becomes an active rather than passive agent and agency is 'congealed' (2003: p. 822). Agency, according to Barad, is an enactment of a process rather than a quality that is possessed by, or attributed to, someone or something (2003: pp. 826–7). Rather than passive and static, bodies are understood as matter*ing*, sensing and relational entities. This new materialist/agential realist perspective foregrounds bodies in both their vulnerability and resistance. The installation engendered an encounter in which materiality and felt registers were entangled rather than separated and/or opposed.

---

17 Immersion is an embodied, intimate and relational presence between audience and artwork, 'an experiential unification of the present in space and time through an immediate experience of sonic flux or vibration' (Schrimshaw 2017: p. 2).

18 These sounds were generated through the sonification of a screen grab from one of the videos I was watching on YouTube. The image was imported into Audacity, an open-source sound-editing program, and converted into a sound file.

Wait – can you still see me? I can see you

You're breaking up a little bit hang on

I've lost you. It's a poor connection

Unruly Bodies

I could feel that my eyes were open... considered how bodies, both human and non-human, are entangled together in an assemblage, and revealed, through the logic of the glitch, that bodies are unruly, without disregarding techno-scientific practices and ideologies that mark and reconfigure them. This manifested through the digital artefact (or glitch) and the stuttering voice-over conversation. Both artefacts and stutters could be described as vulnerabilities; they were encountered as holes, breaks, errors and openings through the multi-sensory, multi-scalar and multi-perspective registers of the work. Yet these openings were also disruptive of the processes they appeared in; the digital artefacts interrupted the processual, visual and temporal experience of the moving image and the stutter disrupted the narrative integrity of the voice-over. Through these interruptions and the many more frictions and resistances in the work, bodies, both human and technical, were explored, attuned to and modelled as both vulnerable and agential. They were unruly; they resisted categorisation, capture, calculation and predictability. Restaging the operative image through the practice of installation attempted to present an assemblage in which the ideologies and narratives were shifted towards the agentive capacities of bodies. Understanding bodies as unruly shifted the discourse towards in-calculability and unpredictability and away from bodies rendered as passive and subject to techno-scientific control, yet it did not disavow these processes. In this sense, *I could feel that my eyes were open...* considered how bodies are entangled but that this entanglement is power differentiated. Importantly, Barad argues that 'despite the fact that "we" are always deeply entangled in (and thus part of) a close web of human and non-human relations and forces, "we" are still the ones who are responsible and accountable for what matters as well as for what is excluded from mattering' (2007, p. 220). Barad's theory takes into account that any technology of measurement contains within it the influence of the measurer. This applies to both military

Figure 5.9 Kate Fahey, *I could feel that my eyes were open…* installed at ZK/U, 2019. Image credit: Kate Fahey.

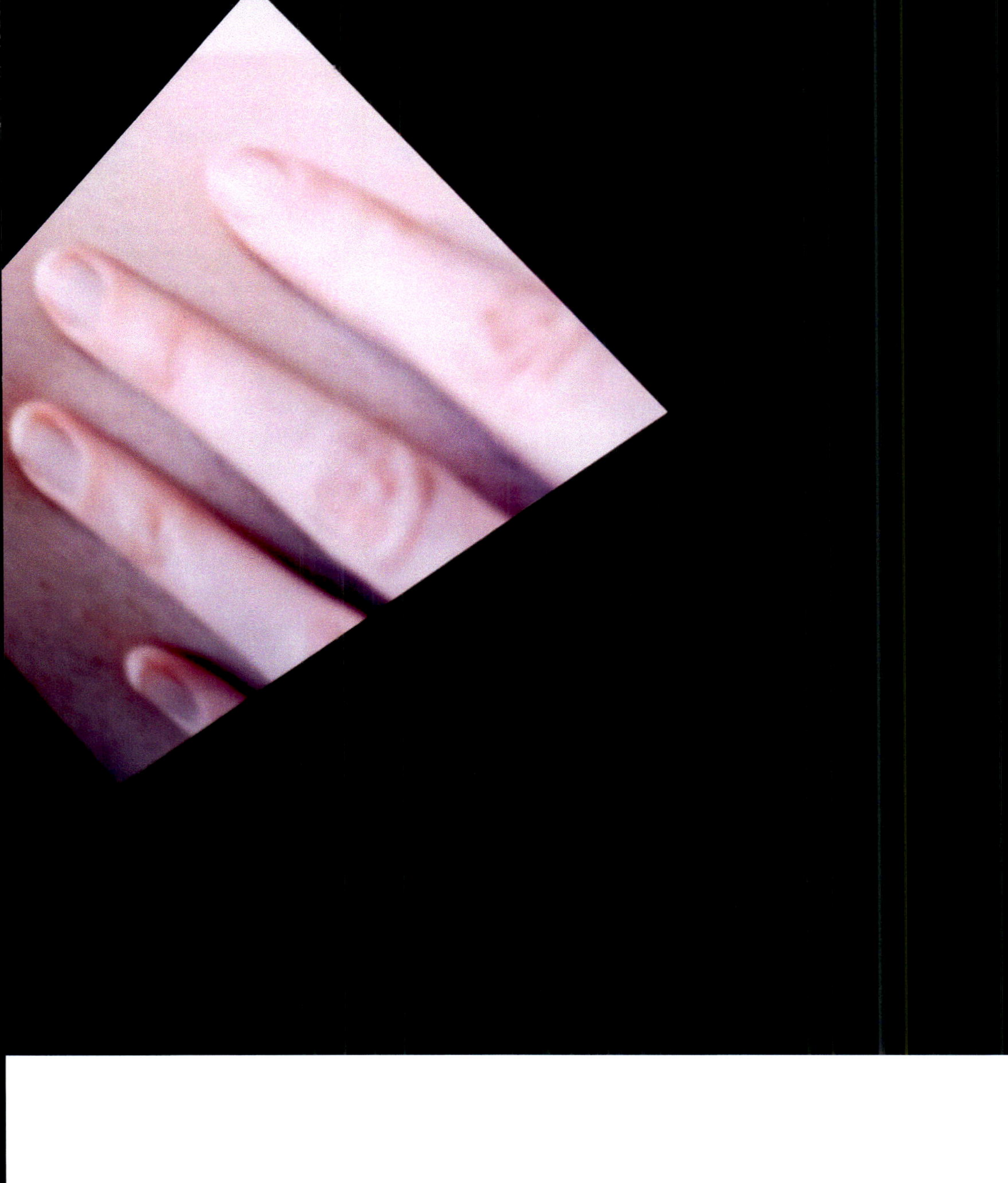

technologies and also my own position, aligning with and adapting Haraway's situated practice and partial perspectives. Creative art practice which does not aim to correct, reveal or represent those marked as *other* but instead is deeply intimate, self-reflective and imaginative can begin to explore this relationality.

Can you hear me?
Can you hear me?

I need to take a break I don't feel comfortable looking at this any more

It was my contention that paying specific attention to the trembling and vibratory quality of materiality could enact a speculative shift from one in which bodies were inscribed by the language and techno-visual qualities of the operative images on YouTube to one where bodies became agential and unruly. This was specifically in response to the ways the footage and the YouTube platform frame drone warfare as omniscient, disembodied and technically precise through such aspects of the thermal gaze, captioning and the notions of persistent presence – *the unblinking eye*. Encompassing a more embodied, *blinking* mode of perception, these felt registers drew attention to relationality and alterity, to the effects of difference and exclusion from mattering. Through these multi-sensory, multi-perspective and multi-scalar perceptual encounters with restaged operative images, viewers' responses were arguably not mobilised through a fixed subject position; subjectivity was continually produced and reproduced from these unfixed relations and intra-actions. This embodies what feminist post-human theorist Rosi Braidotti terms an 'eco-philosophy of multiple belongings', as a 'relational subject constituted in and by multiplicity', one that 'works across differences and is also internally differentiated, but still grounded and account-able' (2013: p. 49). Making direct reference to the deployment of technologically mediated necropolitical violence, she identifies drone operations as post-human, because of the complex technical mediation involved in their operations.[19] However, Braidotti notably

19 Achille Mbembe's concept of necropolitics is a particular theorisation in which racism manages populations based on 'a biological caesura between the ones and the others' (2003: p. 17). It concerns the control of some lives at the expense of

draws attention to the very human network in which lethal weapons are deployed by drone operators. Post-human subjectivity enables an embodied and therefore partial form of accountability which is grounded in relational and collective assemblages (2013: p. 49). In this way, the installation established embodied encounters through hybrid sensory registers rather than re-*othering* bodies marked as *other* as suffering and powerless, by re-presenting bodies through the thermal, weaponised gaze. Braidotti argues against a form of vulnerability through which 'we are recognised as full citizens only through the position of victims, loss and injury and the forms of reparation that come with it' (2013: p. 126). Instead, she embraces a vulnerability that is hopeful rather than 'based on the negative instances of wound and loss' (2013: p. 129). Rather than ideologically predetermined, in the installation, the relations between bodies (human, non-human, technological) were destabilised, generating reconfigured assemblages, instantiations, fictions and reorientations with the potential to stutter pre-existing assemblages.

The installation considered the encounter between bodies and technicality but avoided replicating the ideology of a seamless relationship to technicality, a visual and linguistic strategy used by the military in its uploads to YouTube and evident in much art practice concerned with drone warfare. In attending to the vulnerability of technology through the logic of the glitch, the installation affirmatively interrupted and exposed the ideology of technicality that the operative images and their network generate visually and linguistically. The installation also resisted using didactic and cartographic modes of representation such as infographics. Nor did it rely on spectacular and/or moralising practices such as the presentation of bodies through thermal-imaging camera technology. It revealed the potential of art practice to generate a gap in meaning, subscribing to the logic of the glitch, disrupting the operationality not only of the operative image but of the artwork itself. The glitch is a productive way to think about art as an event that 'interrupts knowledge', 'breaks information' and 'stops making sense' (O'Sullivan 2009: p. 247). Glitches, as 'vacuoles of non-communication' or 'rupturing events' open up a slowness and stillness; they offer an escape from the manipulation performed by 'other affective assemblages' that increasingly operate in a parallel logic to art (O'Sullivan 2009:

others, who is 'disposable' and who is not (2003: p. 27). Necropolitics is a means to understand the armed military drone assemblage as a technology that enacts the sovereign management of populations based on racial distinction in which a 'population is known and audited through the gaze of the drone, but for the purpose of death rather than life' (Allinson 2015: p. 120).

p. 251).[20] I felt that both the vibratory condition of the sound and images and the multi-scalar, multi-perspective and multi-sensory modes through which they were encountered could potentially dislocate or stutter habitual modes of perception of the images. In the many gaps, holes and breakages there was an acknowledgement of what the work cannot say, bearing in mind that the suffering of victims cannot be represented mimetically without violating their integrity as corporeal and individual human beings (Guerin 2015: p. 3). *I could feel that my eyes were open...* was also concerned with what was registered about the body that was not felt and sensed in the multiple gaps and holes in the installation.

You're breaking up - the connection is not good - hang on can you hear me?

Conclusion

In *I could feel that my eyes were open...*, bodies were considered porous – vulnerabilities which allow us to sense other subject positions. This position acknowledged what I am and what I am not – the white, Western position of privilege from which I am practising, and therefore the limits of this artwork. This is especially pertinent in the consideration of bodies marked by institutions and practices as *other*, and the ways feminist intersectional theory is productive of what Jasbir Puar calls 'an ironic reification of racial difference' (2012: p. 53). Puar articulates the problematic aspects of intersectional feminism's corrective 'resecuring [of] the centrality of the subject positioning of white women' (2012: p. 52). Specifically, she argues that many of the categories of intersectionality are derived and employed through 'modernist colonial agendas and regimes of epistemic violence [...] through which the notion of a discrete identity has emerged' (2012: p. 54). Puar expresses the need to consider the friction between

---

20 In addition, O'Sullivan suggests the mass media 'that increasingly operates on a self-consciously affective register – as a kind of nervous system' are one of these assemblages, generating a perpetual state of fear in a 'politics of pre-emption' (O'Sullivan 2009: p. 251). Arguably, this point about the mass media involves an overlap with the military–industrial–media–entertainment network.

intersectional and assemblage theory when read through each other.[21] Friction, in practice, interrupts both the visual and the linguistic. This friction is generated in *I could feel that my eyes were open...* in the graininess, jumpiness, glitchiness, bodily resistance and stuttering (both human and technical). It is thus the encounter itself that is unruly; bodies resist categorisation and representation, and restaging the operative image generates the conditions for a set of relations to occur in which encounters with operative images are potentially re-orientated.

Attending to the materiality of the technical in my practice revealed bodies as sites of agencies rather than exclusively surfaces for inscription. The installation produced a certain discomfort in this unknowing and the unpredictability of bodies that 'can do and think and enact' (Braidotti 2018: p. 21), in their alterity, escape of categorisation and representation, in the irreconciled. It engendered a speculatively agential understanding of all bodies, locating 'the subject in the flow of relations with multiple others' (Braidotti 2013: p. 50). In this sense, *I could feel that my eyes were open...* produced a particular mode of embodiment connected with living and vibratory tensions, rather than embodiment through emotion or affect and the outpouring of grief. Presumptions about other bodies shape how we respond individually and at state level, including responses affected by the media and the military such as indifference and retaliation, but also compassion and hospitality. However, arguably, there is no guaranteed response other than incommensurability, the state of openness and uncertainty. Thus, as a speculative approach to artistic practice, elements of affirmative politics and considering the agency of bodies can begin to sketch a responsible relation to how bodies are considered in the installation. This decentred position 'anchors the subject in an ethical bond to alterity, to the multiple and external others that are constitutive of that entity which [...] we call the "self"' (Braidotti 2013: p. 100). A situated practice concerned with drone warfare that considers these complex relationalities could begin to create a more responsible body of artistic research, one that acknowledges my privilege as a white, Western artist-researcher and generates an embodied encounter with these censored operative images without reinscribing techno-scientific and colonial modes of treating bodies living and dying under drones.

---

21 Puar states, 'intersectionality attempts to comprehend political institutions and their attendant forms of social normativity and disciplinary administration, while assemblages, in an effort to reintroduce politics into the political, asks what is prior to and beyond what gets established' (2012: p. 63).

I can see you can you see me?

I said you're break breaking up

Can you still see me?

References

Allinson, J. (2015) 'The Necropolitics of Drones', *International Political Sociology* 9(2): 113–27.

Barad, K. (2003) 'Posthumanist Performativity: Toward an Understanding of How Matter Comes to Matter', *Signs: Journal of Women in Culture and Society* 28(3): 801–31.

Barad, K. (2007) *Meeting the Universe Halfway: Quantum Physics and the Entanglement of Matter and Meaning*. Durham: Duke University Press.

Barad, K. (2012) 'On Touching – The Inhuman That Therefore I Am', *Differences* 23(3): 206–23.

Blackman, L. (2008) *The Body: The Key Concepts* (English edition). Oxford: Berg.

Braidotti, R. (2002) *Metamorphoses: Towards a Materialist Theory of Becoming*. Cambridge: Polity Press in association with Blackwell Publishers.

Braidotti, R. (2013) *The Posthuman*. Cambridge: Polity Press.

Braidotti, R. (2018) 'A Theoretical Framework for the Critical Posthumanities', *Theory, Culture and Society* 4: 1–31.

Butler, J. (2009) *Frames of War: When Is Life Grievable?* London: Verso.

Butler, J. (2010) *Frames of War: When Is Life Grievable?* (reprint edition). London: Verso.

Butler, J. (2011) *Bodies That Matter: On the Discursive Limits of Sex*. Abingdon: Routledge.

Clark, L. C. (2018) 'Grim Reapers: Ghostly Narratives of Masculinity and Killing in Drone Warfare', *International Feminist Journal of Politics* 20(4): 602–23.

Farocki, H. (2004) 'Phantom Images', *Public*, 0(29). Available at http://public.journals.yorku.ca/index.php/public/article/view/30354 (accessed 11 May 2017).

Fast, H. and Tiainen, M. (2018) *Voice*. Available at https://newmaterialism.eu/almanac/v/voice.html (accessed 29 March 2021).

Gov.uk (2021) 'Update: Air Strikes Against Daesh. The RAF Are Continuing to Take the Fight to Daesh in Iraq and Syria'. Available at https://www.gov.uk/government/news/update-air-strikes-against-daesh (accessed 23 March 2021).

Gregory, D. (2004) *The Colonial Present: Afghanistan, Palestine, and Iraq*. Malden: Blackwell Publishers.

Guerin, F. (2015) *On Not Looking: The Paradox of Contemporary Visual Culture*. London: Taylor & Francis.

Haraway, D. (1988) 'Situated Knowledges: The Science Question in Feminism and the Privilege of Partial Perspective', *Feminist Studies* 14(3): 575–99.

Holmqvist, C. (2013) 'War, "Strategic Communication" and the Violence of Non-recognition', *Cambridge Review of International Affairs* 26(4): 631–50.

LaBelle, B. (2014) *Lexicon of the Mouth: Poetics and Politics of Voice and the Oral Imaginary*. New York: Bloomsbury Academic.

Lloyd, M. (2008) 'Towards a Cultural Politics of Vulnerability: Precarious Lives and Ungrievable Deaths', in Carver, T. and Chambers, S. (eds), *Judith Butler's Precarious Politics: Critical Encounters.* London: Routledge, pp. 92–105.

Marks, L. U. (1998) 'Video Haptics and Erotics', *Screen* 39(4): 331–48.

Marks, L. U. (2002) *Touch. Sensuous Theory and Multisensory Media.* Minneapolis: University of Minnesota Press.

Mbembé, A. (trans. Meintjes, L.) (2003) 'Necropolitics', *Public Culture* 15(1): 11–40.

Ministry of Defence (2015a) 'RAF Strike on ISIL Vehicle in Iraq July 9', 21 July 2015. Available at https://www.youtube.com/watch?v=e9jSEzB2GuA&list=PLMt8dNv5bsl-nIkOvPaLIp_ouaEwDfjxF&index=33 (accessed 3 December 2017)

Ministry of Defence (2015b) 'RAF Strike on ISIL Vehicle in Iraq June 26', 1 July 2015. Available at https://www.youtube.com/watch?v=iUEsnBtlvmg (accessed 4 December 2017).

Mitchell, W. J. T. (2011) *Cloning Terror: The War of Images, 9/11 to the Present.* Chicago: University of Chicago Press.

Noys, B. (2015) 'Drone Metaphysics', *Culture Machine* 16: 1–22.

O'Sullivan, S. (2009) 'From Stuttering and Stammering to the Diagram: Deleuze, Bacon and Contemporary Art Practice', *Deleuze Studies* 3(2): 247–58.

Pasek, A. (2017) 'The Pencil of Error: Glitch Aesthetics and Post-Liquid Intelligence', *Photography and Culture* 10(1): 37–52.

Puar, J. (2012) 'Becoming-Intersectional in Assemblage Theory', *philoSOPHIA* 2(1): 49–66.

Said, E. W. (1979) *Orientalism.* New York: Vintage Books.

Scarry, E. (1985) *The Body in Pain: The Making and Unmaking of the World.* New York: Oxford University Press.

Schrimshaw, W. (2017) *Immanence and Immersion.* London: Bloomsbury Academic.

Spivak, G. C. (1988) 'Can the Subaltern Speak?', in Nelson, C. and Grossberg, L. (eds), *Marxism and the interpretation of culture.* Urbana: University of Illinois Press, pp. 271–316.

Steyerl, H. (2011) 'Documentary Uncertainty', Re-visiones # One. Available at http://re-visiones.net/anteriores/spip.php%3Farticle37.html (accessed 29 March 2021).

US CentCom (2015) 'Airstrike against an ISIL military garrison April 8 near Ar Raqqah, Syria', 13 April 2015. Available at https://www.youtube.com/watch?v=3uxFUMA4GPY (accessed 4 December 2017).

Van Nuffelen, G., De Bodt, M., Vanderwegen, J., Van de Heyning, P. and Wuyts, F. (2010) 'Effect of Rate Control on Speech Production and Intelligibility in Dysarthria', *Folia Phoniatrica et Logopaedica* 62(3): 110–19.

Wall, T. and Monahan, T. (2011) 'Surveillance and Violence from Afar: The Politics of Drones and Liminal Security-scapes', *Theoretical Criminolog* 15(3): 239–54.

Waldby, C. (2000) *The Visible Human Project: Informatic Bodies and Posthuman Medicine.* London: Routledge.

Yancy, G. (2008) 'Colonial Gazing: The Production of the Body as "Other"', *Western Journal of Black Studies* 32(1): 1–15.

6 Embodiment and the Perception of Nonhuman Sentience in Virtual Reality Interactive Art

Nicola Plant

The exploration of our understanding of a human experience is a key function behind art and performance, offering modes of thought that intend to express alternative perspectives on the human situation. As human experience is underpinned by our embodiment, artistic expression is in its form privileged to contribute an insight, as it creates an experience that is inherently visceral and by its very nature deals in direct sensorial engagement with the body.

To be embodied is the fundamental condition of human experience. For each of us our individual embodiment is characterised experientially through direct sensorimotor perceptual feedback and kinaesthetically from a set of movement possibilities, all provided moment-by-moment through our body. We cannot move or act in the world without understanding ourselves as embodied beings. Further, our experience of embodiment extends beyond inhabiting a body to the experience of that body within its environment, but also as a body interacting with other embodied beings.

Immersive and interactive technologies, such as virtual reality, offer a medium for artists to mediate the interconnection between the sense perceptions of our body, the physical environment and other embodied beings with computational processes. Creating a mediated reality in this way lends the potential for artists firstly to envision and imagine alternative ways of perceiving a shared external world but secondly to interrogate our existing processes and approaches of perception.

Embodied Cognition and Interactive Art

The experiential form of interactive art such as that exemplified in *Sentient Flux* speaks to the recent movement in the cognitive sciences

Figure 6.1 Alexandra Adderley and Nicola Plant, title image of *Sentient Flux*, 2015. To experience the artwork, users wear a virtual reality headset and headphones and are instructed to stand in front of a depth camera to track their movement. The virtual environment is a dark, underwater-like scene where users stand in the centre of a round organic cave structure with light flecks floating in the air. Users interact with glowing particles that swim around their hands, arms and body in response to and in time with the user's movements. Users listen to a 3D soundscape of quietly humming machines and bells intended to evoke a sense of meditative contemplation. Image credit: Alexandra Adderley and Nicola Plant, 2015.

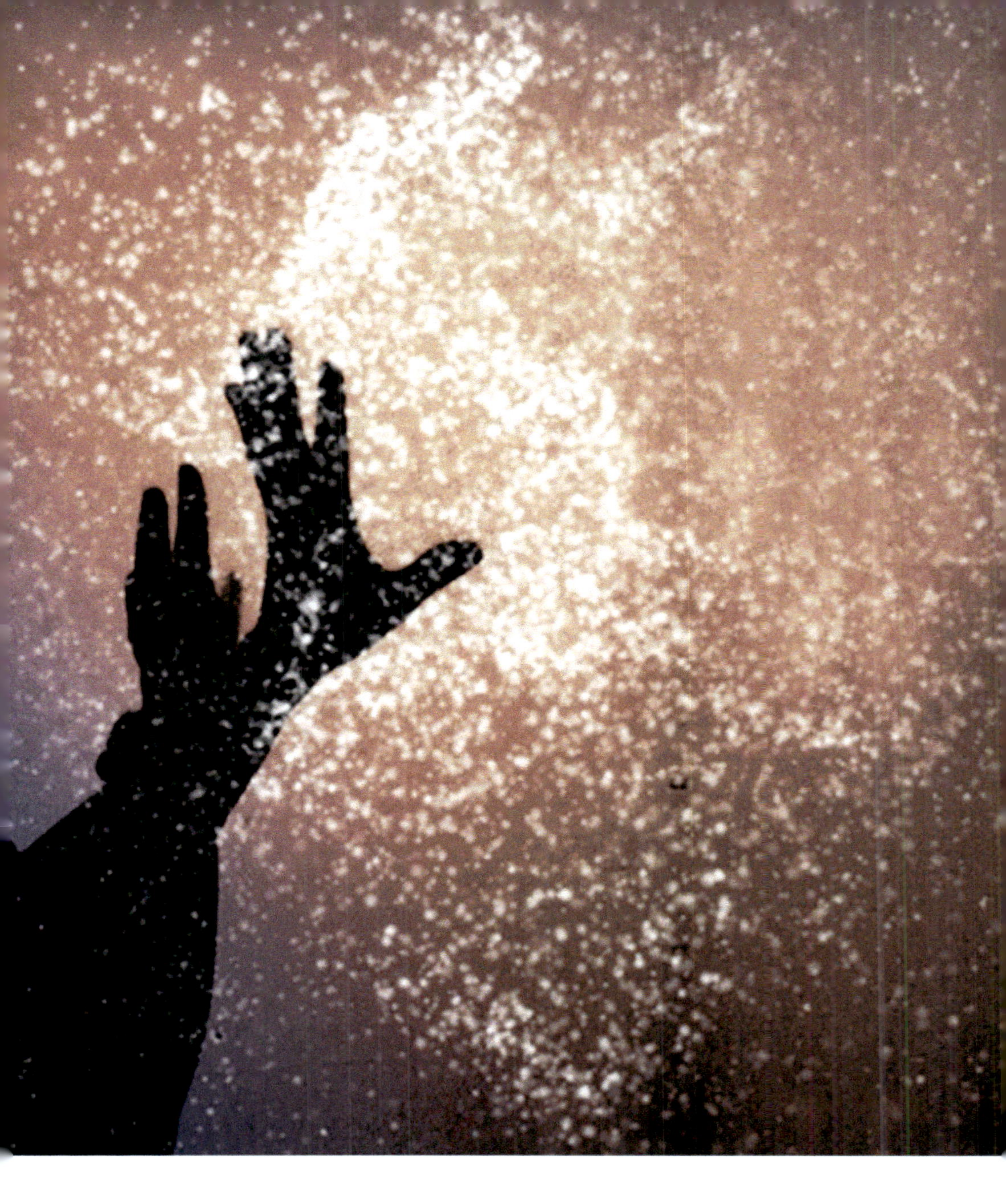

towards an embodied cognition. Taking a phenomenological perspective, embodied cognition asserts that thought is inseparable from the body. Thought is via, through and an act of the body itself (Varela et al. 2017: pp. 147–85). Embodiment is a fundamental component of the experience of reality, or in Heideggerian terminology a sense of 'being-in-the-world', offering the capacity to interact with the world and others in it (Dreyfus 1991: p. 8). The embodied affordances available when creating interactive artwork, especially in immersive media such as virtual reality, leave the opportunity for an artist to create a *not-quite-reality*, presented in a form that can be contemplated in the same embodied way as though it were reality, as a world understanding is not separate from our exploration of it (Penny 2019). Interactive art that presents computationally mediated ways of experiencing our embodiment has the potential to disrupt, alter and enhance the perceptual nuances that hold together the way human experience unfolds, for not only our relationships with the physical but also the social structures with other sentiences within which an understanding of the world is formulated.

Sentient Flux was created out of a curiosity in virtual reality and movement-tracking technology as a medium holding the potential to elicit alternative viewpoints on our reality or, more specifically, a strategy to understand how we perceive embodied reality. *Sentient Flux* is a virtual reality artwork that immersed the participant in glowing particles that interacted with the body and the piece intended to see if users interacted back to the particles as if they were sentient (Figure 6.2).

The piece asks: what are the fundamental conditions for the user to perceive something computer generated or artificial as sentient when the perception of the entity is reduced to its movement alone? This is somewhat like a movement-based Turing test, but instead of testing whether there is a human behind the interaction, the work intends to test the constitution of nonhuman sentience.

The particles' embodiment (or form) is available, as simulated visual information, to the user only via the particles' movements. The piece questions if these particles might interactively move in such a manner that the user perceives a sympathetic connection between the particles' movements and their own. What sort of connection indicates to the user that particles are exhibiting an awareness of the user's existence? Is there a quality of interactive movement dynamics exhibited by the particles that contribute towards expressing a nonhuman or artificial sentience?

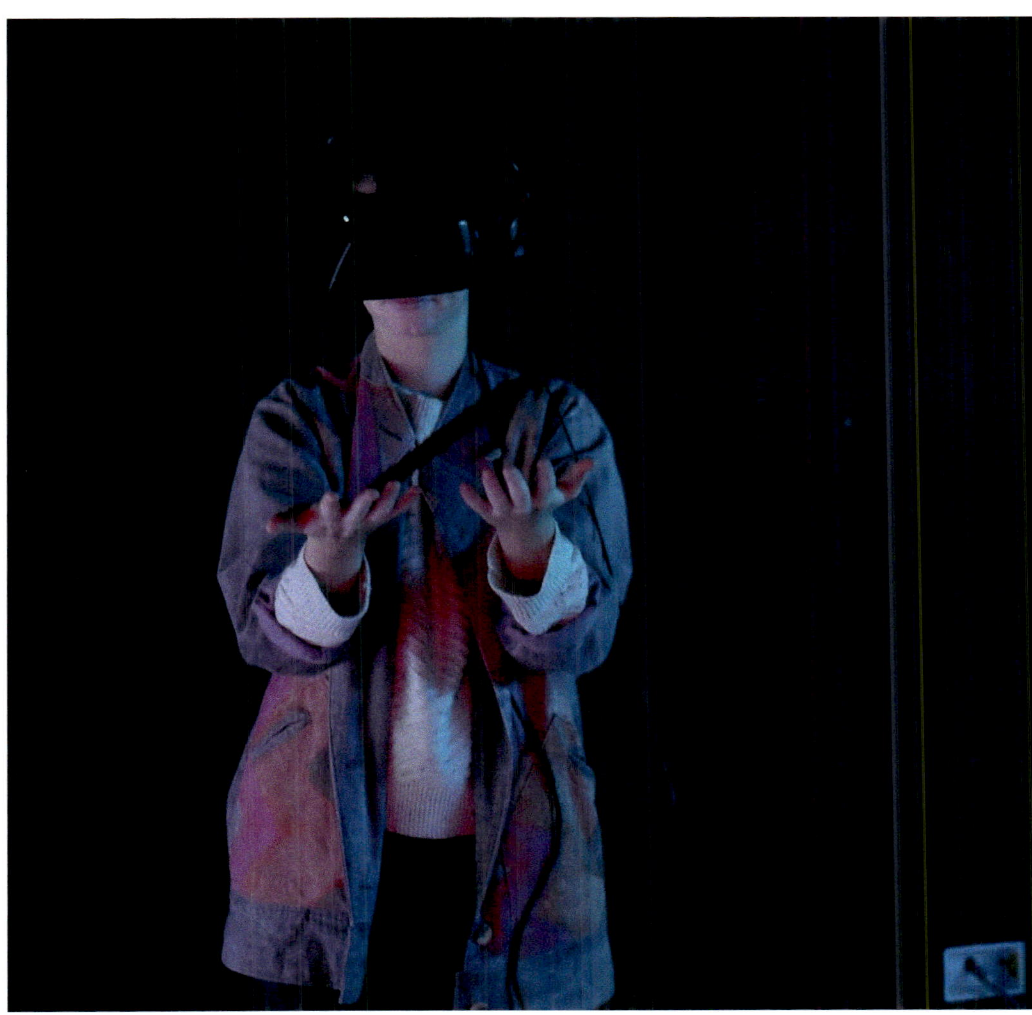

Figure 6.2 Digital photograph of a user of *Sentient Flux* interacting with glowing particles that responded when agitated by the movement of the body.
The particles' reactive movement patterns are generated by using the human user's body as a repellent or attractive force. In this sense, the particles have a three-dimensional awareness of where the user's body is in local space. A representation of the user's body is constructed from a depth map of the real-world surroundings as detected by a depth camera, giving the particles a view of the user's embodiment. A small amount of turbulent movement was added to these forces so their movement was not always towards or away from the user in a linear fashion; this was programmed into the piece with the view to give the particles an artificial sense of their own volition, or possessing a mind of their own, rather than being simply reactive to the movement of the user. Image credit: Alexandra Adderley and Nicola Plant, 2015.

Presence in Virtual Reality

Virtual reality experiences can mimic the affordances of physical reality as spatial and temporal aspects of experience by retaining the conditions to which they are organised. For example, the affordances allowed by our embodied interactions with the real world can be retained, such as our viewpoint changing with the orientation and position of our head and body, or using our hands to manipulate objects in the virtual environment (Gillies 2016: p. 3).

For Michael Madary and Thomas K. Metzinger (2016), virtual reality experiences can be processed by audiences as analogous to everyday experience in all its cultural and social context (Madary and Metzinger 2016, p: 4). However, for a virtual reality experience to be fully immersive and to deliver the impression of being in another world, it must hold a sense of presence. If successful, this sense will cause the user to suspend disbelief and instinctively respond to their environment as though it were real (Slater 2009: p. 5). This is an important aspect in the decision to use virtual reality as a medium for *Sentient Flux*. In order to draw insights about the processes behind our everyday embodied perception of movement and other entities, the experience of the work must be considered in the same way as everyday perception and reality. In other words, experience must be experienced within itself and cannot be experienced from the outside; it must be in first person, and importantly for this piece, an embodied perspective.

In Janet H. Murray's (2020) critical analysis of virtual reality experiences she points out that previous experience with the medium itself will guide how users approach interacting with an immersive experience. This point was reflected in the users' response to *Sentient Flux*, as at the time of exhibition, virtual reality experiences, especially those that involved movement interaction, were novel to the public. This led to the piece needing to be facilitated by the artist or a gallery assistant to instruct users to move their body in order to experience the piece fully. Otherwise, users might not have understood that they had agency over their movements in the virtual environment at all.[1]

---

1   Further, shortcomings of the virtual reality hardware, such as the heaviness of the display mounted on the user's head and face, being tethered by cables limiting the user's ability to walk around very far and the absence of tactility, taste and smell all contribute and shape the experience of immersion and illusions of presence.

Bodily Form in Virtual Reality

Drew Leder (1990) explores the phenomenological experience of being embodied, suggesting sense perception is not regarded as 'thought' but is a more visceral form unique to the body. Leder argues that a sense of self, or the ability to self-reflect, is achieved only in the presence of a 'foreign gaze' (Leder 1990: p. 96). The apprehension of an embodied Self is only defined in the eyes of another or, as originally explored by Maurice Merleau-Ponty and Edie (1971), 'such intersubjectivity draws upon an intersubjectivity implicit within my own body. In gazing upon or touching itself, my body actualizes a sort of reflection' (Leder 1990: p. 23). Leder proposes that 'mutual incorporation', or Merleau-Ponty's notion of intercorporeality, entails an individual's capacities and interpretations to find extension through the lived body of the Other.

Sentient Flux presented the user with a foreign embodiment in the form of a transparent, shadow-like avatar body that flashed with a faint blue light, a material unlike real skin or flesh, not quite human, but other. The avatar body had arms, legs and a torso in the general proportions and with the same movement potentialities of a human body. Although users would look down and observe their avatar perform their full body movement, they would perceive their embodiment in an alternative and alien form to their own. Observing a foreign body performing induces a sense of a foreign gaze, an observation of the user's own movements from an outside perspective that was intended to highlight or make more apparent to the user the nuances behind their own expressions.

Embodiment and a Constitution of Sentience

To constitute is the mental process that forms a concept via the connection of other known structured objects of thought. To constitute another sentience, the experience of our own embodiment is fundamentally implicated in this process as it is both reference point and the means for interacting with the embodiment of other beings. It is this interaction that generates a further layer of expressive phenomena, spanning the social and cultural concepts in which we formulate a shared understanding of each other. Returning to Merleau-Ponty's notion of intercorporeality, there exists a mutual understanding of the body as bearer of expressions and intentions reciprocal to ourselves (Merleau-Ponty 1964: p. 168). This intercorporeal relation within an embodied interaction is primary to us; we understand each other as sentient without theoretical inference or by simulation, but this constitution occurs as a direct relation between people (Scheler 2017: p. 31). *Sentient Flux* considered whether these expressions or intentions can be recognised if the interacting body that bears them is reduced to being represented by movement alone. If so, must there be a specific quality to these movements? What would they look like? Not only this, but what can we understand about how we constitute sentience if we can attribute expressivity and intentionality to a nonhuman entity represented by moving particles?

Zlatev (2007) breaks the constitution of sentience down into different levels of intersubjective understanding, including states like attention, intentions and emotions. The most basic foundation of intersubjectivity is bodily mimesis. He scaffolds intersubjectivity through stages of mimetic representation. The projection of another's sentience out of bodily mimesis occurs during a cross-mapping of another's action onto one's own proprioception in a kinaesthetic sense (Ziemke et al. 2007). Our own embodiment is crucial as a reference for understanding the actions of others through bodily mimesis. Further, *Sentient Flux* suggested that for there to exist a sense of intersubjectivity within an interaction with a sentient entity then this mimetic process would be reciprocal; the act of mimetically moving together would allow the user to consider that a sentient entity is producing the particles' movements.

Sentient Flux was intended to reveal the affective movement features that are prerequisites to recognising sentience in movement. The movement of the interactive particles manifested without any iconical or indexical content, such as gesturing symbols or objects. In other words, any expressive phenomena depicted by the particle system was not in the form of gestures of physical objects or actions, but instead took on a more abstract representation of the affective dimension in its movement dynamics. The movements were generated out of a particle system that possessed no bodily form but emerged energetically around the user's hands, arms and body (Figure 6.3). The movement of the particles responded mimetically to the user's expressions, with a view to determining whether this simple mimetic movement evoked a sense that the essence portrayed by the particle system was empathetic to the user's inner experience. An expression of our affective or emotional states is manifest in how we navigate the external world. The dynamic qualities of our expressions and actions go toward revealing the affective dimension that produced them. Take the example of getting up from a chair: when the sitter gets up out of the chair in a slow and careful manner, we can infer they are feeling tired or weary. In contrast, by getting

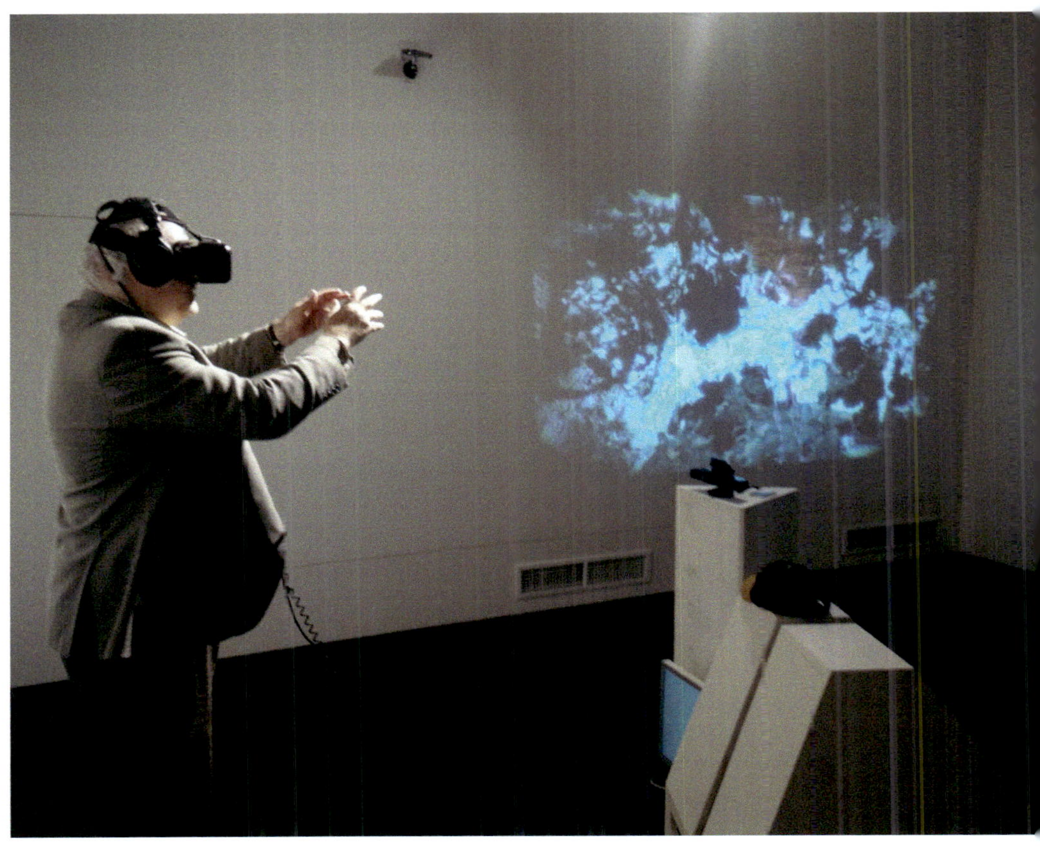

Figure 6.3 Digital photograph of a user interacting with *Sentient Flux* with projection of viewpoint on an adjacent wall.

Once the users of *Sentient Flux* entered the virtual environment it was not always immediately obvious to them that they could interact by moving. Users took time to look around first and it was only when they noticed that they had a bodily form that they would start to move their arms and legs. Judging from the vocal exclamations and surprised facial expressions, the moment that the user discovered their body, the movement affordances they had and the presence of the particles reacting to their movements was a marked moment in the experience for many. Users extended their arms and reached out as if to grasp the particles, starting the interaction by waving their hands around or flicking the particles away with their fingers. These exploratory acts led to dancing or performing with the particles as though the particles were an entity sharing the virtual space. Although the experience is presented to the user through vision – users seeing the virtual environment in the stereoscopic lenses of the head mounted display – by viewing their moving body users could sense their own embodiment and the computationally mediated experience unfolding around it. In this sense, virtual reality served as a virtual interface offering the possibility for external phenomena to be presented in nonhuman ways and human embodiment to be abstracted and interrogated. Image credit: Alexandra Adderley and Nicola Plant, 2015.

up out of the chair quickly our sitter might be excited to attend something or perhaps they are jumping up in a panicked frenzy. It is argued that a reaction to the world can be manifest physically and emotionally and that these manifestations are perceived unmediated by others (Foster 2005: p. 89). Returning to Zlatev's bodily mimesis and moving together as indicative of sentience, the particles in *Sentient Flux* mimetically reflect the user's movements, revealing an affective dimension; does this contribute to the illusion that the particles are sensitive to the emotions behind the movements?

Social Processes and Expressive Movement

Susanne Langer (1953) argues that it is the expressive manifestations, or the dynamic forms of our direct, sensuous, mental and emotional life that are congruent with artistic and expressive form. This form is not thought, but felt and experienced (Langer 1953: p. 215). In the field of theatre and performing arts, Simon Shepherd interprets Langer's writing to suggest that emotions are performative bodily expressions (Shepherd 2006: p. 79).

Shepherd argues that through the body's direct experience of both the emotional and unconscious realms of the psyche, movement is endowed with a special charge and emotional states are transmitted through bodily movement. The emotional or mental state of each other comes inherent in interaction, which is composed of gestures, signals and bodily movements. For Shepherd, rhythm plays an important part in this transmission, proposing that emotions can have a familiar physiological pattern, recognisable to some degree across cultures. In performance, rhythm is considered intensely affective in comparison with mere imitation as rhythm bypasses the intellect and connects directly with basic bodily processes (Shepherd 2006: pp. 77–97). This goes towards dissecting what the act of *moving together* between the particles and the users of *Sentient Flux* might look like. Critical here is that the particles' movements are more than a straight imitation; the timing or pattern of the mimetic interactions reflect the emotional charge present in the expressive movement performed by the user.

When observing interactional behaviour in a study on normal conversation (between humans), William Condon and William Ogston (1966) suggest that 'patterns of change' emerge as an ongoing behaviour. Rhythm is danced by both interacting parties, termed 'interactional synchrony'. Condon and Ogston argue that there are complex and numerous 'configurations of change' that appear to be responsible for the creations of patterns of expressive behaviour. Interlocutors converge and echo these patterns by sustaining and changing movement together in an ordered fashion in a mutual performance of synchrony (Condon and Ogston 1966: p. 4). Patterns of interactional synchrony were simulated in *Sentient Flux* as a function of the computational processes governing the particles' mimetic movement.

In addition, anthropologist Lorna Marshall (2002) states that rhythm is used as a primary mode of communication, especially emotional communication. In a real sense, rhythm is emotion. It is in rhythm – how quickly or how slowly you do the actions, how long you wait between them – that is the prime conveyer of thought and feeling (Marshall 2002: p. 188). Thus, for *Sentient Flux*, even though the particle system responded only with simple computational processes that moved the particles mimetically, as these were based on the rhythm of the user's movements, the structures of meaning were already embedded.

When interacting with *Sentient Flux* the exploratory nature of users' movements indicated that they did not feel as though they were controlling or performing using the particles as a simple system but that they were dancing with particles moving in a reciprocal fashion (Figure 6.4). For Merleau-Ponty and Zlatev, as discussed above, an awareness of this reciprocity pointed to the user's apprehension of particle sentience.

Conclusion

The possibility of a computationally mediated reality in virtual reality holds the promise of presenting nonhuman ways of perceiving not only the external physical world but also sentience in external phenomena and the social processes that underpin this constitution. *Sentient Flux* exploited the embodied affordances of virtual reality to interrogate how a sense of agency, sentience and intersubjectivity with a nonhuman entity is constituted. Users' interactions with the piece indicated that moving together is fundamental within intersubjective interaction. When thinking about how a computer-generated entity might be perceived or might communicate expressive phenomena, the concept of embodiment is the key component. *Sentient Flux* asked: What are the movement qualities in these expressions that describe the dynamics of a human experience of the world? What is required for abstracted movement to communicate sentience?

The interactive coordination that users exhibited when moving expressively with the particle system in *Sentient Flux* is aligned with the

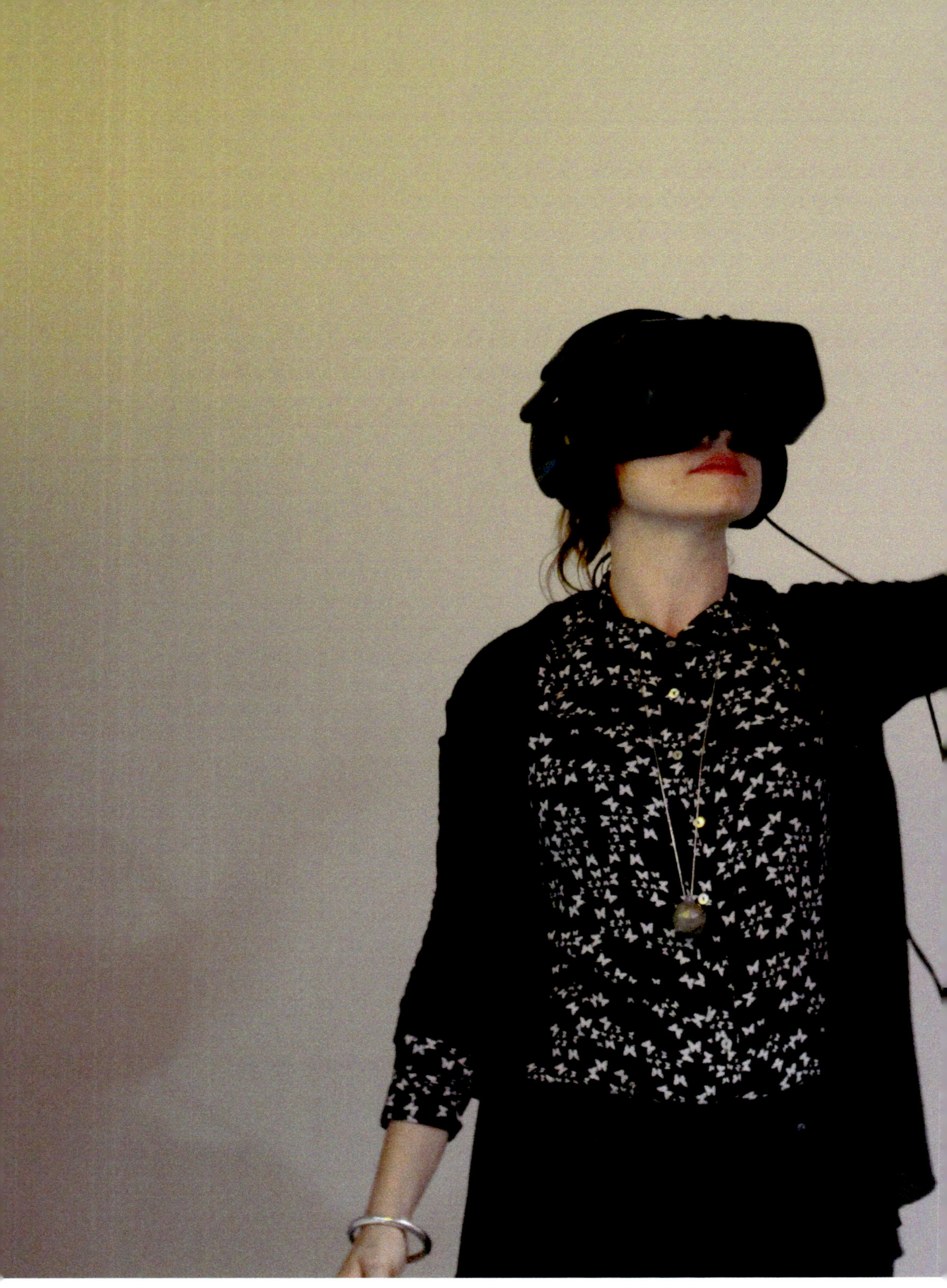

Figure 6.4 Digital photograph of a user interacting with *Sentient Flux*.
Users of *Sentient Flux* exhibited exploratory and investigative expressions that often appeared like dancing in a form that was intrinsically expressive and organic. Expressive rhythm was reflected in the mimetic movements of the particles, but only as they responded to those rhythms produced by the

user. Quick movement elicited quick flashes of brightness. Changes in hue, brightness and the quantity of particles oscillated in relation to the dynamic properties of the user's movement. The speed at which the particles were attracted towards or repulsed by the user's body were approximated by the speed in which their body moved. Image credit: Alexandra Adderley and Nicola Plant, 2015.

interpersonal coordination found in real human interaction. Interpersonal coordination refers to the degree to which the behaviours in an interaction are not random but patterned or synchronised in both time and form (Lakin et al. 2003). The vital qualities of expressive movement that portray sentience are in simple but dynamic mimetic and synchronous interaction with the user's body. The crux of determining a sense of agency, sentience and intersubjectivity in a virtual entity is by embodied movement.

References

Condon, W. and Ogston, W. (1966) 'Sound Film Analysis of Normal and Pathological Behaviour Patterns', *Journal of Nervous and Mental Disease* 143(4): 338–47.

Dreyfus, H. (1991) *Being-in-the-World: A Commentary on Heidegger's Being and Time, Division I.* Cambridge, MA: MIT Press.

Foster, S. (2005) 'Choreographing Empathy', *Topoi* 24(1): 81–91.

Gillies, M. (2016) 'What Is Movement Interaction in Virtual Reality For?', in *Proceedings of the 3rd International Symposium on Movement and Computing, MOCO '16, Thessaloniki, GA, Greece.* New York: ACM Press, pp. 1–4.

Lakin J. L., Jefferis, V. E., Cheng, C. M., et al. (2003) 'The Chameleon Effect as Social Glue: Evidence for the Evolutionary Significance of Nonconscious Mimicry', *Journal of Nonverbal Behaviour* 27(3): 145–62.

Langer, S. (1953) *Feeling and Form: A Theory of Art Developed from 'Philosophy in a New Key'.* Boston: Allyn and Bacon.

Leder, D. (1990) *The Absent Body.* Chicago: University of Chicago Press.

Madary, M. and Metzinger, T. (2016) 'Real Virtuality: A Code of Ethical Conduct, Recommendations for Good Scientific Practice and the Consumers of VR-Technology', *Frontiers in Robotics and AI* 3(3).

Marshall, L. (2002) *The Body Speaks.* New York: Palgrave Macmillan.

Merleau-Ponty, M. (1964). *Signs: Studies in Phenomenology and Existential Philosophy.* Evanston: Northwestern University Press.

Merleau-Ponty, M. and Edie, J. M. (1971) *The Primacy of Perception: And Other Essays on Phenomenological Psychology, the Philosophy of Art, History and Politics.* Evanston: Northwestern University Press.

Murray, J. H. (2020) 'Virtual/Reality: How to Tell the Difference', *Journal of Visual Culture* 19(1): 11–27.

Penny, S. (2019) *Making Sense: Cognition, Computing, Art, and Embodiment.* Cambridge, MA: MIT Press.

Scheler, M. (2017) *The Nature of Sympathy.* London: Transaction Publishers.

Shepherd, S. (2006) *Theatre, Body and Pleasure.* London: Routledge.

Slater, M. (2009) 'Place Illusion and Plausibility Can Lead to Realistic Behaviour in Immersive Virtual Environments', *Philosophical Transactions of the Royal Society B: Biological Sciences* 364(1535): 3549–57.

Varela, F., Thompson, E. and Rosch, E. (2017) *The Embodied Mind: Cognitive Science and Human Experience* (revised edition). Cambridge, MA: MIT Press.

Ziemke, T., Zlatev, J. and Frank, R. M. (eds) (2007) *Body, Language and Mind.* New York: Mouton de Gruyter.

Zlatev, J. (2012) *The Shared Mind: Perspectives on Intersubjectivity.* Philadelphia: John Benjamins.

7 On the Meaning of Virtual Environments and the Evolution of Life

Stephen R. Ellis

A virtual environment, often described as virtual reality, is an interactive multisensory system that produces in its users a sense of being in a virtual reality through a coordinated display of sensory-motor content within a consistent geometry and subject to comprehensible interactive dynamics. The interactions of the hardware and software elements of these systems with their human users involves information flows of such complexity that control structures to manage them must be introduced for realistic and credible user interaction. The required control and filtering, in fact, resemble analogous structures that have evolved within living organisms to similarly manage complex interaction. This analogy suggests that the advent of virtual environments may actually represent a new phase of organic evolution on earth, the earlier phases of which have been associated with the diffusion of life to ever expanding spatial environments. Consequently, the advent of virtual environments may be seen as an event leading to the beginning of life's further expansion into the physical as well as virtual universe.

In this chapter, virtual environments will be discussed in terms of: (1) their physical components and technological origins; (2) their specific connection to vehicle simulation and teleoperation technologies; (3) some of their design challenges for their practical, scientific or aesthetic use; and (4) how they provide an example of a creative historical process like those in the past that have shaped the evolution of life on earth. This process, which is termed recursive leaky encapsulation, is at the heart of the capacity of the random selection processes of biological evolution to allow ever more complex life forms to adapt to ever expanding spatial ranges and varied environments in a manner suggested by Herbert Simon. His essay 'The Architecture of Complexity' (Simon 1996) explains how complex systems made up of hierarchically, partially independent sub-elements can develop the degree of complexity that is evident in living organisms. The basic idea from his analysis principally applies to the control and management of the interactive complexity of interconnected systems, but its application to organic evolution is probably its most far-reaching application.

The complexity of virtual environments as understood through Simon's analysis actually has three separable aspects. In addition to interactive complexity his analysis applies to the environment's compositional and semantic complexity. Compositional complexity arises from the variety of elements, their properties and appearance that appear within an environment. Semantic complexity arises from the ambiguity of the meaning of the observer's actions within their enveloping environment, which necessarily are at least two distinct environments.

A Grandiose Claim!

Virtual environment technology, a communication technology that can lead users to have a sense of being within a 'virtual reality' (VR), has certainly become widely fascinating. For example, a simple Google search for the term 'virtual reality' gets, over 532,000,000 hits.[1] Indeed, this number would be even larger for a more thorough search. But this technology may represent more than a current example of popular infatuation with contemporary 'high tech'; as discussed below, it may actually represent a recent inflection point in human history – indeed, it may represent an inflection point in the history of earthly life as it continually spreads to new environments!

At first blush these claims may seem incredibly grandiose, but the technology they refer to can be argued to be more than just a passing fad in that it can be connected to James Hutton's classic uniformitarian theory of the deep history of the earth, itself a theory containing an idea perhaps as equally surprising, even grandiose, at its time.

In his text 'The Theory of the Earth' Hutton (1788) held that the causes of the geological events leading to the earth's present geography were gradual and slow changes (over millennia) due to processes and events still presently evident. Among these were the well-established geological processes: erosion, sedimentation, compaction, uplift and so on. His observations set the stage for the development of the theory of the evolution of life by Darwin and Wallace. Following Hutton, the discussion below proposes that some of the characteristics of virtual environment technology may be seen as providing a new example of such a creative process for the evolution of complexity similar to

---

1   Search conducted via Google on 13 April 2021.

those which have been evident in the past, continue into the present, and are likely to extend into the future.

But not all of Hutton's claims are supported by this chapter. In his text's final conclusion Hutton also remarked that, with respect to human observation, the geological record showed 'no vestige of a beginning or prospect of an end'. This claim will arguably be countered. And in order to understand this refutation it is important to understand what virtual environments are, where they came from and how they are experienced.

Virtual Environments

A virtual environment may be defined as an interactive, optical virtual image display enhanced by other multisensory displays and feedback to convince its users that they are personally and directly immersed in a represented space which is other than the one they physically inhabit (Ellis 1994). When the presented environment is produced by remote cameras, rather than being synthesised by computer graphics, the experiences provided can be described as telepresence. In either case, users experience the virtual environment by wearing or inhabiting a technology that presents coordinated sensory inputs that appear to originate in an actual, or possibly totally synthetic, environment and which ideally allows them to interact naturally within it as if it were real.[2]

When the alternative environment is completely synthesised by computer graphics, it is now conventionally called virtual reality,[3] referring to the users' experience in the synthetic environment (Wikipedia 2019a, 2019b). When the synthesised content is mixed in some way with real-world content, either by optical or by video camera-based techniques, the resulting system is usually described as augmented reality (AR) instead of VR.

Importantly, the user experience produced by the sensory displays of these systems results from two major types of user interaction: (1) vehicular interaction, in which users move about within the

---

2   Discussing virtual environments in terms of their physical components differs from the approach sometimes used (e.g. Steuer 1992) which defines them in terms of what they do for their users (e.g. creating an experience of immersion). Focus on the technology rather than its effects, however, provides a better basis for understanding how its functioning leads to the experience it produces and what that capacity really means in terms of the history of life.

3   Unfortunately, this term was first used primarily as a marketing term, concealing the extremely poor technical performance of many of the early systems.

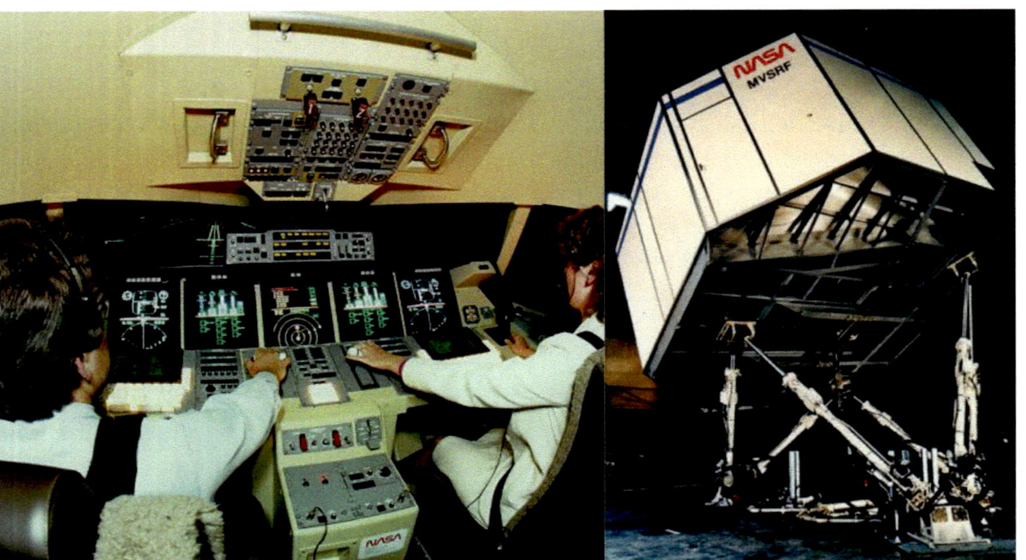

Figure 7.1 *Left:* A digital FSAA flight simulator cockpit at NASA Ames Research Centre, 1980. *Right:* A moving base flight simulator mechanism, 2000.
Image credits: Stephen R. Ellis (left) and NASA Ames Research Center (right).

synthesised space as if they were moving around in the space controlling a vehicle; (2) manipulative interaction, in which the users move elements within the environment, as if they had them in hand. Interestingly, and probably not accidently, these two modes of interaction, as discussed below, are associated with the two primary technological origins of the technology: digital vehicle simulation and telerobotics.

Digital Vehicle Simulation

In their computer-based incarnation the display technologies for vehicle simulation (Figure 7.1) originated with the birth of digital visual simulation technology, largely within the head of Ivan Sutherland (Sutherland 1965), who went on to found Evans and Sutherland, one of the first digital flight simulation companies. But at its birth, Sutherland's invention was not just a conventional vehicle simulator. It was also a personal simulator. A vehicle simulator such as a flight simulator makes a room look and feel as if it were a cockpit of a vehicle located elsewhere. A personal simulator, such as that invented by Sutherland, makes operators feel that they are personally encapsulated by a real or synthetic remote space that is now called a virtual environment, or more colloquially virtual reality, a term popularised by Jaron Lanier. Lanier was one of the founders of a company called VPL, which sought to broaden the commercial application of VR systems beyond vehicle simulation and teleoperation. VPL systems were initially commercially used briefly beginning in the late 1990s. The Matsushita Corporation, for example,[4] incorporated 'virtual reality' as part of an immersing visualisation system to help customers design purpose-built private kitchens in a Tokyo show room (Nomura 2000, personal communication).

As Sutherland and his colleague David Evans realised, the range of possible applications for such vehicle simulation hardware, especially those for the computer graphics systems they pioneered, is large and could extend beyond their initial flight simulation application. Their systems were, after all, a totally new communications medium.

But they also knew at the time that such technology got its value from its specificity. They realised that one way the unique value of their technology could be commercialised would be in aircraft flight simulation, which could allow pilots to practise interaction within a specific aircraft cockpit, like that of a Boeing 747.[5] While a generic aircraft simulator might be fun to play with, real value would particularly accrue if the simulator incorporated the details of a real aircraft. Others, in fact, took the same step, even including development of a head-mounted system for a real helicopter simulator (Barrette et al. 1990). In fact, times have changed and the simulation of physically real vehicles is not as central to the technology as it once was. Consequently, the large majority of applications that run on commercial VR technology today do not necessarily include detailed, validated physical simulations of real vehicles. But the myriad details incorporated into the software still are important to note because, if not properly managed through design choices, they can make the experience of virtual reality difficult. This in turn can make the underlying virtual environments uninhabitable and potentially the source of

4   An example of a VPL headset of the type used by Matsushita, the Japanese manufacturing conglomerate, is marked by an asterisk on the right-hand side of Figure 7.4 (p. 167).
5   The 200 pages of detailed course material in Professor Frank M. Cardullo's (1993) short flight simulation course at SUNY Binghamton gives a sense of the extent of specific simulation details needed for simulation of the real aircraft that carry passengers. These requirements greatly exceed those to make a generic flight simulator as might be run on a personal computer, but probably more importantly point to the inherent overall high level of complexity and detail of virtual environment software.

dangerous sensory-motor aftereffects of the kind that concern the manufacturers of vehicle simulators.

Evans and Sutherland eventually went on to become one of the major North American vehicle simulation companies by developing highly specific simulators for particular aircraft. These simulators were useable for design analysis, personnel training and accident investigation, primarily with respect to civilian applications; a parallel track of development was also pursued more covertly within a US military context (Furness 1986).[6]

Those familiar with the origins of visual flight simulation cannot avoid noting that the complex, amazing multisensory realism, once available only in expensive, industrial-quality flight simulators, is now widely available in inexpensive, self-contained, head-mounted displays that can run the required simulation software without an additional host computer, such as the Oculus Quest (Oculus 2019). A number of these systems are now available, surprisingly, for the cost of a high-end mobile phone and a few cups of fancy coffee!

But what is even more surprising about the recent crop of commercial VR systems, especially those including experiential interaction with lifelike virtual beings, is that their inherent complexity of interaction appears to approach that of life itself and leads to a system design architecture which is also adopted by living organisms. I will discuss this later in the chapter.

Teleoperation

Because of the manual aspect of the user interaction needed for the full range of possible interactions in virtual environments, many of the technological innovations they include have come from another source: teleoperations, also known sometimes as telerobotics. This technology originally focused primarily on remote environmental interactions using hand controllers to operate remote robot manipulator arms (Figure 7.2). The manual interaction supported by these systems allows industrial virtual environments to capture the full range of the complexity inherent in normal human behaviour. Indeed, this full range of human interaction with an external environment is but an instance of the kinds of interaction characteristic of all animate creatures.

---

6   For a more detailed academic review of the origins and development of 'virtual reality' see Bowman (2018).

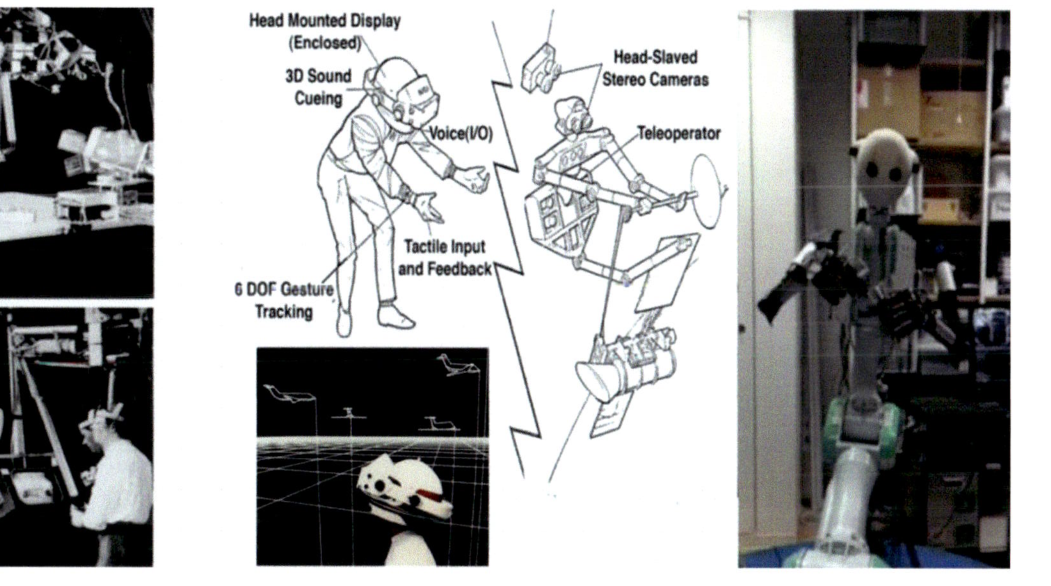

Figure 7.2 (a, left, top) Ray Goertz's electromechanical telemanipulators and hand controllers (Goertz 1964; Goertz et al. 1965). (b, left, below) The first digital computer-based virtual environment/augmented reality viewing system and examples of displayed images (Sutherland 1965). (c) Virtual environment display system used to visualise commercial aircraft traffic at the NASA Ames Research Center started by Michael W. McGreevy. This was initially used to visualise three-dimensional commercial air traffic interactions and later considered for telerobot operation and planetary exploration. (d) A contemporary high-performance teleoperated humanoid robot, the most recent in a series of ever increasing fidelity, humanoid telerobots developed by Susumo Tachi's lab, 2016.

Telerobotics had its origins in various types of remote handling devices for dangerous material and is often associated, at least in the US, with Ray Goertz of the Argonne National Laboratory (Goertz 1964). Some of his initial devices for remote operator interaction were based (amazingly) on almost entirely mechanical linkages. They were used to control remote manipulators within a few metres of their human operators, but they later were electrified and became operable over greater distances.

Development of the technologies underlying telerobotics and vehicle simulation provided a kind of dry run for all the innovations needs to produce the full illusion of virtual reality. For example, parallel development of telerobotic viewing systems, as illustrated in Figure 7.2, led to similar human-interface concepts for wide-field-of-view stereoscopic viewing optics such as those optical characteristics incorporated into the LEEP™ viewer developed by Eric Howlett (1983). It was probably first used to view animated computer graphics by Robert Kenyon in the late 1980s, though a formal report of the resulting research was published only much later (Kenyon and Kneller 1993). Mor natural viewing systems were subsequently developed at the NASA Ames Research Center as part of a programme originally organised by Michael McGreevy (McGreevy 1984; Fisher et al. 1986). Such remote viewing systems of real or virtual content are now to some extent 'in the field', in that they are used, for example, for remote telerobotic mining (Duff et al. 2009) as well as for remote manipulation of dangerous radioactive material, which was one of the early applications for Goertz's devices. But until recently (ca. 2014) most currently fielded systems generally still did not have the anthropomorphic fidelity and dexterity exhibited by the current experimental very high-performance material-handling systems such as that demonstrated by Susumu Tachi (Tachi 2016). Video clips of its operation give only a hint of its demonstrated high visuo-haptic realism, when it is used either as a teleoperator interface or as a multisensory telerobot simulator (Figure 7.2).

Users of such a high-fidelity telerobot system are essentially experiencing a virtual environment, albeit one created by stereoscopic cameras and sensor-driven haptic displays rather than digital simulation. Thus, a fully multisensory synthetic virtual environment also is essentially a telerobotic simulation, though at a potentially differing level of interactive realism, fidelity and detail. The major feature that the telerobotics background provided to virtual environment technology was the realistic manual interaction that was needed for materials handling. This type of user interaction can significantly augment their sense of presence in a virtual environment. But like actual multiaxis dexterous manual interaction in the real world, the user interaction is complicated because of the large number and variety of simultaneously interacting degrees of freedom that must be controlled, especially when the users may need to provide manual backup to automatic control systems. This high level of system complexity is reminiscent of the inherent interactive complexity of living biological processes during environmental interaction.

In fact, the combination of the influences of digital vehicle simulation technology and telerobotics to make virtual environment systems points to their great compositional complexity, since their subsystems must manage, through varied specific hardware, visual, auditory, haptic, vestibular inputs and displays in response to all types of potential user motion, involving for example the hands, limbs, torso or eyes. This plethora of interaction types define the incredible variety of information processing and display that needs to be managed by designers of physical environments.

The Virtual Environment as a User Interface

Creating a complete illusion of a remote presence with a virtual environment has turned out to be hard (Brooks 1999). Today, the illusion is still somewhat incomplete though the originally poor performance of these system has dramatically improved and we now know much of what is needed for a convincing, and relatively safe, persistent sense of remote presence at an amazingly low price (Oculus 2017). The Oculus Quest, for example, is a stand-alone, head-mounted display system which, because of its low interaction latency, high resolution, wide field of view display and detailed widely varied available content, presents interesting, perceptually stable, bright, highly useable virtual environments that begin to closely approximate complex human visual experience. It gives its users a strong sense of presence. Such devices have become very convenient for presentation of virtual experiences and practically usable for information display, data visualisation or a wide variety of interactive story telling (Rogers 2019; Oculus 2019; Ellis 2016).

But meeting the performance needs of the head-mounted display cost-effectively with acceptable form factors still remains challenging, especially for those hoping to develop and standardise cost-effective, widely used, safe technology with a reach comparable to that of cell phones. There is, for example, a remaining need to standardise effective and convenient 3D interaction techniques, analogous to the windows, icons, mice and pointer (WIMP) user interfaces. These WIMP interfaces were first fully developed for two-dimensional screens by researchers at the Stanford Research International and Xerox PARC. Also known as 'graphics' user interfaces, they were intended to reduce (and largely succeeded in reducing) the complexity of personal computer use. They consequently supplanted the earlier, typed text command interfaces through which operators 'talked' to their computers. The 'replacement' of the command line interface, nevertheless, has remained incomplete since typed command input, or similar declarative input systems, still persists.

The WIMP interface turned human–computer interaction from something resembling a spoken conversation into something more akin to a dance in which communication is achieved through the interplay of human-controlled and computer-controlled objects and text. But this 'dance' took place in the restricted space of a two-dimensional display in front of the user, as a kind of restricted world-in-itself, which could be easily discerned, entered and exited. It could, accordingly, still be conceptually spatially separated from the immediate real environment inhabited by both the user and the computer screen. However, the advent of the virtual environment as a user interface involved a much greater step in interface development. In this new case, the computer embodying the interface presents itself as multiple objects and other synthetic elements in a surrounding environment that may or may not be congruent with or conveniently mapped to the user's existing physical environment. The mapping may indeed be spatially conformal and metrically accurate, but alternatively it may be presented in often seemingly complex, arbitrary ways depending upon the communicative intent of the software developers. However this new interface format is presented, it is inherently more complex, varied and extended than its WIMP predecessor. It embodies a much bigger new dance: the dance of life.

It is hard to overstate the revolutionary impact of this aspect of virtual environments. The software generating the immersing environment – that is in effect the system's user interface – synthesises human experience, surrounds and encapsulates its users in an environment that competes with their physical environment for attention and influence. It, in fact, challenges their intuitive sense of what their enveloping environment may afford. Indeed, in some respects this encapsulation accomplished by the virtual environment is both physical and computational, because the technology producing it mediates both the transfer of energy as well as the transfer of information between users and their surroundings.

Furthermore, the virtual environment presents challenges even to language itself because it raises the possibility of simultaneous, potentially temporally convoluted, personal existence in at least two places at one time in a more complete way than earlier forms of telecommunication such as the telephone. This sense of dual simultaneity, which is a kind of semantic complexity, may even encourage the introduction of a new tense for the verb 'to be' to denote this new dual reality as it becomes more commonplace. This duality of presence is somewhat captured by the current sense of being 'online' when using the internet but is qualitatively more complete and explicit in virtual environments. Perhaps this new personal sense of simultaneity may make some of the temporal paradoxes of quantum mechanics more comprehensible? In any case, the technology can most certainly give its users a more concrete ability to see from the viewpoints of others.[7]

Interestingly and somewhat paradoxically, this technology provides this extension of human experience by partially isolating its users from their immediate physical environment in the manner of a leaky encapsulation. Such an encapsulation allows only some of the energy or information in the surrounding physical environment to interact with the users who are also inhabiting the virtual environment. These users may also curiously be somewhat isolated as well from the specific virtual environment they experience, in that their interaction within it is limited by the imperfection and incompleteness of their user interface.

As discussed below, the kind of leaky encapsulation associated with the experience of virtual reality is not totally new in the evolution of life. In the past, it has had more of a physicochemical rather than an informational basis. Its informational/computational aspect, however, makes the virtual environment somewhat distinct since it is not necessarily constrained by the principles of physics, chemistry or biology of our physical environment.

The virtual environment's computational arbitrariness is on the one hand, its enormous strength because it can be used for story telling or human augmentation to give its human users uniquely powerful physical or mental powers. But, on the other hand, the arbitrariness of potential user interaction poses numerous new, sometimes unique, design questions because virtually any aspect of voluntary human movement can be used for environmental

---

7   Developing the ability to 'see though the eyes of others' (Boas 1920) is a key goal of the study of ethnology, though it usually refers to the semantic elements of experience rather than its geometric aspects.

interaction. This great variety of possible control inputs consequently introduces potential interactive compositional complexity normally absent during personal interaction within real environments. It must, however, be noted that telerobotic control with a conventional remote-control system is itself also inherently complex due to the duality of an operator's sense of presence at their control site and their work site.

Probably the most significant general uses for these new interactive capacities include procedure development for vehicle operation and training, data visualisation and, perhaps most obviously, in entertainment, video games and immersive cinema. These three use cases are illustrated in Figure 7.3. However, the generality with which virtual environments can be designed implies that future designs and applications, and their costs and benefits, are likely beyond current imagination.

But these potential future applications are well beyond the scope of this chapter, which will focus now on some of the details of information flow within a virtual environment, a pattern of information flow that can be seen as analogous to information flows across nested substructures within natural organisms, for example subcellular structures recursively nested in cells, nested in tissues, nested in organs and nested in bodies.

Design Complexity of Virtual Environments

The fact that users of virtual environments are simultaneously experiencing interaction within their virtual environment as well as within their actual physical environment is a source of very significant design and usability issues. Three such issues are: (1) motion sickness and/or unwanted shifts in sensory-motor coordination, which are examples of interactive complexity (Lackner and DiZio 2003); (2) possible attentional confusion or, more concretely, tripping hazards because of spatially overlapping real and virtual environments – though these can be mitigated by features such as the Oculus Guardian©[8] (the problems resolved by the Guardian© are examples of compositional complexity); and (3) kinematically unusual control laws that affect the dynamics of user interaction

---

8   The Guardian is a user interface concept employed by the Oculus Quest head-mounted display to protect its users from stumbling into real-world objects. It appears to its users as a cage-shaped, virtual object enclosing a predetermined safe volume within which they may move.

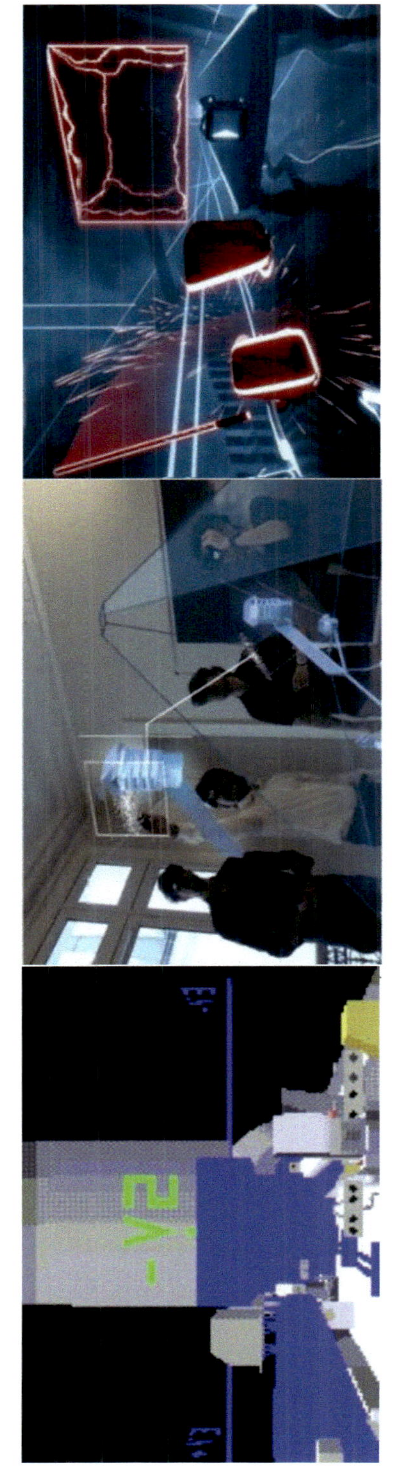

Figure 7.3 Three more recent examples of the applications of virtual environments and related technologies. An interactive image of the Space Shuttle Orbiter (Loftin et al. 1993) that was viewed as a virtual environment by the ground crew to practise procedures for in-flight operations in the Space Shuttle Orbiter bay (left). An augmented reality visualisation of muon 'x-ray' data possibly revealing a previously unknown void within the Great Pyramid at Giza (Sample 2017; Seide 2018) (middle). Beat Saber, a screen shot of a virtual reality game for the Oculus Quest headset in which participants use the Oculus Quest to play an immersing video game in which virtual swords (left within frame) are used to slash approaching virtual objects, 2019 (see Robertson 2018) (right).

(examples of interactive complexity – a specific example of such a law would be a nonlinearity in the control of a vehicle introduced to capture more of a user's attention).

Interestingly, when such changes affect users' social interactions, they also contribute to semantic complexity. I recall an example of this kind of aftereffect from the video game world mentioned to me by John Wharton. While attending an Asilomar Workshop on Microprocessors, he had a chance go on a video game binge, playing *Hard Driving* endlessly for free.[9] The game rewards aggressive driving. He found later when driving home through the Santa Cruz Mountains that he fell into speeding around curves as if he were racing at Le Mans. Slater et al. (1997) have commented more formally on other types of the semantic complexities of virtual environments.

The system complexity of virtual environments, of course, depends on the specific design of their various component software and hardware. But probably their most prominent component is each systems' head-mounted display.[10] Somewhat surprisingly, this one part probably has the longest developmental history (Figure 7.4), partly because of its connection to very much earlier optical systems, for example Galileo's head-mounted telescope and its optical successors.[11] More recently, the design of night vision viewing systems has stimulated the optical developments needed for virtual environments (Wiseman 1992). However, because virtual environments incorporate both computationally created and real imagery, these systems greatly increase the number and variety of the design questions well beyond those of their predecessors. The details of these questions are also largely well beyond the scope of this chapter.

We can, however, get some sense of the degree of overall development difficulty by looking historically at the head-worn component of virtual environments and comparing it to that of

9   The Asilomar Workshop on Microprocessors took place in Pacific Grove, California, in 1976. It was held initially every year or so, but eventually became irregular. It was attended by the major microcomputer innovators in Silicon Valley, did not publish proceedings, and swore all attendees to silence and to promise not to steal each other's work. But it was a significant incubator for the 'Valley's' meteoric technical advances.

10 The head-mounted display should probably be described as a head-referenced viewer, since back-projection systems without a head-mounted display are certainly a possible format for virtual environments that can produce an illusion of virtual reality (e.g. Cruz-Neira et al. 1992).

11 Galileo's head-mounted system was part of a proposed system to determine longitude at sea (Stefani 2013). It was called a Celatone and is shown in the lower left corner of Figure 7.4.

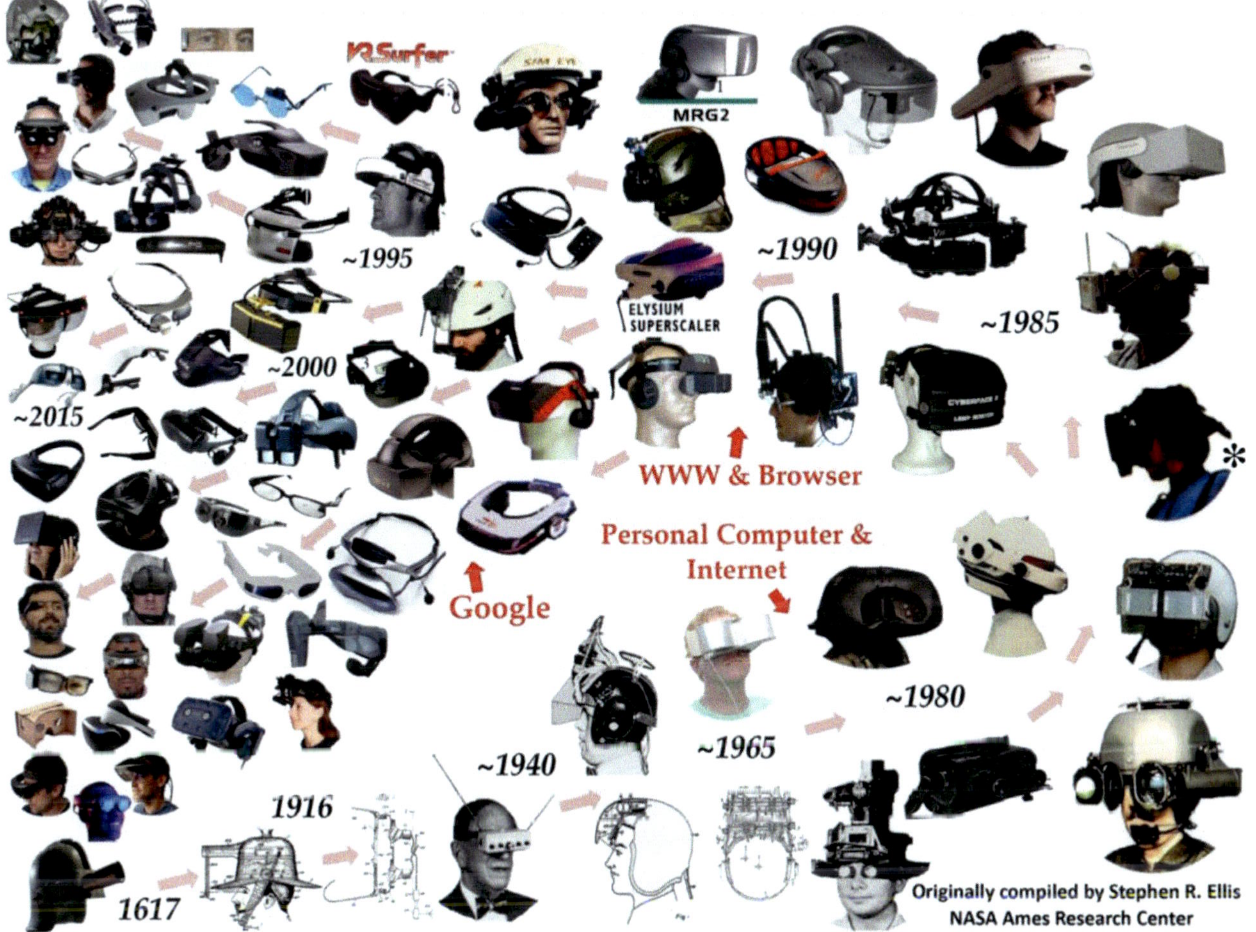

Figure 7.4 Some examples of head-mounted viewing from Renaissance times to the present. Image credit: Stephen R. Ellis.

other contemporaneously developed information technologies, as shown in Figure 7.4. Overlaid on this cornucopia of displays are marks showing the introduction of several IT milestones that have to date already clearly changed the world: the personal computer, the World Wide Web with an associated browser, and the Google search engine. All of these key developments have clearly had major societal impacts. So, it is reasonable to ask why VR has taken much longer to have a similar social effect.

One of the reasons for the relatively slower cultural impact of virtual environments is the large amount of variably detailed content which needs to be recoded or simply created to make them interesting, useful and valuable. The wide variation of detail and precision that must be used to model the content, geometry and dynamics of the environmental simulation in these systems complicates and delays application development. This complication is especially salient in display systems incorporating real-world objects, which must be scanned and edited for display.

An example of the amount of detail used for specifications required of a validated, certified aircraft simulation is that of an existing aircraft.[12] Admittedly, such a specification, were it to be made for a head-mounted aircraft simulation, is on the high end of virtual environment. Nevertheless, this example points to the range and precision of virtual environment systems that designers must address in some way.

A virtual environment user interface cannot be thought of as simply a three-dimensional version of a computer interface. Users of virtual environments do not just send a simple key press but literally send multiple, simultaneous signals to the system from potentially every part of their body, many possibly without conscious awareness. The number of these signals is large, potentially hundreds or more. After receiving these signals, the system software and hardware return the consequences of their inputs by updating the users' view of the virtual space, their body pose, and myriad other positions and states of elements within their virtual environment. Because of the great variety of the possible inputs the users may give, the responses from the system can be correspondingly more complex. In fact, much of the design of habitable virtual environments is largely focused on controlling this complexity.

Figure 7.5 explains some interesting user–system communication symmetries that are present in virtual environments. The centre of

---

12 For specific examples of detailed content, geometrical and dynamic considerations behind vehicle simulation see Cardullo (1993).

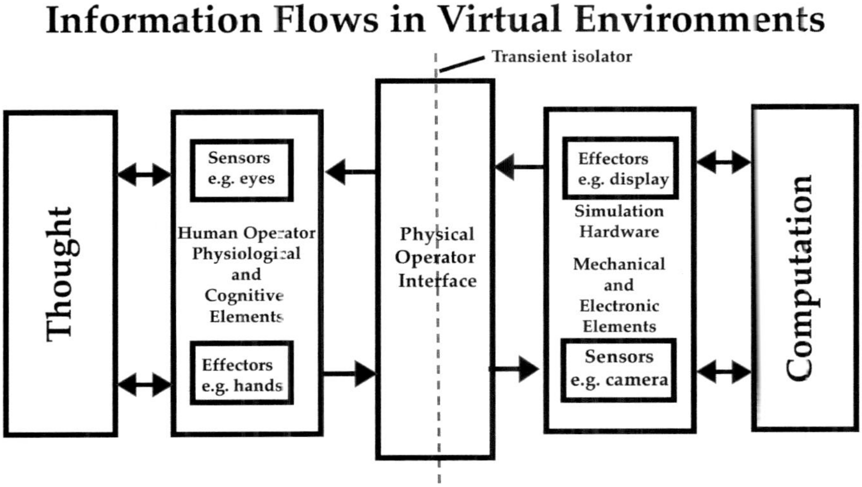

Information Flows in Virtual Environments

Figure 7.5 Directional information flows represented by arrows within and between human users and virtual environments.
Image credit: Stephen R. Ellis.

the figure represents the conventional interface between users and in this case the hardware of the virtual environment they inhabit. Interactions at this interface are physical. The control information moves through this interface as physical signals and responses, initiated either by the user or by the system. The way the figure is constructed presumes that the initial signal originates with the user. But once the process of interacting within the virtual environment begins, its closed-loop nature makes the determination of causation ambiguous. In this figure, causation may be considered to begin with some movement of the user's hands.

Once a hand movement starts the process, the resulting signals circulate from user effectors to system sensors and then to system effectors and then to user sensors, and so on. The process continues as a feedback loop modulated by the user's future responses and the system's reactions. This low-level control loop could describe, for example, a user's hand movement from one place in a virtual environment to another. What is significant about the feedback control process illustrated is that higher-level control processes within the user and within the system modulate the lower-level interaction. On the user side, the speed with which the movement is made could be increased over time. On the system side, the resistance that a user might feel to the intended movement could be analogously produced by the computer simulation.

What is significant for virtual environment systems is that there is potentially a massive amount of computation running to determine the overall system response and the correspondingly considerable thought within the user to respond to the system as the overall interaction between the two progresses. The thought and computation modulate the lower-level interaction in changing the complex ways the user becomes familiar with the system and as the system develops an understanding of the physical and interactive characteristics of its users.[13]

In fact, it will be seen that a particular design innovation needs to be introduced to manage the dynamic complexity of the user–system interaction. This innovation provides an example of a process analogous to those which created the geological record, as alluded to in the introduction to this chapter. Obviously, this discussion cries out for a great deal of formalism for adequate description but this detail is clearly beyond the scope of this chapter. Figure 7.5's basic graphic portrayal, however, can reveal an intriguing aspect.

Consider, for example, what happens when the various interacting control–display loops displayed in Figure 7.5 are not properly synchronised. Under such conditions, the users' estimates of the internal state of the systems' top-level control loop might not correctly correspond to the actual system state, and thereby cause the user to issue a movement command that is inappropriate for the actual virtual environment state. These mismatches could arise either from incorrect assumptions made by the system of its user or by the user of the system. Alternatively, they also could have simpler causes such as unappreciated transmission latency so that a correctly produced response simply arrives late. One consequence of such delays in human motor control, for example, is that they can produce unwanted tremor in an effector such as a hand. But in either case, the result is a degradation of user–system interaction as the consequences of the erroneous actions propagate.

Another way to think about the effect of delay in user–system interaction is as a specific class of general mode errors in which the users do not correctly recognise the actual state of the system they are trying to control. This mode-based interaction difficulty is often mitigated by some kind of signal to unambiguously indicate a system's true interaction mode.

---

13 The nature of this understanding is captured by J. J. Gibson's concept of 'affordances' (Gibson 1975) as interpreted by Norman (1988), in that he points out that the affordances of an object may be indicated by its physical or other characteristics.

The problem of mode errors is particularly troublesome to address in the complex user interfaces found in virtual environment systems since not only do users end up needing to develop a mental model of the system they use, which essentially represents their understanding of the system, but also the systems themselves correspondingly develop models of the users, representing the understanding of their users' system knowledge, current status and likely future inputs. In so-called smart systems, the systems themselves explicitly maintain a model of their users. This user model is intended to assist the user. However, for improperly synchronised systems, when the system has an incorrect estimate of the state or intention of the user, the prediction and inference process can backfire and interfere with user interaction. Clearly, these two types of error can also interact with each other and thereby present significant problems for coordinated control in ways studied in control engineering.

Formal approaches of control, information and queuing theory[14] are needed to resolve these asynchrony questions in detail and provide system performance requirements to manage the resulting control difficulties; however, the high-level graphic description in Figure 7.2 supports some qualitative discussion regarding how the potential control instabilities may be managed. Because these instabilities essentially arise from incorrect error feedback passing back and forth between the user and virtual environment, one technique used is to remove them by episodically blocking the connection between interacting parties (i.e. the user and the system). This interruption allows time for more stable interaction to emerge as the two interacting parties attempt to re-establish synchrony. This blockage may be selective but it can be pervasive. It is as if a semipermeable functional barrier is introduced to separate the user and the system as two encapsulated entities so that their internal processing can, in a sense, relax to resynchronise and subsequent unwanted interactions can be minimised.

One example of such an isolation technique is the so-called move-and-wait[15] strategy used in telerobotics (Sheridan and Ferrell 1963). It is by nature inefficient since it involves intentionally introducing a time delay before user feedback is provided in response to user

14 Control theory, information theory and queuing theory are all branches of applied mathematics used to analyse patterns of information flow and control.
15 In a move-and-wait strategy a user makes some kind of controller input and then waits to see its effect before making a subsequent control input. Typically, the user is operating a remotely controlled system with considerable lag, so that the effects of the control input cannot be detected immediately.

action. The basic point is that the partial isolation of the interacting subsystems provided by the delay can make the overall system operation more resilient and tolerant of error or unexpected input. This resilience results from the user waiting for any transient untoward interactions triggered by their action to abate. Hence the name of the technique: move-and-wait.

Virtual Environments and the Evolution of Life

Interestingly, the evolution of life on earth also provides examples of such biological leaky encapsulation. In the case of early organic evolution, the interacting sub-elements are biochemical, with putative encapsulated structures evolving to contain small islands of interacting chemical reactions, allowing those reactions to progress before the immediate internal reaction products disperse and interfere, potentially halting the reactions. But no matter how the problems resulting from the user–system de-synchrony arise, the solution may be thought of as a leaky computational barrier that is introduced surrounding the interacting elements to partially isolate them from each other. The consequent partial isolation enables such complex systems to evolve and adapt more rapidly than those without such partial isolation of their internal potentially interacting subsystems, as described by Simon (1996).

We, of course, do not yet know exactly how life evolved, but its chemical origin clearly required a basis for the initial encapsulation to keep all the interacting autocatalytic chemicals together so that the intermediate products needed for the process of reproduction did not simply float off. Consequently, to address the requirement of some type of initial containment, some theories have, for example, proposed that the pores on structures, such as those present on undersea hydrothermal vents, provided the initial necessary containment for primitive life to begin (Wang et al. 2018). Other theories would see the surface adhesion associated with clays or other physical substances as the substrate for the original containment (Cakmak and Keating 2016). With subsequent development, living processes eventually could provide their own encapsulation by producing their own enveloping cell membrane that could result in cells with separable identities. The initial prokaryotic cell type that could have developed from these early processes is thought to be the oldest form of cellular life. An example of such cells, the cyanobacteria have produced some of the oldest geological structures identifiable as fossil evidence of life (Awramik 1971).

The process of encapsulation may be thought to have continued recursively through the development of internal closed substructures within the prokaryotic cell with the development of the cell organelles which gave rise to the more modern eukaryotic cell. The most prominent internal structure is the cell nucleus, a defining characteristic of this more advanced cell type. Like other forms of leaky encapsulation that serve to isolate subsystems that would otherwise interfere with each other, even the nucleus within the eukaryotic cell seems to exhibit further internal encapsulation, producing even more deeply differentiated structures, for example the nucleolus within the eukaryotic nucleus itself. The physiochemical mechanisms producing this recursive encapsulation are not all well understood. But in the case of the mitochondria, a substructure within the cytoplasm of the eukaryotic cell, there is some evidence from the mitochondrial DNA that it may have arisen as a consequence of some kind of symbiosis (Gray et al. 2001). Thus, symbiotic inclusion seems to be an example of a process that can lead to hierarchical substructure. But it is not clear whether this is the only possible basis. Once an initial recursive hierarchical structure has developed, there are system-level evolutionary arguments which imply further adaptive advantage for the organisms with hierarchical structure of organs versus those that lack it. These kinds of hierarchical evolving structures have been argued to enable greater cellular resilience and ultimately more successful evolution (Simon 1996), which may be conjectured to drive faster adaptive change, giving those organisms exhibiting the encapsulation a survival advantage when environmental conditions alter. Thus, by the curious backwards logic of evolution, the adaptive advantage of recursive encapsulation may be seen as an explanation for its own development.

Interestingly, the process of recursive leaky encapsulation may be seen to continue after cells, which had formally aggregated into relatively amorphous colonial masses, began to form encapsulated clumps of cells with similar or at least correlated functions. Such structures would be the predecessors of the first distinct organs. The first of the specialised organs was possibly a skin-like structure similar to that which has been determined to electro-physiologically encapsulate masses of cells making up the ancestors of today's sponges (Adams et al. 2010). In fact, the benefits in terms of faster evolutionary change associated with the continuation of this hierarchy of encapsulation could be one of the factors behind the so-called Cambrian explosion, which saw a rapid colonisation all around the globe by a large variety of organ-exhibiting creatures with more and more well defined organs which embody the principle of recursive encapsulation.

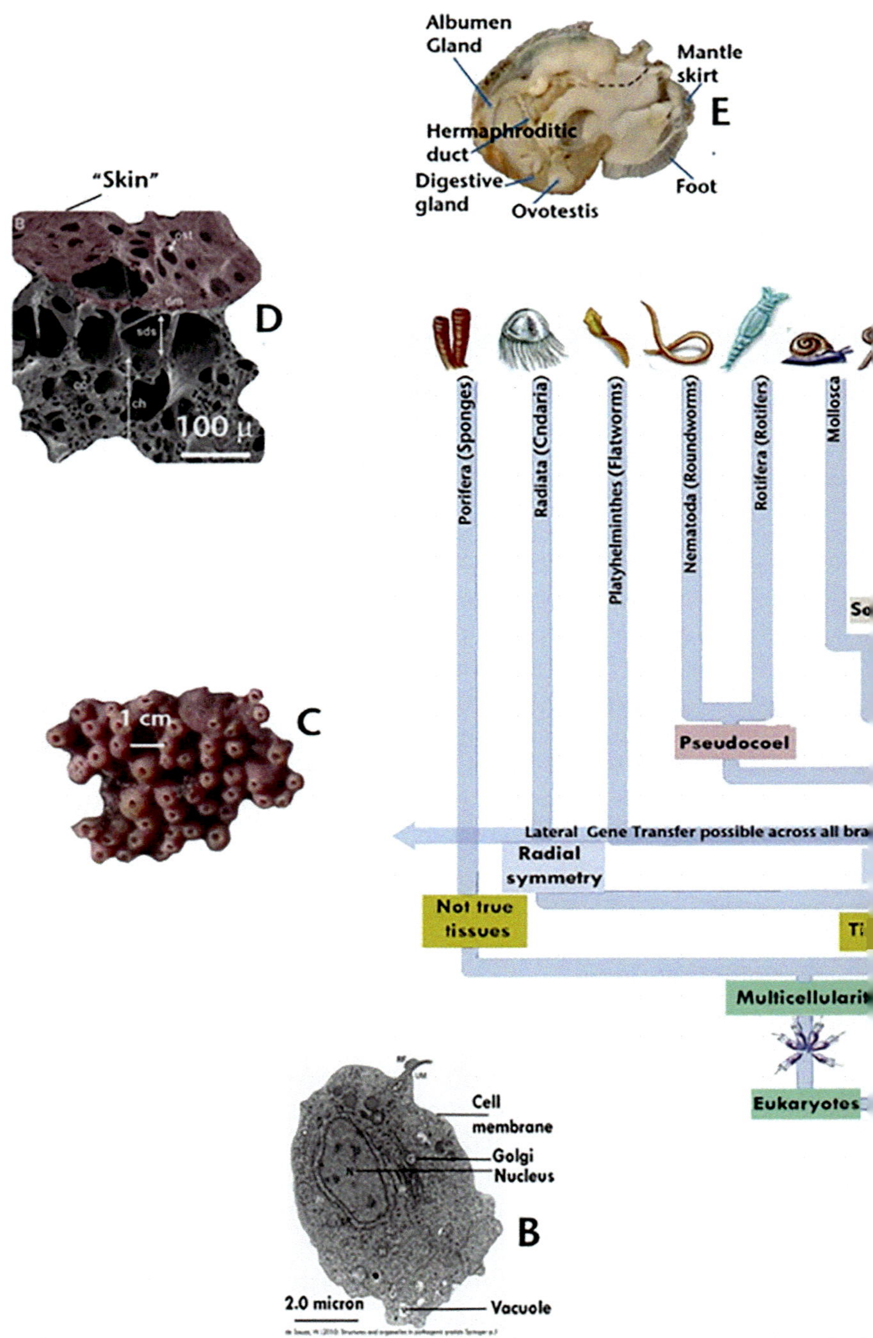

Figure 7.6 The development of personal information display technologies that place users within a virtual environment represents a new cycle of recursive leaky encapsulation that has characterised life repeatedly since its inception. The prokaryotic cell (A) represents the first cycle after the containment associated with life's origin. The internal membranes of the eukaryotic cell, for example

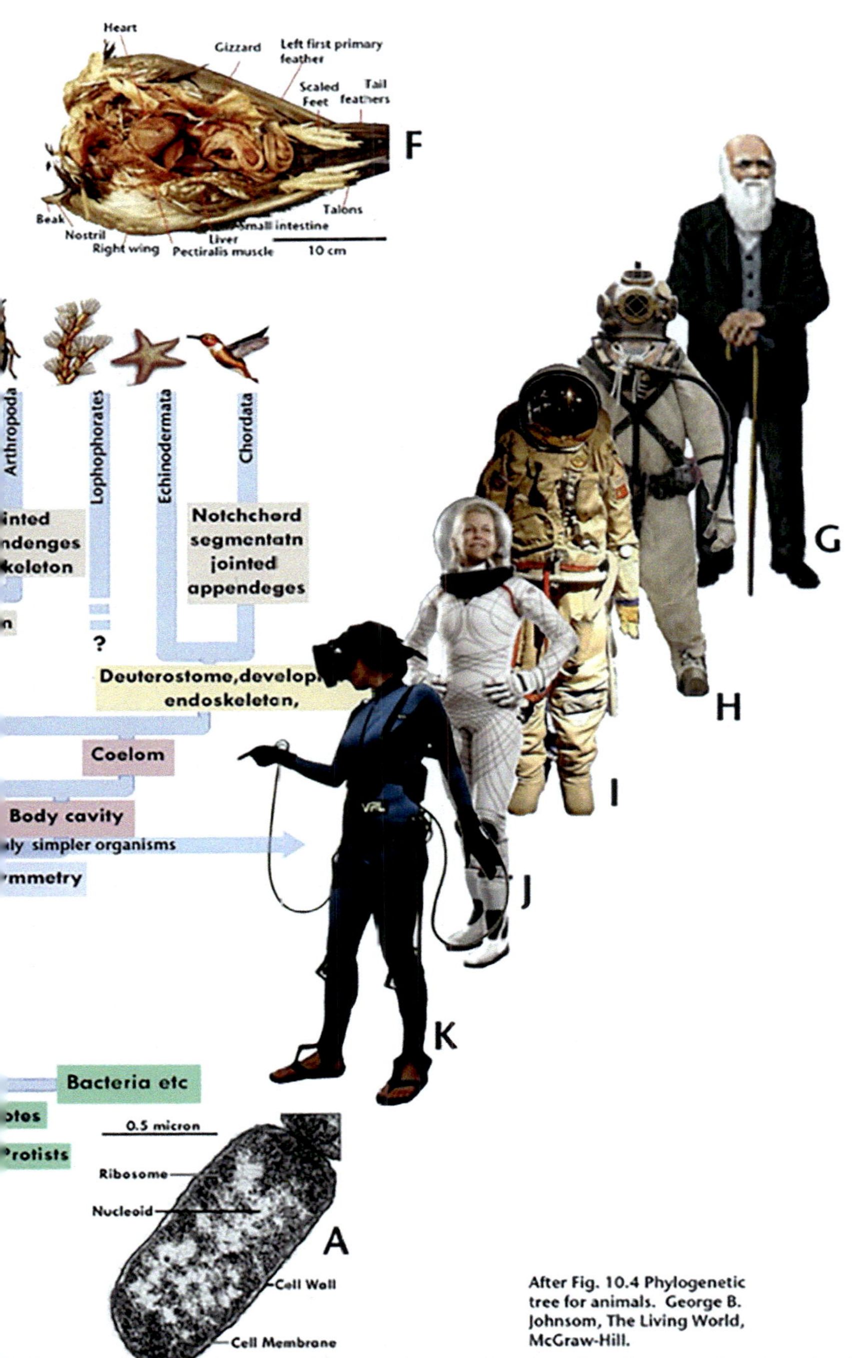

of the encapsulation of the cell nucleus (B), represents the second cycle, the protoskin (C) of the sponges represents the third cycle, the distinct internal organs of higher life forms such as the molluscs (D) the fourth cycle, and the development of various forms of body enclosing suits (H-K) represents the fifth and most recent cycle.

Image credit: Stephen R. Ellis.

Throughout the overall course of the evolution of life on earth there thus seems to be an association of geographical spread with the cycles of recursive leaky encapsulation, beyond the site of the initial origin, putatively the undersea vents: initially to the immediate vicinity of the vents as life began to spread with more complex cellular biology development; then throughout the oceanic environment, as the great bloom of various body types allowed the exploration, indeed, the definition of new ecological niches around the globe; and finally, with more complete encapsulation, onto the land and into the air. And we may see yet another cycle of encapsulation in the development of various types of suits and associated helmets that allow human underwater or high-altitude exploration, including diving suits, spacesuits and most recently the head-mounted displays and body suits worn by users of virtual environments. Indeed, contemporary head-mounted displays can be seen as another round of this kind of development, albeit in this case enabling exploration now of virtual rather than real environments. The newest displays and helmets may be seen as a reprise of the older virtual reality suit and helmet demonstrated as a prototype by VPL Research in the late 1980s and early 1990s. These all can be seen as part of the newest round of recursive leaky encapsulation. Each of these suits and the corresponding internal display systems open up new real and virtual environments for human exploration and experience, just as the preceding layers of encapsulation supported the diffusion of life again and again into new environments.

Admittedly, this story is somewhat fanciful, but at least it should have some appeal and it does lead us to the promised refutation of Hutton's observation concerning the evidence he amassed to support his uniformitarian theory of the earth. So what exactly did he say? In reference to the evidence regarding the pre-existing geological conditions on the surface of the earth, which he referred to as a 'succession of worlds', he wrote:

> But if the succession of worlds is established in the system of nature, it is vain to look for anything higher in the origin of the earth. The result, therefore, of our present enquiry is, that we find no vestige of a beginning, no prospect of an end. (Hutton 1788: p. 304)

But we can now see that those processes which he observed to have shaped the surface of the earth have, in fact, not left us totally without a vestige of the beginning. They have.

Life itself is that vestige.

Unlike physical processes which exhibit successive change but do not seem to have an explicit memory, living creatures do, in that they at least attempt to 'remember' and carry the structure of their ancestors forward as a vestige of the past.

And it will be life that caries the evidence of its own recursive structure through new cycles of the encapsulation expanding the biosphere, as it did from the sea to the land, from the land to the air, and now off the earth into the solar system with the potential for ultimate spread throughout the universe.

Awareness of the meaning of this expansion can, in fact, provide another way to look at the famous Apollo 8 *Earthrise* photograph. This mission is sometimes considered equal in significance to the Apollo 11 moon landing mission, in that Apollo 8 represented the first departure of humans from the earth.[16] But we can now also recognise that it may not just be about the first human departure from earth but may more significantly also represent the most recent purposive expansion of life itself into a new environment, the universe at large.

Now if this is not a grandiose vision, nothing is!

References

Adams, E. D. M., Goss, G. G. and Leys, S. (2010) 'Freshwater Sponges Have Functional Sealing Epithelia with High Transepithelial Resistance and Negative Transepithelial Potential', *PLoS ONE* 5(11). Available at https://doi.org/10.1371/journal.pone.0015040 (accessed 10 October 2019).

Awramik, S. M. (1971) 'Precambrian Columnar Stromatolite Diversity: Reflection of Metazoan Appearance', *Science* 174(4011): 825–7.

Barrette, R., Dunkley, R., Kruk, R., Kurtz, D., Marshall, S., Williams, T., Weissman, P. and Antos, S. (1990) 'Flight Simulation Advanced Wide FOV Helmet Mounted Infinity Display (AFHRL-TR-89-36)'. Air Force Human Resources Laboratory.

Beat Saber (2019) *Beat Games*. Available at https://twitter.com/beatgames studio?lang=en (accessed 26 October 2019).

Boas, F. (1920) 'The Methods of Ethnology', *American Anthropologist* 22(4): 311–21.

Bowman, T. (2018) *Fate Amenable to Change: A Technical and Social History of Virtual Reality in the United States of America, from 1965 to 2005*. Oxford: University of Oxford, 2018.

Brooks, F. P. (1999) 'What's Real About Virtual Reality?', *IEEE Computer Graphics and Applications* 19(6): 16–27.

Cakmak, F. P. and Keating, C. D. (2016) 'Combining Catalytic Microparticle with Droplet Formed by Phase Coexistence: Adsorption and Activity of Natural Clays at the Aqueous Interface'. Available at https://www.nature.com/scientific/reports (accessed 20 November 2019).

Cardullo, F. M. (1993) 'Flight and Ground Simulation Update', Course notes presented at the Watson School of Engineering and Applied Sciences, 11–15 January, SUNY Binghamton, NY.

16 As astronaut Michael Collins said, 'If Apollo 11 was about the "arriving" and Apollo 8 was about the "leaving", the two were about equal in significance' (Collins 2018).

Collins, M. (2018) 'Apollo's Most Dangerous Mission', PBS's *NOVA* episode, 26 December.

Cruz-Neira, C., Sandin, D. J., DeFanti, T. A., Kenyon, R. V. and Hart, J. C. (1992) 'The CAVE: Audio Visual Experience Automatic Virtual Environment', *Communications of the ACM* 35(6): 64–72.

Duff, E., Caris, C., Bonchis, A., Taylor, K., Gunn, C. and Adcock, M. (2009) 'The Development of a Telerobotic Rock Breaker', in *Field and Service Robotics: Results of the 7th International Conference* , pp. 411–42. Doi: 10.1007/978-3-642-13408-1_37 (accessed 6 June 2022).

Ellis, S. R. (1994) 'What Are Virtual Environments?', *IEEE Computer Graphics and Applications* 14(1): 17–22.

Ellis, S. R. (2016) 'So You Are Going to Make a Robot That Looks Like a Human Being? Really!', *Presence* 25(4): 1–9.

Fisher, S. S., McGreevy, M., Humphries, J. and Robinett, W. (1986) 'Virtual Environment Display System', in *ACM 1986 Workshop on 3D Interactive Graphics, Chapel Hill, North Carolina, 23–24 October 1986*. New York: ACM, pp. 77–87.

Furness, T. A. (1986) 'The Super Cockpit and Human Factors Challenges', in Ung, M. (ed.), *Proceedings of Human Factors Society 30th Annual Meeting*. Washington, DC: Human Factors and Ergonomics Society, pp. 48–52.

Gibson, J. J. (1975) 'Affordances and Behaviour', in Reed, E. S. and Jones, R. (eds), *Reasons for Realism: Selected Essays of James J. Gibson*. Hillsdale: Lawrence Erlbaum, pp. 410–11.

Goertz, R. C. (1964) 'Manipulator System Development at ANL', in *Proceedings of the 12th RSTD Conference*. Lemont: Argonne National Laboratory, pp. 117–36.

Goertz, R. C., Mingesz, S., Potts, C. and Lindberg, J. (1965) 'An Experimental Head-Controlled Television to Provide Viewing for a Manipulator Operator', in *Proceedings of the 13th Remote Systems Technology Conference*. La Grange Park: American Nuclear Society, pp. 57–60.

Gray, M. W., Burger, G. and Franz, B. F. (2001) 'The Origin and Early Evolution of Mitochondria', *Genome Biology* 2(6). Available at https://www.ncbi.nlm.nih.gov PMC138944 (accessed 6 June 2022).

Howlett, E. M. (1983) US Patent Number 4406532, Wide Angle Color Photography Method and System, 27 September.

Hutton, J. (1788) 'Theory of the Earth', in *Transactions of the Royal Society of Edinburgh*, 1 (NuVision Publications, LLC, 2007).

Kenyon, R. T. and Kneller, E. W. (1993) 'The Effects of Field of View Size on the Control or Roll Motion', *IEEE Transactions on Systems Man and Cybernetics* 23(1): 183–93.

Lackner, J. R. and DiZio, P. (2003) 'The Cyber Adaptation Syndrome', in Adelman, G. and Smith, B. (eds), *Encyclopaedia of Neuroscience* (3rd edition, CD-ROM version). Amsterdam: Elsevier Science.

Loftin, R. B., Loftin, N., Engelberg, M. and Benedetti, R. (1993) 'Applying Virtual Reality in Education: A Prototypical Virtual Physics Laboratory', in *Proceedings of the IEEE 1993 Symposium on Research Frontiers in Virtual Reality*. Los Alamitos: IEEE Computer Society Press, pp. 67–74.

McGreevy, M. W. (1984) 'NASA Ames Virtual Environment Display: Applications and Requirements', unpublished internally distributed technical document, Aerospace Human Factors Research Division, NASA Ames Research Center.

McGreevy, M. W. (1992) 'Virtual Reality and Planetary Exploration. Humans and Machines in Space: The Vision, the Challenge, the Payoff', in *Proceedings of the 29th Goddard Memorial Symposium, Washington, 14 & 15 March 1991 (A93-54305 23-12)*. Springfield: American Astronautical Society, pp. 93–115.

Norman, D. (1988) *The Design of Everyday Things*. New York: Basic Books.

Oculus (2017) *Oculus Rift Developer Guide Version 1.4.0*. Available at https://developer.oculus.com/documentation/unity/book-unity-dg/?locale=en_US (accessed 11 March 2020).

Oculus (2019) 'Oculus Quest Head Mounted Display'. Available at https://www.oculus.com/quest (accessed 10 August 2019).

Robertson, A. (2018) 'Why Beat Saber Is My Game of the Year, Star Wars Meets Guitar Hero in VR', 18 December. Available at https://www.theverge.com/2018/12/18/18145103/beat-saber-game-of-the-year-psvr-oculus-vive (accessed 6 June 2022).

Rogers, S. (2019) 'Oculus Quest: The Best Standalone VR Headset, Forbes', 3 May. Available at https://www.forbes.com/sites/solrogers/2019/05/03 (accessed 10 September 2019).

Sample, I. (2017) 'Archaeologists Discover Mysterious Void Deep Within Great Pyramid of Giza', The Guardian, 2 November. Available at https://www.theguardian.com/science/2017/nov/02/archaeolgists-discover-mysterious-void-deep-within-great-pyramid-of-giza (accessed 6 June 2022).

Seide, J. (2018) 'Great Pyramid "Hidden Chamber" May be a Muon Illusion'. Available at https://www.news.com.au/technology/science/archaeology/great-pyramids-hidden-chamber-may-be-a-trick-of-perspective-egyptologist-warns/news-story/d02e9021caf6233a265c0d84b7277812 (accessed 5 April 2018).

Sheridan, T. B. and Ferrell, W. R. (1963) 'Remote Manipulation Control with Transmission Delay', *IEEE Transactions on Human Factors in Electronics* 4: 25–9.

Simon, H.A. (1996) 'The Architecture of Complexity', in *The Sciences of the Artificial* (3rd edition). Cambridge, MA: MIT Press, pp. 183–215.

Slater, M., Pertaub, D. P. and Steed, A. (1997) 'Public Speaking in Virtual Reality: Facing an Audience of Avatar', *IEEE Computer Graphics and Applications* 19: 2.

Stefani, M. (2013) *Galileana, X, 169–185* (original in Italian). (See also https://brunelleschi.imss.fi.it/itineraries/multimedia/Celatone.html https://catalogue.museogalileo.it/indepth/Celatone.html.)

Steuer, J. (1992) 'Defining Virtual Reality: Dimensions Determining Telepresence', *Journal of Communication* 42(4): 73–93.

Sutherland, I. E. (1965) 'The Ultimate Display', in *Proceedings of IFIP* 65(2) 506–8.

Tachi, S. (2016) 'Telexistence: Enabling Humans to be Virtually Vbiquitous', *Computer Graphics and Applications* 36(1): 8–14.

Wang, D. T., Reeves, E. P., McDermott, J. M., Seewald, J. S. and Ono, S. (2018) 'Clumped Isotopologue Constraints on the Origin of Methane at Seafoor Hot Springs', *Geochimica et Cosmochimica Acta* 223: 141. doi: 10.1016/j.gca.2017.11.030 (accessed 6 June 2022).

Wikipedia (2019a) 'Virtual Reality'. Available at https://en.wikipedia.org/wiki/Virtual_reality (accessed 5 August 2019).

Wikipedia (2019b) 'VPL Research'. Available at https://en.wikipedia.org/wiki/VPL_Research (accessed 14 September 2019).

Wiseman, R. S. (1992) 'Birth and Evolution of Visionics', *Proceedings of the SPIE, Infrared Imaging Systems: Design, Analysis, Modeling and Testing III 1689,* 16 September.

8 Sweeping Away the Dust: Mars as Reconstructed Image

Luci Eldridge

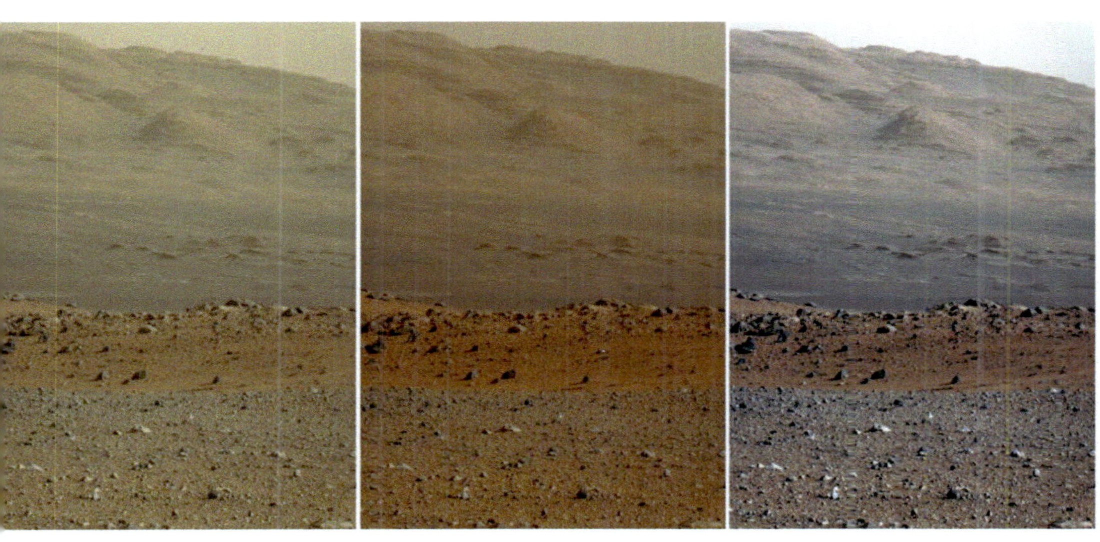

Figure 8.1 *'Raw,' 'Natural' and 'White-Balanced' Views of Martian Terrain*. This image was taken by *Curiosity* on 23 August 2012 (sol 19) looking south-west to Mount Sharp.
Image credit: NASA/Jet Propulsion Laboratory (2013).

Digital dust veils the landscape with otherworldly debris; the sunlight is muffled through a thick atmosphere. Switching on the Earth-like filter in the third version balances out the image in white, artificially clearing the red haze from the sky, settling the dust. Features seem purer through Earth-light: vision is no longer blurred through the Martian haze; layers of sediment reveal themselves. I can see more than *Curiosity*. The touch of the machine transforms the landscape into something other; it alters it, pervades it with its vision. Earth-light estranges the landscape; repetition brings it closer to home, but further from its original. The split screen delays the white from seeping through and contaminating the raw, unprocessed landscape.[1]

The single image from which the three versions shown in Figure 8.1 were reconstructed was captured by the MastCam on NASA's Mars rover *Curiosity* on 23 August 2012 looking south-west from the rover's landing site in Gale Crater towards Mount Sharp. The slope in the distance is the rover's goal (NASA/Jet Propulsion Laboratory 2013). This triptych has been used in NASA press releases and has been cited in newspaper and online articles discussing the variability of colour perception in vision and photography and in articles discussing the 'true' colour of the Martian surface. But it is also an example of the kind of representational practices geologists working on Mars rover missions are engaged in. Recent images from NASA's rovers offer us technological windows onto ostensibly familiar yet remote and hostile terrains; the cameras on board capture and relay a telerobotic vision, framing for the viewer what the rover 'sees' on Mars. These images are studied in great detail by scientists around the world and interrogation of what they show often goes beyond simply looking at a jpeg file on a desktop computer or tablet. In Mars exploration, post-processing enables scientists to reveal the chemical

---

1   Maurice Merleau-Ponty's (1964) studies on the phenomenology of perception emphasise the importance of experiencing the world from 'the inside', with the body as the locus of perception. As Mars cannot be explored in this way what we see is a post-phenomenological approach in which remote devices enable a form of mediated perception. In order to make scientific discoveries, scientists must learn how to imaginatively inhabit the images they work with. As distillations of thought that play with this notion of stepping into the image of Mars, the sans serif portions of text in this chapter represent my subjective accounts of prolonged periods of looking at the three-part image of Mars titled *'Raw', 'Natural' and 'White-Balanced' Views of Martian Terrain*. These speculative intervals offer moments of contemplation, considering what it may be like to step into the image as an imaginative and immersive encounter.

compositions of rocks or to make stratigraphic comparisons between geology on Mars and Earth. It is an investigative activity that relies on the image-editing skills of the geologist to know what might be present within the image and exactly how to reveal it.

These are visions captured by robots on the surface of another world, visions that are then re-capitulated by the trained eye. And while this kind of manipulation of images prevents us from seeing what any human might perceive on Mars (in terms of a particular colour, for instance), it enables a new way of looking. In fracturing the relationship between what might be seen on Mars (what the camera records) and what is seen in the image (after colour balancing has taken place), we switch between different modes of seeing: between the robotic, the human and the imagined. This fracture – or 'glitch' as I will later determine – can be seen as a method towards another kind of visibility connected to knowledge and understanding in relation to what we know of Earth.

In this form of remote sensing, images become malleable entities, constantly being reworked and reconstructed to uncover the history and make-up of this distant land.[2] It is a process that is intuitive and creative, in which the practice of working with images to see, sense, shape and reshape our knowledge of this alien terrain facilitates a virtual encounter with Mars and its image.

Invisible Vision and Re-presentation

In *Camera Lucida*, Roland Barthes states that the photograph 'always carries the referent within itself'. It is a trace of the moment it represents; indexically linked to its subject, it points to the object, signifying its presence in some past moment (Barthes [1981] 2000: p. 5). He writes:

2   Such practices also include the use of panoramic displays, giving the viewer a sense of what it might be like to experience Mars in full 360°. Three-dimensional imaging techniques and terrain modelling enable rover drivers to accurately plan safe traverses as well as giving scientists a more intuitive sense of the topography. Colour balancing images in certain ways reveals the geological or chemical make-up of rocks. And large, physical reconstructions of the Martian terrain become rehearsal spaces for rover testing. Such image forms are essential for new science investigations and remote navigation, yet they are indebted to a deeper history of virtual art. Painted panoramas, stereoscopic devices, painted dioramas and museum dioramas attempted to envelop and captivate viewers of the eighteenth, nineteenth and early twentieth century, providing opportunities for immersive encounters with historical moments and distant lands. It is in this same way that imaging technologies on Mars rover missions attempt to transport scientists and engineers virtually to a landscape we cannot witness first-hand.

It is often said that it was the painters who invented Photography (by bequeathing it their framing, the Albertian perspective, and the optic of the *camera obscura*). I say; no, it was the chemists. For the *noeme* 'That-has-been' was possible only on the day when a scientific circumstance (the discovery that silver halogens were sensitive to light) made it possible to recover and print directly the luminous rays emitted by a variously lighted object. The photograph is literally an emanation of the referent. From a real body, which was there, proceed radiations which ultimately touch me, who am here. (Barthes [1981] 2000: p. 80)

Barthes' 'that-has-been' is key to establishing the photograph's indexical link with the object represented – the light bouncing off the object touched the film within the camera, validating that this moment occurred, in the past, for the photographer who was there at that specific moment and stood in that exact spot. As proof, memory, framed by photographic perspective. This of course becomes far more complex with digital imaging and editing software, when images can be manipulated in ways that make them appear realistic. And this discussion around photographic 'truth' is being exacerbated by debates around 'post truth' and 'alternative facts' whereby we are seeing a direct engagement with photography's claim to truth, be they manipulated photographs or not. Importantly for this text, the idea that the photographic image forms an indexical link with the thing photographed is further complicated when images claim to represent some kind of unseen reality, when the referent exists in a different kind of reality altogether, requiring a device or series of devices to make visible that which would otherwise remain unseen.

This notion of 'invisible vision' is something that predominates throughout scientific discourse, be it in microbiology or astrophysics. Whether from the number of photons hitting the light detecting charge-coupled device (CCD) on *Curiosity*, or the Hubble Space Telescope capturing invisible wavelengths of light in the infra-red and ultraviolet, imaging technologies are making the invisible, visible.[3] And while 'invisible vision' may refer to images captured at a distance through remotely operated vehicles or high-powered telescopic lenses, it may also describe how scientists transform data

---

3   Instead of using a photographic plate that changes when exposed to light, the electronic photographic detector called a charge-coupled device (CCD) captures precisely the number of photons that hit it. These detectors sit like water buckets and count the number of photons that fall into them. Because the CCD relies on counting the amount of light entering it, the pixel can be displayed as either a shade of grey (black having zero photons and white having many) or a number. For more information see https://hubblesite.org (accessed July 2023).

once it is sent back to Earth for processing as image manipulation is employed to make data visible and analysable. *Representation in Scientific Practice Revisited*, published in 2014 and edited by leading scholars in science and technology Catelijne Coopmans, Janet Vertesi, Michael Lynch and Steve Woolgar, examines the broad range of scientific practices of working and reworking images to present and re-present scientific facts. Using image manipulation tools like filters, colour balancing and contrast adjustment to reveal aspects of the specimen that would otherwise remain unseen, these images are considered by scientists as part of the labour process. In his writing on using images for scientific visibility, Michael Lynch (1985) argues that 'objects and relationships which were initially invisible become visible and palpable as a result of highly technical skills and complex instruments' (Lynch 1985: p. 37). He argues that 'what laboratory scientists perceive and work upon' is 'artificial in the extent to which its appearance depends upon such technologies' (Lynch 1985: pp. 37–8). Such 'rendering practices' – which might include 'graphs, photographs, charts and diagrams', constituting 'the material form of scientific phenomenon' – are essential to the data's analysability (Lynch 1985: pp. 38, 62, 43). For Lynch, these technologies do 'not merely *extend* the sensitivities of sensory perception', but 'domesticate' and 'routinise' 'space and time in accordance with the instrument's use', providing a perception that is an 'active reconstruction' of the object under scrutiny (Lynch 1985: p. 59).

Images are built up and whittled down in manners that are processual, requiring a working and *re*-working of data. When Eadweard Muybridge presented his instantaneous photographs of a galloping horse in 1872 there was much controversy as to whether these pictures were 'real'. They were inauthentic images of how the human eye perceives: the 'camera saw too much' (Scharf 1962: p. 186). Yet for Walter Benjamin, the photographic apparatus enabled the limitations of human sight to be overcome; the camera revealed how the horses actually moved through space and it is in a similar vein that scientists use representational practices to 'see' beyond appearances. Just as the photographic camera was used by Muybridge to uncover Benjamin's 'optical unconscious' – dissecting time and space to reveal hidden motions of movement – image processing is used within scientific practices as an unfolding activity (Benjamin [1935] 2008: p. 37).[4]

---

4   Walter Benjamin discussed the notion of using the camera as a technical apparatus to reveal truths about the unseen. In *The Work of Art in the Age of Its*

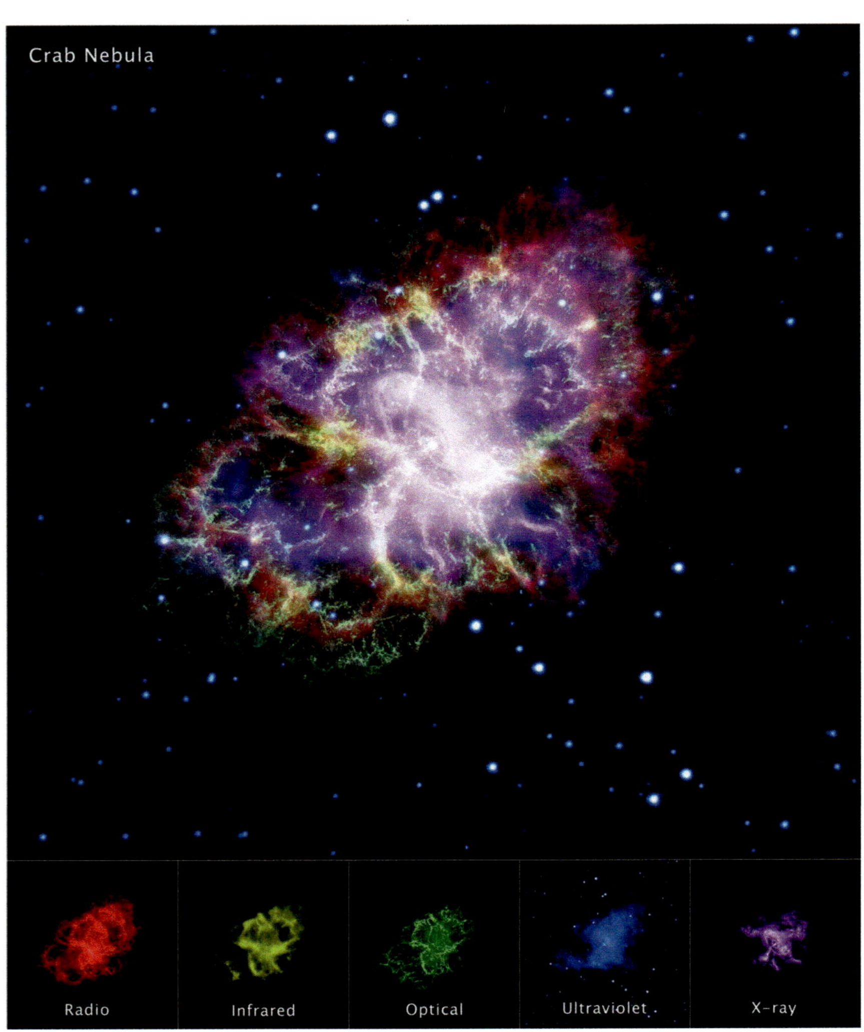

Figure 8.2 *Crab Nebula from Five Observatories*. This image was released on 10 May 2017.

Image credit: NASA, ESA, G. Dubner (IAFE, CONICET-University of Buenos Aires) et al.; A. Loll et al.; T. Temim et al.; F. Seward et al.; VLA/NRAO/AUI/NSF; Chandra/CXC; Spitzer/JPL-Caltech; XMM-Newton/ESA; and Hubble/STScI.

Remote sensing technologies, according to Professor of Cultural Anthropology Stefan Helmreich, give scientists 'perceptual access to the world they are sampling, while simultaneously shaping what they are able to see there' (Helmreich 2009: p. 142). So while these robotic forms of vision enable, they also mediate. A prime example of this are astronomical images; the image of the Crab Nebula (Figure 8.2) for instance was constructed from data obtained by five different telescopes. The resultant image is an amalgamation of telescope optics, digital detectors, computer programs used to render the data, and visual imagers manually processing the data. These kinds of representations, then, are consequently the products of a series of decisions combining scientific and aesthetic concerns.

In line with thinking about the image as something that is dynamic and layered, marked by the potential to unfold into something new, Michael Lynch and Steve Woolgar outline the use of the term 'representation' within scientific discourse and the preference often given to 'mediation', 'enactment' and 'visualisation' in describing scientific images and practices (Coopmans et al. 2014: p. 4). The Latin verb *repraesentare* means 'to make present or manifest or to present again' (Rip and Ruivenkamp 2014: p. 193). The term, then, implies a 're-presentation' of material, that may be re-constituted and re-evaluated to form new re-presentations that reveal information through trained judgement. Furthermore, as social scientists Arie Rip and Martin Ruivenkamp argue, representations

> are constructed in practice, and their acceptance as representative of what is 'out there' is achieved as the outcome of a process rather than a simple assertion of resemblance between a purported original and what an image shows. (Rip and Ruivenkamp 2014: p. 178)

Representation, then, implies a more subjective image, whereby the appearance – and in some cases the existence – of the referent is brought into question.

Technological Reproducibility he claims that it is through the 'optical unconscious' that features perceptually unobtainable by our eyes alone can be revealed:

> It is another nature which speaks to the camera as compared to the eye. 'Other' above all in the sense that a space informed by human consciousness gives way to a space informed by the unconscious. Whereas it is commonplace that, for example, we have some idea what is involved in the act of walking (if only in general terms), we have no idea at all what happens during the split second when a person actually takes a step [...]. This is where the camera comes into play, with all its resources for swooping and rising, disrupting and isolating, stretching and compressing a sequence, enlarging or reducing an object. It is through the camera that we first discover the optical unconscious, just as we discover the instinctual unconscious through psychoanalysis. (Benjamin [1935] 2008: p. 37)

Curiosity is equipped with a series of essential cameras designed for different purposes. There are seventeen individual cameras in total on board the rover: twelve engineering cameras, four science cameras and the Mars Descent Imager (MARDI), all designed to work in sub-zero temperatures. Taking photographs on Mars is not just a simple case of pointing the camera and clicking a button. Because it can take up to twenty minutes for a signal to reach Mars, the rover receives science and engineering activities on a day-to-day basis. Capturing images has to be built into the rover's daily command sequence along with driving and arm activities and other scientific experiments. These command sequences are simulated virtually before being sent up to the rover; it carries them out, and then the data comes down at the end of the day to be analysed. This data is used to plan the following day's experiments and/or drives, and the process is repeated (Wright 2015).

Whereas Apollo astronauts returned their analogue negatives of the Moon to Earth for chemical processing, the *Curiosity* rover beams back electronic data via radio signals which arrive at JPL requiring digital processing. In *Working on Mars,* William J. Clancey (2012) quotes Dr R. Aileen Yingst, a senior research scientist at the Planetary Science Institute, on processing the Panoramic Camera (PanCam) images that were captured by the *Spirit* and *Opportunity* rovers:

> It's a very complex camera that gives you back information in ones and zeroes, instead of an image you can immediately understand. A PanCam image, once it's downloaded – once it's been sent back to us by the spacecraft – has to be looked over and calibrated. You have to know what you're looking at. And then various versions of those images have to be released in formats that computer software can read and understand. That's a lot of background information to digest before you get to a picture of a rock, which is what you're trying to get to. (Clancey 2012: p. 94)

The visual data is subject to varying degrees of alteration in order to create an image that can be read by both scientists and machines. Image data from the *Curiosity* rover comes down to the Multi-Mission Image Processing Laboratory at JPL. Bob Deen (2015) is one of the technical leads, and he explains the role of his team:

> We provide the data that the Mars rover drivers use. We do the image processing and terrain analysis, that's what the scientists use to figure out what's around and which targets they want to select. (Deen 2015)

All data processing happens on the ground; the data comes down and is put through a series of automatic processing pipelines, with algorithms written by Deen and his team, that transfer the ones and zeroes into images. These images are not just pictures and each is encoded with metadata logging the instrument, time, sol, camera model and geometry of the camera. All this information is what makes it a scientifically useful image.

Understanding these images, then, goes beyond surface appearances and happens at a deeper level that is both computational and human centred. We desire to see Mars as we would if we set foot there ourselves and while the data might be readable on a machinic level this transformation of it into images is key for scientists and geologists requiring a 'boots on the ground' approach to investigations. Here, robotic vision relayed as visually readable images – and importantly *sequences* of images – is key to facilitating some kind of intuitive encounter, albeit on a purely virtual level.

Virtual Encounters with Images of Mars: *The Martian Triptych*

Satellite views of Mars capture a sense of the planet as a whole, while also depicting it as distant and remote. Rovers, on the other hand, offer a vision analogous to how we might see Mars, providing windows framed by photographic perspective. Just as Christopher Columbus and Ferdinand Magellan took artists aboard their ships to capture discoveries of the New World, so too do these rovers relay their unique experiences in images. Only now the entire world can bear witness to these exploratory endeavours. These rovers mimic aspects of human form which has been accentuated by their online presence; stereo-vision at human eye height, arms carrying instruments and wheels that enable movement over long distances, the rovers facilitate virtual presence on Mars. With stereo capability referred to anthropomorphically as left and right, the Navigation and Mast Cameras on *Curiosity* are 1.97 metres above the ground and are the 'eyes' of the rover.[5] This ability to be able to see the terrain at human scale and from an Earthly perspective allows us to project ourselves imaginatively into the landscape. By looking upon an image that places the human at the centre of the mediated experience, the Navigation and Mast Camera images make way for the possibility of a virtual experience. Described by many scientists and engineers working on the missions as our precursors to an unknown

5   Average eye height is around 1.44–1.65 metres for women and 1.56–1.77 metres for men.

world, the likening of the rovers to surrogate explorers is a form of psychological immersion in both the missions and terrain. As is highlighted by the image *'Raw,' 'Natural' and 'White-Balanced' Views of Martian Terrain*, scientists rely on processing images to reveal what the landscape would look like under different lighting conditions and the practice of working with images in this way enables a more immersive encounter with a landscape we can only experience *as image*. For ease of reference, I shall rename *'Raw', 'Natural' and 'White-Balanced' Views of Martian Terrain* as *The Martian Triptych*.

In the triptych, the unprocessed colour image on the left is what the MastCam captured. It is the raw, unfiltered photographic data recorded directly by the camera. For all intents and purposes this image is the most neutral: in 'raw' format it is a direct translation of the subject into image, of the light-reflective surfaces apparent to the lens at the moment of capture. Raw images are often compared to photographic negatives and carry with them the implication that post-processing has yet to take place. The central image has been produced after 'calibration' on Earth to 'show an estimate of "natural" colour, or approximately what the colours would look like if we were to view the scene ourselves on Mars' (NASA/Jet Propulsion Laboratory 2013). Although scientists rarely refer to these calibrated images as 'true' colour (recognising that they cannot be totally 'realistic' depictions) the 'natural' image aims to get closest to human vision. The final 'white balanced' image in this triptych shows an estimate of what the terrain would look like under 'Earth-like, rather than Martian, lighting' (NASA/Jet Propulsion Laboratory 2013). Mars is further from the sun, so sunlight is weaker and the red dust in the atmosphere alters the colour of light reaching the ground. Through automatic algorithms, 'white balancing' an image assumes something in the scene is white, but as there are no white objects on Mars (or at least the atmospheric dust give sunlight a different hue to that on Earth) this process takes the lightest portion of the image to make the adjustment. Looking at the 'natural' image of Mount Sharp we can see it is the sky and the highlights on the rocks in the foreground that are the lightest areas: in the 'white balanced' version these portions of the image appear white. As the intensity of the 'white' object can vary from image to image, the overall appearance of the white-balanced image can differ: sometimes it is obvious that white-balancing has occurred (the sky is overtly white and sometimes blue as opposed to a dusty pink) but at other times the colour adjustment can be fairly subtle. By making this adjustment, geologists are able to quickly and accurately identify rock types similar to those on Earth from their colours and textures, enabling the *Curiosity* team to make decisions on potential points for further investigation. Often, white-balanced images are output in press releases as stand-alone images but NASA always makes a point of stating their recalibrated nature, providing links to webpages showing the raw or natural-colour images. In *The Martian Triptych* the white-balanced image of Mount Sharp is displayed alongside its unprocessed and natural counterparts, so the recalibration in this case is immediately evident.

Although there is scientific purpose to these images, this use of imagery also highlights NASA's desire to image the (currently) impossible; that is, 'this is what it would look like if you were stood there' or, in the most drastic case of the third image, 'this is what the landscape would look like if you brought it to Earth, or took Earth's atmosphere to Mars'. This desire to bring the vision of the Martian rover into our Earthly grasp reflects the decision to stitch multiple images together to form Mars panoramas and to experience the planet in 3D through head-mounted displays, 3D-enabled screens or anaglyphs, thus enabling viewers to imagine themselves in the landscape, but all the while standing firmly on Earth. Yet the landscape represented in *The Martian Triptych* is not one we feel we can physically encounter on the same kind of immersive, illusory level provided by head-mounted displays; presenting each iteration side by side and accompanied with explanatory text, we are immediately made aware of the image's reconstructed nature. The three-part picture of Mount Sharp is a scientifically useful set of images for which virtual immersion lies in scientists' abilities to distinguish different features under different lighting conditions. And at the heart of the white-balanced image lies the desire to place our human, Earth-bound vision at the forefront of seeing. Displaying a certain tendency to succumb to an idea of scientific order, the third iteration overtly recalibrates the scene through Earth goggles, and is a vision of Mars that is required in order to 'see' and ascertain some kind of 'truth' from a geological standpoint. But this is also a vision of a landscape that remains trapped within the space of the imaginary, as white balancing the image reconstructs something that does not and cannot exist, both for us as viewers of the image on Earth and for any future visitors to Mars.

In *The Martian Triptych*, superficial colours are imposed onto the surface of the visible and as our eyes traverse the three images we are reminded that no image is stable. As a result of colour balancing, Mount Sharp oscillates between 'raw', 'natural' and 'white balanced', creating a flicker that does not occur within the image but, rather, through the movement of our eyes as we scan the three images. The readability of the three images comes about via repetition and difference, and via the explanatory text: the images must be framed linguistically in order to be understood and this highlights their purpose within a scientific discourse and the subjective nature of the best way to 'see' Mars. Unlike, say, a colour photograph of a scene on Earth, the three-part image of Mount Sharp is clearly influenced by the desire to see in different ways and the ability of the viewer to directly compare the three versions reminds us that there could be many more versions and that perhaps there is no 'pure' version to be had. In *The Martian Triptych*, then, subjectivity is made explicit as we are aware from the outset of our own, and others', acts of looking. In fracturing the relationship between what might be seen on Mars and how it is pictured, a glitch occurs between vision and representation.

Predominantly referring to failure, the term 'glitch' was first used by the astronaut John Glenn in 1962 to describe unknown and un-specified problems, an 'unexpected occurrence, unintended result, or break or disruption in a system' (Menkman 2011: p. 26). The term is inherently digital, signifying a rupture, a loss of transparency which creates an awareness of the interface. Artist and theorist Rosa Menkman elaborates on the glitch as both a break in the transpar-ent portrayal of information and as an aesthetic in *The Glitch Moment(um)*, a study of the theory, practice and social context of 'Glitch Art'. She builds on the assumption that 'technology can be "see through"' – that is, it does not intrude on the process of captur-ing and perceiving information – to consider glitch as some kind of failure (Menkman 2011: p. 14). Menkman describes the glitch as 'an (actual and/or simulated) break from an expected or conventional flow of information or meaning within (digital) communication systems that results in a perceived accident or error' that may be understood as either technical or social (Menkman 2011: p. 9).

The application of filters and colour balancing shifts the image between different modes of seeing. But instead of occurring invol-untarily as some form of accident, in *The Martian Triptych* the glitch takes on special significance, acting as a way *into* the image. Through manipulating the colour of images, scientists are able to reveal features of the landscape that would otherwise remain unseen. The glitch, in this case, can be used as a method of becoming immersed. Central to the mobilisation of the image and making the invisible visible, it does not act to disrupt our immersion in the landscape, but *enables* our immersion in the landscape-as-image. The separate filters are fixed, and scanning from left to right we journey from the unknown to the nearly comprehensible, each repetition a variation on the last. In this flicker between raw, natural and white balanced, the glitch becomes a kind of practice, enabling a human-centred encounter with the Martian landscape. The glitch, then, while rupturing the relationship between what might be seen (on Mars) and what is represented (in the image before us), functions as a method towards another kind of visibility, which is connected to knowledge and understanding in relation to what we know of Earth.

Flicking between these worlds I become immersed in technological alterations; the forms remain but the interplay of light and colour constantly shift the landscape before my eyes. The filtered light comes from one direction, in line with my eyes just behind the luminescent screen; it veils the flattened landscape with a translucent film, painted only onto the surface of the visible.

Stepping beyond the screen, past the barrier into the middle image, walking forwards into the landscape, those particles that were seen upon first entering stay the same and everything else flickers back to its original state of raw unprocessed colour.

Turning over a rock in 'white balanced' reveals the terrain as belonging to two worlds now: the filter over flat appearances is broken; it is not the light falling upon the landscape but a filter upon the window through which I look. No longer three versions of the same landscape, but three versions of the same image.

Revealing the Invisible and Sweeping away the Dust: 'Glitch-as-Method'

The predominant difference between the MastCam on *Curiosity* and the PanCams on the Mars Exploration Rovers (MERs) is the ability to directly record colour images. The PanCams were multispectral, capturing black and white images at various wavelengths (both visible and invisible) through different filters. To obtain a 'true colour' image, the landscape was filtered through red, green and blue and these separate records were then reconstructed into a colour image. *Curiosity*'s MastCam, on the other hand, acquires single colour images in wavelengths visible to the human eye. The wide 34 mm lens and the narrow 100 mm lens making up *Curiosity*'s MastCam can together attain up to 1,600×1,200 pixels using Bayer-pattern filters (RGB). These RGB filters are superimposed on the CCD, resulting in the generation of three-band colour images onboard the rover, an example of which is the raw, unprocessed colour image as seen in *The Martian Triptych* (Alexander et al. 2015: p. 35).

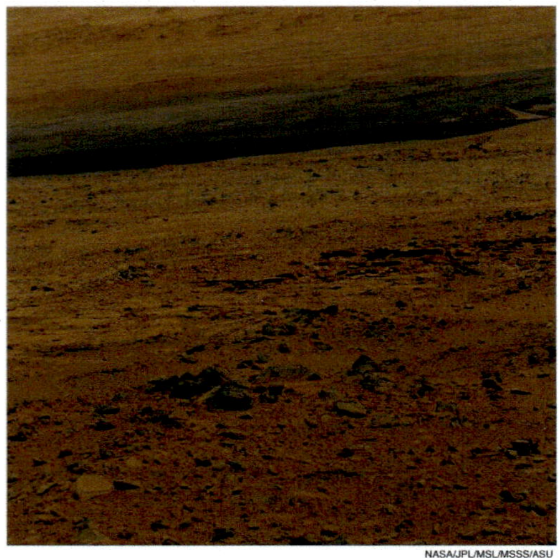

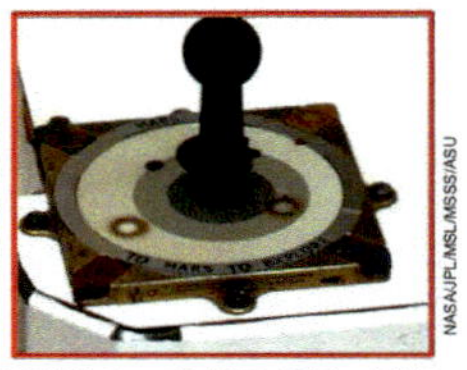

JB-4

Figure 8.3 *Using Curiosity's Mast Camera to View Scene in 'Natural' Color.*
This image was captured on 17 October 2012. Image credit: NASA/JPL-Caltech/MSSS/ASU (2013a).

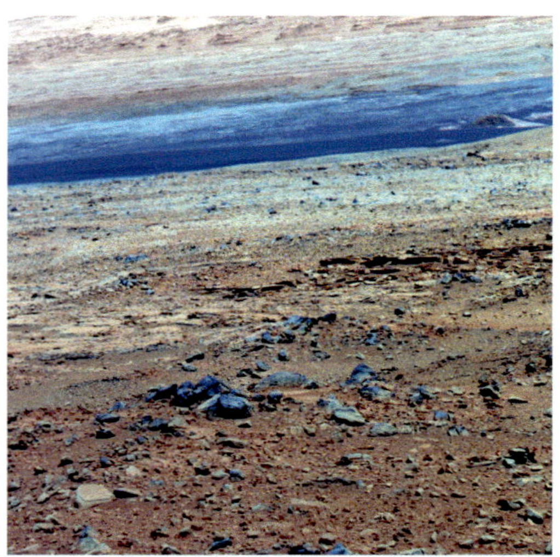

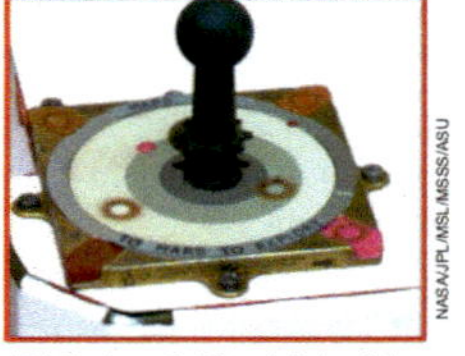

JB-5

Figure 8.4 *Using False Color from Curiosity's Mast Camera.*
This image was captured on 17 October 2012 (sol 71). This red–green–blue composite was generated from images captured using the MastCam's narrowband science filters at wavelengths of 751 nanometres, 527 nanometres and 445 nanometres. Image credit: NASA/JPL-Caltech/MSSS/ASU (2013b).

In *Seeing Like a Rover: How Robots, Teams, and Images Craft Knowledge of Mars* Janet Vertesi (2015) explains that there is a vital distinction between the true and false colour images that were produced during the *Spirit* and *Opportunity* missions. Here, true colour referred to a 'particular combination of filters that approximates the range and type of light sensitivity exemplified by the human eye' (Vertesi 2015: p. 80). By capturing the landscape through filters, images taken by the PanCam had the potential to provide 'information on the mineralogical composition of surface materials that supplement[ed] and complement[ed] data obtained by other MER instruments' (Bell et al. 2003: p. 3). 'False colour' imaging for MER referred to particular combinations of images taken through different filters to reveal colours to which the human eye is not sensitive, including near-infra-red, red and blue. *Curiosity*'s MastCam also has science filters which can be used to capture false-colour images of the Martian terrain (Figure 8.4) but predominantly the images are captured using visible wavelengths and are calibrated to produce 'natural' colour images. These colours can then be stretched during scientific work on Earth to make 'enhanced' colour images.

In order for visual imagers to work out the images on the ground (to create the 'natural' colour image) a calibration target is sent onboard each rover. The Caltarget consists of variously coloured materials and as scientists already know what these colours should look like, it acts as a known quantity and point of comparison against which colours in the image may be measured. In a sense, it becomes a home referent on Mars, enabling researchers to estimate what the landscape would look like if we stood there ourselves. The Caltarget is located on the rover deck, about a metre behind the mast, and the one on *Curiosity* is almost identical to the ones that were onboard the MERs. The sundial design allows scientists and engineers to work out the location of the sun and the base of the target consists of '7 spectrally distinct regions: 3 grayscale rings and 4 coloured chips', which are imaged by the cameras in order to 'derive accurate relative reflectance calibration for scenes of interest' (Kinch et al. 2013: p. 1; Bell et al. 2006: p. 2). When the MastCam images are downlinked to Earth they are processed through a calibration pipeline which was developed based on extensive pre-flight testing and using images of the Caltarget captured by *Curiosity* when it first landed on Mars. *The Martian Triptych*, then, is a product of numerous procedures and desired viewpoints. The data has been captured on Mars, bounced via radio signals to Earth, at which point it is calibrated and recalibrated as an image we can comprehend. The journey the image takes is one of great distance and multiple translations, its final resting place the screen of an office or home computer. The Caltarget essentially acts as an aid to help work out the level of calibration needed and exemplifies our desire to see, understand and negotiate the distance of space and time from our unique human perspective. With the aid of the Caltarget, Mars is brought into the terrestrial realm, into a human grasp.

Despite the inclusion of the home referent, Melissa Rice, Associate Professor of Planetary Science at Western Washington University, explains that because of the difference in the way colour images are produced for *Curiosity* and how they were produced for the MERs, our impression of the colours of Mars on each mission is different (Rice 2016). This is also reflected in the different terms used to describe the images: for the MERs they are 'approximate true colour', while for *Curiosity* they are 'natural colour'. This discrepancy between the rovers' visions of Mars is comparable on a more human-centred level to theories surrounding how individuals each perceive colour. In his 1953 *Philosophical Investigations*, Ludwig Wittgenstein writes:

> Look at the blue of the sky and say to yourself 'How blue the sky is!' – When you do it spontaneously – without philosophical intentions – the idea never crosses your mind that this impression of colour belongs only to *you*. And you have no hesitation in exclaiming that to someone else. And if you point at anything as you say the words you point at the sky. I am saying: you have not the feeling of pointing-into-yourself, which often accompanies 'naming the sensation' when one is thinking about 'private language'. (Wittgenstein [1953] 1958: p. 96)

Considering Wittgenstein's idea of a private language, it is quite logical that each of the Mars rovers has different perceptions of colour.

'False colour' on the MERs used a particular combination of filters to reveal information about the composition or mineralogy of rocks, soils and surface features; in addition, post-processing was used to draw out specific features of the Martian surface. Raw image data can be reconstructed into a variety of images, each presenting a different yet equally valuable vision of Mars. Principal Data Scientist at the Multi-Mission Image Processing Laboratory at JPL Bob Deen (2015) uses the example of an image captured by the *Opportunity* rover in 2004 (Figure 8.5) to explain how enhancing the colours of images can enable invisible vision:

> Enhanced colour intentionally exaggerates. 'Blueberries' on the *Opportunity* mission is an example – if you look at a properly calibrated

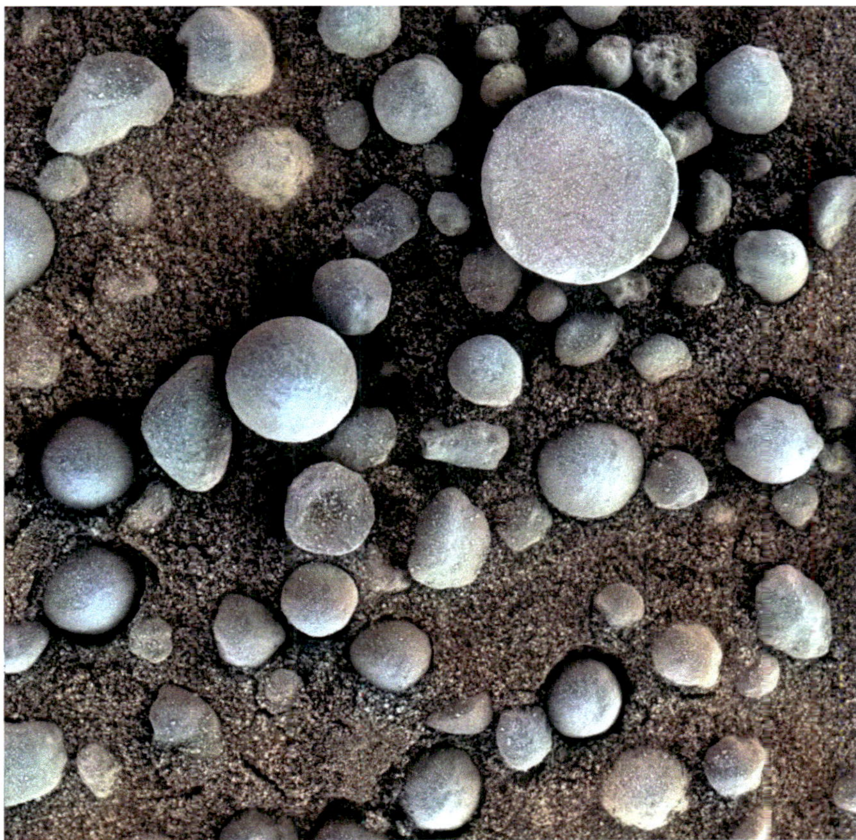

Figure 8.5 These small 'spherules' were captured by *Opportunity*'s microscopic imager with colour information added from the PanCam on 19 April 2004 (sol 84).
The area shown is 3 cm across. Image included in the NASA press release showing *Spirit* and *Opportunity* highlights, 27 January 2015. Image credit: NASA/JPL-Caltech/Cornell/USGS (2015).

> image these round structures aren't blue they are grey. But enhancing the colour makes them blue because there is nothing else blue in the scene [...] what it does is brings out the variations in colour which tells geologists that that area is bluer than that, and that's useful. It's hard to tell that because everything's covered in dust and so it's important to reveal. (Deen 2015)

Here, colour is manipulated in order to reveal useful information for making geological identifications. Janet Vertesi (2014) explains that 'this does not imply a change in the underlying dataset: only a change in visual orientation or aspect due to the combination of filtered images' (Vertesi 2014: p. 25). The practice of image manipulation allows 'objects and relationships which were initially invisible [to] become visible and palpable as a result of highly technical skills and complex instruments' (Lynch 1985: p. 37). In Mars missions, pictures are considered as part of the labour process, and the reconstruction of images using post-production allows the invisible to become visible through immersing oneself in the changing status of the image. It is through the recognition of difference within the process of repetition in *The Martian Triptych* that the glitch disrupts a 'true' perception of what the landscape looks like but also enables us to 'see' Mars differently. In *The Martian Triptych* the image morphs from one filtered view to the next, flickering between a representation of the visible and the invisible. The glitch as the perceptible colour shift viewed in the interchange can be seen as a method of becoming immersed in the landscape-as-image.

For Vertesi (2015), 'false colour' images are on par with 'true colour' when it comes to scientific value. It is often necessary to see 'different things in the same image', so filtering the image through various colours 'represent[s] different ways of seeing and knowing the Martian surface' (Vertesi 2015: p. 78). Vertesi uses the analogy of the duck–rabbit gestalt drawing, likening it to the extrication of numerous datasets from the same image. What occurs in the gestalt flip of the duck–rabbit also occurs by pulling out various colours in Deen's Martian 'blueberries' example, producing different observations by altering the colour balance of the image. Vertesi draws on Wittgenstein's concept of 'seeing as' to demonstrate how it is possible to see different things within the same image. In the duck–rabbit example we at first might see a duck, and then a rabbit, or vice versa. These perceptual shifts are what Wittgenstein calls 'noticing an aspect', and this might also be applied to experiencing a painting or photographic image (Wittgenstein [1953] 1958: p. 193). On one level we see it as representing an object or landscape; on another we see it as paint on canvas or ink on paper. But whereas our interchanging perception of the duck–rabbit alters within our brains through a period of prolonged engagement with the image, scientists working with Martian data manually apply filters to change their perception of the landscape. Vertesi terms this form of image manipulation 'drawing as'; in order to gain different visual experiences, the scientist must 'draw' the image as one thing or another. She argues that the scientific image may only gain 'analysability if it can present its relevant features to analysis', which is to say that 'it can only be recognisable if it has been *drawn as* something recognisable: a presentation of a particular kind of object, or an object with particular features' (Vertesi

2014: p. 18).[6] But whereas Galileo drew the Moon using his own vision and a pencil on paper, *drawing as* for Vertesi means reconstructing images and image data: here, '"drawing" can mean to pull or guide, to reveal or conceal, to work with and around material objects, to produce new configurations of space or movement' (Vertesi 2014: p. 20). Revealing new ways of seeing the same image in order to achieve scientific goals, Vertesi proposes *drawing as* not as a philosophical concept but as a practical one.

In *The Martian Triptych* the raw representational data of Mount Sharp does not inherently change, but our perception of it does. With the duck–rabbit drawing it is impossible to perceive both the duck and the rabbit at once: it is constantly shifting, from one to the other, depending on how we choose to look at it. In *The Martian Triptych*, it is not a case of how we choose to focus our eyes but more of a case of where we choose to look (at this image or the next). Everything is presented at once, together, in a triptych that makes palpable the shifting and unfolding status of the image within scientific discourse. Through the process of repetition, of reworking images and disrupting the relationship between the camera's vision (represented in the 'raw' image) and the 'natural' and 'white balanced' iterations, Mount Sharp is 'drawn' as something perceivable for both a viewer looking at this scene on Mars, and then under Earth-light. The white-balanced image of Mount Sharp has been manipulated by humans, for humans, as a means to understand the Martian terrain through an Earthly gaze. Our expectations of how Mars should look is perpetuated through the calibration of images and once we have an idea of what Mars looks like (its hazy pink sky and dusty terrain) it would be difficult to see it another way. Perhaps, then, we need such images as *The Martian Triptych* in order to destabilise our understanding – without the previous two iterations of Mount Sharp we might easily be tricked into believing that the white-balanced version is a place on Earth.

Scientists attempt to gain clarity by performing image manipulation in order to see and reveal different things; the disruption to the order of the single image – as exemplified so explicitly in *The Martian Triptych* – embodies the notion of the glitch-as-method. The images inevitably stray from what our eyes might see (this is part of the glitch) but they do so in a scientifically beneficial way (as a

---

6   Vertesi exemplifies this through Galileo's use of chiaroscuro in drawing his image of the moon; the craters and mountainous features were only distinguishable as such because of the skill of Galileo's hand, whose representational techniques conformed to those already in existence (Vertesi 2014: p. 21).

method of revealing). The colour filters upon *The Martian Triptych* are like language, drawing out specific aspects of the landscape for the viewer's attention. The scientists and engineers working with such images must know what to look for, and how to 'see'. *Seeing as* and therefore *drawing as* require a certain amount of imagination in order to function. Wittgenstein uses the example of a simple line drawing of a triangle to exemplify this:

> This triangle ◿ can be seen as a triangular hole, as a solid, as a geometrical drawing, as standing on its base, as hanging from its apex; as a mountain, as a wedge, as an arrow or pointer, as an overturned object which is meant to stand on the shorter side of the right angle, as a half parallelogram, and as various other things. You can think now of *this* now of *this* as you look at it, can regard it now as *this* now as *this,* and then you will see it now *this* way, now *this.* (Wittgenstein [1953] 1958: p. 200)

Our interpretation of what the triangle stands to represent relies heavily upon the text that is supplied alongside it. The flexibility to be able to 'see the illustration now as one thing now as another' means that we 'see it as we *interpret* it' (Wittgenstein [1953] 1958: pp. 193–4). Wittgenstein continues:

> It is possible to take the duck–rabbit simply for the picture of a rabbit [...] but not to take the bare triangular figure for the picture of an object that has fallen over. To see this aspect of the triangle demands *imagination.* (Wittgenstein [1953] 1958: p. 207)

Being able to see different features in the Martian terrain requires a level of imagination, one that is trained upon the act of revealing. The scientist or visual imager must know *how* to reveal information invisible in the raw data image, but they must also have an awareness of what *might* be present in order to perform the right kinds of manipulations.

It is through a certain training that scientists and engineers are able to make sense of Mars through such images. Contrary to philosopher and cultural theorist Guy Debord's (1983) view that cinema-goers (and by extension viewers of all kinds of image-based entertainment) are ignorant spectators, philosopher Jacques Rancière (2011) argues that the spectator is not passive but instead enters into a space whereby their subjectivity affects the reading of the image. Rancière's critique of Debord's that 'viewing is the opposite of knowing' serves to argue that 'ignorance is not a lesser form of knowledge, but the opposite of knowledge; that knowledge is not a collection of knowledge, but a position' (Rancière 2011: pp. 2–3, 9). For Rancière, then, the spectator is active in their interpretation of the image:

> Emancipation begins when we challenge the opposition between viewing and acting; when we understand that the self-evident facts that structure the relations between saying, seeing and doing them- selves belong to the structure of domination and subjection The spectator also acts, like the pupil or scholar. She observes, selects, compares, interprets. She links what she sees to a host of other things that she has seen on other stages, in other kinds of place. (Rancière 2011: p. 13)

As this is a landscape without referent, spectatorship is the only means by which we might experience Mars. In order to make the informed transition from seeing to understanding, objective and subjective levels of engagement with images from a range of special- ists are key to obtaining scientific knowledge and figuring out how best to navigate the terrain. The images can tell more than what they show, but this requires knowing exactly how to look at them. In this sense, scientists and engineers working on Mars rover missions are trained as professional lookers. They have an educated and intuitive understanding about how these images should be read and how to reveal more information to help them with the task at hand. Here it is not just a question of what the image does (what we see at face value) but what the viewer brings to the looking experience. What we have here is not the passive viewer that Guy Debord described but Rancière's emancipated spectator in which their subjectivity directly influences their reading of the image (Rancière 2011: pp. 6–7)

As with Eadweard Muybridge's studies on motion, the cameras on *Curiosity* see more than the eye. In this way, the Martian terrain can be seen as and for a number of things: as a cliff face or mountain, as composed of different soils, or for its atmospheric make-up. We can also see it as a picture or as numbers. Using the glitch as a method, scientists become professional lookers and immersion lies in the subjective manipulation of images to reveal the invisible.

The Mars rover is our surrogate, an extension of our vision, albeit a robotic one. In no other field of extra-terrestrial exploration has there been such a focus on attempting to surpass the screen-as-window, to increase immersion and transport the viewer, virtually, to this alien world. Yet despite what the vast mega-pixel panoramic images being returned by the *Curiosity* rover show us of this environment, this is a landscape that remains totally out of reach, millions of miles away. This distance is an impenetrable boundary – both physically and metaphorically – that imaging and sensing technologies are trying to break. In the case of *The Martian Triptych* the viewer must actively engage with the changing status of the image in order to glean greater truth from a representation that depicts a referent that is at its very core separate, distant, existing only within appearance. For the viewer of *The Martian Triptych*, looking, manipulation and engagement occur on the surface of the image.

I see as the rover, I am the rover, its eyes an extension of my own. Together we conjure up a multiplicity of vision, imperfect and weighed down by data. The desire for knowledge infiltrating and fracturing a seamless window, a single unencumbered and authoritative vision.

The precise, unfiltered rover vision appears oddly hazy; a film of dust rests atop these eyes. It is a vision different from my own, embedded with algorithmic intelligence, a sense of its skeletal frame's embodiment in the landscape. Wiping clean the image, exposing the richness of the colours of Mount Sharp I start to see with greater clarity. Sinking into the welcoming embrace of folded hues....

But not for long. Bleached, washed and rung out by an Earthly lens, shadows strengthen, highlights gleam, the blue haze of distant terrain suddenly cold and uninviting. Succumbing to a processing and re-processing of Mars, image, and vision I am thrown from the dusty terrain and into an encircling clean-up operation, an obliteration of all things Martian. The washed-out grains of sand becoming white noise, their tiny abrasive vibrations like grit in my eyes. The ocular affront accompanied by a metallic ringing in my ears.

References

Alexander, D., Crisp, J., Cervantes, A., Allbaugh, A., Maki, J., Blaney D., Delapp, D., Morgan, T., Arvidson, R. and Lavoie, S. (2015) 'Camera & LIBS Experiment Data Record RDR Data Products', in *Mars Science Laboratory (MSL) Software Interface Specification* (online), pp. 1–428. Available at http://pds-imaging.jpl.nasa.gov/data/msl/MSLNAV_0XXX/DOCUMENT/MSL_CAMERA_SIS_latest.PDF (accessed 2 September 2015).

Barthes, R. [1981] (2000) *Camera Lucida: Reflections on Photography* (trans. R. Howard). London: Vintage.

Bell III, J. F., Joseph, J., Sohl-Dickstein, J. N., Arneson, H. M., Johnson, M. J., Lemmon, M. T. and Savransky, D. (2006) 'In-Flight Calibration and Performance of the Mars Exploration Rover Panoramic Camera (Pancam) Instruments', *Journal of Geophysical Research: Planets* 3: 1–38. Available at http://dx.doi.org/10.1029/2005JE002444 (accessed 20 July 2016).

Bell III, J. F., Squyres, S. W., Herkenhoff, K. E., Maki, J. N., Arneson, H. M., Brown, D., Collins, S. A., Dingizian, A., Elliot, S. T., Hagerott, E. C., Hayes, A. G., Johnson, M. J., Johnson, J. R., Joseph, J., Kinch, K., Lemmon, M. T., Morris, R. V., Scherr,

L., Schwochert, M., Shepard, M. K., Smith, G. H., Sohl-Dickstein, J. N., Sullivan, R. J., Sullivan, W. T. and Wadsworth, M. (2003) 'Mars Exploration Rover Athena Panoramic Camera (Pancam) Investigation', *Journal of Geophysical Research* 108, E12 (8063): 1–30. Available at http://dx.doi.org/10.1029/2003JE002070 (accessed 21 October 2015).

Benjamin, W. [1935] (2008) *The Work of Art in the Age of Its Technological Reproducibility, and Other Writings on Media* (eds M. W. Jennings, B. Doherty and T. Y. Levin; trans. E. Jephcott, R. Livingstone and H. Eiland). Cambridge, MA: Belknap Press of Harvard University.

Clancey, W. (2012) *Working on Mars: Voyages of Scientific Discovery with the Mars Exploration Rovers.* Cambridge, MA: MIT Press.

Coopmans, C., Lynch, M., Vertesi, J. and Woolgar, S. (eds) (2014) *Representation in Scientific Practice Revisited.* Cambridge, MA: MIT Press.

Debord, G. (1983) *Society of the Spectacle.* Detroit: Black and Red.

Deen, B. (2015) Interview with Luci Eldridge. 3 November, Pasadena, CA.

Helmreich, S. (2009) 'Intimate Sensing', in Turkle, S. (ed.), *Simulation and Its Discontents.* Cambridge, MA: MIT Press, pp. 129–50.

Kinch., K. M., Morton, B. M., Bell, J. F., Johnson, J. R., Goertz, W. and the MSL Science Team (2013) 'Dust on the Curiosity Mast Camera Calibration Target', in *44th Lunar and Planetary Science Conference, vol. 1*, pp. 1–2. Available at http://www.lpi.usra.edu/meetings/lpsc2013/pdf/1061.pdf (accessed 26 July 2016).

Lynch, M. (1985) 'Discipline and the Material Form of Images: An Analysis of Scientific Visibility', *Social Studies of Science* (online) 15(1): 37–66. Available at http://dx.doi.org/10.1177/030631285015001002 (accessed 22 January 2015).

Menkman, R. (2011) *The Glitch Moment(um).* Amsterdam: Institute of Network Cultures.

Merleau-Ponty, M. (1964) *The Primacy of Perception* (trans. J. M. Edie). Illinois: Northwestern University Press.

NASA/Jet Propulsion Laboratory (2013) '"Raw", "Natural" and "White-Balanced" Views of Martian Terrain'. Mars Science Laboratory Curiosity Rover. Available at http://mars.jpl.nasa.gov/msl/multimedia/images/?ImageID=5148 (accessed 10 January 2015).

NASA/JPL-Caltech/MSSS/ASU (2013a) 'Using Curiosity's Mast Camera to View Scene in "Natural" Color'. Photojournal. Available at http://photojournal.jpl.nasa.gov/catalog/PIA16801 (accessed 30 June 2015).

NASA/JPL-Caltech/MSSS/ASU (2013b) 'Using False Color from Curiosity's Mast Camera'. Photojournal. Available at: http://photojournal.jpl.nasa.gov/catalog/PIA16802 (accessed 30 June 2015).

NASA/JPL-Caltech/Cornell/USGS (2015) 'Martian "Blueberries"'. NASA Mars Exploration: Spirit & Opportunity Highlights. Available at http://mars.nasa.gov/mer10/multimedia/images/?ImageID=6944 (accessed 3 December 2015).

NASA, ESA, G. Dubner (IAFE, CONICET-University of Buenos Aires) et al.; A. Loll et al.; T. Temim et al.; F. Seward et al.; VLA/NRAO/AUI/NSF; Chandra/CXC; Spitzer/JPL-Caltech; XMM-Newton/ESA; and Hubble/STScI (2017) 'Crab Nebula from Five Observatories'. Available at https://www.jpl.nasa.gov/images/crab-nebula-from-five-observatories (accessed 15 September 2020).

Rancière, J. (2011) *The Emancipated Spectator* (trans. G. Elliott). London: Verso.

Rice, M. (2016) Email correspondence with Luci Eldridge, 20 July.

Rip, A. and Ruivenkam, M. (2014) 'Nanoimages as Hybrid Monsters', in Coopmans, C., Lynch, M., Vertesi, J. and Woolgar, S. (eds), *Representation in Scientific Practice Revisited.* Cambridge, MA: MIT Press, pp. 177–200.

Scharf, A. (1962) 'Painting, Photography, and the Image of Movement', *Burlington Magazine* 104(710): 186–95. Available at http://www.jstor.org/stable/pdfplus/873665.pdf (accessed 20 October 2016).

Vertesi, J. (2014) '*Drawing as:* Distinctions and Disambiguation in Digital Images of Mars', in Coopmans, C., Lynch, M., Vertesi, J. and Woolgar, S. (eds),

Representation in Scientific Practice Revisited. Cambridge, MA: MIT Press, pp. 15–35.

Vertesi, J. (2015) *Seeing Like a Rover: How Robots, Teams and Images Craft Knowledge of Mars.* Chicago: University of Chicago Press.

Wittgenstein, L. [1953] (1958) *Philosophical Investigations* (trans. G. E. M. Anscombe). Oxford: Basil Blackwell.

Wright, J. R. (2015) Interview with Luci Eldridge, 2 November, Pasadena, CA.

9　The Overview Effect

Brian Black

Figure 9.1 User interaction with *The Overview Effect.*
Image credit: Samual Philpott.

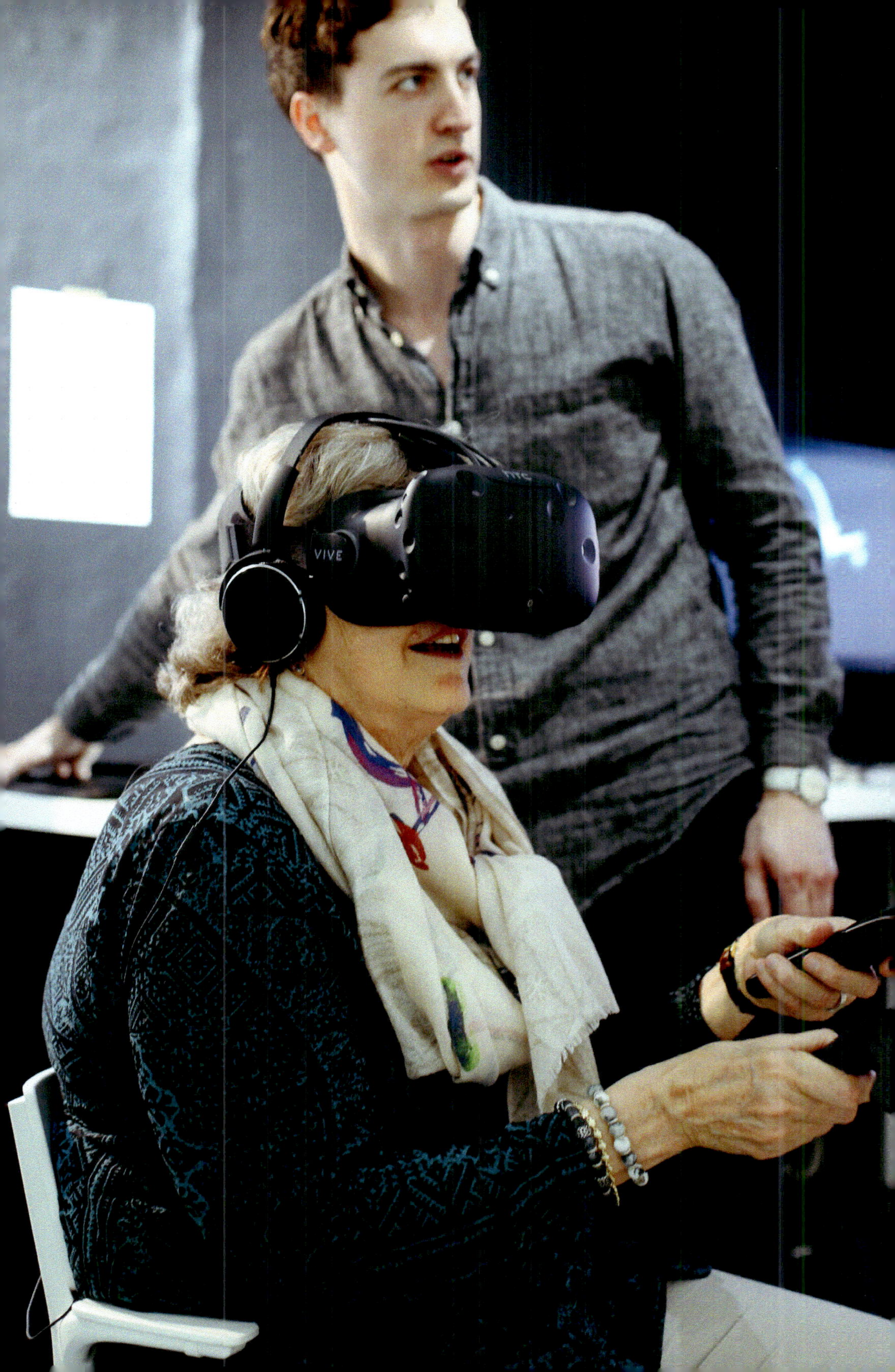

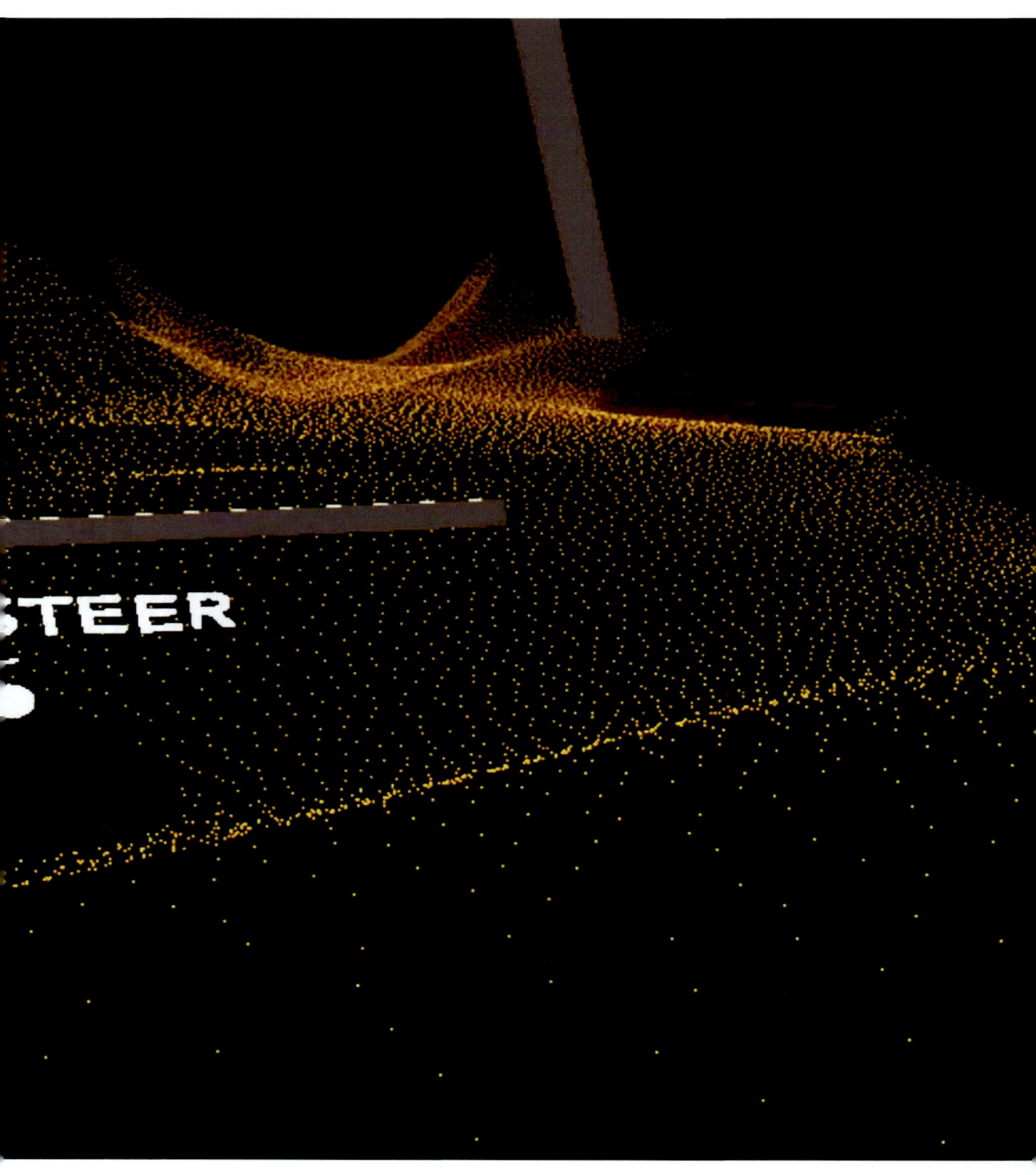

Figure 9.2 Screen capture from virtual environment showing what users of the tool see upon donning the headset.
Image credit: Brian Black.

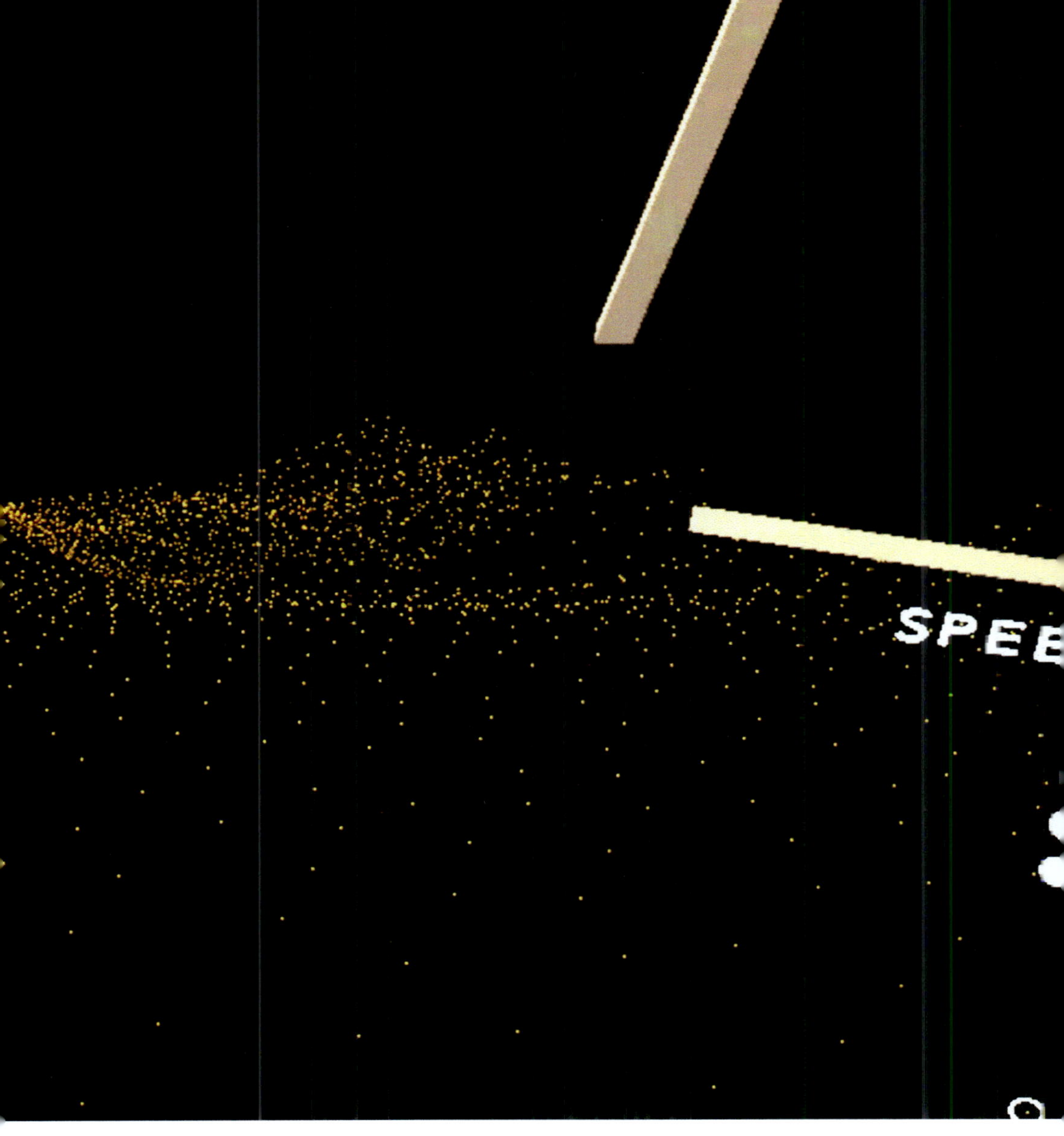

SPEE

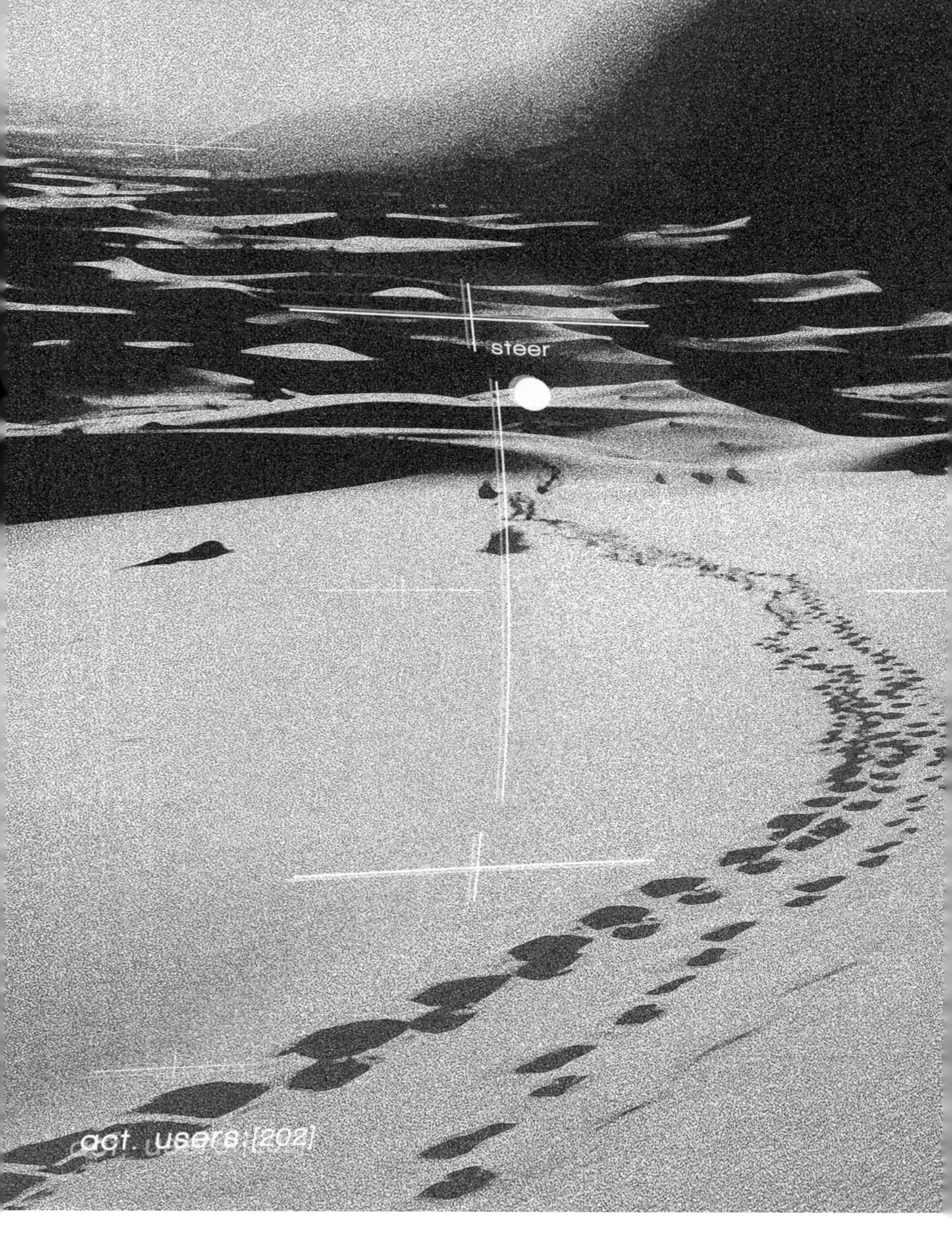

Figure 9.3 Screen capture from the VR simulation developed by Black to show users what it might be like to traverse the surface of Saturn's moon Titan. Image credit: Brian Black.

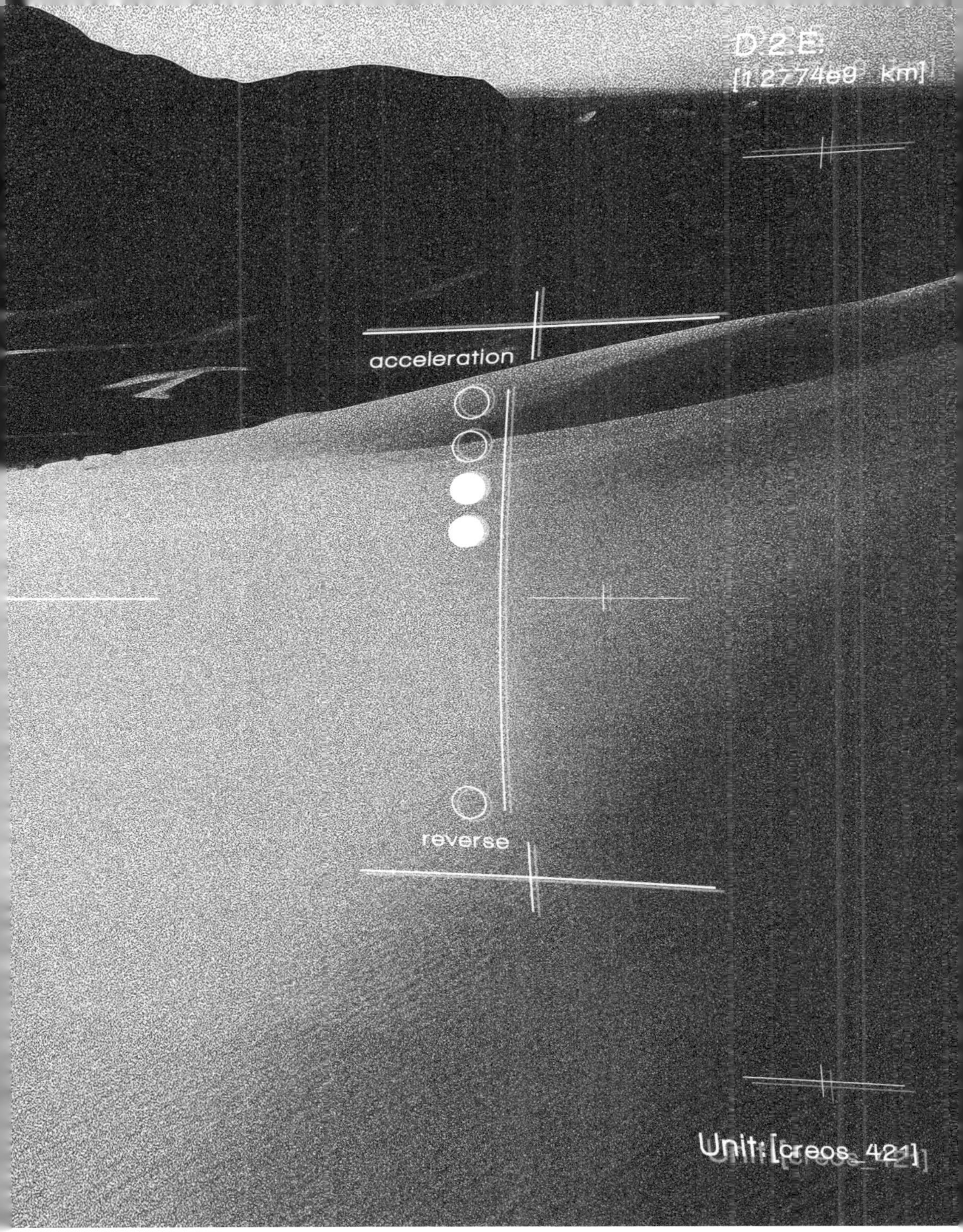

D 2 E
[127740 km]
acceleration
reverse
Unit:[creos_421]

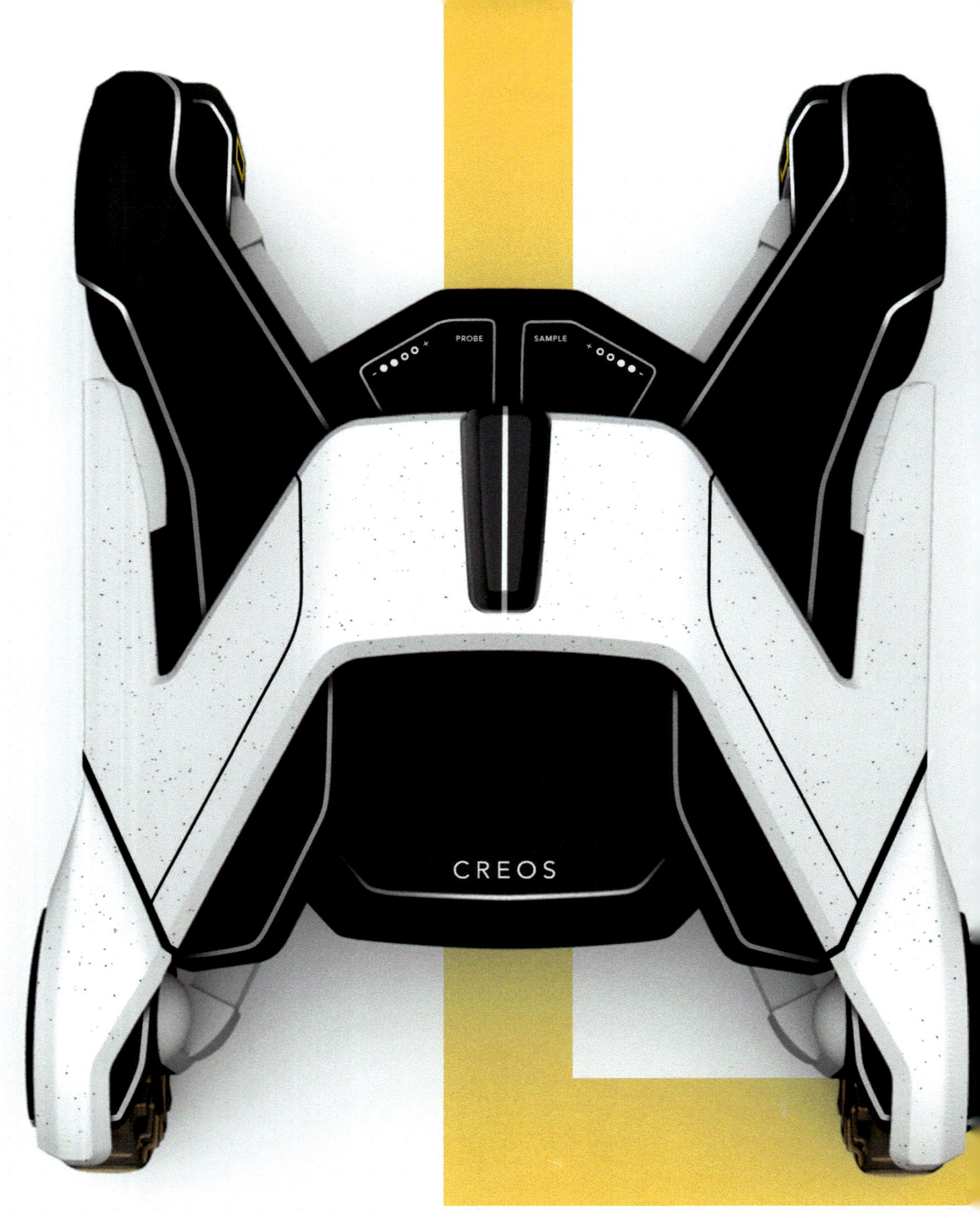
PROBE
SAMPLE
CREOS

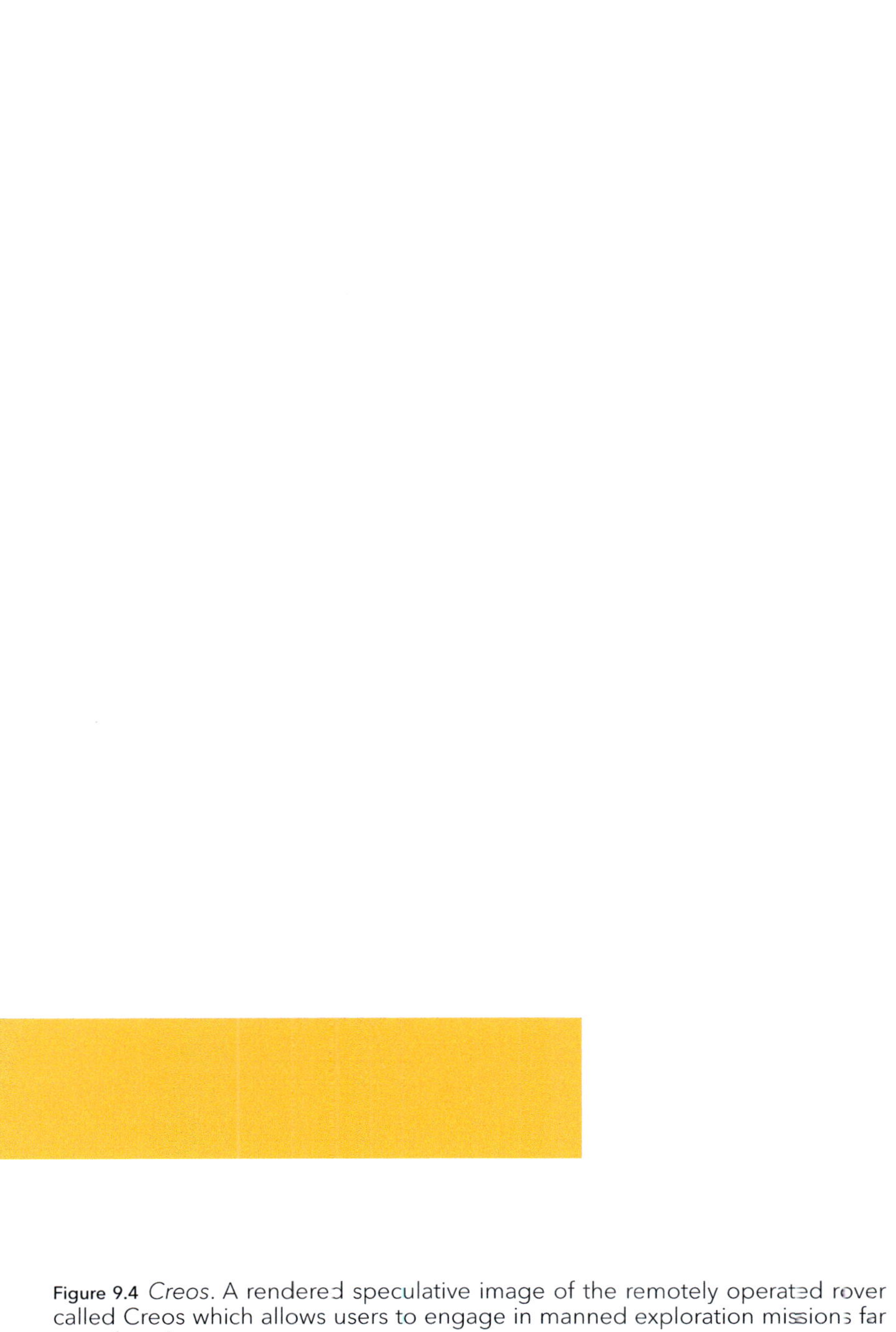

Figure 9.4 *Creos*. A rendered speculative image of the remotely operated rover called Creos which allows users to engage in manned exploration missions far away from home.
Image credit: Brian Black.

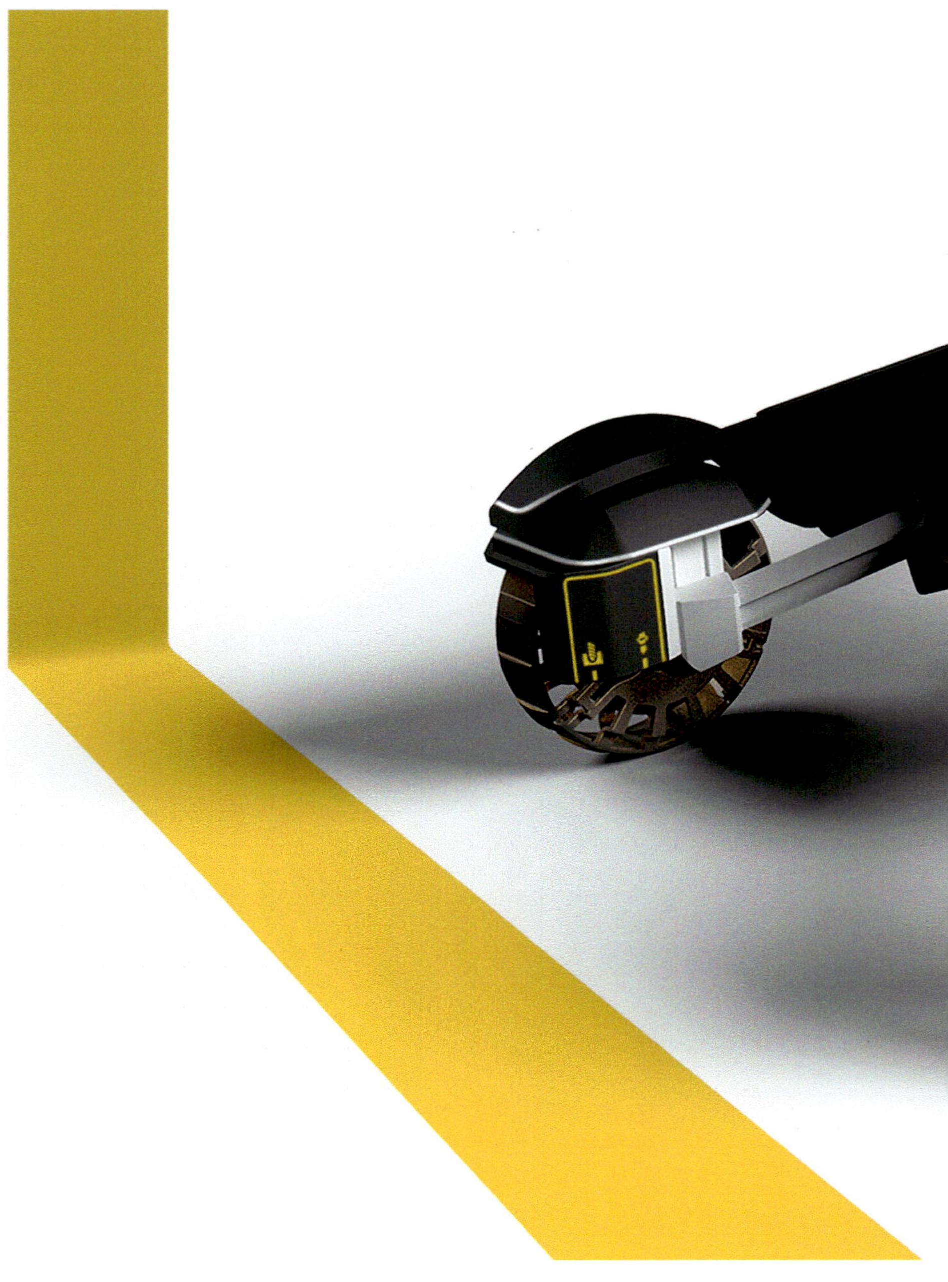

Figure 9.5 *Sonar*. Creos carries a suite of sensors to connect its users to the environment it is travelling through and allow them to feel like they are actually there. Image credit: Brian Black.

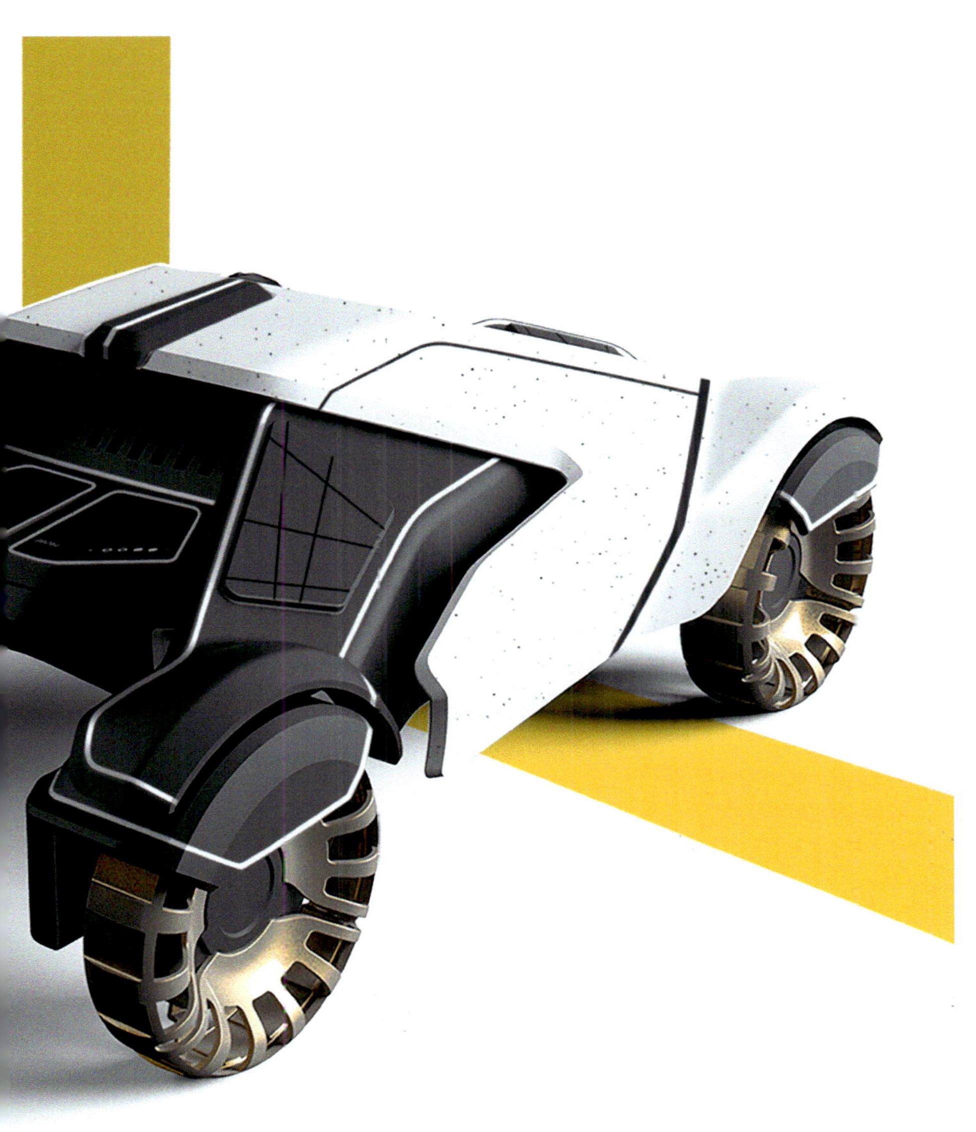

The Overview Effect

Brian Black

Interactive virtual reality experience concept shown on HTC Vive, 2017

This speculative project was inspired by vehicle designer Brian Black's fascination with space exploration, and impacted by the increasing xenophobic behaviour observed among communities and politicians around the world. A weakening in global empathy has occurred and individuals more and more exist inside echo-chambers of fear and intolerance. The resulting symptoms risk destroying the public's ability to understand the philosophical or long-term meaning behind costly and seemingly unimportant initiatives such as manned space exploration. *The Overview Effect* is not intended to be a replacement for human space exploration but, rather, a way to empower space agencies and engage the public. Some could argue that much of the struggle NASA faces with its budget has to do with its ability to advertise and demonstrate what it is doing in an engaging and exciting way. It is one thing to read about the accomplishments from NASA or ESA in the news, but something completely different if you could be placed inside the mission and allowed to experience, interact and contribute to a portion of it.

The Overview Effect is set in a near future where manned space exploration has blossomed and missions to our moon, Mars, and beyond have become feasible and commonplace. The concept imagines that a network of access terminals has been installed at museums and universities around the globe which allow the public to view and participate in manned inter-planetary missions alongside the on-site astronauts. The users of these systems are transported to far-off worlds as they take control of one of many unmanned rovers using virtual reality. To overcome the time delay of remotely operating robots millions of miles away, the concept imagines its users operating the device in a pre-scanned virtual representation of the actual environment. Actions and feedback happen 'in real time' from the user's perspective, while the inputs are sent to a centralised control system to coordinate with other users and apply safeguards for the rovers. The actions are then sent to the rover, with the real feedback later being transmitted back as a confirmation of its actions. An important aspect of this concept is its immersive element. Stereo-scopic cameras, binaural microphone technology and synchronised stimulus of the limbic system allow operators to see, hear and feel as the rover. The vehicles are equipped with a multitude of scientific instruments and participants are granted the ability to contribute to ongoing studies conducted by the astronauts through mapping, sample collection and seismic data gathering.

The phrase 'overview effect' was borrowed for this project from author Frank White, one of the first to publish writings describing the cognitive shift in awareness many astronauts report after their first encounter seeing Earth as a whole from outer space (Overview Institute 2022). The phenomenon marks a fundamental change in their perception of the Earth, humanity, and how they themselves relate to it. The overview effect has been described as both spiritual and secular, depending on the individual. One thing, however, is constant: all report a similar realisation of the fragility and oneness that exists for our species and the planet we inhabit. Black's goal with this project is to explore how one could capture a similar mental shift to engage the public and increase their understanding of the long-term impact of costly manned space exploration projects.

In a near future where manned missions to Mars and beyond become feasible and common, how do space agencies share their accomplishments and engage with the public? *The Overview Effect* is an experience concept designed to increase public understanding by allowing users to remotely operate unmanned rovers on other worlds using a virtual reality interface. The intention is to provide the public with a more visceral and meaningful experience in hopes this will elicit a greater understanding for the intention behind manned space exploration, and our place in the universe.

—

Black is currently a design manager at Volvo Cars, in the strategic and brand design team, working across car programmes to formulate and execute longer-term product strategies while also building the tools their designers use to make sure their portfolio of cars is ever more customer-centric and sustainable. They are also a main connecting point for design to the broader Volvo cars business (marketing, product planning, customer experience) as well as facilitators of longer-term external brand collaborations.

Reference

Overview Institute (2022) 'Frank Wright'. Available at https://overviewinstitute.org/dt_team/frank-white (accessed 6 June 2022).

Shaping

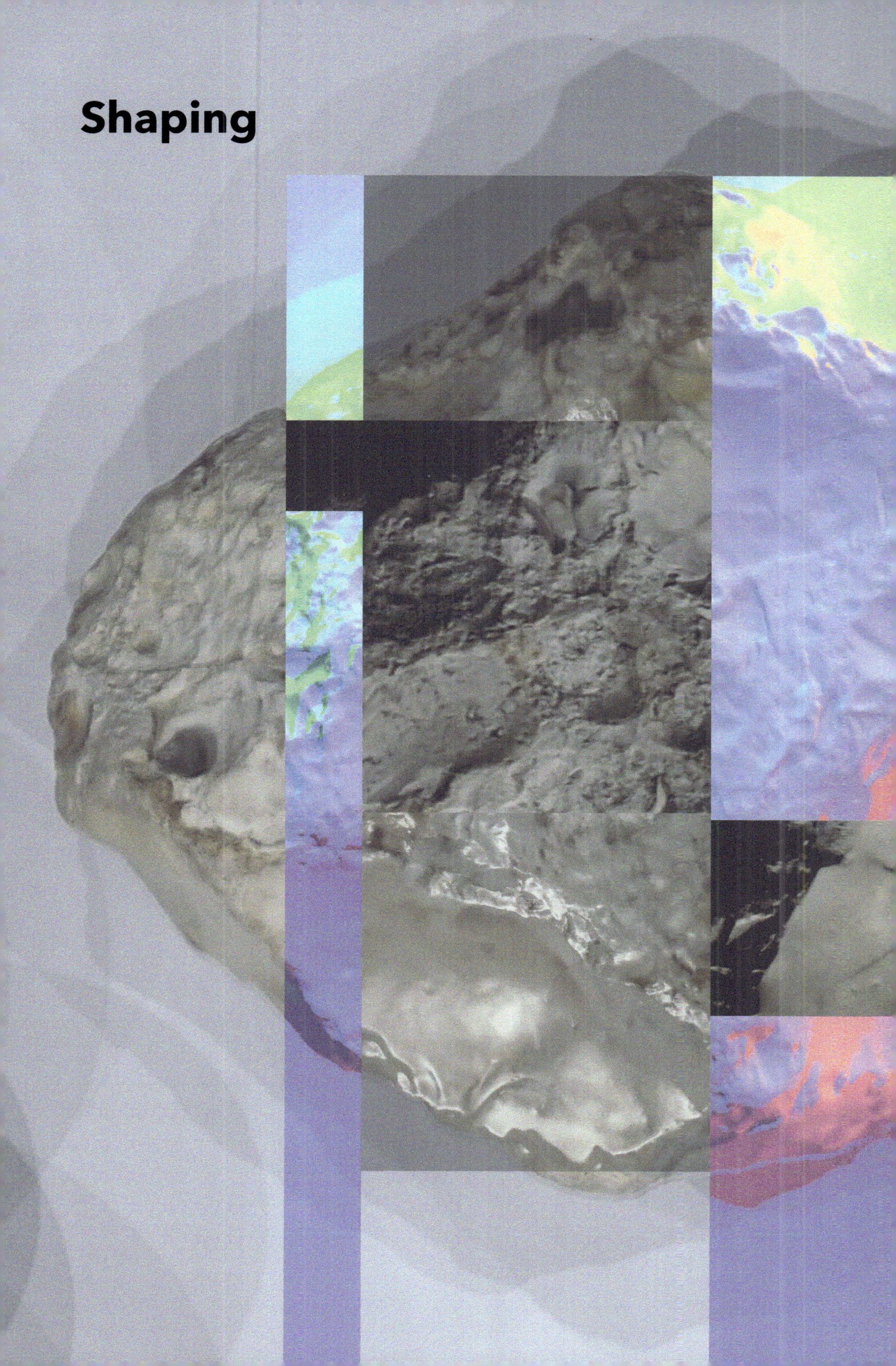

10 Robotic Presences: Encounters with Artificial Social Companionship and Embodied Representation

Bianca Westermann

The Cultural Conception of Robots

Robots have been part of our culture for almost 100 years.[1] The word, as well as the idea of a tireless artificial worker, was created in the humanistic drama *R.U.R. – Rossum's Universal Robots* (*R.U.R. – Rossumovi Univerzální Roboti*, 1920/1) by Czech writer Karel Čapek. Only a few years after the fictional figure was born, the first precursors of industrial robots became a reality (cf. Ichbiah 2005 p. 207; Nocks 2008: p. 59f; Rosheim 1994: p. 70; von Randow 1998: p. 10). As a result, the common understanding of robots has since been formulated through a combination of fictional representations in film and literature, and industrial machines. What is important to note is that neither has directly been present in the average human's everyday life. This will change, with social robotics on the brink of becoming a common technology – that is, robots are not only now being designed for a human environment but are being designed to interact and communicate with humans on ever greater levels (cf. Bartneck and Forlizzi 2004). As robots increasingly start to populate everyday life, the question of human–robot interaction receives heightened attention. To avoid the highly charged question of whether or not social robots can be a meaningful replacement for social interactions, this chapter focuses on how encounters with artificial social machines can reshape our concept of presence and being present.

As noted, until recently real-life robots have been a special kind of machine few people came into contact with. For example, industrial robotics worked safely contained in factory buildings where their operating areas were separated and protected by sensors. If a human

---

1 For a pre-history of automata stretching back to ancient Greece see Riskin (2016).

entered that security zone any action was immediately shut down, to avoid accidents. Of course, in the meantime, a broad variety of robots have been populating the science-fiction genre. Robots have always been, in terms of a cultural concept, a distorted mirror of the human that does not strive for mere comparability to the human but threatens to (partially) overcome the human: being stronger and more intelligent are the most prominent attributes (see a detailed discussion in Westermann 2012). As a result, these fictional adaptations of the robotic theme have always discussed the impact robots might have on society and everyday life. Alongside dystopian stories depicting a war between humans and (intelligent) machines that originated from fear of machines subduing humans – the most prominent example movie being *The Matrix* (1999) as well as the *Terminator* films (1984–2019) and the more recent television series *Westworld* (since 2016) – there are diversified plots that posit the question of how more (seemingly) friendly robot–human encounters may change our everyday life as well as discuss the social status of (fictional) robots – like *The Bicentennial Man* (1999), *Her* (2013), *RoboCop* (1987/2014) or *Ex Machina* (2015), to name a few.

Regarding robots as a cultural concept, this tension between the reality of robotics and a fictional examination is being challenged anew with social robots on the brink of becoming an everyday reality. Social robots augur to become part of society's everyday life; they promise to live with us, as well as to directly collaborate with us at work. This entering of robots into the human sphere is the turning point between what we have come to know as 'robotics' and 'social robotics'. The new promise of the social robot is that there will no longer be a clear separation between human and robotic areas of action. Lawnmower and vacuum-cleaner robots have already become a widespread technology in the human home; their promise is to be followed by much more sophisticated robots in the tangible future.

Of course, this development has produced concern, specifically in fields like care work and autonomous driving. The common point of quite a few critics (Turkle 2011 or Sparrow 2015 for example) is a fear that the user will misinterpret the machine's responsiveness for real social interaction. From a media scholar's point of view, this chapter is based on a different assumption that offers a new perspective: the core point to this view on human and robot interactions is that something similar to how Samuel Taylor Coleridge's willing suspension of disbelief has shaped the usage rather than presuming that the majority of users are misreading these encounters. This means that for human–robot interaction, although the *gestus* of human–human interaction is transferred to human–robot interaction, the fact that robots are machines is not automatically completely lost but marginalised due to advantages in usability.

This approach takes the computer literacy most users have into account. Social robots, like mobile media, trace back to computer technologies. The development of computers from calculating machines to media machines was accompanied by an increasing opacity of computers' technical nature (e.g. in the invention and spread of graphical user interfaces to the point of tablets, which can be understood as the transformation of computers into screens). This development, one might argue, was the beginning of society's need to somewhat socialise technology as well as its range of capabilities and the area of application grew simultaneously: smartphones, for example, not only offer a welcoming start screen like computers but, based on our daily routines, suggest the best route to work or inform their users of today's weather even without being asked. Computer technology developments in terms of input devices like speech recognition software (e.g. Microsoft's Cortana or Apple's Siri) make it easier to anthropomorphise technology. However, that does not mean the average user is not aware s/he is asking a phone for the weather forecast or petting a robotic cat or seal for comfort (or to be entertained by their pet-like artificial behaviour). Applying the same behavioural routines as in human–human or human–animal interactions is, then, just the most intuitive and, therefore, familiar way to use technology, to which the user willingly complies. Of course, there is still room for misreading these human–robot interactions and misperceiving them as real social interactions. But rather than assuming most users cannot differentiate between the living and the technological, this proposition presumes most users willingly engage in this illusion. Therefore, these interactions can be described as para-social, to underline that these are, in fact, a reference to social interactions but are in no way to be mistaken as such.[2]

The potential functionalities social robots offer might raise the idea that we are on the verge of a machine generation that superficially could no longer be described as trivial machines in the sense of Heinz von Foerster. According to von Foerster, a machine is trivial if the given input predicts the output, while in order to be non-trivial, it has to be impossible to predict the output based on the given input (cf. von Foerster 1992: p. 62ff.). Of course, this perspective is not

---

<ol start="2">
<li>It is important to note that the usage here of the term 'para-social' does not reference the 1950s concept that was coined to describe the relationship between TV personas and their viewers (cf. Horton and Wohl 1956).</li>
</ol>

aimed at the actual technical design, which is still based on a trace-able correlation between the robot's programming and behaviour, but at the possible ways to understand this behaviour while perceiving the robot as a black box. In other words, to grasp the complexity of social robots in terms of machinery, one needs an advanced understanding of technology or robotics; as only experts are capable of doing so, a common ground to comprehend their complexity and agency has always been a comparison to the human. The reason for this analogy is that robots, real as well as fictional ones, have always been programmed to perform human tasks, be they tasks they could do better than humans (in terms of accuracy and endurance) or tasks that would be too dangerous for humans. Therefore, humans have always been a compelling reference, and robots have always been machines that mimic humanness.

For these reasons, robots have always been open to certain attributions an observer might make to the machine when encountering it. Their connection to the human as a biased analogy is why robots have been so regularly featured in science fiction. They can be understood as an ambivalent cultural concept that questions the status of the human. However, with social robotics on the brink of entering everyday life, their seeming autonomy and their apparently techno-social potential for a certain degree of decision-making prompts the question of their potential responsibility for their actions.[3] It becomes apparent that their entering into the social sphere takes place on two levels: a spatial level as well as a social one. Entering the human sphere, the assignments robots promise to be tasked with include not only household chores like vacuum cleaning, which could still be understood as a compulsory service, but more social tasks, such as being present or offering companionship. A transformation of the interface accompanies this shift. Pressing buttons or programming commands is more and more replaced by natural-language interfaces. Taking the real and potential capabilities of social robots into account, the cultural connotation of the para-social interactions social robots offer becomes intelligible. This transition lays the foundation for social robots no longer to be considered tools but rather to become more and more artificial companions that seem to simulate presence. Their social standing can therefore be anticipated as oscillating between being social surrogates and alternative companions that most users consciously

---

3   In fact, from a humanist approach, one interesting, continuative question concerns how these robots reshape our concepts of intelligence, autonomy and the social.

accept in terms of a para-social willing suspension of disbelief not to fulfil a social desire but to benefit from technological functionalities these machines offer (that sometimes can easily be reduced to the charm of a new interface for known functions).

Therefore, this chapter suggests an analysis of social robots as media machines. One can argue about whether or not computers, and subsequent social robots, do or do not inhabit media qualities on their own, but this chapter aims to follow the assumption that they do. Analysing robots as a form of media offers two main insights. First, it allows us to consider how human and machine notions mutually are shaped to influence a robot's design and capabilities. Second, the transfer of agency onto the machine becomes traceable not as an empowerment of the machine but as an expression of particular needs and amenities society has. This chapter places importance on analysing social robots as a medium of presence. Central to this analysis will be two examples: the 'adorable home robot' Kuri, produced by Mayfield Robotics, that, despite being highly featured, never made it to the market; and Carl, a telepresence robot built by Orbis Robotics, who refer to it as an 'Avatar robot'.

What It Means to be Present

With their presence being central to the ways social machines might be understood, it is necessary to contextualise the notion of presence this chapter is based on. Hans Ulrich Gumbrecht has proposed a differentiation between cultures of meaning and cultures of presence. He locates the basis for his differentiation in distinct ways of acquiring the world. More intellectual ways of grasping one's world, like communication and interpretation, are associated with cultures of meaning, while more embodied ways to understand one's surroundings, like penetrating and consuming, are marking cultures of presence. Mysticism is, according to Gumbrecht, a mode of gaining access to the world that is balanced between meaning and presence: here, bodily presence can still be experienced, while this feeling is not directly linked to a physical presence. This contrast between cultures of meaning and cultures of presence is an ideal or typical one, as 'real' cultures always share both forms. The pressing question therefore becomes: How are the ratios of meaning and presence balanced?

Gumbrecht describes the Western culture as a culture of meaning with a fundamental longing for presence (cf. Gumbrecht 2012: p. 143; Gumbrecht 2004: p. 58):

> For us, presence phenomena always come as 'presence effects' because they are necessarily surrounded by, wrapped into, and perhaps even mediated by clouds and cushions of meaning. (Gumbrecht 2004: p. 105f.)

Gumbrecht's contradiction between meaning and presence is informed by a striving, maybe even a longing, for a more direct grasp of the world than the humanistic (in this case this means hermeneutic) interpretation can offer. As he does not approach the confrontation of meaning and presence as a simple antagonism, his aim is not to replace hermeneutics but to complement the approach in order to gain a much more complex grasp of the world. In other words, in exploring the dynamic tension between meaning and presence Gumbrecht 'ultimately argues for [...] a relation to the things of the world that could oscillate between presence effects and meaning effects' (Gumbrecht 2004: p. xv). His notion of presence is therefore quite literally informed by its Latin origin, *prae esse*, which means *being in front of* and therefore relates to a spatial (and special) proximity. In other words, presence requires not only materiality and sensory perception but also a specific spatiality and temporality: the here and now.

Focusing on the social presence or interaction that robots provide allows for avoidance of the judgemental question of whether or not social robots can be a meaningful replacement for social interactions. Analysing how the encounters with artificial social machines can reshape our concept of presence offers a far more sophisticated approach, rather than tapping into David Collingridge's dilemma, which states that the outcomes of technical developments are appreciable only to a certain degree, so that its effects have already hardened once a technology has taken hold (Collingridge 1982). This double-bind problem describes how society can be shaped by technological developments without being fully able to assess its consequences on society. Focusing on how a robot's individual presence shapes the interaction between the user and the robot offers a different understanding, which in turn can be the bedrock of efforts to actively form the relationships society wants with robotics.

Taking Gumbrecht's notion of presence into account, the aim here is to pay close attention to the robot's embodiment strategies: not only in asking how s/he/it is situated but also how social robots contribute to the interacting person's perception and constitution of embodiment. Social encounters with robots simulate the presence of another being, while there is actually only a machine present, one that offers different kinds of connectivity. Therefore, the machine's embodiment is the focal point, whether it is in the sense of a telepresence device, like Carl, that could be read as an embodied tele-representative, or in the sense of a corporeal, but artificial and limited interlocutor, like Kuri. The question of analysing these quite different examples of a robot's embodiment is not only to discuss how these robots can embody the presence of a distant person or simulate the presence of a social other, but also to interrogate how these encounters reshape our notions of interacting and communicating.

Meet Kuri

Despite being in pre-order for $800 in 2016 in the US, Kuri has never overcome its developmental status. In 2018 Bosch, a major financier behind Mayfield Robotics, withdrew its support. Regardless of being featured on the 2017 Consumer Electronics Show in Las Vegas, the startup failed to convince other investors. One might speculate that the reasons for Kuri's lack of further funding included the lack of a certain degree of functionality, which makes Kuri an even more interesting example to consider.

Kuri's embodiment is quite ambivalent, as the robot's developer aims to equip it with a personality while at the same time emphasises its 'machineliness'. The robot's body is based on abstractions of human bodily features. Advertised as 'a home robot for life', it has a white, cone-shaped body, on which a ball-shaped head rests. All in all, the little figure is almost sixty centimetres high and lacks any bodily extremities, as its 'arms' are reduced to painted-on shadows and its 'legs' are reduced to three small wheels.[4] Kuri's most prominent feature are its comic-like eyes, which dominate its head and can even give the little robot a smile.

Reporter Aki Ito describes Kuri in a short video for Bloomberg Technology: 'Think of her as Amazon's Alexa surfing on a roomba. She doesn't do a whole lot. The phone in your pocket can probably do a lot more' (Bloomberg 2017). In this quote, Ito has adopted a female gendering of the robot, referring to Kuri as 'her'. As the robot's body does not imply any gender it is up to the user encountering s/he/it to ascribe one or none at all. In fact, it is rather interesting to note the situations in which Kuri is given a gender and by whom, as the gendering expresses a social placement ascribed to the machine. Ito's decision to feminise Kuri can be understood as a way of restricting

---

4   As of July 2023, the marketing webpage, with pictures of Kuri, was still online. See https://www.heykuri.com/life-with-kuri.

the robot's influence. Not to forget: referring to Kuri as 'she' places her in the line of ancestry of the fictional dream of mechanical housemaids. Simultaneously, the comparison with a smartphone points out that there already is a technology fulfilling Kuri's functionality. One significant difference between smartphones and social robots are the fundamentally different ways of embodying functionality; while smartphones are kept close to the user's body, which can be understood as a form of incorporating their functional capacities into the user's body, social robots can be read as autonomous excorporations and biomorphisations of certain techno-functional capacities (see Westermann 2020). Here, the significant difference between social robotics and smartphones becomes obvious: while smartphones and their functionality are incorporated into the user's body, social robots are biomorphised to subject their agency into some kind of para-social being. Kuri's failing to reach marketability can consequently be read as demonstrating that a robotic presence itself was not seen as a marketable feature by investors. Conversely, it becomes apparent that Kuri is indeed designed as a presence-robot.

Kuri's development was featured and accompanied by the extensive website Mayfield Robotics created to advertise its product. Underlying its advertised functionality – which incorporates reading stories to children as well as watching the owner's property – Kuri's presence is the robot's core feature: 'With emotive eyes and a friendly disposition, Kuri will always inspire and create connections in your home' (Mayfield Robotics 2019). Additionally, Kuri offers to be virtually present at home: 'Whether you're reviewing the day's video adventures, or streaming Kuri's view real time to your phone, Kuri's app keeps you connected to your home and life at home' (Mayfield Robotics 2019).

Considering Kuri's embodiment, Mayfield Robotics' main aim is to present Kuri as a non-frightening being: this starts with its height as well as its overall appearance. From this point of view the missing limbs, though probably primarily due to the fact that artificial arms and hands are challenging to design, can be read as part of the effort of making Kuri less alarming. The lack of limbs means a specific restriction of possible actions the robot could perform. A similar decision was made concerning Kuri's ability to communicate: the designer's explicit choice to reduce Kuri's own voice to a friendly chirping and beeping not only tasks the user to learn to interpret these non-verbal vocalisations but as well inscribes conformable restriction of possible actions in the robot's body. In other words, considering these different aspects that all follow the same concept, the design of Kuri's body in general can be interpreted as a way to stress Kuri's status as a presence-machine and restrict the robot's possible range of actions beyond being present.

In order to fulfil the expectations society – and in this case potential buyers – have of robots, Kuri's machineliness has to be matched with a certain degree of likeness to the human, or, as the chief executive officer of Mayfield Robotics, Mike Beebe, has put it: 'a personality' (TechCrunch 2017). The robot was designed to 'create dynamic interactions that bring out a real sense of personality' (Mayfield Robotics 2019). Described in a TechCrunch article as 'designed to be a companion first, and an assistant second' (Etherington 2016), a Pixar animator was responsible for Kuri's movement design of rolling around on three wheels, which allows the robot to move in any direction. Kuri is fitted with mapping sensors that facilitate the recognition of obstacles, including stairs:

> Mapping sensors enable Kuri to navigate your house autonomously. A sensor array helps Kuri learn and remember where everything is located, and also stay away from cliffs and obstacles in his path. (Mayfield Robotics 2019)

All in all, the developers aimed to create an animal, or maybe a child-like personality, to maintain a certain distance from the human. When patted on the head, Kuri will look up and start chirping like a purring cat. In addition to the non-verbal chirping and beeping, the 'heart light' in its chest that 'helps Kuri convey a sense of mood' (Mayfield Robotics 2019), as well as the robot's comic-like eyes, are the only ways of it 'communicating' with humans. Of all of these features, the eyes might be the most expressive, being basically big black dots with a pair of artificial movable eyelids. They allow Kuri to blink and create the impression of smiling eyes that we have come to know from comic figures. While Kuri's design is catering to interaction, Kuri's potential to communicate is quite restricted: unable to speak, the little robot's ability is reduced to playing media content.

Even more, Kuri's relatively restricted possibilities to communicate are made up for with much more sophisticated recording abilities. The robot's left eye is, in fact, a high-definition camera that allows for high-level face and pet recognition. Moreover, the robot is equipped with four sensitive microphones to locate sounds. Kuri's surveillance abilities are based on the robot's technical skill to see and hear for the user as well as to inform the user immediately of any detected motion. The associated app allows real-time access to Kuri's live feed, completing the robot's surveillance capacities. It is noteworthy that the ability to detect potential intruders or be notified of one's child's or pet's movements is directly connected to the technical capacity to see, mirroring Western culture's primacy on visuality.

Clearly, Kuri's functionalities cover two main fields which add to its ambivalence in embodying presence as well. First, it is an entertainment companion. Its built-in speakers allow its users to listen to their favourite songs, audiobooks and podcasts. This feature is highly stressed, as Kuri is presented as a family member of a different kind, one that explicitly interacts with children and even reads bedtime stories to them. That the latter feature is mentioned is remarkable, as reading bedtime stories to children is a communicative ritual of social bonding that is given high social priority in Western society. Second, Kuri is a surveillance robot that monitors one's house in everyone's absence as well as informs via the app when a family member comes home or sends pictures of any intruder. Given the overall aim to present Kuri as a friendly home companion it is not surprising at all that this feature is a rather passing mention rather than the centre of its advertisement.

Surveillance as well as reading bedtime stories are (on a cultural level) quite powerful functionalities the little machine is advertised to perform. Both are capabilities directly linked to the human. Against this background, all of the choices that formed Kuri's design function, indeed, to mark these technologically performed but human coded abilities as being as non-frightening as possible. Kuri's whole embodiment is aimed at being a presence that is non-human but non-machine as well. It is important to note that shifting the design to either extreme (more human-like or more machine-like) would amplify its potential to irritate the user, as a human-like machine surveilling one's house and telling a story to one's children can be perceived as concerning as a machine-like machine performing these human tasks. Thus, the design places the robot as close as possible to a mere thing that still reacts to human interaction in order to allow its usage. In other words, Kuri's design aims at restricting its presence to a certain non-threatening level while simultaneously still enabling its ascribed functional potentials: Kuri's whole embodiment is aimed at interaction without trying to simulate communication at all.

Meet Carl

In contrast to Kuri, Carl is a telepresence robot built by Orbis Robotics and has been advertised as having the ability to virtually attend funerals or visit elderly family members who live far away. While telepresence robots are per se a very special case of social robots that start to populate the realm of our social interactions more and more, Carl's special field of activity makes him unique. Like Kuri, Carl's body can also be described as a somewhat bodily figure, yet it is even more abstract than Kuri.[5] Carl's 'head' is a high-resolution seventeen-inch monitor completed by a high-definition webcam and an amplified-speaker system. The body is a pole, which is adjustable in height and is positioned on a movable platform. Just like Kuri's, Carl's body is reduced to a minimalistic shape and its main functionalities are to move around and perceive the world for its user(s).

Like one of quite a few other telepresence robots advertised on Telepresencerobots.com (like *BotEyes – Pad* or *AVA 500*) that can already be bought, Carl's architecture can be described as an embodied and mobilised conference call. Some contemporary telepresence robots are, in fact, mobile stations, on which one can mount a commercially available tablet. As noted by Telepresencerobots.com the feature that

> separates the Carl robot from many of the other telepresence robots is that multiple users can log in and take part in the remote presence experience. One person controls the movement of the robot while the others can view (and be viewed) from their own locations.

Given that Carl's functionality depends on lending his machine-body to allow one to six humans a 'virtual instant presence' (Telepresencerobots), it is noteworthy that someone felt the need to name the robot with a Christian name. This naming is an act of personification. It reveals that the robot is perceived differently from the technology enabling a conference call that almost disappears during the calls as long as there is no technical breakdown. Naming Carl underlines his own presence as an agent or intermediator.

The fact that Carl lends its body to several people at the same time emphasises the primary conditions its embodiment implies. Though one can use Carl's body, that body offers only limited capabilities, as one can move around and see and hear the world while it is im-possible to touch, feel or smell the surroundings. Similar to Kuri, Carl's embodiment emphasises visuality as the primary mode of approaching and grasping the world. And even further development will not change this in the near future but instead underlines the primacy of a visual approach to the world:

---

5   Pictures of Carl can be found at https://telepresencerobots.com/robots/orbis-robotics-carl (accessed 13 July 2019).

> Currently, Orbis Robotics is preparing to implement integration of biometric sensors (including heart monitors), improved optics for visual observation of patients, and family participation. This last feature is exclusive to the Carl robot and allows members of a patient's family to participate in the Carl video call while the doctor is using the Carl to remotely visit the patient. (Telepresencerobots 2019)

This concentration on audio-visual senses is especially noteworthy as Carl is advertised to allow virtual attendance at embodied social practices. Funerals are a cultural ritual that is not only watched and semiotically understood, but also felt. To express one's condolences is an act of speech and, in most cases, an embodied gesture. The same holds for visiting the sick, which often includes the comforting or healing potential of human touch. Considering these embodied practices, Carl's restrictions become palpable, as the robot is not designed to provide any of these. What is important to note is that Carl does not provide access to an augmented or virtual reality but instead doubles the user's embodiment by simultaneously allowing them to be present in two places at once: using Carl facilitates one shared and yet split experience.

The search for what one might call a robotic touch opposing a visual approach has led to inventions like Hiroshi Ishiguro's Elfoid. The roboticist has built a robotic mobile phone that relies on touch in order to 'figure out the best means of conveying human presence, in a mobile variant of "presence in a pocket"'. Timo Kaerlein analyses the immediacy of Ishiguro's Elfoid when he states:

> It seems that it is not so much the communication partner at the other end of the line who is the true object of desire, but rather the artefact of the mobile phone. The prospect of immediacy is subtly shifted from access to the interlocutor's mind to an intimate relationship with the device itself. (Kaerlein 2012)

In fact, one could argue whether or not Carl is a social robot at all. On a technological level, Carl consists of robotic parts but, unlike other robots, which are controlled by algorithms, Carl is controlled by a distant human brain. It is a mechanical body temporarily controlled, offering presence as well as a shared experience. Therefore, Carl, or at least his technologically improved successors, may provoke cultural controversy on a different level to robots like Kuri. It becomes apparent that in considering Carl's presence, two perspectives need to be differentiated: on the one hand, there is the perspective of someone who meets up to six different corporeal distant and possibly geographically distributed people who share the robot's body; and on the other hand, there is the perspective of those up to six people who share the mediated experience of being present in the distance in one joint artificial body while potentially being spatially scattered in different places. As only one can take control of the robot's body, the other five users' mediated presence is in addition reduced to a unique form of passiveness that diminishes the being in two places at once to a visual, externally controlled experience.

Carl's own presence is reduced to the absolute minimum: it is just a technological body that allows bodily distant users to be there in a literal yet virtual sense. To what extent these corporeal distant users borrowing Carl's machine-body can figuratively be there depends on the ability to perform social rituals with only a broadcast voice, lent eyes and no chance to touch or feel the other or the distant surroundings. With these limitations Carl's embodiment restricts the mediated presence it offers in a way that modifies the offered possibilities of interaction and communication. These restrictions are even intensified when a user does not control the robot's body but is a passive guest on a robot's body that is externally controlled by someone else. Carl only allows its users to interact and communicate through its artificial body, while, stripped of the steering user's capabilities, this body itself does not even allow interaction.

Conclusion

Both robots, Kuri as well as Carl, inherit a certain immediacy in their presence, meaning they both simulate presence, but each one is doing so in a different mode. Carl offers to be in two places at once as a shared yet limited group experience. As a telepresence robot, Carl separates the user's attention from his/her own fleshly presence by inhabiting a somewhat restricted mechanical body that one can simultaneously share with others (while only one can take the lead and actually pilot the robot's body). Though Carl simulates a direct presence and a direct communication he still is a medium that is only suggestive of presence, as the ways to interact through and with him are limited to the mediation of presence, as the telepresence Carl offers is reduced to a moving, hearing and seeing body that cannot feel or smell its surroundings. This might change when telepresence bodies not only allow their users to move and perceive through them but begin to directly interact with other human beings and machines through a fully functional body. Nevertheless, telerobots like Carl raise the question of bodily presence, as its design undermines being in the here and now by doubling the places in which the user is physically located.

Kuri's presence is seemingly immediate as well. S/he/it does not simulate one being there but instead is *there* for you and simulates a presence of her/his/its own rather than a human user's presence. The home robot's real technological potential are her/his/its surveillance capabilities as a passive presence-function. Simultaneously her/his/its potential of being actively present in terms of simulating subjectivity is reduced to modes of interaction and performing as a media machine.

Both robots' abilities to mediate interaction and communication mirror their embodied concept of presence. Carl is a representative through which up to six users can communicate, while Kuri is a limited interlocutor with a restricted set of active ways in which to interact but has an elaborated functionality to record, replay and distribute media data. In sum, both forms of presence differ from a human presence that does not simulate immediacy but is immediate. Yet, both robots require (each in its own way) a human user to simulate immediacy. However, remembering Gumbrecht's characterisation of Western culture as a culture of meaning that can best experience presence as mediated effects, this might just come 'naturally' to the Western culture. That is why each robot in its own way can act as a bodily representation of the visual as formative cultural technique (someone logging into Carl to 'be' somewhere else as well as Kuri's surveillance function) and equally as an artificial imitation of subjectivity (meeting someone through Carl as well as Kuri as media machine). In short, both robots are designed to facilitate effects of presence in terms of effects of meaning.

References

Bartneck, C. and Forlizzi, J. (2004) 'A Design-Centred Framework for Social Human–Robot Interaction', in *Proceedings of the Ro-Man 2004, Kurashiki*, pp. 591–4. Available at 10.1109/ROMAN.2004.1374827 (accessed 10 April 2021).

Bloomberg (2017) 'Your New Robot Roommate BFF'. Available at https://www.bloomberg.com/news/videos/2017-01-06/your-new-robot-roommate-bff-video (accessed 13 July 2019).

Collingridge, D. (1982) *The Social Control of Technology*. London: Frances Pinter.

Etherington, D. (2016) 'Home Robot Kuri Is Like an Amazon Echo Designed by Pixar'. Available at https://techcrunch.com/2017/01/03/home-robot-kuri-is-like-an-amazon-echo-designed-by-pixar (accessed 13 July 2019).

Gumbrecht, H. (2004) *Production of Presence: What Meaning Cannot Convey*. Standford: Standford University Press.

Gumbrecht, H. (2012) *Präsenz*. Frankfurt am Main: Suhrkamp.

Horton, D. and Wohl, R. R. (1956) 'Mass Communication and Para-social Interaction: Observation on Intimacy at a Distance', *Psychiatry* 19(3): 185–206.

Ichbiah, D. (2005) *Roboter. Geschichte, Technik, Entwicklung*. München: Knesebeck.

Kaerlein, T. (2012) 'Presence in a Pocket. Phantasms of Immediacy in Japanese Mobile Telepresence Robotics', *Communication +1* (1): article 6.

Mayfield Robotics (2019) 'Hey Kuri'. Available at https://www.heykuri com/life-with-kuri/ (accessed 13 July 2019).

Nocks, L. (2008) *The Robot. The Life Story of a Technology*. Baltimore: Johns Hopkins University Press.

Rosheim, M. E. (1994) *Robot Evolution: The Development of Anthrobotics*. New York: Wiley.

Riskin, J. (2016) 'Frolicsome Engines. The Long Prehistory of Artificial Intelligence', *Public Domain Review*. Available at https://publicdomainreview.org/essay/frolicsome-engines-the-long-prehistory-of-artificial-intelligence (accessed 22 August 2022).

Sparrow, R. (2015) 'Robots in Aged Care: A Dystopian Future?', Working Paper. Available at http://profiles.arts.monash.edu.au/robert-sparrow/files/2017/05/RobotsInAgedCare_ADystopianFuture_Web.pdf (accessed 13 July 2019).

TechCrunch (2017) 'Mayfield Robotics' Kuri Is an Adorable Home Robot'. Available at https://www.youtube.com/watch?v=Gvle_O4vD18 (accessed 13 July 2019).

Telepresencerobots (2019) 'Carl'. Available at https://telepresencerobots.com/robots/orbis-robotics-carl (accessed 13 July 2019).

Turkle, S. (2011). Alone Together: Why We Expect More from Technology and Less from Each Other. New York: Basic Books.

von Foerster, H. (1992) 'Entdecken oder Erfinden. Wie läßt sich Verstehen verstehen?', in Gumin, H. and Meier, H. (eds), *Einführung in den Konstruktivismus*. Munich: Piper, pp. 41–88.

von Randow, G. (1998) *Roboter: Unsere nächsten Verwandten*. Reinbek: Rowohlt.

Westermann, B. (2012) Anthropomorphe Maschinen. Grenzgänge zwischen Biologie und Technik seit dem 18. Jahrhundert. Frankfurt am Main: Fink.

Westermann, B. (2020) 'Social Encounters with Symbiotic Media Technologies', in Burkhard B., Shayien, M. and Grashöfer, K. (eds), *Explorations in Digital Cultures*. Lüneburg: Meson Press.

11 The Robotics Division of the Dramaco Instrument Company Introduces the Ensocellorator Reliance Pro 2

maya rae oppenheimer

CORPORATE ARCHIVES OFFICE
Public Event Record Form

This is an internal document ONLY.
All questions should be addressed to the listed Dramaco company representative.

EVENT DETAILS:
'Call for Papers – Robot Futures: Vision and Touch in Robotics sympos um
Deadline for submissions – Friday 3rd March 2017

This one-day symposium, to take place at the Science Museum, London, or 8th July 2017, will bring together engineers, scientists, cultural theorists and artists to explore notions of embodiment and telepresence in the field of robotics and in virtual and augmented realities.

Humans are embodied ir robotic explorers; endowing them with 'eyes and hands' robots are able to relate perceptions and experiences of places and objects physically unavailable to us. Although such robots might not 'look' human, it is the desire to see stereoscopically, and to feel through all the senses that grant robots anthropomorphic qualities; we see and feel through the robot. In this way robots enable a more embodied experience, which is nonetheless mediated. The development of virtual reality technologies is increasingly enabling us to see and feel as the robot in order to get closer to a more immersive experience.

We invite established and emerging researchers to submit abstracts for paper presentations that address notions of embodiment, telepresence, vision and touch specifically regarding robotics and virtual and augmented realities. We welcome proposals from the arts & humanities and the sciences, particularly from researchers whose work spans both fields.'

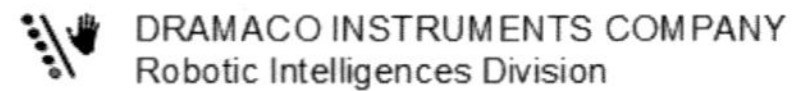

DRAMACO REPRESENTATIVE:
Maya Rae Oppenheimer
Head of Research & Development, Robotic Intelligences Division

PROPOSAL:
A preliminary soft pitch of the ERP2 prototype to a specialist audience in London, UK. This symposium will provide a platform for Dramaco's infiltration of the high-end robotics research market due to its proximity to and involvement with the following institutions: The Science Museum, the Royal College of Art, Imperial College, which are all robot engineering and research vanguards. Will gather valuable insight into overseas market perceptions and potential contacts for shaping robotic intelligences.

REPRESENTATIVE SIGNATURE   DATE: 3/03/17

ARCHIVAL ACQUISITION   DATE: 11/04/21

DRAMACO INSTRUMENTS PRESENTS
Slide deck.

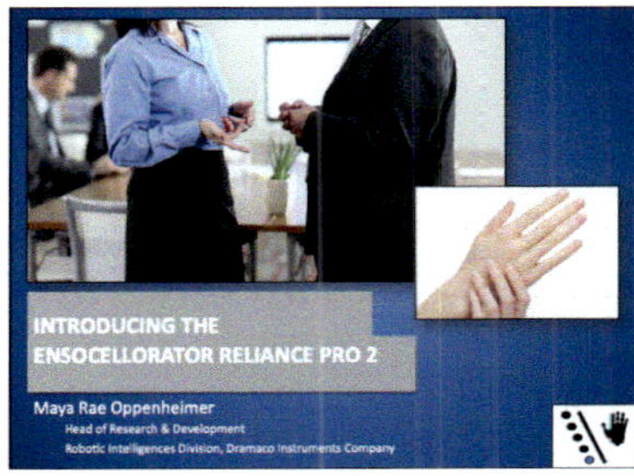

1.

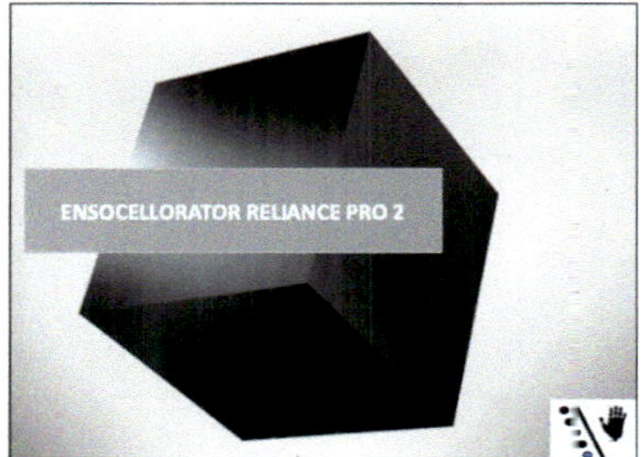

2.

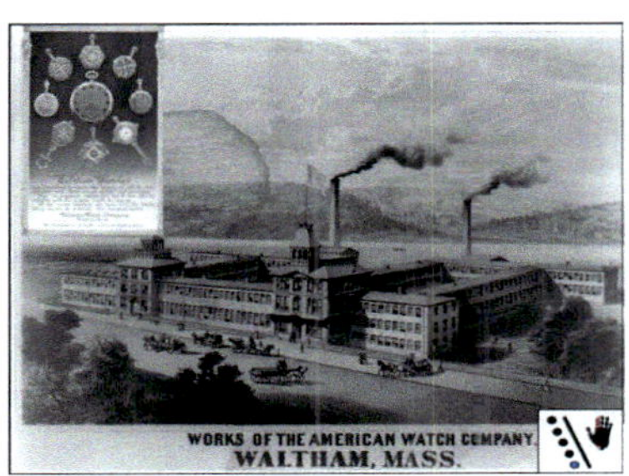

3.

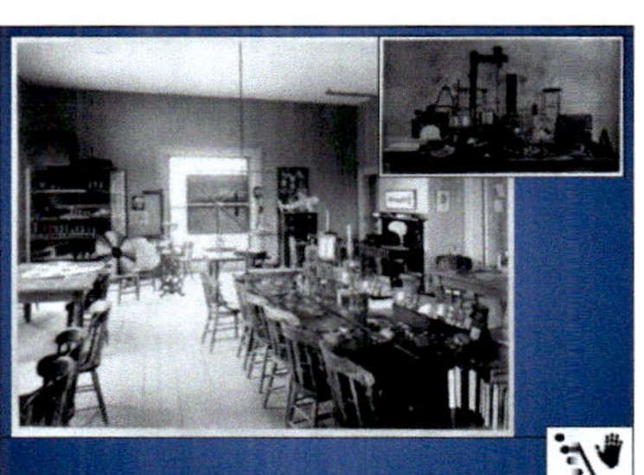

4.

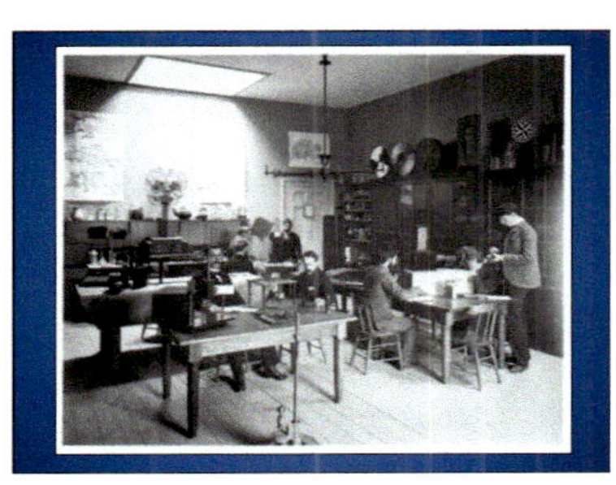

5.

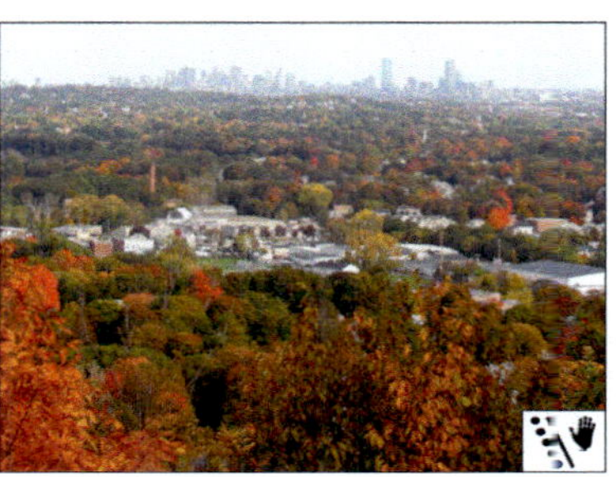

6.

DRAMACO INSTRUMENTS PRESENTS
Slide deck.

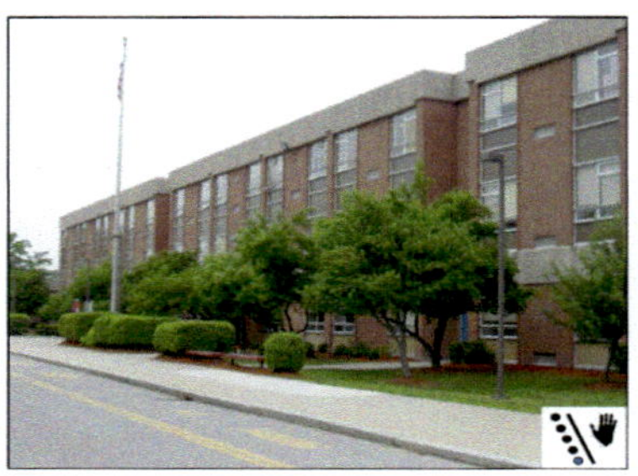

7.

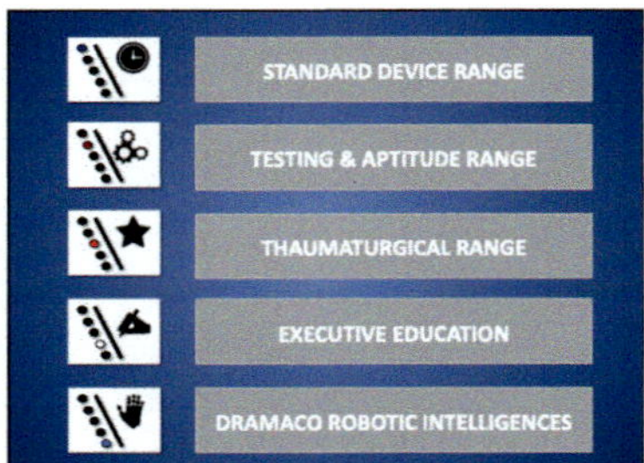

8.

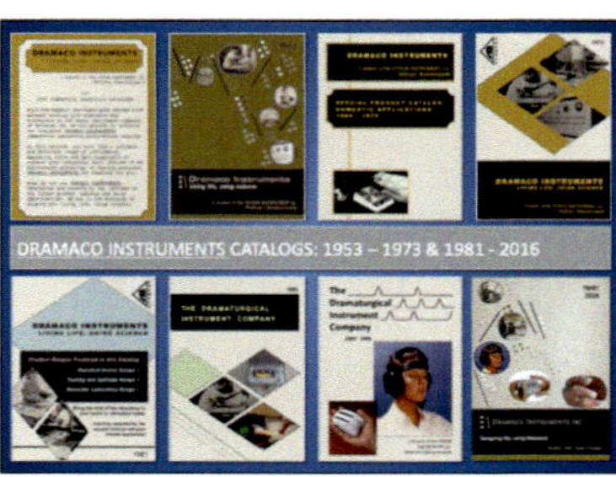

9.

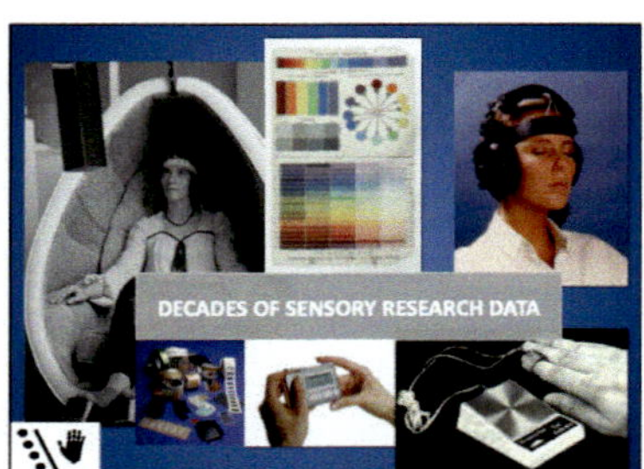

10.

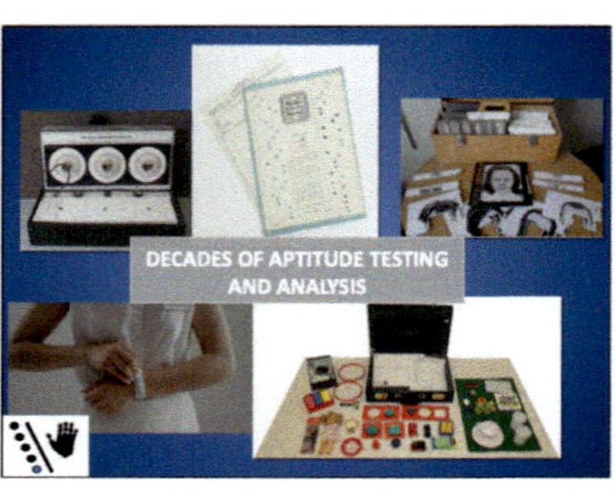

11.

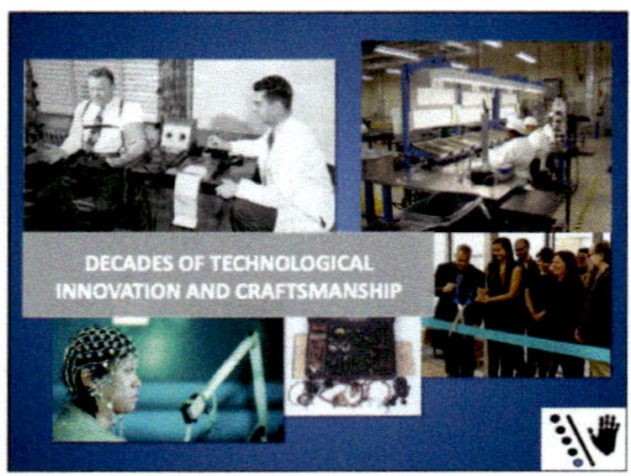

12.

DRAMACO INSTRUMENTS PRESENTS
Slide deck.

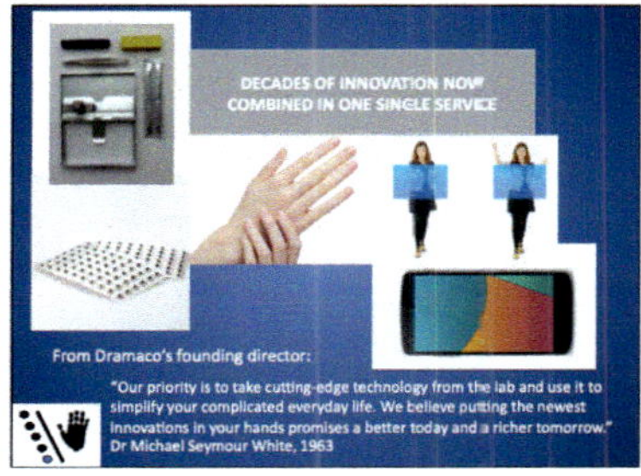

13.

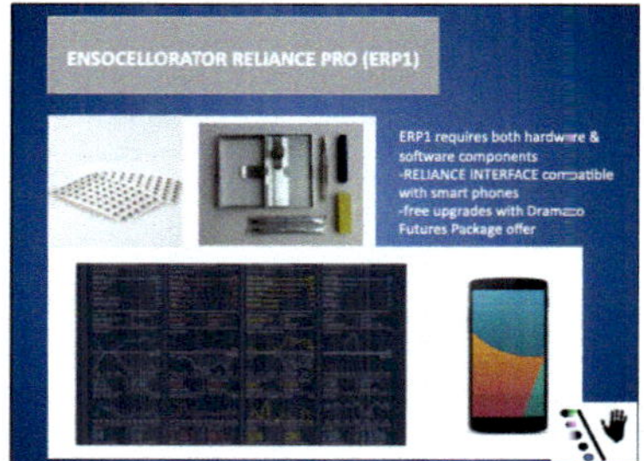

14.

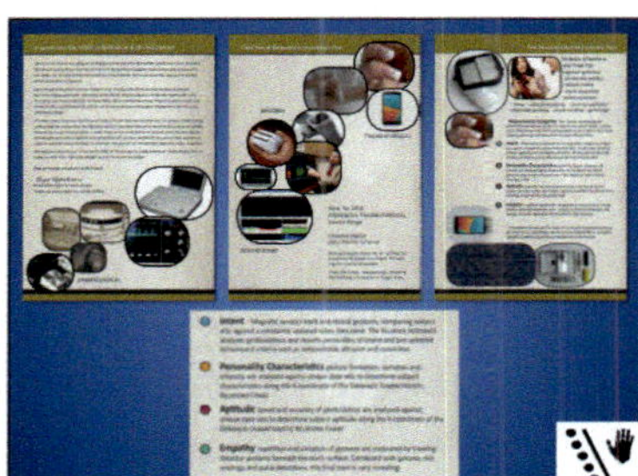

15.

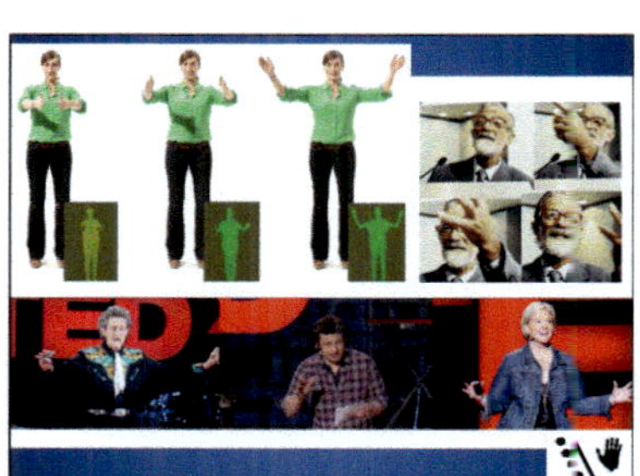

16.

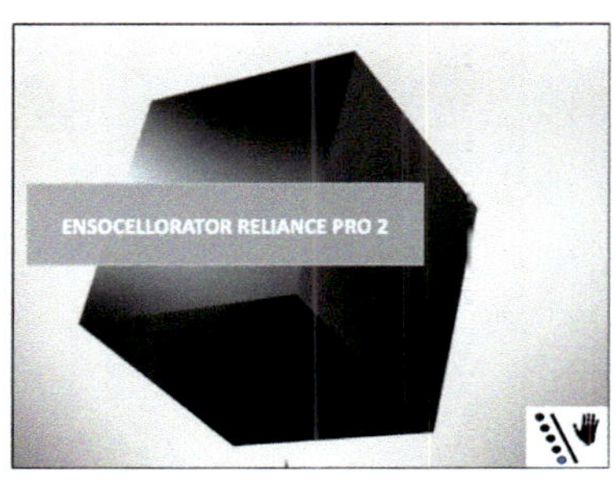

17.

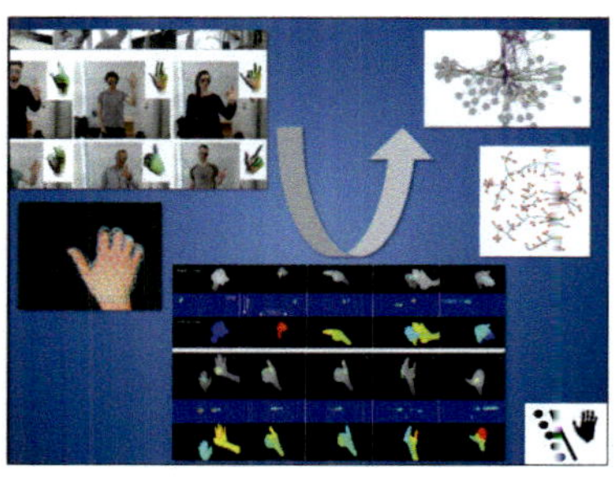

18.

DRAMACO INSTRUMENTS PRESENTS
Slide deck.

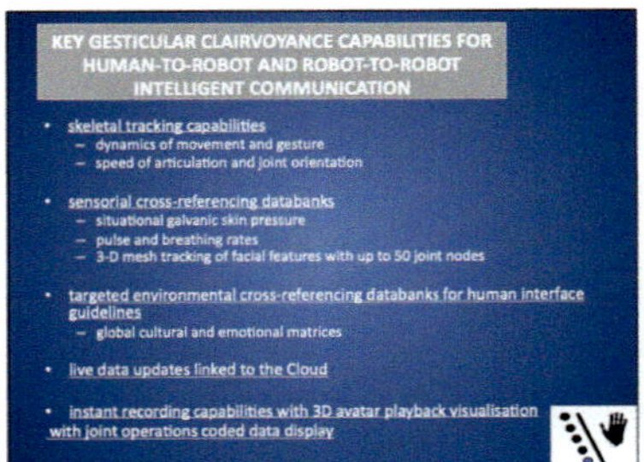

19.

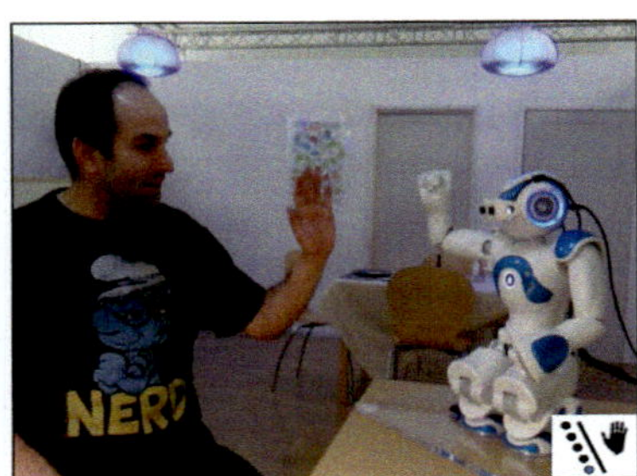

20.

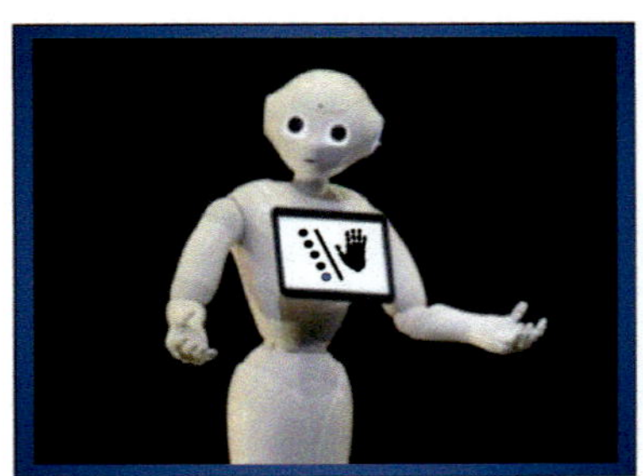

21.

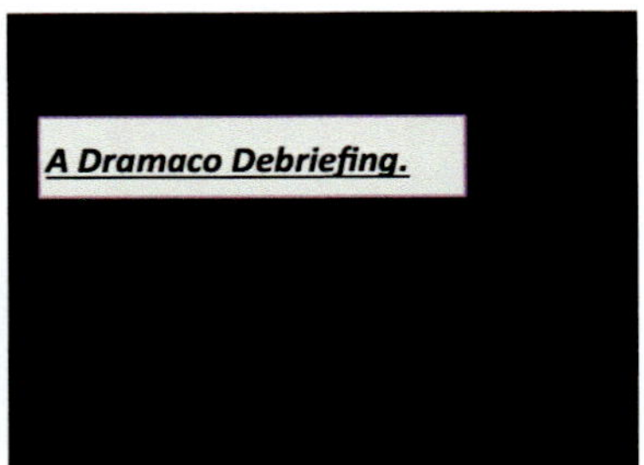

22.

Dramaco Instruments Project does several things:

• 'If we can, should we?'

23.

Dramaco Instruments Project does several things:

• critiques vanguards of innovation and
  investment: time, capital, laboratory space,
  infrastructure costs, knowledge-transfer
  and societal care;

24.

DRAMACO INSTRUMENTS PRESENTS
Slide deck.

25.

26.

27.

28.

NOTES:

SCRIPT FOR:

Dramaco Instruments Presents: The Ensocellorator Reliance Pro 2
Maya Rae Oppenheimer
8 July 2017, The Science Museum, London

Property of DRAMACO INSTRUMENTS COMPANY

[Slide 1]

What comes to mind when you hear the adjective 'robotic'?
Here are some results from a brief online dictionary search:
+ 'awkward'
+ 'clumsy or stiff'
+ 'devoid of human feeling'; 'cold'
+ 'speaking without feeling or expression'

My company, Dramaco Instruments, and I are here to help change that!

Good afternoon. My name is Maya Rae Oppenheimer, and I am the Head of Research and Development of the Robotic Intelligences Division of the Dramaco Instruments Company. It is with much excitement that I join you today in order to present our latest contribution to the robotics and AI innovation landscape: the Ensocellorator Reliance Pro 2, affectionately known as the ERP2.

[Slide 2]

The ERP2 finished a rigorous pre-release trial period earlier in the spring of 2017, and this product – never before seen on a commercial business market – is set to launch in September 2017. So, it is with this innovative moment in our company's and in the industry's development that have the pleasure of introducing you to the ERP2, a unique Gesticular Clairvoyance Platform.

There is no question that we are witnessing extraordinary developments in the robotic engineering field. We have surpassed the ambition of automating low-level tasks and introducing robots to human society or environments too perilous for human activity. Now, our attention lies on the emotional cultivation of humanoid robot counterparts. As robots become more supple, more functional, more invaluable to our everyday lives, we at Dramaco believe working in the social psychology of robots and their emotional training is the future of the industry.

Dramaco has decades of experience working across laboratory instrument development and social, human interaction. We are perfectly positioned to break into this new and expanding, necessary field that will shape the future of robotic intelligences: software detection and analysis software that allow robots to interact with human counterparts effectively and accurately.

In sum: by implanting the ERP2 to your robot models (any model with a USB or Wi-Fi connection), you can enjoy an emotionally intelligent interaction with your robot, which will respond, with guidance, from the patented Dramaco Reliance Interface (DRI). The ERP2's DRI combines intent, personality characteristics, aptitude and empathy quotients from any social interaction scenario, and provides your robot with socially appropriate and emotionally intelligent responses.

It is our belief at Dramaco that steady and responsible innovation develops over time. From where I stand, the heritage of our company and its decades of servicing domestic and commercial psychological needs with cutting-edge devices and tests, all honed in professional laboratories, is inseparable from our latest vanguard of innovation in robotic and artificial intelligence fields.

[Slide 3]

But first things first. I won't blame you if you haven't yet heard of Dramaco Instruments, or our parent company, the Dyson Instrument Corporation. We have a long history in the north-eastern United States, and we are only beginning to grow globally.

We are at the beginning of a new international marketing campaign supported by service branches in our home-town of Waltham, Massachusetts, where we still occupy our original factory floor. Extending offices to London and Tokyo and developing administrative outposts in Mauritius and marketing branches in India, Brazil and Saudi Arabia by 2020, means we have the global infrastructure in place to continue our tradition of service and innovation across growing and complex market demands.

We trace our roots to 1881 Waltham, home of the American watch-making industry and a community with generations of skilled craftsmanship, instrument manufacturing experience and the spirit of technological modernisation. Our company is a multi-generational family business with deep roots in the American dream. Jeremiah Dyson immigrated to the United States from Ireland in 1853 as a boy, and he was one of seven siblings. He settled with his family in Brooklyn, where he worked as a local errand boy and eventually a runner in jewellery shops. Young Dyson would pick up and deliver pocket watches for winding and repair, eventually gaining enough skill in the movement of watches and clocks to take a seat at the repair benches of Bauman's Time Service in Queens, New York.

Rumour has it that Dyson's skill extended to locks and safes, and he supplemented his daily wages by winning bets over cracking all manner of securities, from bank vaults to back doors. What a metaphor for a true American beginning: open your own doors by any means necessary! Eventually, in 1875, Dyson gained employment at the American Watch Company factory in Waltham, and in 1880, he took the next step towards realising his dream: owning his own business and giving back to his community.

[Slide 4]

Lucrative as watch-making was in Waltham, Jeremiah Dyson, now a young man, was ready to exercise the entrepreneurial spirit that America is so well known for cultivating. Dyson was an avid reader, and after his shifts at the watch factory, he would pour over newspapers and trade journals at his local public library. Dyson became aware of the growing industry of scientific instrument development, which had much in common with his own trade.

The so-called Brass Age of Psychology had come to America, and with it, a growing client base of amateur and institutional clients prospecting truths about the human body and human nature. With early psychologists determined to quantify their field, and to bring it in line with the data-objectivity of the natural sciences, Dyson saw a new application for his talents with precision and mechanisation: combine them with the measurement imperatives of social scientists.

[Slide 5]

Here we see students in Munsterberg's lab researching the effect of attention and time on colour perception. Notice the elaborate instrument on the table to the right, the one at the centre of the experiment conducted by three men in suits. This is the only known live documentation of Dyson's Diagnostic Colour Lantern captured in its moment of application. The Diagnostic Colour Lantern was designed on Dyson's personal drafting table and was assembled in our Waltham factory: it was a hybrid design that combined the then common Magic Lantern brass chassis with precision measurement tools that could document reaction times to subtle stimuli introduced into a subject's field of vision. While the original photographed here is lost to time – perhaps it will still show up in an antique shop along the Hudson! – we cherish this photographic evidence of our heritage.

In fact, our corporate archives number among the largest holdings of early psychology material – from extensive inventories of the earliest psychology laboratories in America to prototypes of nineteenth-century instrumentaria. The photo you are looking at here depicts Hugo Munsterberg's famous Harvard Psychology laboratories wherein young psychologists app ied new instruments to human behaviour conditions for the first time. This often meant on each other!

We also have folders of correspondence letters in our archives sent between Dyson and widely respected philosopher-psychologists like William James and the doctor-turned-criminologist John Augustus Larson, who, along with the genius of his predecessor William Moulton Marston, went on to tighten the fabric of our country's civil service and legal system with the famous lie detector device. We are so privileged to be part of this crucible of American psychology history.

[Slide 6]

How many of you have been to Waltham, Massachusetts? Well, aren t you all lucky? It's a wonderful place that you can look forward to visiting.

This is Waltham today, and you can easily see the beautiful landscape we call home. Between the autumn turning leaves, you can make out the clusters of homes and local industry that comprise this thriving town. Note the brick smokestack, a beacon for the original American Watch Company's factory. You can also see Boston in the distance and other surrounding towns with their illustrious Ivy League institutions whose laboratories have made Waltham such a lucrative industrial playground of instrument manufacturing.

[Slide 7]

Speaking of making history, this is what we are here to do today. So let's have a look at Dyson Instruments today, specifically its specialist branch, Dramaco Instruments, my direct employer.

Here is the Dramaco Instruments Company building, which was set up under the umbrella of the Dyson Instruments Corporation in 1953. Dramaco specific-ally sells instruments that draw upon the precision and expertise developed in our laboratory instrument trade, but for a non-specialist consumer market.

That is: in your personal home; at your private business enterprise; for all your everyday needs. You can, as our early logo suggested, 'Live life, using science!'

Our headquarters consists of three storeys of in-house testing labs, prototyping facilities, manufacturing floors, customer service branches (including our 24/7 call centre support lines), in-house marketing team, employee day-care and onsite tennis court. We have fifteen hundred employees spending time with us every day in these four walls.

[Slide 8]

We consider all of our employees to be part of the Dyson–Dramaco family, and this ethos spreads into the spirit with which we have grown as a company. Today, there are five branches all within the Dramaco family, which remember, is only one constituency within the Dyson Corporation. Here is a list of all of our current branches, which developed, one by one, starting with the first branch you see on this slide.

Like all good things, Dramaco started small, and kept things reliable. This was the ethos behind the Standard Device Range. Launched in 1953, we saw this inaugural Dramaco range as a chance to test the viability of selling our laboratory instruments on the domestic consumer market. Once we secured our reputation with a reliable and innovative business plan, the Dyson Corporation expanded their future investments for Dramaco, and we began to grow.

Next came the Testing & Aptitude Range, which built upon the applications of household instruments marketed through the Standard Device Range. Our customers could practise the art of psychology and behavioural analysis right in their living rooms! With an ever-increasing line of tests and applications, parents and business owners across the country were really benefiting from the new theories pouring out of our nation's psychology laboratories and into newspapers and magazines. From improving your reaction times to external stimuli and exercising your memory capability, to assessing the capabilities of new babysitters, employees or boyfriends, cutting-edge research was truly palpable and applicable.

Our third line hit the market in the 1980s, and we named it the Thaumaturgical Range. Hailing from the Greek words thaûma, meaning 'miracle' or 'marvel', and *érgon*, meaning 'work', this range was a real game-changer for Dramaco and separated us from our competition. Every product in this line earned its place in our catalogue as a wonderworker, and in turn, transformed consumers into miracle workers themselves! These instruments had the power to change the physical world by changing you and your loved ones. From exploring everyday applications of classical conditioning, to vision enhancement capabilities to early smart-home circuitry, this home-laboratory grew so quickly that within a year of its launch, we founded the Executive Education Range. We updated and refreshed classic Dramaco products for the sophisticated demands of the corporate, global office. Beneath the walnut, teak or burnished metal encasing of your Dramaco devices lay the signature science of our experts.

In 1961, we expanded our research and development activities once more, bringing our in-house profile to a family of five acclaimed product and service ranges. This remains our model today.

[Slide 9]

Our aforementioned archive documents this growth, and we have catalogues from all of Dramaco's ranges. While our logo has changed, and our graphic identity and language has altered as taste and fashion dictates, our commitment to heritage and innovation has never wavered.

I would like to draw your attention to the catalogue cover on the bottom right. This catalogue documents a special fifty-five-year anniversary collection of the Dramaco Robotic Intelligences Range: it archives the launch of ERP1, the predecessor of the ERP2, and the reason we are here today. I'd like to present the ERP1 to you now, so that you have a very clear perspective on the build-up to this afternoon's launch.

[Slide 10]

The ERP1 and ERP2 build upon decades of sensory research data that Dramaco gathered via its free customer service analytics branch. This service was set up in 1963 to support our Dramaco ranges, from optical tracking devices to timers and neural mapping analysis. This resulted in decades-worth of data-banks for contextually specific applications, which we have converted into a mass of invaluable data capital. We also harvested our consumer complaints, testing results, questions and sales data for development purposes, pre-dating smartphone and social media analytics by decades.

[Slide 11]

Dramaco's devices and their requisite services are also enriched by decades of aptitude testing and analysis, allowing us to constantly build up our knowledge of our consumer bases and their psychological and social profiles. Thanks to our in-house test processing facilities and help lines, we have reams of information about our customers, which we can funnel into the next-generation technologies that help solve real-world, wicked problems.

[Slide 12]

Finally, with decades of technological innovation and craftsmanship, the Robotic Intelligences Division (RID), which is a commercial research and training centre, can confidently ensure these products have the functionality and craftsmanship to back up our claims.

We do not just build robots or design hospitable AI programming – we focus on the software and minimal hardware that will enhance any market model. Our RID products can be uploaded to many existing robot devices in order to render their interactions more human and more empathic.

[Slide 13]

In the words of Dramaco Robotics Intelligences Division's first Director, Dr Michael Seymour White, 'Our priority is to take cutting-edge technology from the lab and use it to simplify your complicated everyday life. We believe putting the newest innovations in your hands promises a better today and a richer tomorrow.' Over fifty years later, we haven't stopped.

[Slide 14]

The ERP1, launched in 2015, is a business-to-business Gesticular Clairvoyance Platform that runs on cutting-edge algorithmic software and minimal hardware. The product consists of a pocket-sized installation toolkit, 120 discrete and remote micro-magnetic sensors, and a complex RELIANCE INTERFACE app that is compatible with current market smartphones.

Since our tomorrow promises uncertainty – with the prevalence of alternative facts, post-truth, and fake news – we at Dramaco Robotics asked ourselves how could we function amidst such deception? We built upon our landmark Thaumaturgical Range, with product stars like the PERSONALITY EVALUATOR and the TRUTH DETECTOR 4000 with its CHARACTERISTIC RELATIONS CHART to create the Gesticular Clairvoyance Platform, an intent and personality decoder that works like the lie detectors of yore. However, this device is more nuanced, more reliable, live-tracking, discreet and irrefutable.

To activate the ERP1, simply attach the state-of-the-art, micro-magnetic tracking sensors to any subjects' fingertips using the kit's invisible adhesive system. You can see from these slides that the sensors are roughly the size of a pen-tip. The ultra-sensitive adhesive, combined with 1,000 fibre-optic tips/0.01mm, collects a complex combination of biofeedback and relays diagnostic data to the in-app receptor, the RELIANCE INTERFACE. Data point translations include 3D motion-tracking matrices that calculate speed, intensity and gesticular tremors, galvanic skin pressure levels, pulse speech-to-gesture velocities, and vocal intonation abnormalities. A patented Dramaco Robotics heuristic feeds thousands of data points per second through our patented RELIANCE INTERFACE to create an easy-to-read subject report that translates invaluable, non-verbal communication truths. By using the ERP1, you have evidence-based proof concerning your subject's moral intent, personality characteristics, learning aptitude and empathic capacities. Results are communicated to the administrator in the form of a colour-coded graphic interface, diagnostic break-down across each of the four previously mentioned measurement categories and a free Dramaco CHARACTERISTIC RELATIONS CHART.

What the ERP1 does, which no other device on or off the market can, is cross-reference all known capacities of meaning making, mediation and communication. Linguists like J. L. Austin have been telling us for years that our use of imperative language is socially explicit and rife with meaning and intent beyond the utterance. Tone modulation and speech speed are untapped diagnostics in our investigative and surveillance interests. Furthermore, studies show that 65% of non-verbal communication – fodder that lies at the heart of meaning – is unintelligible to the average social subject. Imagine what potential for subject-understanding is suddenly unlocked when all these factors are decoded via the ERP1.

In short, the ERP1 unlocks the motive and social frame of any subject.

The wonder really lies in the RELIANCE INTERFACE, which compiles, analyses and translates meaning from gesture into immediate data at your fingertips.

[Slide 15]

Let me tell you a bit more about this feature.

To assess subject intent, the ERP1 cross-compares subject gestures against a live databank of context-dependent gesticulations and their narrative outcomes. Testing modes can consider pre-selected behavioural criteria such as malevolence, altruism and conviction. Personality characteristics are assessed and weighted using gesture-field formation, variation and repetition to yield diagnostic x–y coordinates. Aptitude relies upon Dramaco's algorithm of speed and accuracy versus continuous gesticulation vis-à-vis eye movement. Finally, empathy measurements result from a delicate cocktail of embodied repetition and variation compiled against galvanic skin pressure and pulse detections.

Since releasing this product on the B2B market, we had incredible interest from a range of lucrative enterprises including human resources organisations and civil service contractors, private prison administrations, political campaigns, school boards, private security and logistics corporations and Hollywood film studios. All of this consumer data has accumulated in our servers, and this means our computing algorithms are becoming stronger and stronger.

We at Dramaco have also teamed up with high-profile public-speaking platforms to secure the cultural relevance and breadth of today's consumer market. This level of exposure has led us to collaborate with several industries at the vanguard of speech-to-motion graphic technologies, including the gaming industry, virtual reality, digital communication services and various social media and streaming platforms.

What is key for our clients is the ERP1's capacity to assume the burden of assessment, measurement and judgement. We know this evidence-based support matters to our clients, and this is clear with our own happy evidence: record uptakes in sales on this product and its bespoke, accompanying service. In our first quarter alone, we sold 250,000 product units with our signature five-year Dramaco Futures Package service bundle.

And it is with this volume of growth, this confidence and unprecedented intelligence born of sheer data that we present to you, the ERP2!

[Slide 16]

We see AI doing the risky work of interstellar exploration, the careful work of excavating ocean treasures, but what about the nuanced and invaluable work of making one's meaning clear? Of discerning trust? Of learning to behave empathically? We as humans are fallible here. Why should our robotic counterparts be, too? Why not teach our robots how to model good social behaviour, sourced from the hive-mind of our best communicators and thinkers?

[Slide 17]

Imagine yourself on a hiring committee, buying a new car, at a conference. Can you really believe what people say? Are you understanding all the coded messages? What if there was a latent robotic witness crunching that data for you and determining not only interview questions but forecasting the compatibility of a human candidate in your office environment?

This is precisely where the ERP2 comes in. It builds on all that data gathered through the use of the ERP1, but renders it actionable when embedded in robotic devices.

[Slide 18]

The composite diagram, pictured on this slide, roughly illustrates how the ERP2 functions. Let's focus on the human hand as an example site of enquiry, while also noting that the ERP2 can generate readings on any human body part or facial feature.

The ERP2 gathers its gesticular input data via a comprehensive 3D infra-red laser mesh that is projected onto the subject's body. The mesh is not discernible to the human eye and can function in any light or weather conditions both as a live feed or on recorded media. Thousands of gesticular coordinates, skeletal tracking velocities and sensorial cross-referencing intensities are abstracted onto a digital plane and recoded according to a patented cluster-model algorithm with virtual imaging processing that allows derivative algorithms to represent the subtle, social nuances of conversational modes, exculpatory utterances and implied human engagements.

In simple terms, the ERP2 is a digital truth serum that is stealthier, stronger, completely remote and runs on deeper data analysis than any other product on the market. This data is then processed into responses actionable by the host robot carcass.

[Slide 19]

One of the features that makes the ERP2 so desirable for current markets is its AI cross-referencing data capacity. ERP2's sophisticated computing has the capacity to cross-reference global coordinates with comprehensive databanks that account for global cultural and emotional matrices.

Furthermore, the ERP2 capabilities are constantly updating, and live data package updates are available to all ERP2 users. Because Dramaco Instruments appreciates the importance of documentation for legal purposes, the system is also equipped with instant encrypted recording capabilities with 3D avatar playback visualisation and joint operations coded data displays: this means your data is instantly replayed and translated into various surveillance modes, making your readings immediately legible to criminal, legal and non-specialist audiences.

[Slide 20]

This may sound unapproachable to some of you, so I've included this image of Benny, one of our lab technicians, testing an early prototype of the ERP2 imbedded in a Nao robot. We aren't involved in building robots, but we are interested in enhancing them. With the ERP2 Gesticular Clairvoyance Platform, the Nao robot now has sophisticated social functionalities that help it understand complex human behaviours and intentions.

[Slide 21]

Our robot client base has become one of the fastest-growing markets for Dramaco's ERP2. Here is an image of Pepper talking to an auditorium of hundreds of Peppers, extolling the uses of her new ERP2 implants! As far as we can tell at Dramaco, there is only room for more innovation as we continue 'Designing life, using Dramaco!'

**

A Dramaco Debriefing

In the summer 1991 issue of *October*, Andrea Fraser published 'Museum Highlights: A Gallery Talk'. While published in an academic journal, which holds a reputation for esteemed – if not, for some, exclusive – articles on art theory, criticism and aesthetics, the twenty pages from Fraser include a script for a performance across several dates in February 1989. The script occupies most of each page, aligned to the left margin, with physical actions or details pertaining to setting and activities rendered in italics:

> *At three o'clock, Jane Castelton enters the West Entrance Ha'l and begins to address whoever appears to be listening. She is dressed in a silver-and-brown houndstooth check double-breasted suit with a skirt just below the knee in length, an off-white silk button-down blouse, white stockings, and black pumps. Her brown hair is gathered into a small bun held in place with a black bow:*

Good afternoon, uh ... Everyone? Good afternoon. My name is Jane Castleton, and I'd like to welcome all of you to the Philadelphia Museum of Art. I'll be your guide today as we explore the museum, uh, its history, and its collection. (Fraser 1991: pp. 105–6 italics in the original)

This excerpt gives a flavour of Fraser's script and how she constructs documentation of her museum tours. Fraser, appearing as Castelton, gives every impression of being a reliable host, and as the tour unfolds, she follows a typical museum docent script with triumphal language and praise of the building, patrons and artworks. Eventually, however, doubt manifests as her exaggerations become increasingly absurd. She applies institutional language and sweeping gestures to infrastructure features such as the water fountain, the toilet facilities and the café and museum shop. In so doing, the infrastructure of the institutional narrative is exposed as staged and equally contrived. In the published form of this critique, Fraser includes documentation of the February tours, showing Castleton, suited and pumped, surrounded by persuaded and uncertain museum visitors, alike. The right-hand column of the article carries a series of explanatory footnotes that indicate Fraser's research and exposure of institutional hypocrisies in funding, collecting and programming.

Fraser creates a double narrative here: one of the tricked and one of the wizened. Of course, to move from one to another is to be receptive to a deception – to be aware of the ruse. Both experiences are valid, but one is intended to catch out not only the subject of critique (the museum) but also those who have been unaware of their own duping (the museum visitor). A debrief, in this case, is a disillusionment, and that can be a high-stakes process to navigate for both the author of a critique as well as the disillusioned.

While Fraser works on the museum institution and has done so for decades, including what she argues is a co-opting of institutional critique by institutions themselves (Fraser 2005), my project, 'The Dramaco Instruments Company', has a different target. Dramaco is a counter-archive project that uses the language and visual culture of business pitches and commercial catalogues to highlight the history of psychological instrumentaria and laboratory methods in a consumer market and the subsequent normalisation of human-subject targeting for study, surveillance and deception for the sake of a 'larger' abstract goal: national security, civic obedience and individualised complacency (Chew et al. 2018). 'Counter-archive' in this context picks up on several qualities of an inherently critical enquiry into the work of archives and their generating bodies: they 'can be political … resistant, and community-based. They are embodied differently and have explicit intention to historicize differently, to disrupt conventional … narratives, and to write difference into public accounts' (Chew et al. 2018: p. 9). Through the counter-archive of Dramaco, I use invented documentary traces and performative modes to infiltrate specialist spaces of knowledge exchange that – like Fraser's critique of museum spaces of initiation and dissemination – often go unchecked. These spaces include to date: the tech symposium, the academic conference, the job interview, the academic publication. All scenarios relate to potentially coercive applications of social psychology laboratory instruments updated for twenty-first-century use in the robotics field.

As a counter-archival project, Dramaco occupies a fictional and plausible space that relies upon – in the first instance – a suspension of disbelief followed by a de-hoaxing by way of debriefing. This is not unlike the psychological methods the project critiques, which are discussed below. As a counter-archive, it does the work of de-centring the accepted application of technology on human subjects, one that has a long lineage in the history of psychology (Capshew 1999; Cetina 1992). Following Brett Kashmere (2010) on the qualities of this mode, 'the counter-archive represents an incomplete and unstable repository, an entity to be contested and expanded through clandestine acts, a space of impermanence and play'. Kashmere continues to articulate the tone in which this unfolds, which in my view, is a key aspect of such a mode of critique:

> Taken as an action, the term [counter-archive] entails mischief and imagination, challenging the record of official history. Employed as an artistic strategy it pushes our archival impulse into new territories, encouraging critique and material alteration/fabrication, and emboldening anarchivism. To counter-archive is to counter-act, to rewrite, to animate over. (Kashmere 2010: n.p.)

Creative authorship and supplementation of a documentary narrative make this mode of archival art distinct from many methods explored by artists since what Hal Foster calls the 'archival impulse' of the 1990s (Foster 2004): a postmodern need to work with history as material.

When I started the Dramaco Instruments Company project in 2014, I was a postgraduate student building a PhD thesis focused on Stanley Milgram's research on obedience to authority, and a large portion of my enquiry centred on the material culture of contemporaneous laboratories and deceptive laboratory instruments (see Stanley 1974, 2017). I was also teaching part time at the Royal College of Art (RCA) in London, during a period wherein my pedagogical seat, the School of Humanities, was shrinking: meanwhile, courses related to robotics and engineering in the School of Design were burgeoning. To those knowledgeable in either constituency – that of 'Milgram Studies' or the RCA – the spectre of Dyson as a brand does not ring hollow.

In the case of the RCA, Sir James Dyson is an esteemed alumni, former provost and donor. Inventor of several household gadgets, notably one that harnesses cyclonic separation to stylishly vacuum clean the house, Sir Dyson's name and brand of design continues to influence pedagogy at the well-known art and design college. New facilities and partnerships with Imperial College and Dyson support many new building projects and course pathways, and there is, of course, the recently added RCA Robotics Laboratory. There is no question that I was influenced by what I perceived to be a culture of 'innovation' over criticality, while working at the RCA.

The connection of Dyson to Milgram is narrower but key for me. An influential American social psychologist, Stanley Milgram is widely recognised for his Yale University research on obedience to authority (Milgram 1974, 2017), which disseminated a laboratory model claiming to prove that individuals will follow orders under certain conditions even when their actions will harm another person.[1] As I

---

1   Harper Perennial's 'Resistance Library' series re-published Milgram's 1974 text in 2017 with a jazzy and contemporary cover and introduction from famous psychologist and former friend and colleague of Milgram, Philip Zimbardo. Zimbardo led the infamous Stanford 'prison' experiments in August 1971.

read more and more about Milgram's experiment methods and laboratory designs during my doctoral research, I became increasingly interdisciplinary in my approach to unpacking his famous obedience work. I interviewed artists who had explored Milgram's laboratory design through model reconstructions from photographs (Gaskin 2008; Dickinson 2005) and consulted 'human factors' engineering models commensurate with industry standards for commercially available lab instruments (Chapanis et al. [1949] 1961; Morgan et al. 1963). I visited Milgram's archives at Yale University to find copious planning notes and sketches that revealed Milgram's instrument designs. Most writing on Milgram's obedience work focuses on his data or possible recreations that match contemporary ethics protocols (Burger 2009; Blass 2000; Cohen 2008) and little focus falls upon the material design of the laboratory, which was filled with incredible stage props and scripted procedures.

The original shock generator, or 'Shock Box' as it became known, is permanently enshrined at the Center for the History of Psychology at the University of Akron, Ohio. Milgram designed and built this device to construct a deceptive scenario wherein subjects thought the generator delivered increasingly dangerous electric volts when they depressed levers that traversed the expanse of the device's façade. The device would buzz and lights would go on and off, but no shocks were delivered.[2] It, when compared to other instruments in the collection from university laboratories, stands out as aesthetically striking but rather ineffective as a quantifying device: there were too many bells and whistles compared to contemporaneous, efficient models. Given this discrepancy in design history, the whole infrastructure of laboratory investigation could, in turn, be queried as a performance piece. The pivot of Milgram's obedience research becomes a rather spectacular, fake shock generator that subjects had to engage with throughout an endurance scenario of inflicting (what they thought were) electric shocks on another (complicit) subject.

As I researched Milgram and his contemporaries, his colleagues and critics, I became aware of an amazing heritage of deception in psychology with legacies in nineteenth-century mesmerism. Both share an obsession with science, administrations of electricity and instrument tinkering during the historical 'Brass Age of Psychology' (Popplestone and McPherson 1994). To cling to performed veracity, Milgram took care to design all minutiae of this shock generator.

2   For a deeper analysis of the device's design features, capabilities and images from the archive, see Oppenheimer (2019).

He designed the entire device himself and enlisted technicians to help him do the wiring. Sourcing toggle switches from the Radio-Shack store and bits from Yale laboratories, Milgram budgeted the largest amount of the Shock Box's assembly costs to have a small steel plate engraved with a fake instrument company brand: Dyson Instruments of Waltham, Massachusetts. The brand plate exists on the upper left-hand side of the device like an authenticating stamp (Oppenheimer 2019).

This material fiction, which lies at the heart of the infamous experiment on obedience to authority, an iconic psychology experiment that continues to resonate in popular culture and Psychology 101 textbooks, planted the seed for my own forays into deception in my practice: that of artist-researcher.[3] Following the methods of historians of science like Lorraine Daston (1999), historians of psychology Thomas Sturm and Mitchell Ash (2005), and sociologist of technology Sherry Turkle (2007), I was preoccupied with imagining a biography around this object to unpack its subjective influence on Milgram, his collaborators and human test subjects. What kind of agency did this device bring into the laboratory design? Sturm and Ash challenge researchers to consider what role instruments play in the results of experiments and to acknowledge that the design of instruments is never value-neutral. While Milgram alluded to his interest in theatrical staging in his personal notes, he did not acknowledge the value-laden design of the Shock Box.

For the past four years, I have approached archives, including the Sterling Memorial Library at Yale and the Archive of the History of American Psychology (part of the Center at University of Akron) and instrument collections at McGill University and the University of Toronto, as creative sites of historical research and story-telling. Recently, I tend to regard these fonds as scripts for performance art, leading to themes of dramaturgy crossed with scientific discourse. More specifically, I am mining twentieth-century social psychology experiments that involve deception strategies as part of the experimenters' test conditions. Questions such as 'what was an acceptable

---

3   Recent popular culture examples include the 2015 film *The Experimenter*, directed by Michael Almereyda and staring Peter Sarsgaard as Stanley Milgram and Winona Ryder as Alexandra Milgram; various reality television re-enactments, including the Discovery Channel's *How Evil Are You?* (2011) and the BBC's Horizon series (2009). Book and graphic designer Chip Kidd published a graphic novel about Milgram (2008). Affiliated experiments, including Zimbardo's Stanford 'prison' experiment, have also recently become films, and Zimbardo continues to narrativise his and Milgram's work on 'good and evil' on YouTube and the TEDtalk platform (2008).

threshold of deception for subjects?' and how tone, planted stooges or physical props upheld deception are insightful examples for my own counter-archival work.

Deception is intertwined with the history of psychology. Researchers have and continue to use disinformation, illusions, coercions and props to construct a social situation that is put in motion, quantified, analysed and then generalised to lay claims upon everyday behaviour.[4] Institutional reviews have rendered many such practices unethical, particularly experiments that administer doses of medication, electric shocks or physically and emotionally compromising scenarios. Contemporary practitioners, however, argue that 'research deception' is a necessary method of attaining accurate data (Kimmel 2007; Rosenthal and Rosnow 2008). These range from repetitions of 'bystander effect' scenarios in undergraduate psychology labs to assessing stress under invented testing or competition scenarios. The American Psychological Association (APA), which governs North American standards of practice, dictates that experiment designs using deception must include an essential and standardised debriefing of all subjects. This process must provide 'a prompt opportunity for participants to obtain appropriate information about the nature, result and conclusions of the research' and that potential harm should be mitigated with humane values upheld over scientific priorities (2017: section 8.08). Many such debriefs involve a 'dehoaxing' wherein the deception is revealed to the subject in order to prevent future harm to the subject and remove any confusions or social tensions generated during the research.

It is this history of deception and its parallel emergence of robotics that I am interested in conflating and narrating in order to host conversations about the ethics and equity of robot futures. Whose motives are shaping these devices and what methods beget the products that reach consumers?

The ERP2: Critiquing Robot-to-Human Empathy

While I am the Head of Research and Development at Dramaco Robotic Intelligences, I am not a business person nor a roboticist. In fact, on paper, I have little to do with robotics aside from thinking about them a lot and in atypical ways. I do so from an

---

4   This is also a popular entertainment model as seen in programme concepts including *Candid Camera* (of which Stanely Milgram was a fan: see Milgram and Sabini [1977] 1992) and the Canadian platform 'Just for Laughs'.

artist-archivist and cultural studies perspective.[5] Dramaco which started as an experimental method of thinking critically about the language, visual culture and ethical intent of histories of twentieth-century psychology, has since grown to also encompass discourses in robotics. Dramaco Instruments Company now has a specialised robotics division, which is harnessing its decades of data collection via its customer service and data analysis support systems. This behavioural data is a treasure trove of programmable aptitudes for engineers who seek to make artificial intelligence (AI) interfaces and robot interactions more humanoid.

The ERP2 and its range of devices are plausible. Some of the things I have written about in this expository tone do exist and are emergent product prototypes. As such, I am interested in taking my counter-archival project to constituencies outside galleries and artistic discourses, where this kind of critical play is more intuitive and is more digestible. By pitching to interdisciplinary forums or by accepting the 'come be an artist/humanities representative/critic on our panel of roboticists' invitations, I am finding a different tenor of debate and resistance.[6]

My interjections thus far have led to awkward, combative, competitive and curious discussions. I always begin presentations or pitches as the Head of Research and Development and do not provide the dehoaxing until the final minutes of whatever forum I can gain. This endured confusion – built upon by planned hints and jargon-laden passages of word-salad – pivots into an earnestness of reflexive discussion. Of particular interest for me is the ever-important, elementary ethical query: 'If we can, should we?', as seen in Slide 23 in the PowerPoint deck.[7]

Dramaco's products and the way they are framed are deeply uncomfortable, but they are also not complete inventions. Devices like the ERP2 and its predecessors draw upon language and device functionality encountered in the literature of lie detector devices (Lykken 1998; Bunn 1997), law-enforcement manuals and training guides (O'Toole 1975) and contemporary writing on triumphal innovation,

---

5   Similar tones and methods come to mind in Althea Thauberger's work 'Althea, Lorraine' (2018), which mixes the National Film Board of Canada's Still Photography Division, the persona of its gatekeepers and the work of archiving that requires critical review (see Thauberger 2020).

6   I commiserate with Siri Hustvedt's frustration at being invited to interdisciplinary events to represent the humanities at neuroscience and psychology forums – often finding herself positioned as an apologist, afterthought, defender of ethics (Hustvedt 2016).

7   Slides 24–8 of the counter-archival Slide Deck published here document discussion points I keep in slides to help structure Q&A periods when presenting.

optimisation and 'reproducing the lessons of the market' (Tolentino 2020: p. 63).

Questioning vanguards of innovation (Slide 24 lists time, capital, laboratory space, infrastructure costs, knowledge-transfer and societal care) should be constant areas of critical and ethical investment. We need to be asking whose interests are represented in robotics industries and critiquing how robotics and AI industry players approach language, frame and utilise living subjects, and communicate/share/sell their knowledge as well as data capital. Shannon Mattern's writing around the encoding of racialised bodies captured by robotic surveillance devices at border-crossings is a case in point (Mattern 2018). Robots do the horrific work of removing identity and humanity from figures, reducing them to patterns and digital silhouettes for threat detection and possible annihilation. Such applications of robotic vision are the violent side of the empathy robot-to-human relation coin. These come together and are insidious products of leaping at the vanguard of innovation before we know how to ask careful questions of what robotic entities are doing (with or without us, as suggested in Slide 25).

The ERP2, as a project within the larger counter-archive of Dramaco, targets the ever-depleting membrane between AI-infused robots and human capacities/capabilities. Current vanguards of robotics research explore ways of making technology more comfortable, familiar and emotive: soft robotics is one such constituency (Rus & Tolley 2015), as is the service robot industry (Price 2011). If robots can share more humanoid traits via AI processing, like grasping socialised behaviours and emotional competency, in addition to deep learning, what does this mean for present relations? What models, in particular, are the source material for behaviour? Underlying these queries, especially, is a deep concern for any projection of social responsibility onto devices that are positioned as value-neutral.

Speculative futures and science fiction have long been used when complicating and germinating these debates, and they prove to be areas of creative enquiry that bridge what could otherwise remain localised concern to real-world activism. Queering robotic vision and robot–human relationships (Slide 26) is my current (as of 2021) preoccupation with this work. Legacy Russell's introduction to *Glitch Feminism* succinctly names the issue: 'who defines the material of the body? Who gives it value – and why?' (Russell 2020: p. 9). If a concerted effort is not made to ensure non-normative models, algorithms and critiques are accommodated in robotic innovation (from the human to the robot body), we will see homophobic as well as racist and ableism patterns nascent in heteronormative systems of capital ownership and institutional power reproduced. Furthermore, neuroscientists, biologists, psychologists and medical professionals are still re-learning (and staking claim) to queer ways of being that should and must be translated – culturally, emotionally, intellectually (Roy 2018). This becomes increasingly urgent as robotics research claims to use nature as a source for learning functional, ethical use but dominant readings of nature are still Western European-, Enlightenment- and heteronormative-informed (Slide 27).[8]

It is no accident that the ERP2 concept-device is a literal 'black box' (Slides 2, 17). Part of the Dramaco project involves play with the visual culture of business stock photos and PowerPoint graphic templates: cool blues, modulated greys and curated balance of capability and trade secrets. The metaphor for grasping a system's inputs and outputs but not the workings of its insides is rather 'on the nose' for the fictional devices of Dramaco. It also brings me to the meta-motive for this project, which is to experiment with different methods of writing about these issues, performing warnings and troubling the triumphs.

Dramaco is a collage of various constructions: myths of nation and productivity, narratives of innovation, historical contexts of data surveillance, technological trajectories of capital gain, visual aesthetics and culture of the business pitch, visual culture of corporate environments, and the translation of social interactions into algorithms.

In closing, adopting this persona when writing, speaking and designing – a company history, production and service mandate, commercial products and affiliated archives of adverts and catalogues – allows me to explore urgent tensions around commercial ethics in robotic innovation, as mentioned, but also ritualised structures of knowledge formation and transfer, including the academic chapter or article or conference. The 'fooled you' tactic of counter-archival work can provoke audiences into acknowledging their reactions and uncertainty. If I remember correctly, the particular contribution of Dramaco to the Robot Futures symposium in July 2017 was mixture of low-key frustration on the one hand and curious

---

8   I am indebted to the work of Orphan Drift for this thinking through affect and the digital for decades and across immersive modes. Also recent Zoom discussions with two artists and their work made revisionist edits of this submission more sensitive: Marissa Sean Cruz and her 2019 video piece *PLAY(ing) IN MY PEN(ding doom)* that glitches the Boston Electronics dog robot; Mary Maggic's contribution to the Vera List Center's 'Lab Work – The Art of the Experiment', where she led a meditation on eco-plastics and queer embodiment (see Maggic 2021).

amusement on another: it is difficult to read expressions in the moment, and there is no single way to respond to a glitch in the system. Such is its potential.

References

American Psychological Association (2017) 'Section 8: Research and Publication', *Ethical Principles of Psychologists and Code of Conduct*, pp. 10–12.

Blass, Thomas (2000) *Obedience to Authority: Current Perspectives on the Milgram Paradigm*. New York: Routledge.

Bunn, Geoffrey C. (1997) 'The Lie Detector, Wonder Woman and Liberty: The Life and Work of William Moulton Marston', *History of the Human Sciences* 10(1): 91–119.

Burger, Jerry M. (2009) 'Replicating Milgram: Would People Still Obey Today?', *American Psychologist* 64(1): 1–11.

Capshew, J. H. (1999) *Psychologists on the March: Science, Practice and Professional Identity in America, 1929–1969*. Cambridge: Cambridge University Press.

Cetina, K. K. (1992) 'The Couch, the Cathedral, and the Laboratory: On the Relationship Between Experiment and Laboratory in Science', in Pickering, A. (ed.), *Science as Practice and Culture*. London: University of Chicago Press, pp. 113–38.

Chapanis, A., Garner, W. R. and Morgan, C. T. [1949] (1961) *Applied Experimental Psychology: Human Factors in Engineering Design*. London: Wiley & Sons.

Chew, M., Lord, S. and Marchessault, J. (2018) 'Introduction: Archive/Counter-Archives', *Public* 57: 5–9.

Christensen, L. (1998) 'Deception in Psychological Research: When Is Its Use Justified?', *Personality and Social Psychology Bulletin* 14(4): 664–75.

Cohen, A. (2008) 'Four Decades After Milgram, We're Still Willing to Inflict Pain', *New York Times*, 28 December, A24.

Cruz, M. S. (2021) 'Conversation #4: We Are Still Processing 2020'. Convened by CiCA x FoFA Gallery, Concordia University. Available at https://cuatfofa.gallery/we-are-still-processing-2020/conversation-4 (accessed 9 April 2021).

Daston, L. (1999) 'Introduction', in Daston, L. (ed.), *Biographies of Scientific Objects*. Chicago: Chicago University Press, pp. 1–14.

Dickinson, R. (2005) 'The Milgram Reenactment', in Lütticken, S. (ed.), *Life Once More: Forms of Reenactment in Contemporary Art*, exhibition catalogue. Rotterdam: Witte de With, pp. 109–16.

Foster, H. (2004) 'An Archival Impulse', *October* 110 (autumn): 3–22.

Fraser, A. (1991) 'Museum Highlights: A Gallery Tour', *October* 57 (summer): 103–22.

Fraser, A. (2005) 'From the Critique of Institutions to an Institution of Critique', *Artforum*, September: 278–83.

Gaskin, V. (2003) 'Subjects in Search of an Author', in Ruston, S. (ed.), *The Milgram Re-enactment: Essays on Rod Dickinson's Re-enactment of Stanley Milgram's Obedience to Authority Experiment*. Maastricht: Jan van Eyck Academie, pp. 6–15.

Gundlach, H. (2007) 'What Is a Psychological Instrument', in Ash, M. and Sturm, T. (eds), *Psychology's Territories: Historical and Contemporary Perspectives from Different Disciplines*. London: Lawrence Erlbaum Associates, pp. 195–224.

Havemann, E. (1957) 'The Age of Psychology in the U.S.', *LIFE Magazine*, 7 January: 68–82.

Havemann, E. (1957) 'Tools Psychologists Invented', *LIFE Magazine*, 14 January: 106–20.

Havemann, E. (1957) 'The Psychologist's Service in Solving Daily Problems', *LIFE Magazine*, 21 January: 84–102.

Hustvedt, S. (2016) *A Woman Looking At Men Looking At Women; Essays on Art, Sex, and the Mind*. New York: Simon and Schuster.

Kashmere, B. (2010) 'Cache Rules Everything Around Me', *Incite Journal of Experimental Media* 2. Available at http://incite-online.net/intro2.html (accessed 30 October 2019).

Kidd, C. (2008) *The Learners*. New York: Simon and Schuster.

Kimmel, A.J. (2007) *Ethical Issues in Behavioral Research: Basic and Applied Perspectives*. Cambridge, MA: Blackwell.

Lykken, D. (1998) *A Tremor in the Blood: Uses and Abuses of the Lie Detector*. New York: Perseus.

Maggic, M. (2021) Seminar 6: Lab Work – Art of the Experiment. Convened by Jeannine Tang. Workshop part of As for Protocols Series, Vera List Center, Zoom, online.

Mattern, S. (2018) 'All Eyes on the Border', *Places*. Available at https://placesjournal.org/article/all-eyes-on-the-border (accessed 30 October 2019).

Milgram, S. (1974) *Obedience to Authority: An Experimental View*. New York: Harper and Row.

Milgram, S. (2017) *Obedience to Authority* ('Resistance Library Series'). New York: Harper Perennial.

Milgram, S. and Sabini J. [1977] (1992) 'Candid Camera', in Sabini, J. and Silver, M. (eds), *The Individual in a Social World: Essays and Experiments* (2nd edition). London: McGraw-Hill.

Morgan, C. T., et al. (1963) *Human Engineering Guide to Equipment Design*. New York: McGraw-Hill.

Oppenheimer, M. R. (2019) 'Dramaturgical Devices and Stanley Milgram's Hybrid Practice', in Cateforis, D., Duval, S. and Steiner, S. (eds), *Hybrid Practices: Art in Collaboration with Science and Technology in the Long 1960s*. Berkeley: University of California Press.

O'Toole, G. (1975) *The Assassination Tapes: An Electronic Probe into the Murder of John F. Kennedy and the Dallas Coverup*. New York: Penthouse Press.

Popplestone, J. and McPherson, M. (1994) *An Illustrated History of American Psychology*. Madison: Brown and Benchmark.

Price, L. (2011) 'NurseBot: Personal Mobile Robotic Assistants for the Elderly', The Index Project. Available at https://theindexproject.org/stories/nursebot (accessed 4 November 2019).

Rosenthal, R. and Rosnow, R. L. (2008) *Essentials of Behavioral Research: Methods and Data Analysis* (3rd edition). New York: McGraw-Hill.

Roy, D. (2018) *Molecular Feminisms: Biology, Becomings and Life in the Lab*. Seattle: University of Washington Press.

Rus, D. and Tolley, M. T. (2015) 'Design, Fabrication and Control of Soft Robots', *Nature* 521: 467–75.

Russell, L. (2020) *Glitch Feminism*. New York: Verso Books.

Sturm, T. and Ash, M. (2005) 'Roles of Instruments in Psychological Research', *History of Psychology* 8: 3–34.

Thauberger, A. (2020) 'Interview', *CanadianArt*, 26 February. Available at https://canadianart.ca/interviews/althea-thauberger-2 (accessed 9 April 2021)

Tolentino, J. (2020) *Trick Mirror: Reflections on Self-delusion*. New York: Random House.

Turkle, S. (2007) *Evocative Objects: Things We Think With*. Cambridge, MA: MIT Press.

Zimbardo, P. (2008) 'The Psychology of Evil', TEDtalk. Available at https://www.ted.com/talks/philip_zimbardo_on_the_psychology_of_evil?language=en (accessed 4 November 2019).

12 Metalithic Postcards During the Pandemic

Ian Dawson and Paul Reilly

Robotic vision should come as no surprise. After all, the siliceous revolution has been evolving for quite some time. In fact, silicate technology is one of the oldest and most enduring examples of human ingenuity. In the chalklands of southern Britain, flint has been the material of choice for a wide range of lithic tools and technological developments for prosthetic extensions to dexterous hands and multimodal embodied intra-actions from the palaeolithic period onwards (e.g. blades for cutting and skinning, axes for carving and felling, and picks for digging). Flint is a very hard material which when fashioned produces incredibly persistent artefacts that can retain their identity and carry the memory of their own fashioning and subsequent uses almost indefinitely (Lord 1993). Until recently, such objects were generally recorded, analysed and fixed within typological and functional categorisations by archaeologists using standardised 2D hand-drawing and photographic practices (e.g. Raczynski-Henk 2017). While these long-established methods allow scholarly classification and comparisons to be made, few would argue that such methods of (re)presentation convey anything like the full multidimensional, multisensorial, material character or presence of the lithic tools themselves. Moreover, such depictions say almost nothing about the environment and setting from which these artefacts emerged. However, 3D digital photogrammetry, scanning, and automated drawing and rendering methods are beginning to address some of these limitations (e.g. Barone et al. 2018; Gatt 2019).

For Paul Reilly, an archaeologist, and Ian Dawson, a sculptor, our transdisciplinary art/archaeology encounters with, and studies of, such beautiful handcrafted stone artefacts are instantaneously and endlessly fascinating. Besides being aesthetically, technologically and culturally intriguing, lithic artefacts wear the marks of their making as 'impact scars', displaying interesting and beautiful patinas which recall different aspects of their long life journeys. It is not unusual, for example, for so-called Stone Age tools to be (re)used and retouched in later periods such as the Bronze Age or the Roman period (e.g. Adkins and Adkins 1985; Manclossi et al. 2019; Devièse et al. 2020). They are pluritemporal, that is, they have multiple overlapping pasts (Olivier 2011), ongoing presents and imminent futures. They are not finished objects, for they are still in the making, and their biographies and itineraries are ongoing. They continue to spawn new genealogies of mattering and, regardless of how ancient and durable any particular artefact may be, it remains an 'object in motion' (Gillespie and Joyce 2015). One particular artefact from a pluritemporal scatter, or surface assemblage (Harrison 2011), of lithic artefacts found by Paul Reilly in a cornfield on the Hampshire Downs, UK, is being (re)shaped, (re)apprehended and (re)contextualised, sometimes disruptively, in a transdisciplinary project exploring post-human (Braidotti 2013, 2019) and post-photographic (Zylinska 2017) *phy*sical and di*gital* (i.e. *phygital*) 'art/archaeology' practices (see Bailey 2017, 2018).

This chapter explores our expanding cyborgic apprehension of a flint artefact encountered by the authors during the pandemic of 2020 and the phygital perturbations exerted from this moment of serendipity. We call the extreme skeuomorphic[1] artefacts that emerge from our intra-actions with this Mesolithic artefact and the non-human visual technologies (Zylinska 2017) enfolding this cognitive assemblage (Hayles 2017) of mattering (Barad 2007) *metalithics*. The twelve postcards in this chapter document our plastic and digital responses to this individual but persistent lithic artefact, retaining many aspects of this inspirational cryptocrystalline prototype, including the affordances of wonder, enchantment (Perry 2019) and novel acts of discovery (Edgeworth 2015). The postcards also comment, diffractively, on our purposefully disruptive transdisciplinary, technology-based and subversive art/archaeology practices.

What do we mean by 'diffractively'? The term has several connotations. In physics, diffraction (or interference) refers to the different ways waves combine when they intersect, and the apparent bending that occurs when a wave encounters an obstruction. Here, though, following feminist theoretician and physicist Karen Barad (2007), diffraction also refers to the way in which phenomena dynamically intra-act and entangle. According to Barad, these encounters produce reconfigurations that produce a 'differencing' and a 'space-timemattering' (Barad 2014: p. 168). This inspires our art/archaeology approach.

---

1   Skeuomorphism is a reference to objects whose formal characteristics and properties were derived from an earlier prototype made with different materials with material affordances not associated with that of the new object – for instance, a ceramic pot shaped with sharp angles that looks like a hammered metal container (see Conneller 2013). One might think of skeuomorphism as remediation; a popular example is the trash can on a computer desktop.

During the coronavirus lockdown the authors were isolated from one another, our respective departments, and much of the shared technology and collegiate expertise we normally relied on in our previous collaborations. Fortunately, communication and exchanging digital artefacts in this partnership was very productively disrupted by the pandemic. The physical exchanges of these artefacts, and their surrogates, held many generative surprises along their journey from, and back to, a field in Hampshire, via a home office in a small nearby village, and a home studio in south-east London. In addition to the internet, the Royal Mail was crucial to delivering our post-human metalithic intervention, and it is important that we acknowledge this quotidian physical dimension in our material discursive dialogue by sharing our insights through the set of postcards presented here.

Art/Archaeology Postcards from the Field

Postcard 1

> [T]here is more to photography than meets the (human) eye [because]
> *all photography bears a nonhuman trace.* (Zylinska 2017: p. 51)

It is amazing what you can find if you know where and how to look. Recognising an ancient lithic tool in a ploughed field covered with broken stones, or under a crop of corn, is not straightforward. Potential artefacts are indicated, initially, by tell-tale shapes. It takes patient practice to 'get your eye in' and recognise objects of interest, as they are inevitably partially obscured by the soil (regolith) still attached, and may also be screened by plants. Normally, the field archaeologist must pick up, clean and handle the suspected stone to confirm its status as an artefact. In other words, the act of discovery is a multistage, multimodal process. The Mesolithic artefact of interest here was found just off a footpath running across a cornfield on the chalklands of the Hampshire Downs. When we say 'Mesolithic' we mean that its technical style suggests that the lithic tool we can now hold in our hands was fashioned in the Middle Stone Age (i.e. c. 10,000 BCE to c. 4,000 BCE). However, since flint is incredibly hard, durable and useful, this persistent artefact could have been in and out of use in the succeeding millennia before it started mattering to us at 13:31 hours on 24 September, CE 2020. This initial act of discovery was photographed in situ by Reilly in collaboration with his Honor 8X mobile imaging device, which also logged the metadata just referenced. The intra-acting assemblage that is implicated in Postcard 1 includes a veritable cornucopia of entangled silica: the lithic artefact

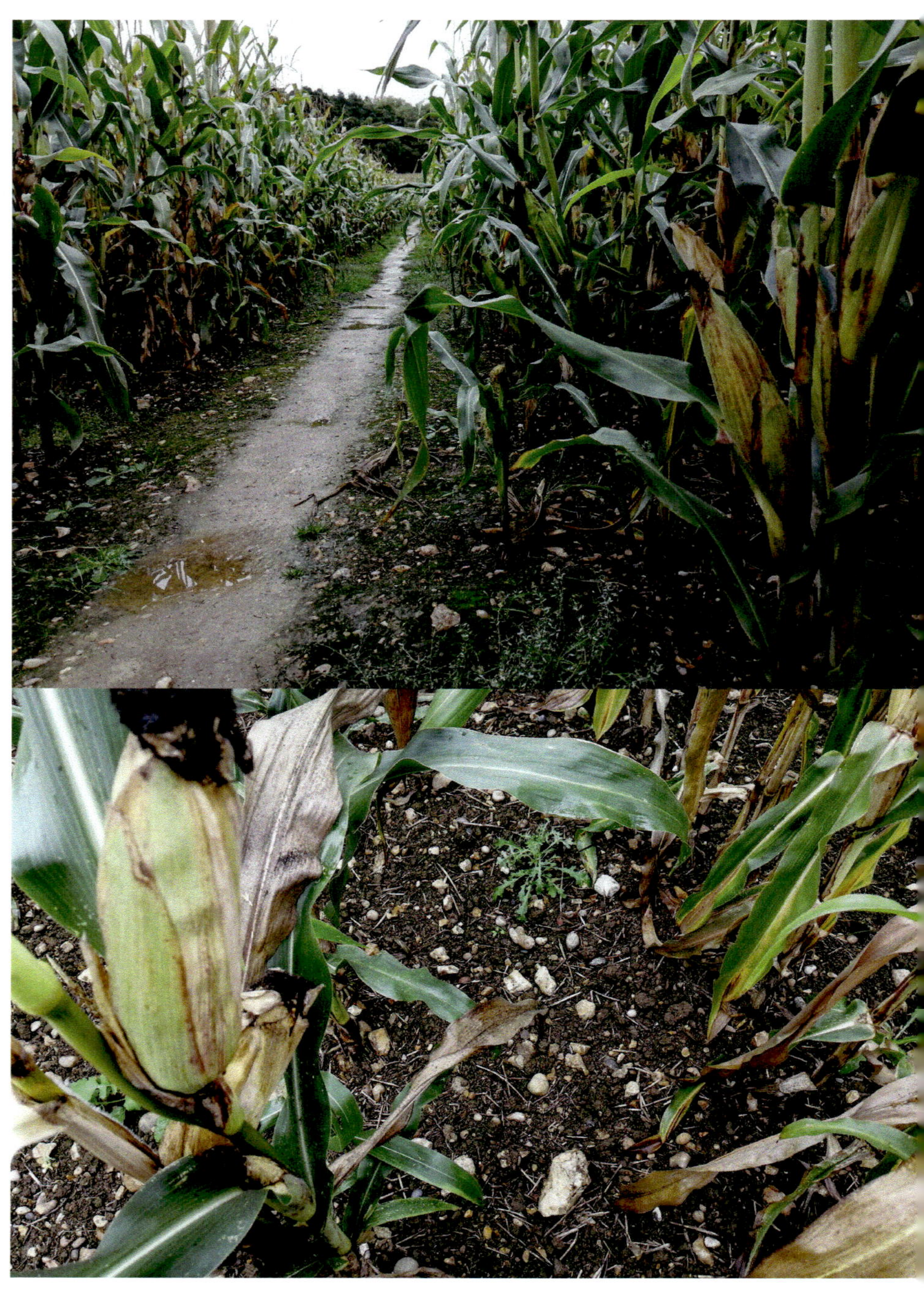

Postcard 1 'A silica-entangled act of discovery', image montage, 2021.
Image credit: Ian Dawson and Paul Reilly.

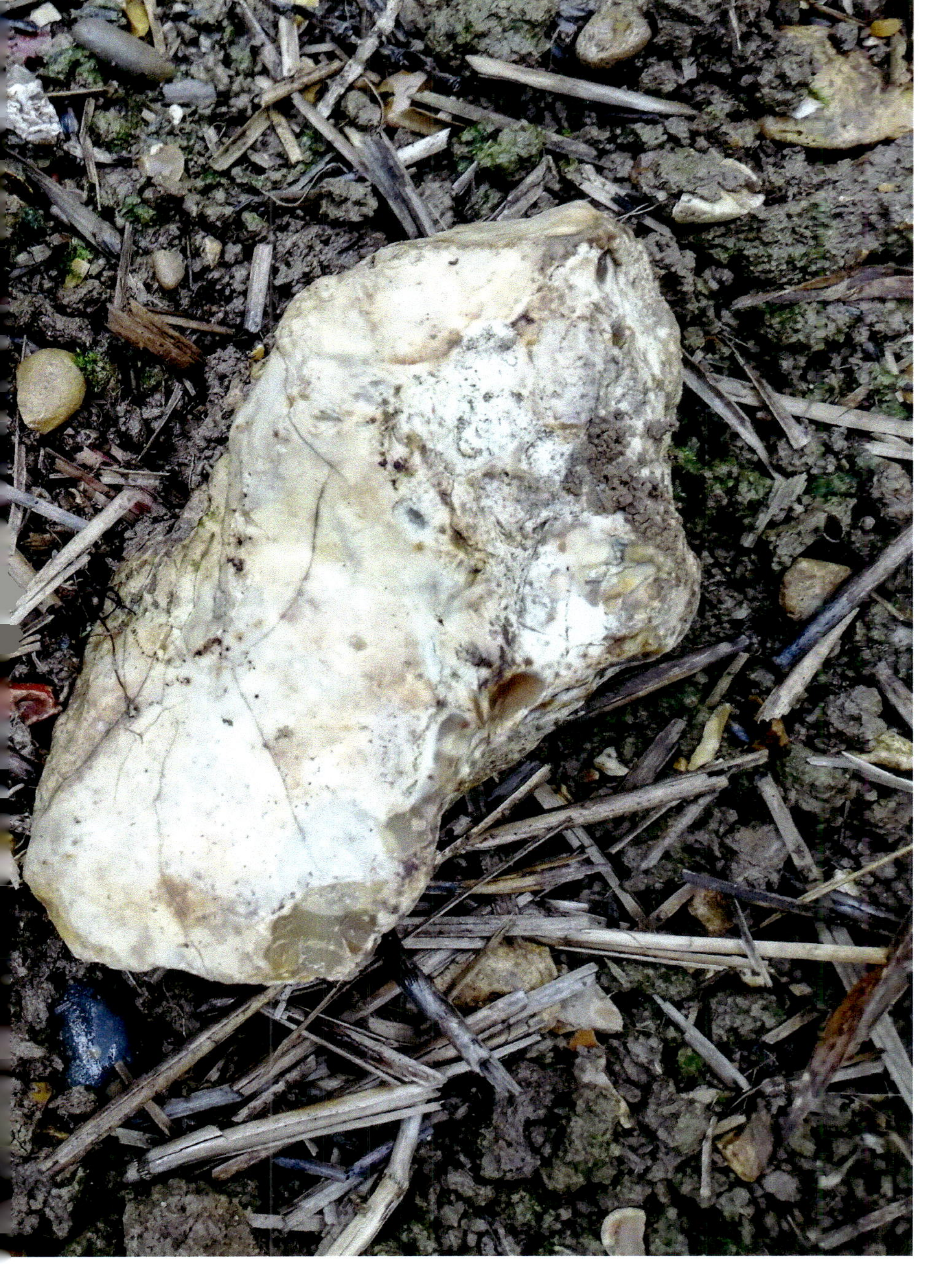

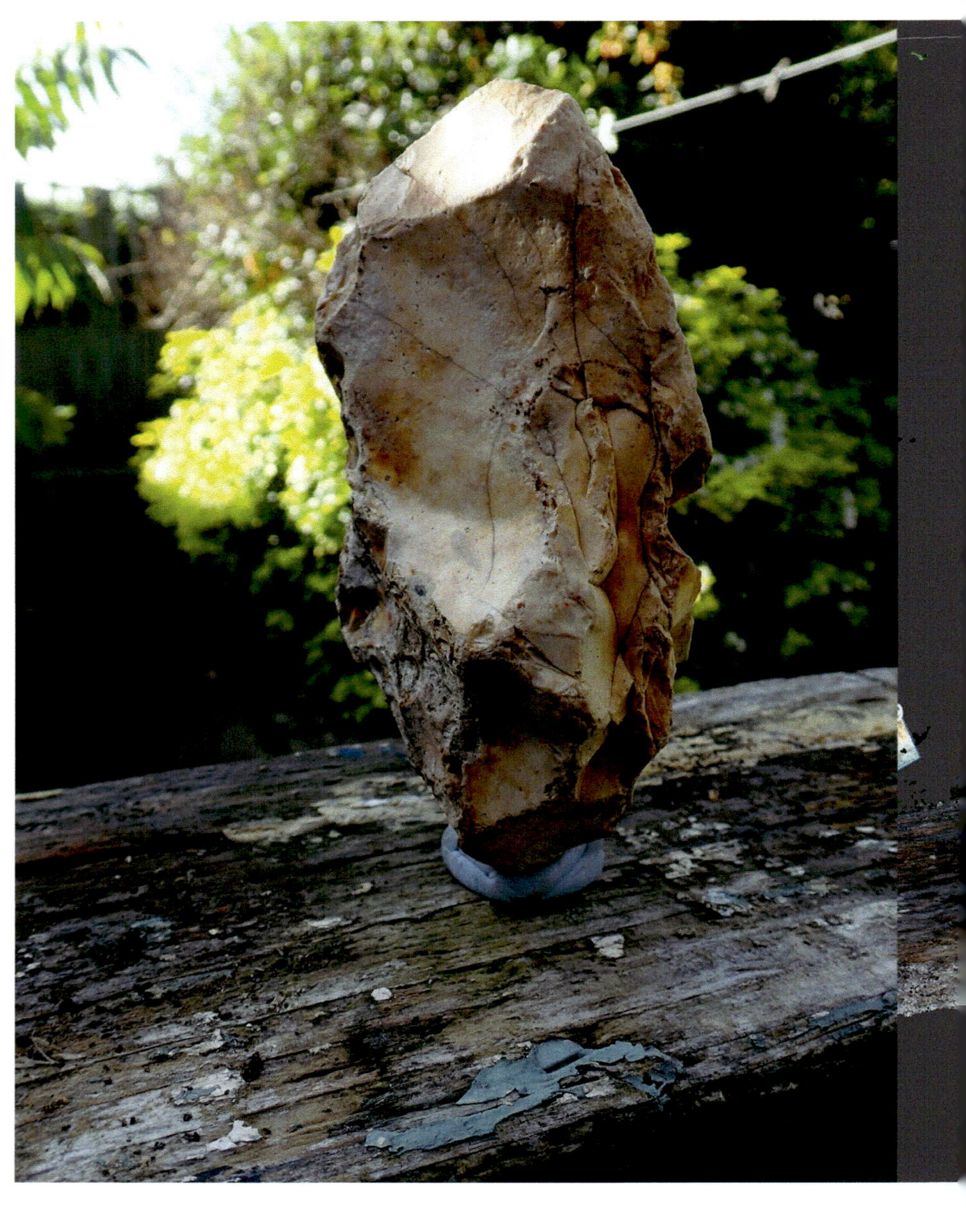

Postcard 2 'Structure from motion (SfM)', image montage, 2021. Left side (above): photographic still. Right side (opposite): screenshot using Agisoft Metashape. Image credit: Ian Dawson and Paul Reilly.

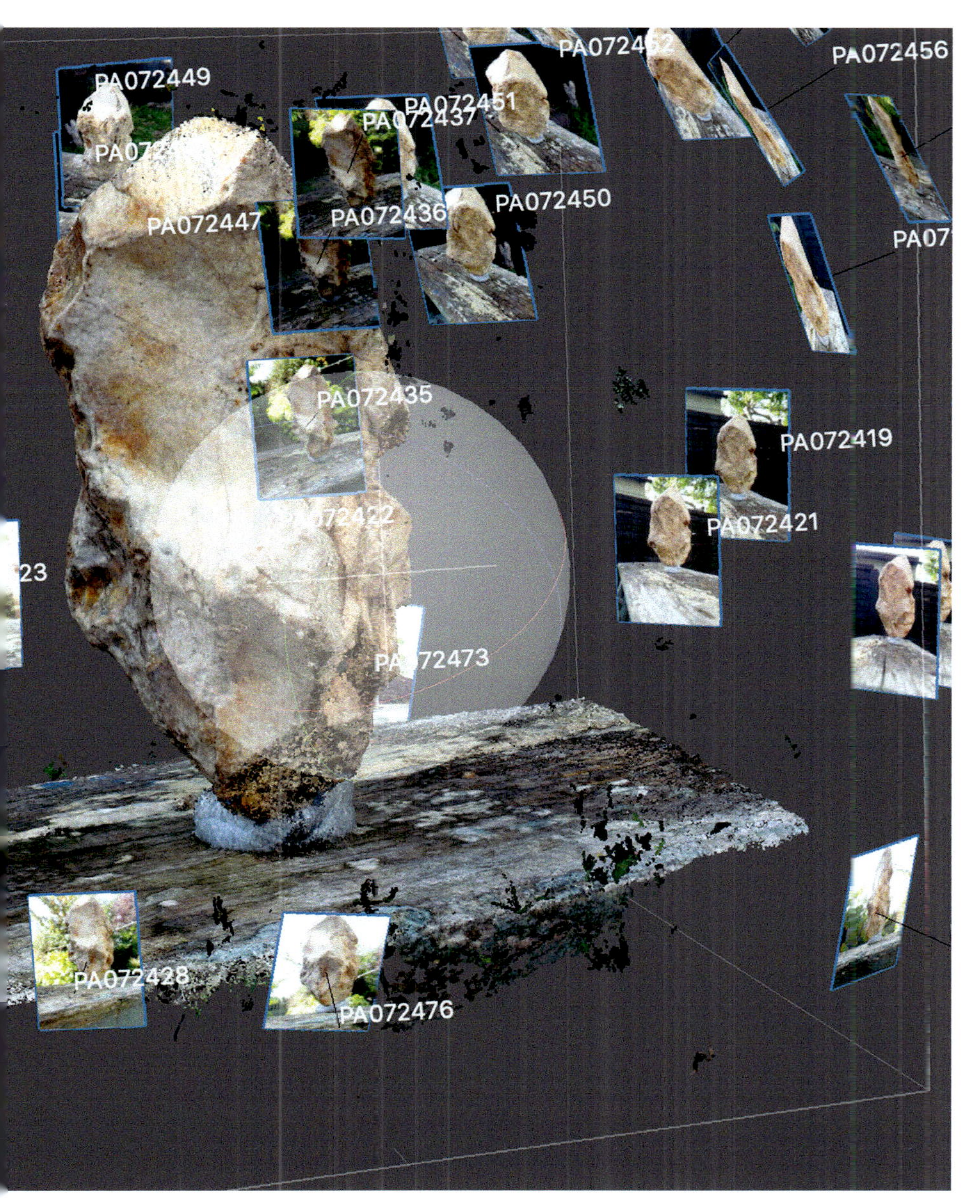
PA072449
PA072462
PA072456
PA072451
PA072437
PA07
PA072447
PA072436
PA072450
PA07
PA072435
PA072419
PA072422
PA072421
23
PA072473
PA072428
PA072476

was fashioned from a cryptocrystalline flint nodule; the lithic and its context were transmitted via photons through the glass lens of the camera; next the flux of light was sampled over the period of exposure and registered as numerical readings via an array of epitaxial silicon-based light-sensitive 'eyes' on the charge-coupled device (CCD); after which, the array of data was relayed for processing to produce an image using a HiSilicon Kirin 710 chipset, and displayed on a glass screen, or stored on a silicon solid-state drive (SSD); and later transmitted over a network to further silicon-based devices.

When measured, our lithic weighed 510g, and its longest dimensions were 130 mm × 77 mm × 46 mm. Neither the metrics nor the static 2D digital photographic record or adequately convey what it feels like when you grasp the artefact in your hand and appreciate its heft and subtle balance. Nor does it explain how your fingertips instinctively find the slightly softer and rougher pads of cortex that the maker left in place to offer a good comfortable grip, while keeping the hard and sharp business end of the tool projecting well clear of the user's palm and fingers when wielding it.

Sharing this artefact remotely and virtually was an unexpected challenge to our collaboration efforts, due to the disruption caused by the Covid-19 pandemic.

Postcard 2

> Form is henceforth divorced from matter. In fact, matter as a visible object is of no great use any longer, except as the mould on which form is shaped. Give us a few negatives of a thing worth seeing, taken from different points of view, and that is all we want of it. (Holmes 1859)

More than 150 years after Oliver Wendell Holmes made this prescient observation, our first step was to register the object in the round by applying the widely used archaeological technique known as 'structure from motion' (SfM) photogrammetry (e.g. Historic England 2017). To accomplish this, Reilly took the flint into his back garden and placed it on a stepladder, using Blu Tack to create a temporary armature or prosthetic support, in order to allow navigation around the artefact. With the object now bathed in natural light and centred in its makeshift amphitheatre, Reilly then ritually circled the object, intermittently taking photographs with a digital camera, and produced a sequence of sixty-one images that formed a rough spherical overlapping mosaic. This performance echoed François Willème's pioneering rapid prototyping techniques known as photosculpture in the 1860s (Cubitt 2014: p. 240; Minkin and Dawson 2014), which sets out an alternative path towards parallel processing, and one distinctly different from that of the sequential narrative of cinematic film history – 'a wholly noncinematic, but rather precybernetic mode of visual analysis' (Cubitt 2014: p. 240). Whereas Willème's capture process utilised twenty-four cameras situated in a circle around a sitter to create daguerreotypes with a ten-second exposure, Reilly used an Olympus Tough compact digital camera with its aperture set to f3.2 and the exposure time set to 1/60 s (so, cumulatively, just over one second of imaging). 186.4 MB were downloaded from the CCD in packets of 3456×4608 pixels in jpg format, via a USB2 cable connected to a Lenovo W540. Then on 7 October 2020 this data was uploaded to a Google folder by Reilly from his home office in a Hampshire village via a WiFi router, and downloaded by Dawson in his garden studio in London on a 4G tethered Apple Macbook Pro, and then processed using Agisoft Metashape. The sixty-one images were aligned, creating 27,138 tie points, processed into a dense point cloud of 2,236,753 points, and finally meshed as a 3D model with 447,330 faces. The processing in the SfM software took 9 minutes and 45 seconds.

Rotating our new/old digital object inside our software portal we navigated its various orthographic views. The image is pseudo-orthographic as the flint's surface – with its structure of cracks and knapped fissures – is reinscribed with a new set of gestural parameters attached. The skeuomorphic flint we now encounter appears 'just enough as it used to be' (May 2019: p. 87). As the pixel information derived from the Mesolithic flint was processed we reconsidered the unfolding of different temporalities and how 'distinct technical ages are bound up with distinct conceptions of time' (May 2019: p. 39). We created a three-dimensionally navigable file format for future digital handling, assembling a *mnemotechnical* image by a process of signals and as an aggregation of data. Although we might think of the digital camera and the sixty-one images as having composed this photogrammetric composite, this is a process more akin to modes of telemetry in the format of an electrical image (May 2019: p. 50). We can think of these images as having new forms of dynamism as data are transmitted across great distances and at speeds we cannot grasp, and as part of an energetic process, like Nipkow's scanning disc of 1884, a patented imaging device to make visible 'object A at any location B' through the reassembly of 'tiny oblongs of light suspended in a whirling rectangle of brilliance in the machine's gaping mouth' (Kittler 2009: p. 208).

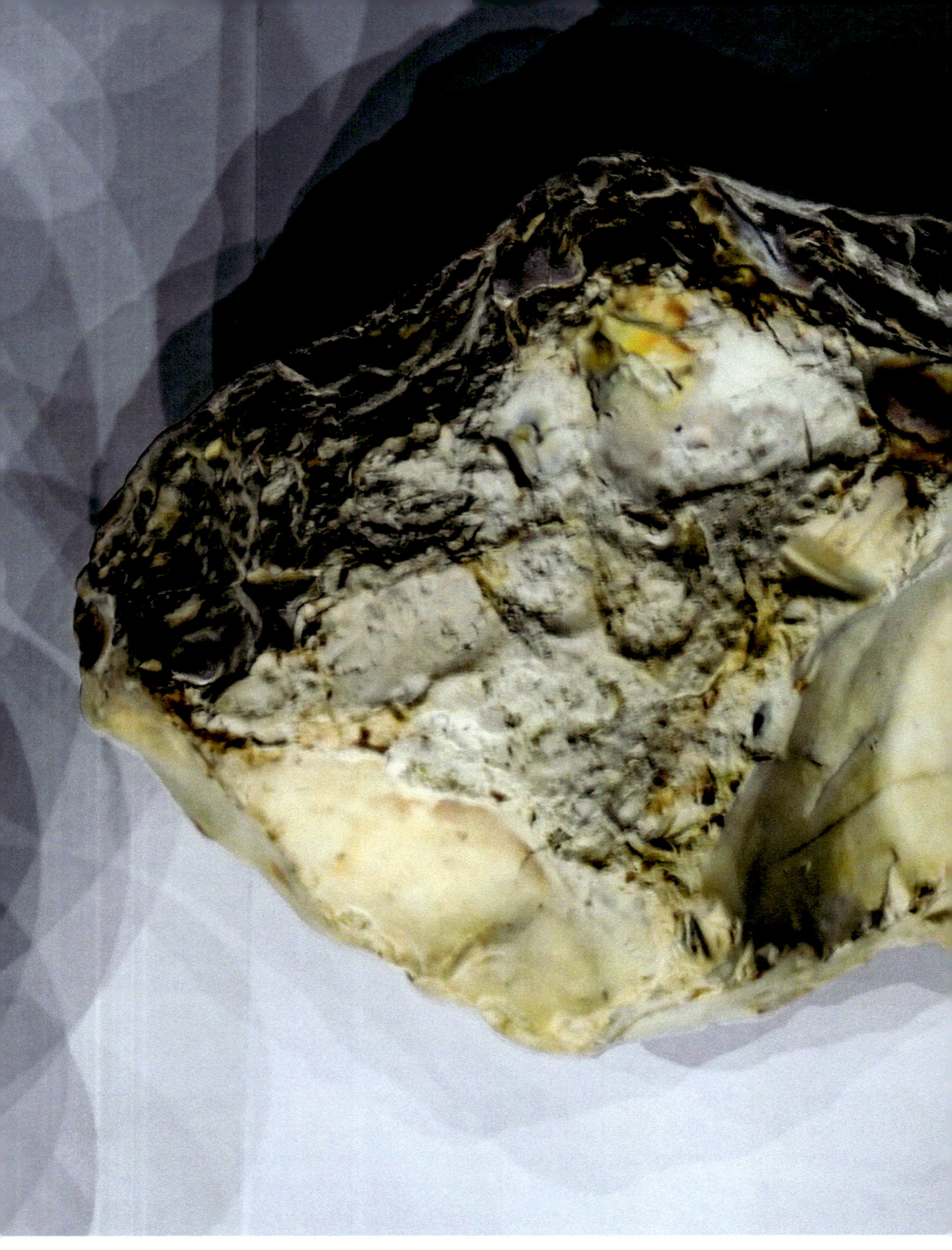

Postcard 3 'This is not a photograph of a Mesolithic artefact', PTM file exported as JPG from the RTI Viewer, 2021.
Image credit: Ian Dawson and Paul Reilly.

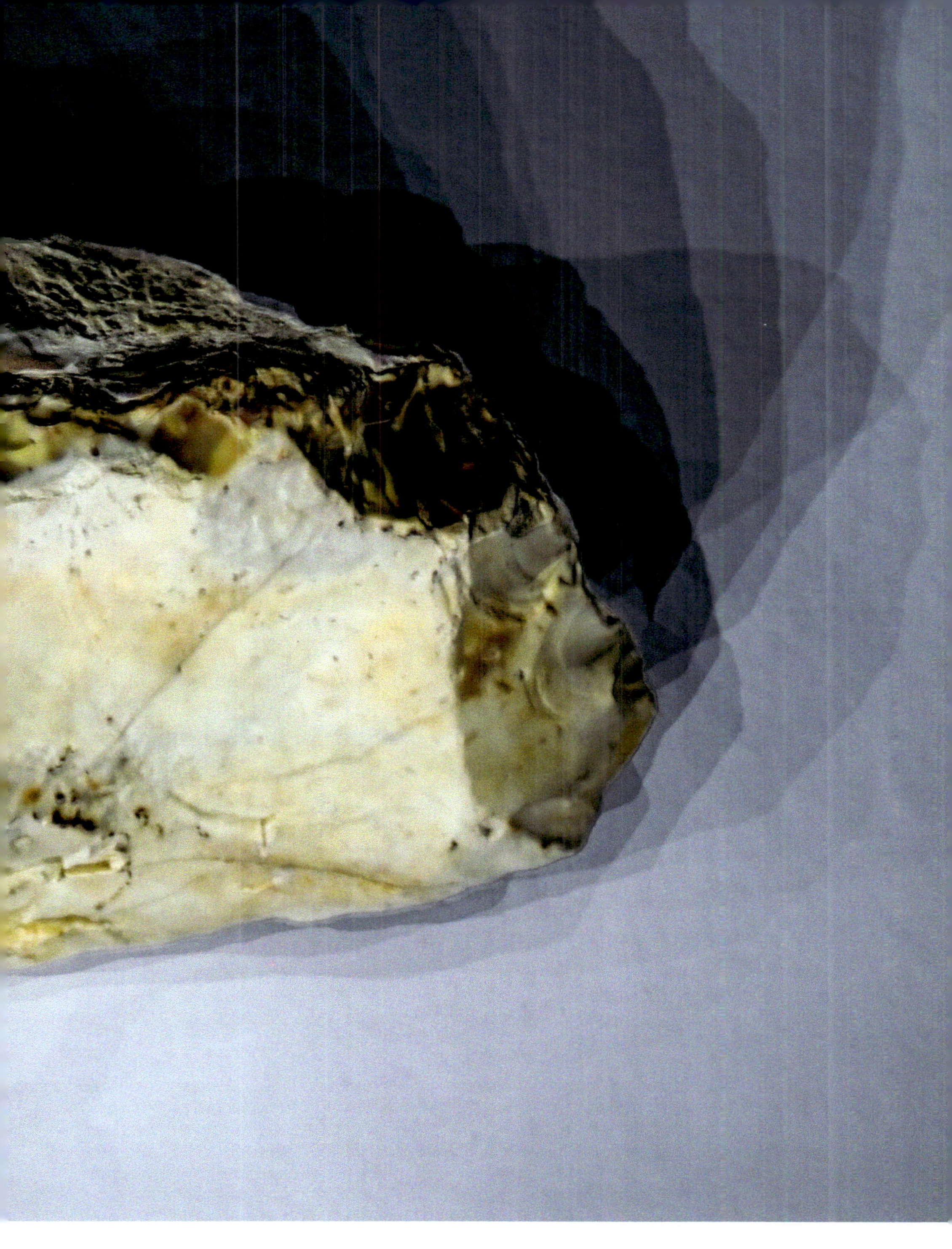

Postcard 3

> Digital images are not innocent, they carry genealogies of practices
> of looking and recording. (Jones and Díaz-Guardamino 2019: p. 211)

Postcard 3 appears to be a traditional static photograph of our post-Mesolithic artefact. It is a misleading image, for the depiction is a synthetic or, in Vilém Flusser's (2011) terms, a 'technical image'. It is a *compiled* frame produced by employing another archaeological computational photographic technique, called reflectance transformation imaging (RTI), developed by the non-profit organisation Cultural Heritage Imaging (CHI n.d.). Put simply, RTI is a technique which uses multiple light positions to extract the surface morphology and colour properties of a subject in extremely intimate detail, allowing relighting and reinvestigation.[2] This frame is just one of many possible visual instances obtainable from a volatile quantum mosaic of algorithmically defined individual pixel states, modelling morphological, colour and textural properties (specifically, colour and surface normal), of a digital surrogate of the prototype artefact. The data required to create this polynomial texture map (PTM) were derived from a sequence of fifty-four photographs taken from a fixed camera (actually, a photon detector) in which, with each successive shot, the position of the strobe lighting the object was incrementally moved to produce a hemispherical array of lighting positions. Highlights due to the strobe's flash, which are detected on a fixed reflective sphere, in every frame, allow surface normal and lighting angles to be calculated. Once the PTM is compiled, the artefact's simulated surface morphology can be relit interactively with new (virtual) reflective properties, such as highly directional reflections due to specular enhancement or, more or less, scattered reflections modelled with diffuse gain filters. The changing interplay of light and shadows, while intra-acting with the virtual artefact with the different rendering filters provided by the RTIViewer interface, allows the user

2   For a full description of various forms of RTI see CHI (n.d.). English Heritage (2018) also gives a convenient and accessible introduction to best practice and the different forms of RTI. In the method practised here, a static camera takes multiple images, while a direct light source is moved to a different position for each shot. This is usually a tethered strobe which can be placed at acute angles to accentuate the shadows cast across the object. Many photographs are then processed, extracting the light information to form a polynomial texture map (PTM). A PTM file is a viewable interactive image where the viewer can retrace the different amalgamated lighting positions and view the object through an array of different filters, such as specular enhancement, diffuse gain and normals visualisation, each of which is able to bring out specific aspects of the subject being studied; these all are synthesised images. See also Dawson et al. (2021).

to discover and record fine informative surface details which would be missed by the unassisted human eye. For instance, low-incidence, or very shallow, raking light is very effective for emphasising surface relief such as retouched edges and fine scratches. Incidentally, the associated fringe of interlaced shadows, due to the sequence of fifty-four changed lighting angles, is a kind of temporal diffraction pattern in which 'different times bleed through one another' (Barad 2017: p. 68). Dimensions of time, such as duration, past, present and future, are blurred in this unique unfolding cognitive assemblage.

Postcard 4

> Photographs, never intrinsically calculable, remain thoroughly visual. Images, structurally calculable, are only apparently visual. (May 2019: pp. 50–2)

Postcard 4 is a *diffractive image* (Dawson et al. 2021) of the same RTI image in Postcard 3, in which 'artistic', or qualitative and observational, renderings are interlaced with 'scientific', or quantitative, computational or mathematical, renderings (see Carusi et al. 2014). The image is a collage of what we consider to be the 'best' viewing combination to bring out important archaeologically diagnostic and aesthetic details. For example, without going into technical details, in the bottom left of the image the shiny metallic-appearing oval indent is produced using 'specular enhancement' and a pseudo-raking light, which brings out the subtle ripples in the facet indicating the direction of percussive force applied to detach a bulbous flake and develop an edge on this section of the tool. Immediately above, a 'diffuse gain' filter was judged to be the most effective rendering mode for defining the rough surface of the unworked cortex of the flint nodule from which the tool emerged. Equally, 'luminescence unsharp masking' allows a more intimate examination of the pitting and cracks across the large facets in the central right section between the two upper vertical colour-coded blocks mapping the computed surface normal topology of the lithic. All the visualisations in this collage reveal significant morphological and post-fabrication details. Each of the rendering algorithms used (i.e., default, specular enhancement, luminescence unsharp masking, diffuse gain and normals filtering) are standardised functions (CHI n.d.), but their application – when and where to apply them, and under what lighting angles so as to make and register the most informative or surprising observations – depends

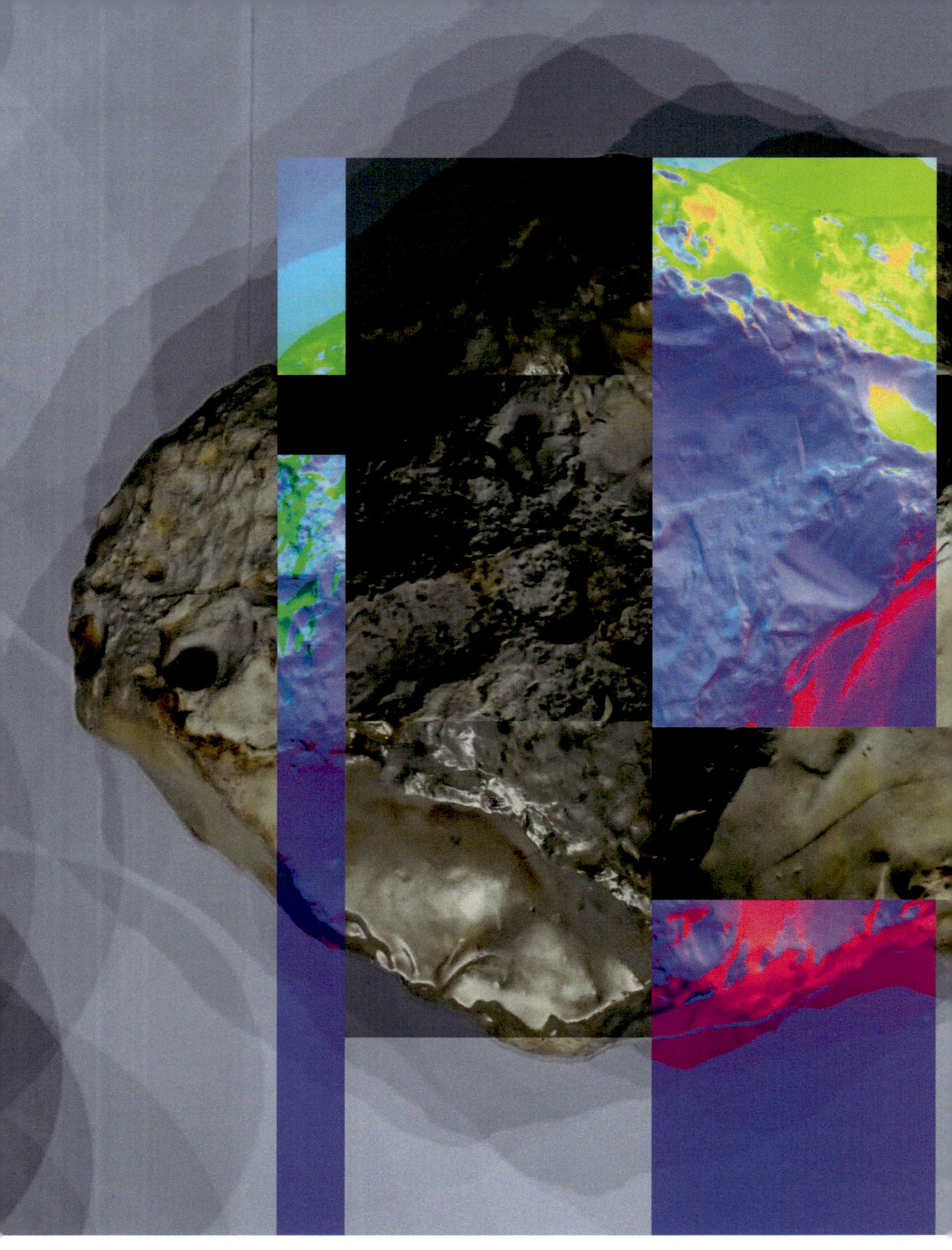

Postcard 4 'Reflectance transformation (diffractive) image', composite images exported from a PTM file on the RTIViewer, 2021.
Image credit: Ian Dawson and Paul Reilly.

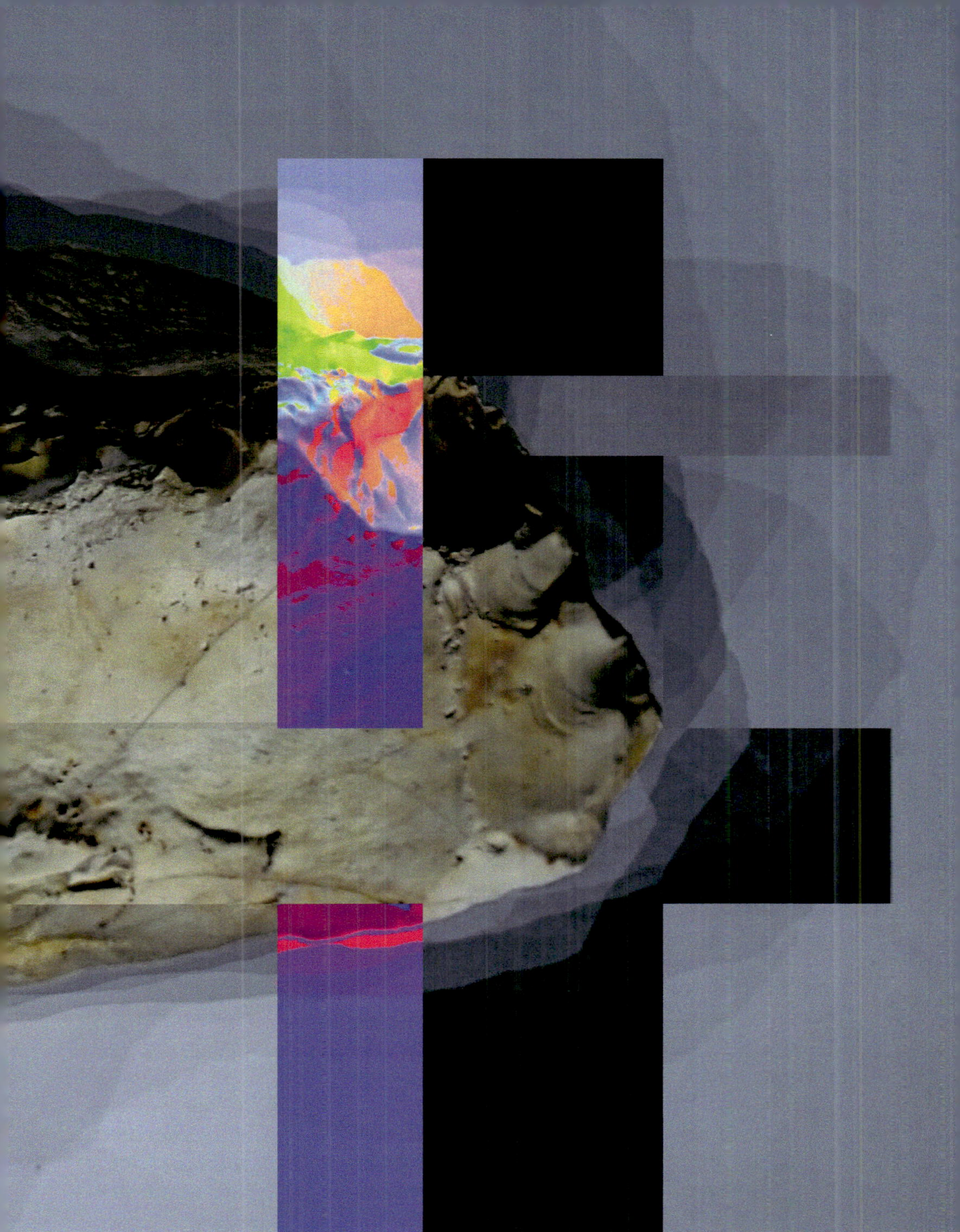

much more on what is being looked for in the first place and how that changes when one's visual searches need to be recalibrated and reframed by the individual researcher, as new details suggesting new avenues needing (re)searching are identified. Most RTI users will start their visual investigations using the default settings of the RTI apparatus and software. Very quickly, they will start to pan and zoom into details and experiment with different filters to better bring out features of interest to them in the context of their own research perspective and ambitions. Changing wavelengths (to, e.g., IR, UV, or multispectral) will sometimes disclose previously invisible details, which then catalyse a completely new series of visual interrogations at higher resolutions (e.g. Kotoula 2016; Giachetti et al. 2017). As Karen Barad puts it:

> Apparatuses are not preexisting or fixed entities; they are themselves constituted through particular practices that are perpetually open to rearrangement. This is part of the creativity and difficulty of doing science: getting the instrumentation to work in a particular way for a particular purpose (which is always open to the possibility of being changed during the experiment as different insights are gained). (Barad 2007: p. 203)

Postcard 5

> Only when we focus on computer-synthesised images, images of the nearly impossible because [they are] ungraspable, unimaginable, and incomprehensible, can we start to suspect what sort of hallucinatory power is at hand. (Flusser 2011: p. 37)

Postcard 5 adds another layer of machine/human cognitive diffraction onto the image in Postcard 3, exploiting the computer vision technique of image 'style transfer', which is readily available on the internet. Style transfer relies on sophisticated 'neural algorithms of artistic style' (Gatys et al. 2016) using a very deep convolved neural network (CNN) (Simonyan and Zisserman 2015) to extract the *style* of one image and transfer it onto the *content* of another (Miller 2019, chapters 7–12; Wang et al. 2020). It produces another form of diffractive image which, in this case, interlaces different styles and subjects through a machinic way of seeing. Our 'content image' is once again the compiled RTI frame shown in Postcard 3, featuring the fringe of interlaced shadows that materialise a temporal diffraction pattern. The applied style image is a Nomarski differential interference contrast microscopy rendering of a partially etched silicon integrated circuit wafer (Richstraka 1979). The result of this diffraction experiment is 'Silicon alchemy I' (Postcard 5), which is quite a departure from standard representations of lithic objects (e.g., Lord 1993; van Gijn 2010; Raczynski-Henk 2017). This is one of a series of diffractive digital studies exploring the recursive intra-action of light, shadows, silicon and artificial neurons (Reilly 2020). In this study, the archaeologist's usual analytical gaze upon the 'impact scars' that shaped the flint tool, through the RTI image, is radically disrupted when it is convolved with the machinic gaze of a *style transfer* deep neural network. The outcome of this exercise is a diffractive image in which the RTI multi-lit flint artefact, including its spacetimemattering *compound shadows*, is seemingly transmuted and rematerialised as backlit stained glass. The artefact is rendered recognisable as a multitemporal, multiscaler phenomenon by an eclectic post-human cognitive assemblage.

Postcard 6

> The 'eyes' made available in modern technological sciences shatter any idea of passive vision; these prosthetic devices show us that all eyes, including our own organic ones, are active perceptual systems, building on translations and specific ways of seeing, that is, ways of life. (Zylinska 2017, p. 17)

Finally, on 4 December 2020, we were able to get some studio time in the Covid-secure Winchester School of Art. The session was remarkable for many reasons, not least being Dawson's first physical encounter with the lithic artefacts. The objective of the session was to look at the lithics and metalithics afresh using a legacy, but still useful, Creaform EXAscan hand-held 3D laser scanner connected to a laptop running the accompanying Geomagic Studio software. The lithics were placed on a mat covered with reflective position targets, which are automatically identified by the system to ensure precision scanning. The EXAscan can perform 25,000 readings per second at a resolution of 0.05mm and accurate to 0.04mm. However, the accuracy of the machine also depends on the dexterity of the operators, who must work within the tolerances of the set-up. The optimum distance from which to hover, twist and sweep the thin red flickering line, the haptic gaze, of the laser over the artefacts was about 30 cm. Initially, the operator's eyes track the red line of the laser sweeping across the surface of the flint. However, a quick glance away from the 'subject' to the Geometric Studio screen revealed unwanted 'holes' in

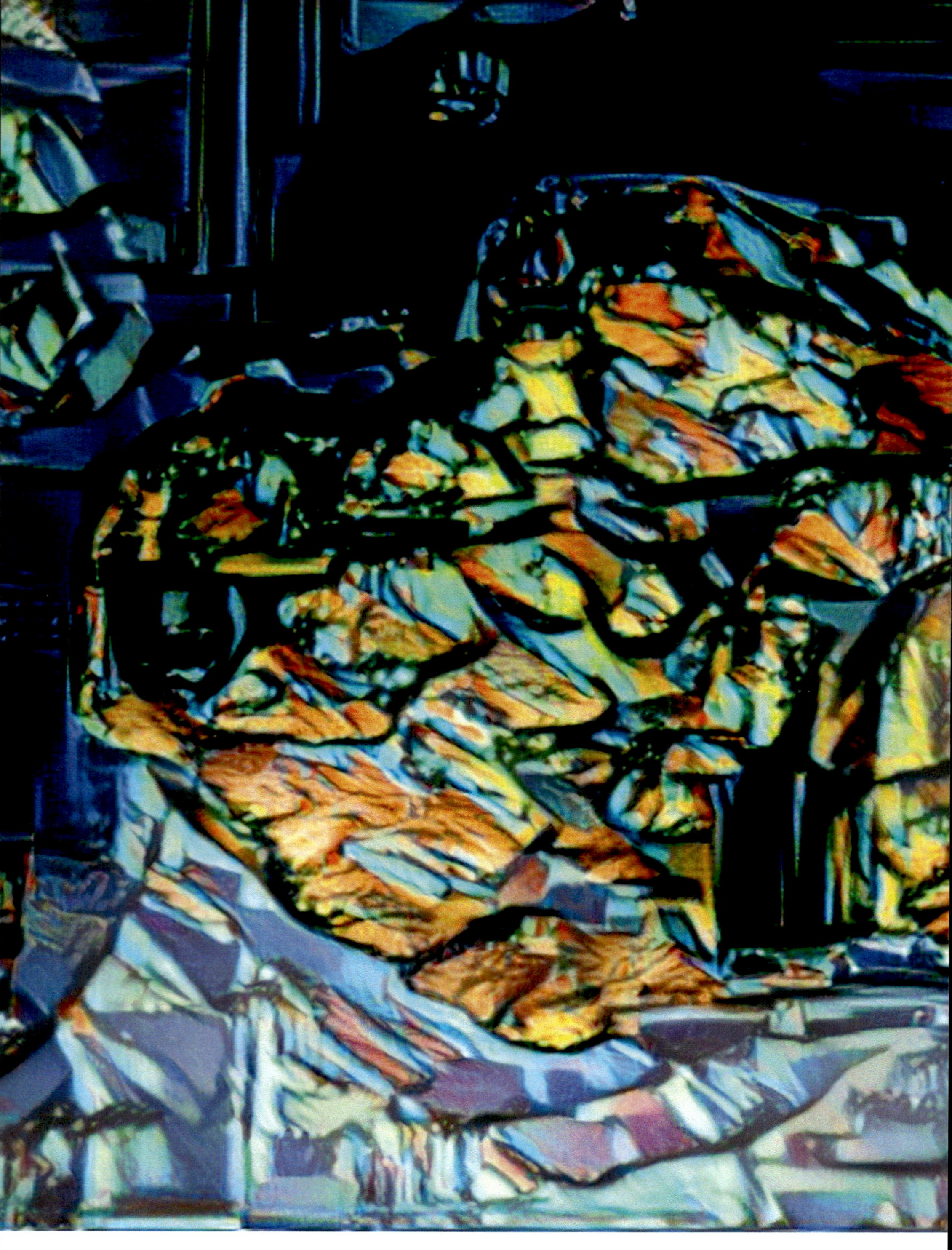

Postcard 5 'Silicon alchemy I', composite image using style transfer software, 2021. Image credit: Ian Dawson and Paul Reilly.

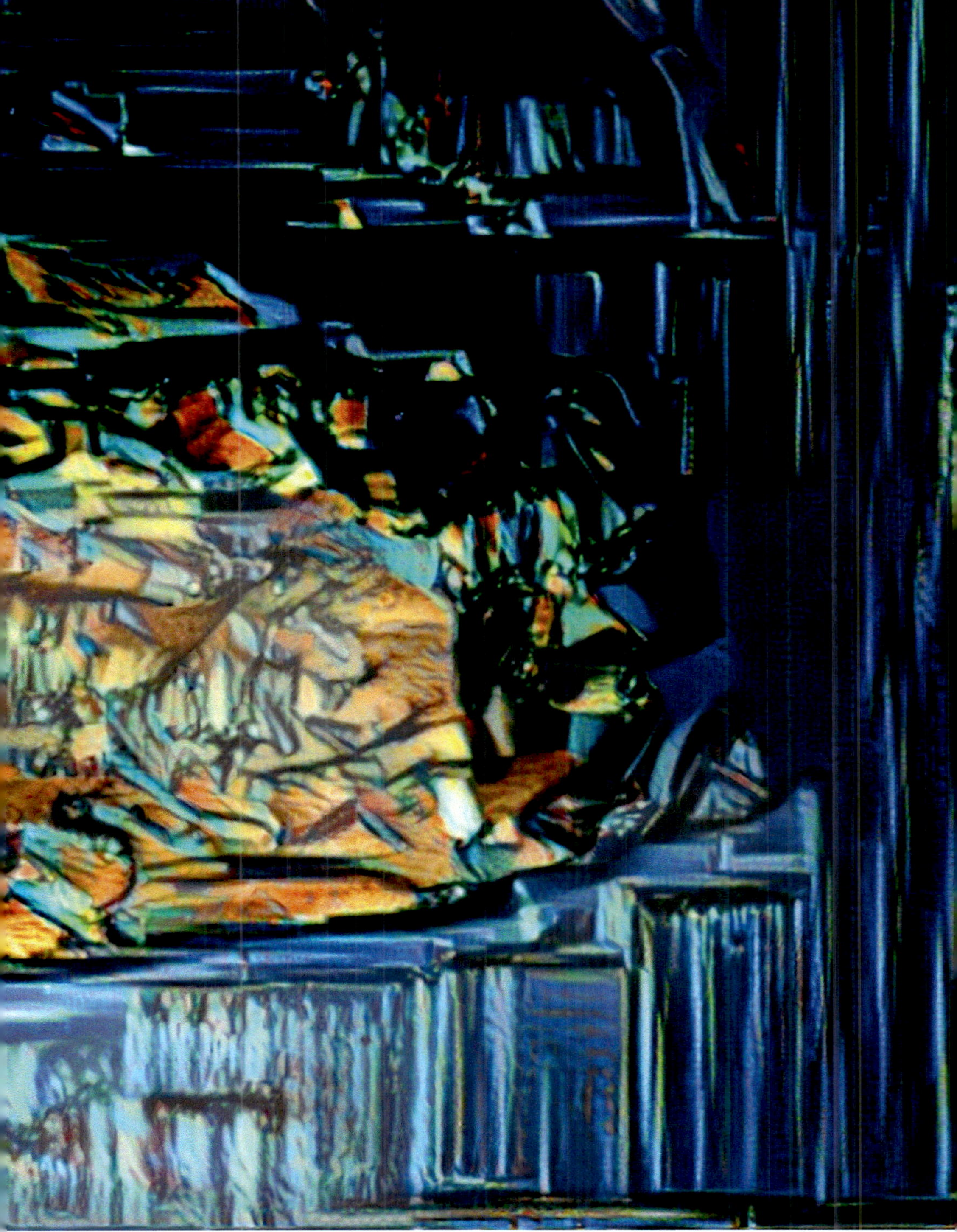

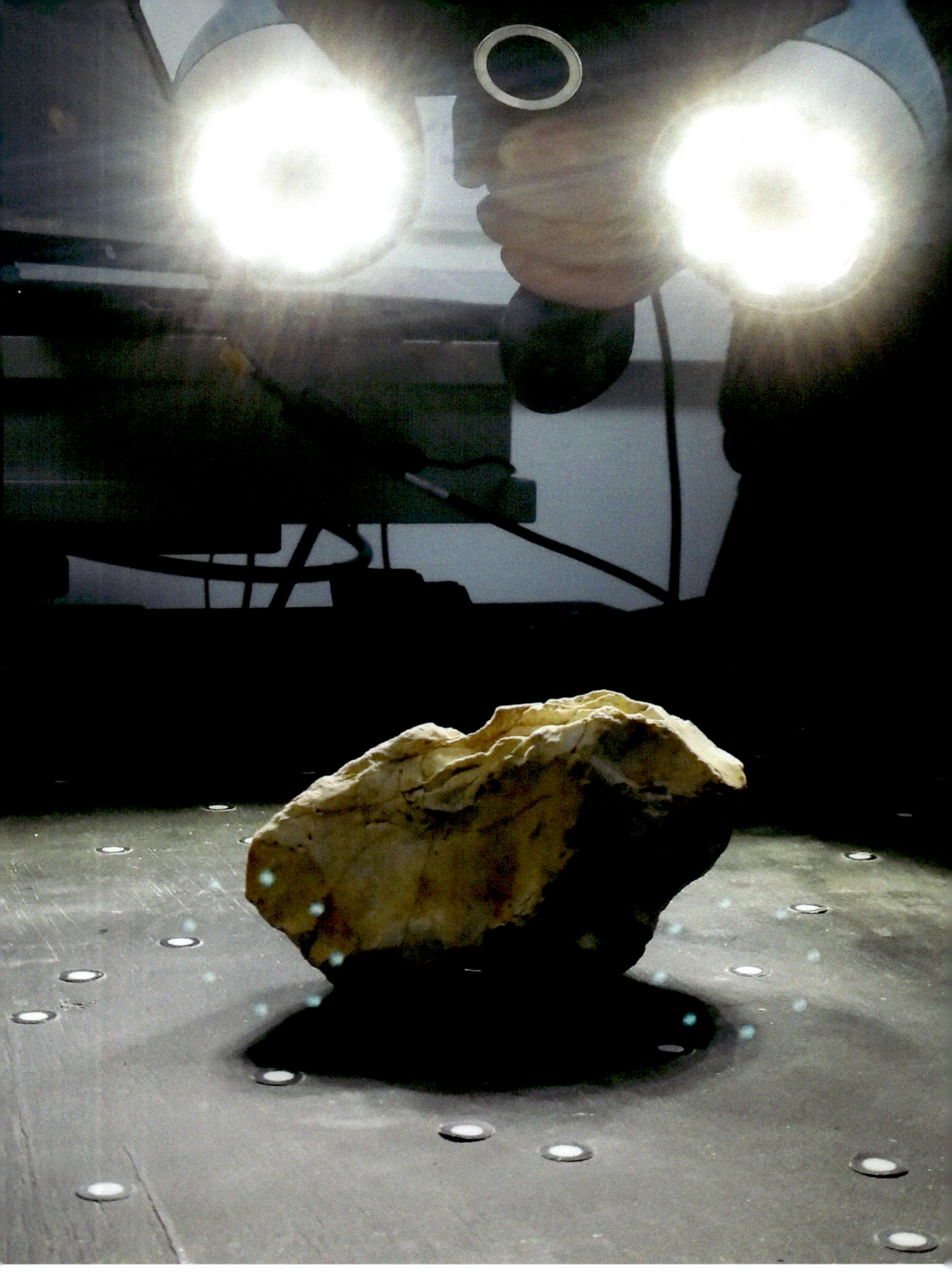

Postcard 6 'Gaze of the machines; grasping the artefact remotely', Creaform EXAscan, 2021.
Image credit: Ian Dawson and Paul Reilly.

the scan data. When this happened, a profound change occurred in how the operator intra-acted with the apparatus, the other researchers in the studio and the artefact being scanned. The operator now engaged with the scanning activities through feedback indicators displayed on the screen was is no longer looking directly at the lithics. Besides exposing missing data, a colour-coded depth indicator shows when the instrument is too close or too far from the object to get optimal data. Next, keeping their face turned away from the subject and towards the screen, the operator uses fine adjustments of proprioception within the hand, wrist and forearm to delicately control the movements and gestures of the scanner in relation to the artefact and fill in the tiniest gaps in the data. On screen, individual blank pixels alert the operator to unscanned regions of the artefact. Using only the interactive screen image as a direct visual feedback loop, the human operator, non-consciously (Hayles 2017), deploys a kind of multimodal, but unsighted, haptic vision, or image-making via proprioception. In other words, the operator is able to navigate around the artefact using deft movements, gestures and onscreen feedback to target the scanner at 'gaps'. These gliding hand-held scanning actions bear an uncanny resemblance to the gestures of the trowelling archaeologist when trying to define buried artefacts and deposits hidden from direct view. Whereas the latter results in weighty tangible stuff one can feel with one's own hands, the haptic scanning produces a much less tangible digital trace, which is out of reach, within the screen.

Postcard 7

> The surface of identification in a digital model has no thickness and contains nothing. (Minkin 2016)

In her discussion of the anatomy and pathology of digital images, Louisa Minkin draws attention to the empty cores of many digital models, including those produced using SfM photogrammetry and laser scanning. We consider this analogy as we further fossilise the flints, creating new hollow-bodied forms. As we scan we also output new diagrammatic images from the scanning process; these are projection bitmaps that are created for the 3D software to read in order to re-texture and rewrap the mesh models. They are not really made for humans to see: they are fragments for other machines to analyse and assemble (Zylinska 2017), yet their ordering and pathology are fascinating to us. To 'see' this 2D composite image of a 3D space requires a

Postcard 7 'Robot vision meets Lucretius; collage of sloughing off digital skins', composite image, 2021. Left side; BMP file. Right side; screenshot of the render mode on MeshLab.
Image credit: Ian Dawson and Paul Reilly.

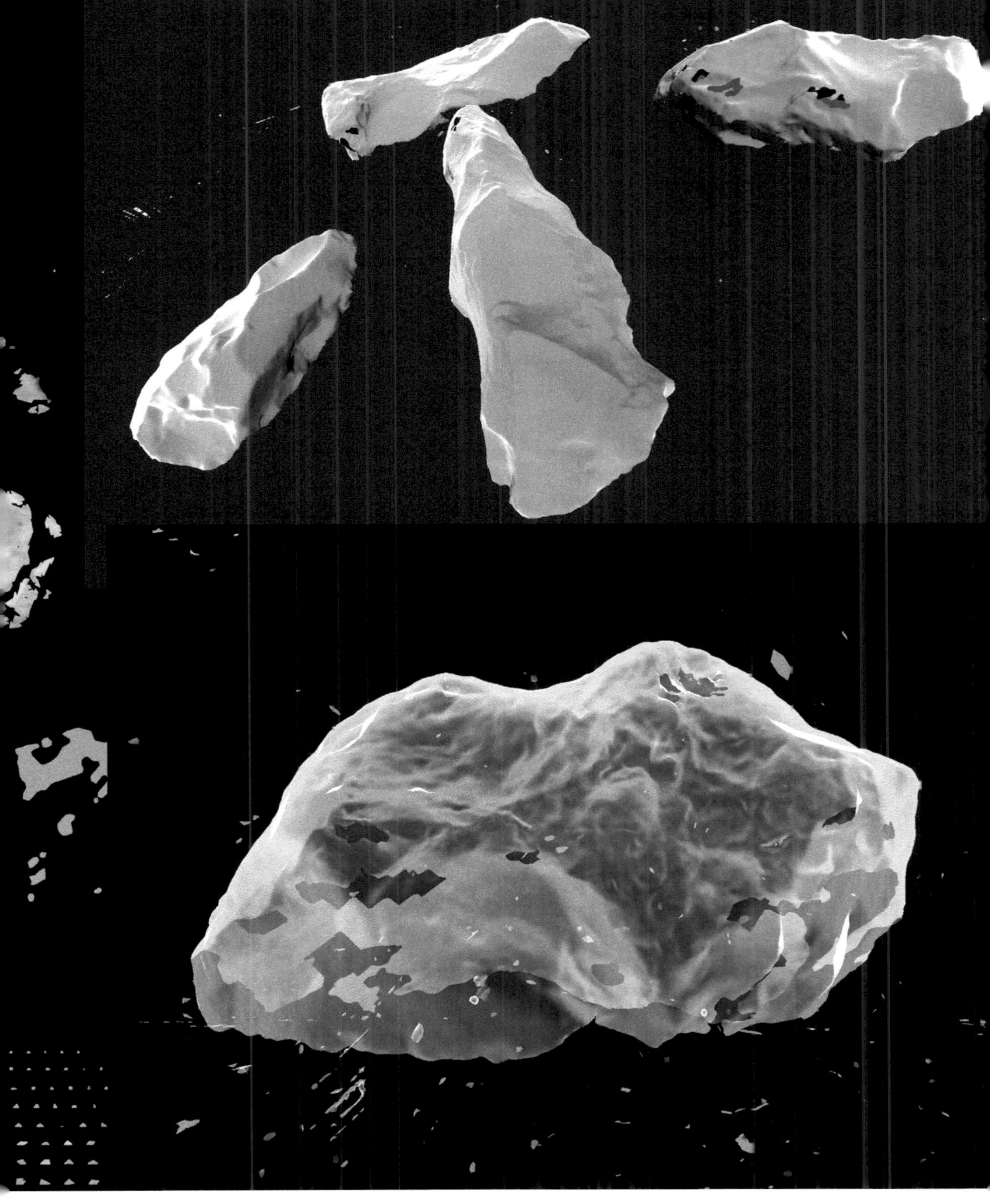

different ordering of space. The robotic *perspectiva naturalis* (Cubitt 2014: p. 210) of an 'image' is a digital description made to be projected inwards in order for the '(re)viewer', that is the software program, to be able to perceive and engage with it. This collage reveals how the computer has become engaged in the construction of visibility, in how the silica eye of the software is active in its vision, in what it sees and how it displays its nature.

We can, then, think of this postcard as showing us the essence of the scanner–computer combination as it peels and removes the surface of the object, thinking of Lucretius' Epicurean model of vision,[3] its atomistic materialism. We can see these images not just as a fossilised empty shell, but as part of a skinning and flaying process. There is also an uncanny relation to Claude Heath's (2010) *First Thing Rotated*. In this work, Heath wraps and then unwraps a flint artefact in paper, using a technique of unsighted rotation, to haptically trace and transfer the object's surface. This is a process we mimic when we scan with the Creaform EXAscan scanner, since we perform our very own sequence of sightless rotations producing a version of Heath's *First Thing Rotated* in the form of this bitmap image. Unlike Heath's approach, which used the flint to draw itself onto the wrapping paper to create something new and affective, this laser flaying acts more like a spoliation, which sheds and shreds any remaining scales of aura that our object had retained before it was emptied out. We therefore feel the need to put the materials back into our increasingly ephemeral artefacts, and to reconnect them with the physical world, the original place and setting of their (im)material becoming.

Postcard 8

> Agentic capacity is now seen as differentially distributed across a wider range of ontological types. (Bennett 2010: p. 9)

The compiled SfM data were cleaned in MeshLab and Meshmixer and then sliced and sent as gcode to be 3D printed in Dawson's

---

3 In *De Rerum Naturum* Lucretius explores images as the cause of vision, describing an image which becomes visible to the human eye only because matter, as 'likeness' or simulacra in the form of a film or skin, is given off from the image during processes of growth and replenishment. Written between 99 and 55 BCE this is one of the earliest accounts linking image and vision (see Dawson et al. 2021).

London studio. Several silica flint tools found in a cornfield, then turned into images in a home office in Hampshire, were now (re)instanted in colourful polylactic acid (cornstarch) using a fused filament 3D printer. More than any other process, 3D printing exemplifies the idea of object-as-trace, as a continuous plastic line is drawn across a three-dimensional field. The creation of these metonymic objects makes the experience and performances of Reilly in his garden more tangible. This 3D printing performance recalls the assembly section of Willème's photosculpture process, where the silhouettes of his daguerreotypes were translated by pantograph into a block of clay.[4] On Dawson's 3D printer, 0.5 mm slices of the model are profiled one after another. Both processes reveal the uneasy interface, or rather complex intraface, between artisan and the machinic array. In fact, Dawson actively joined in the 3D printing performance, spontaneously turning the printer off to introduce different colours of filament, thereby creating stochastic interruptions within the merging patterns that develop on the surface of the print. The stop-starting was arbitrary and often conducted between videoconferences, marking both the day and the duration of the printing process. Each metalithic surface that emerged was a colourful, indeed dazzling, plastic amalgam of prehistoric flint tooling and post-historic 3D fabrication.

It was time for the metalithics to go home. So, on 29 October 2020, Dawson made a journey to a post office and sent a parcel of these new/old objects back to Reilly through the hybrid digital/analogue, semi-automated, indeed phygital system known as the Royal Mail postal delivery process. Incidentally, some other sensors noted that it was 14°C and there was a 14 m.p.h. south-westerly wind with spells of drizzle (https://october-2020.meteoguru.uk).

Through this postcard we implicate an extended assemblage (Deleuze and Guattari 1987; DeLanda 2006). This assemblage does not consist solely of the objects wrapped inside the parcel. It is a much messier, ontologically itinerant, phygital assemblage (see Dawson

---

4   François Willème's photosculpture apparatus is an obscure machine which provides a genealogical ancestor for 3D prototyping. Developed in Paris in the 1860s, it produced 3D models of sitters quickly and seemingly by enchanted means. The sitter entered a top-lit room and posed on a podium for a few moments. Three days later they collected a perfect, detailed portrait statue. How was it done? Twenty-four hidden cameras were triggered simultaneously around the periphery of the space which produced a set of silhouettes. Each was projected sequentially onto a screen where a craftsman used a pantograph to trace the outline into a block of clay, rotating it 15° each time. Willème's device is an assemblage of machines and machinic arrays (see also Dawson and Minkin 2014, 2017).

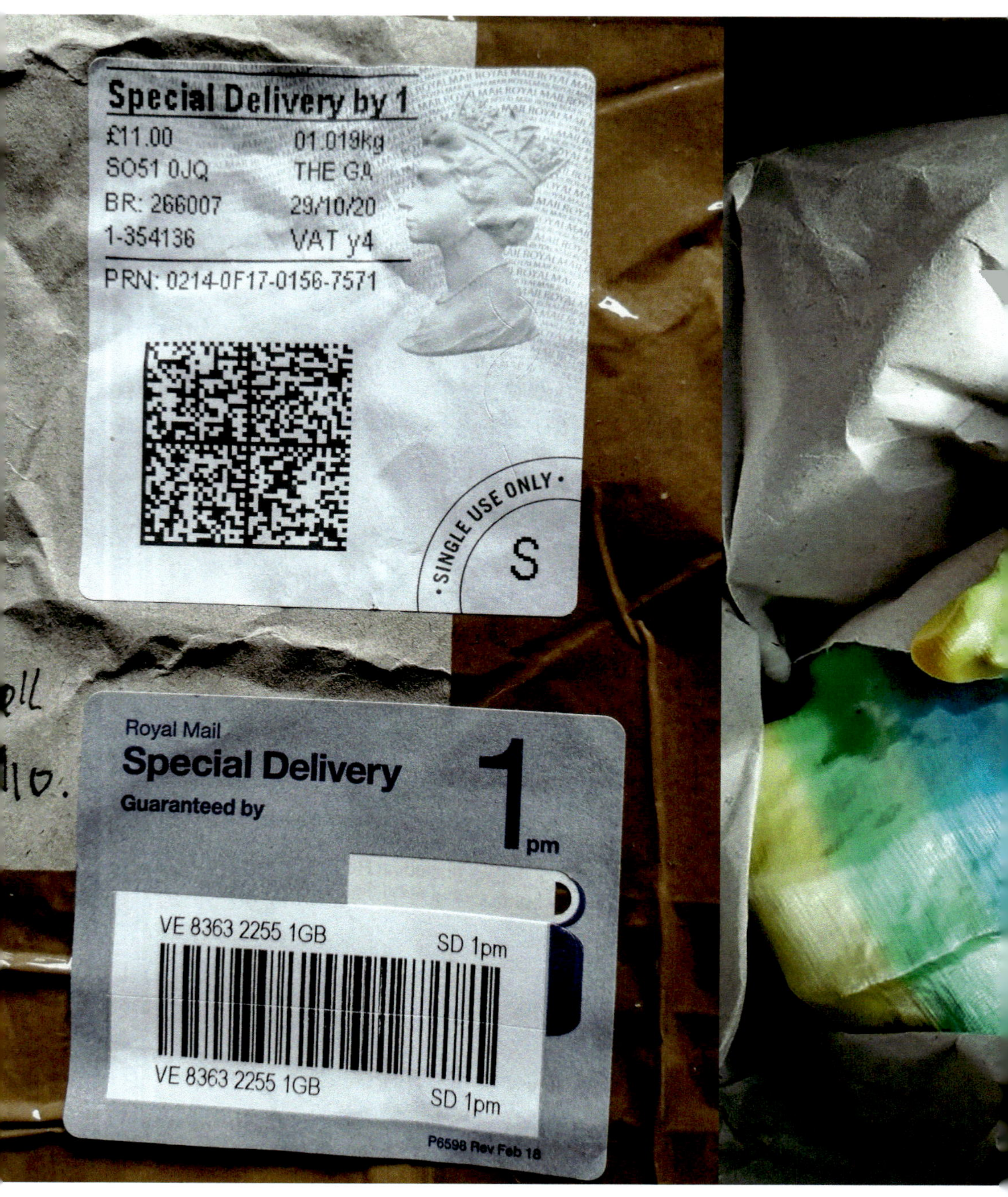

Postcard 8 'Track and trace – ontological itineraries' wrapper detail and contents, 2021.
Image credit: Ian Dawson and Paul Reilly.

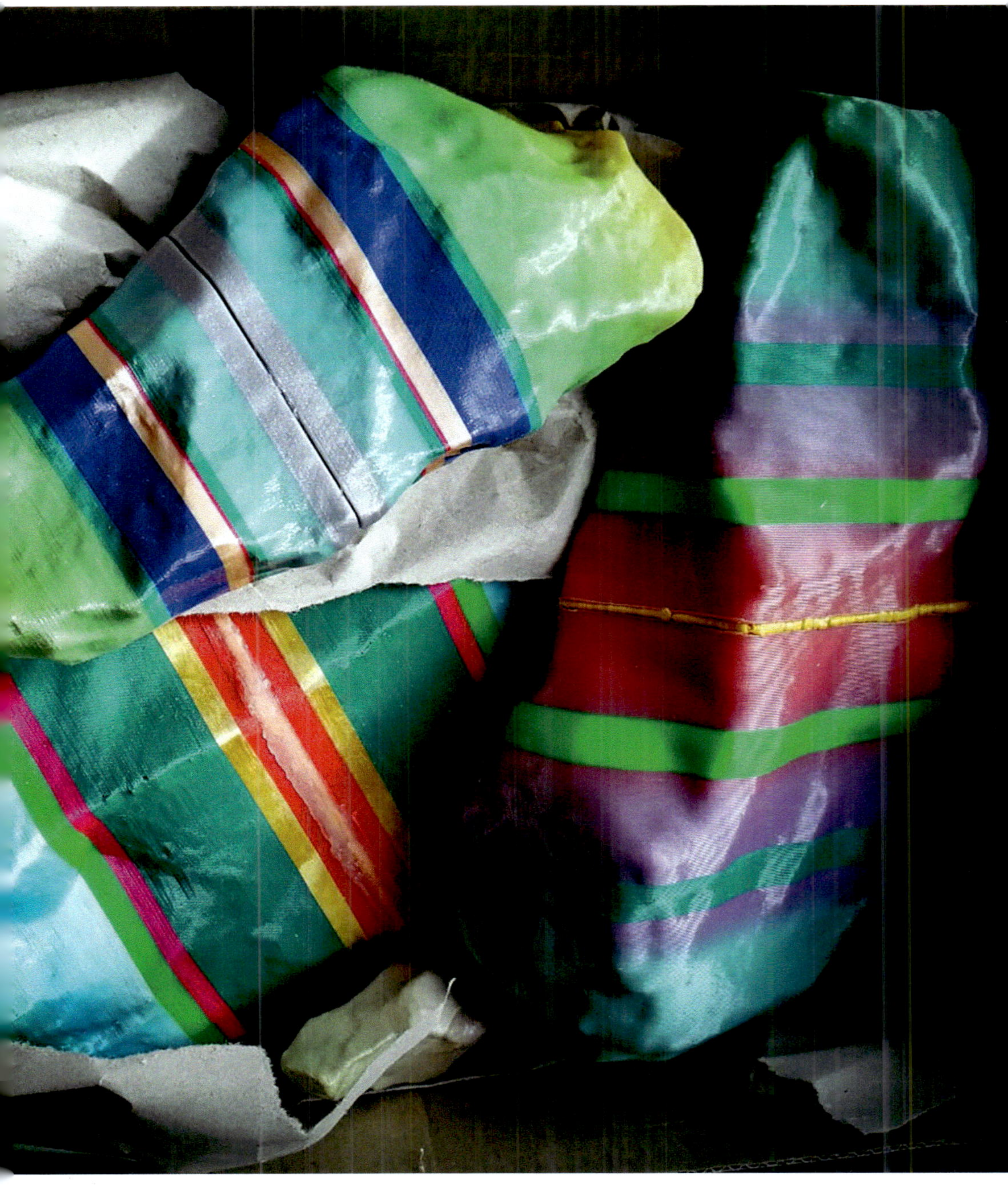

and Reilly 2019), which includes a post box, the Post Office, a Royal Mail distribution depot, the cardboard box and tape, a barcode, a barcode reader, postcodes, gcodes, 3D printer (or gcode reader), both office and studio environments being animated together, digital cameras and images, stepladders, in addition to the human actants (i.e., the delivery driver, depot workers, postman, as well as the artist and the archaeologist). These artefacts cannot be thought of as non-conscious subjects or static entities. Instead, they demonstrate very clearly the vibrancy of matter and the distribution of agency. Following Bennett (2010: p. 36), we can consider the agency of this extended human and nonhuman assemblage to be distributed over a 'confederacy' of intersecting and resonating actants ex-isting separately and together, bringing order and disorder, assembly and disassembly, to the material world. In this postcard, we have sought to place ourselves inside a string of ongoing events.

Postcard 9

> The assumed distinction between the visible and the invisible needs to be replaced with studying the ways of generating eccentric con-figurations of visibilities simultaneously with anaesthetic fields of invisibility. (Dvořák 2021: p. 57)

Our metalithics are home again. This art/archaeology intervention was installed unannounced under the cover of 'The Kindness of Rock Project' begun by Megan Murray in 2015 on Cape Cod, that went viral around the world, and received fresh impetus in Hampshire during the coronavirus pandemic. In this project and its successors, people wanting to promote well-being in their communities leave colourful hand-painted pebbles and cobbles wherever they think is suitable for others to discover, ponder, perhaps photograph, or move to new contexts of discovery (https://www.thekindnessrocksproject.com).

A what3words geocode[5] location triplet is combined with the x,y,z coordinates of the 3D printed object to enable these cornstarch meta-lithics to inhabit the area in the cornfield where they first cropped up. The heavy grey and white silica artefacts are replaced by these light and vibrant skeuomorphs. Whereas their lithic forebears are

---

5   what3words is a geocode system which combines three English-language words to permanently encode any 3 m² geographic location across the globe.

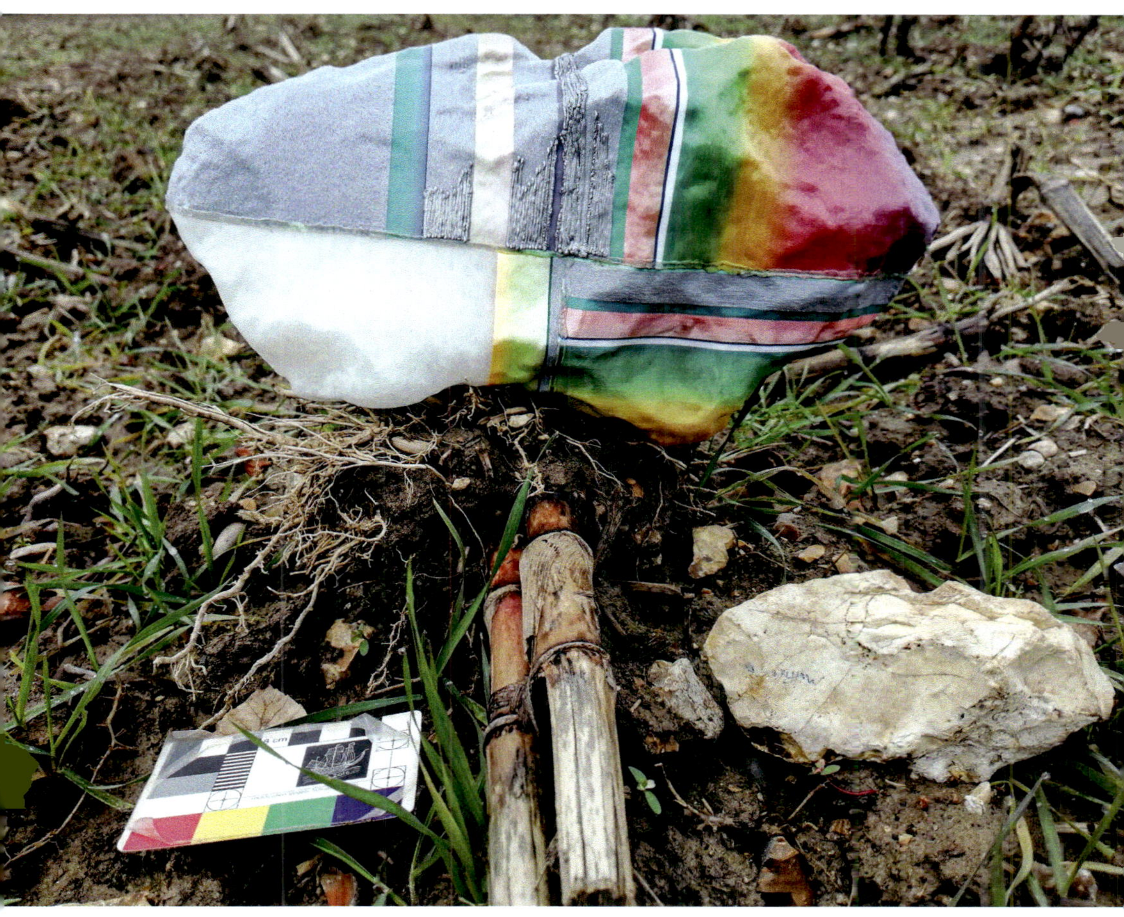

Postcard 9 'Ontological crossroad', photograph, 2021.
Image credit: Ian Dawson and Paul Reilly.

for all intents and purposes invisible to the average person walking across these fields, our much larger, dazzling metalithics visually jump out of the stony soil, as they await a new crop of corn and new passers-by to attract. Frequent return visits to the site showed that the metalithics have been recognised, picked up and moved around a considerable number of times. Some, indeed, are no longer in the field and their whereabouts are unknown to the authors. No matter, more will be introduced when the latest lockdown has been removed. Others will find their way to new contexts of contemplation.

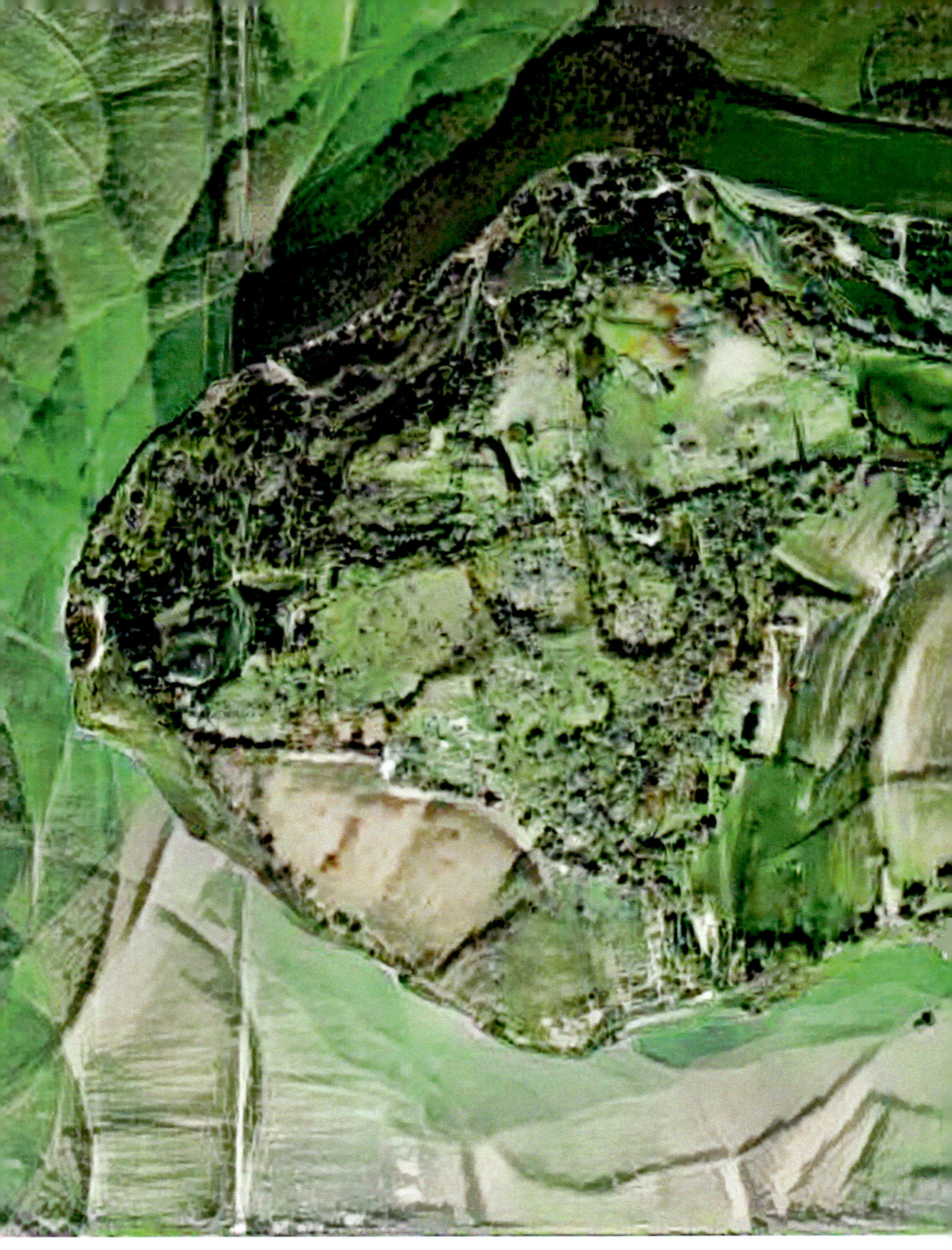

Postcard 10 'Off-the-scale (non-)human (meta)lithic landscape', composite image using style transfer software, 2021.
Image credit: Ian Dawson and Paul Reilly.

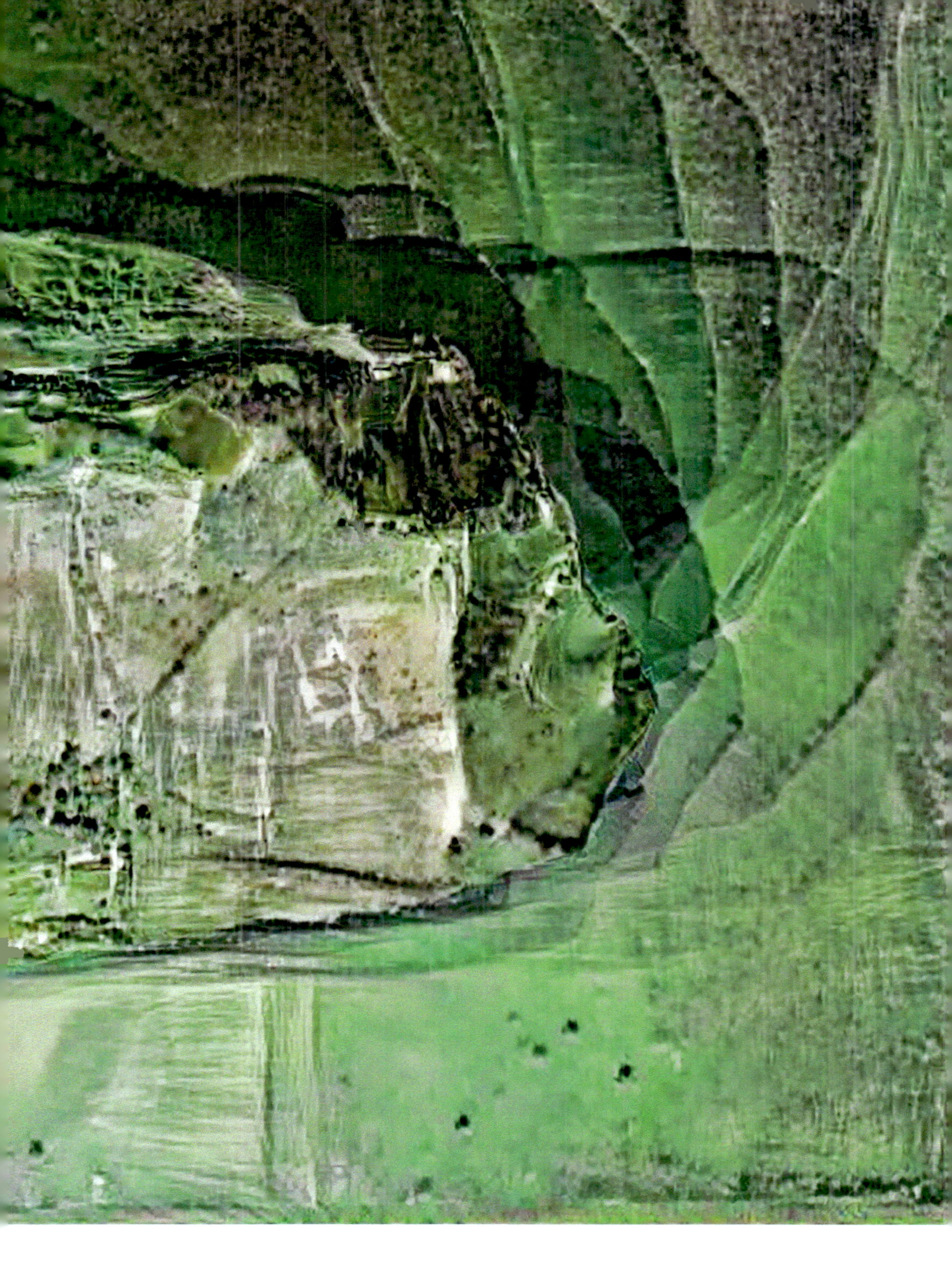

Postcard 10

> We are all chimeras, theorised and fabricated hybrids of machine and organism; in short, we are cyborgs. (Haraway 1991: p. 150)

Postcard 10 is the result of diffracting an RTI image of a hand-held mesolithic 'pick' with a satellite image of several square kilometres of the landscape in which the artefact was found. It was produced using the style transfer algorithm we employed earlier. The 'content image' in this postcard is a frame from a compiled RTI image of the pick also used in Postcard 5. The 'style image' is a satellite image of the local area. The pale marks exposed in the ploughed fields 'on the surface of the pick' are called macula. They are traces of archaeology within the wider landscape. These so-called autographic 'planetary diagrams' (Likavčan and Heinicker 2021) are now interlaced with the topography of a hand-held Mesolithic flint pick found in the setting of that very landscape remotely sensed through the gaze of a 'space archaeologist' cyborg (see Parcak 2009, 2019). The result can therefore be described as a post-human diffractive image. By that, we mean that human and machinic vision, human and much-bigger-than human scales, contemporary and ancient temporal ripples, and art and archaeological practices have been diffracted through one another to produce a totally new conception of the place, setting and scale of the artefact and its contemporary landscape.

Clearly, diffractive images call for new and previously unfamiliar modes of viewing and interpretation. However, our postcard should not be thought of as some kind of static record of an object, place or event. Rather, we offer it as – to borrow a term from Richard Siegesmund and Kerry Freedman (2018: p. 39) – 'a provocation'.

Postcard 11

> In every case imaging is about not representation but metamorphosis. (Ingold 2020: p. 69)

Postcard 11 presents another technical image in which we try to help the 'functionary' escape the shackles of automated image-making apparatuses, and the requirement for them to produce images that correspond to certain general conventions and configurations (Flusser 2011). This image is an assemblage with many layers of recursion creating numerous phygital perturbations and will take a little effort to unpick. At a top level, Dawson has compiled himself and

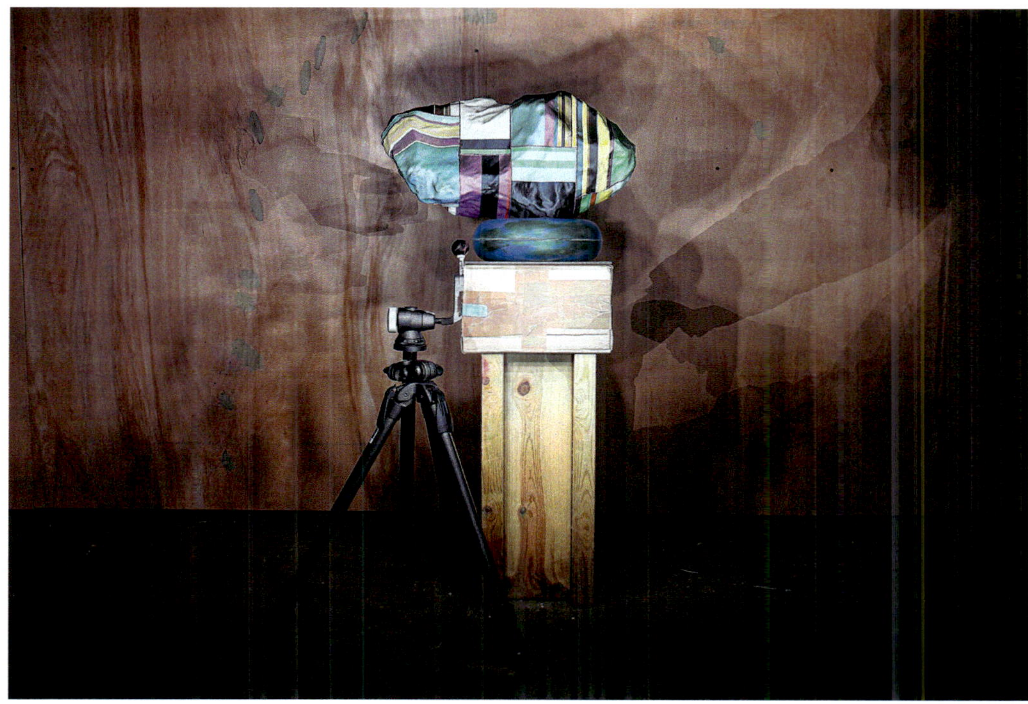

Postcard 11 'Reflections on a diffractive (meta)lithic assemblage', PTM file exported as JPG from RTIViewer, 2021.
Image credit: Ian Dawson and Paul Reilly.

his making processes recursively into this dirty RTI image (Dawson 2021)[6] of a large, colourful metalithic. The diffractive shadows he casts on the data underpinning this image ironically illuminate the many different positions he adopted during the shoot. We can think of dirty RTI images as a form of 'autographic' image (Offenhuber 2020). That is to say, it contains 'a trace of the process itself: it retains some interpretive authority, and it is taken as a product of the phenomenon at its face value' (Likavčan and Heinicker 2021: p. 212). Autographic images, which include timelapses, live streams from space and the

6 Conventional RTI requires subject and apparatus to be static, Dirty RTI refers to a deviation from these rules. The term was coined by Marta Diaz Guardamino in response to the art and archaeology experiments of Dawson and Minkin when they first started to bend the process at Taplow House, a derelict South London housing estate in 2014 (Dawson 2021).

RTI images that we have practised here, become phantom operational images (Farocki 2004) as human labour is joined with the labour of computational algorithms. Autographic images are sensitive to their socio-material context and, just as in this RTI image, they reveal material phenomena as visible traces which draw the viewer's attention back to the ways in which the previously opaque reality of the process of imaging can now unveil itself in the productive alignments between human and nonhuman elements. These are 'images in the making', containing things in motion, involving processes of assembling and reassembling, and reimaginations of the world. As Ing Marie Back Danielsson and Andrew Jones point out, 'if we understand *imaging* as a process of assemblage making, subsequent processes of viewing and intra-action are also components of the continuous process of *imaging*' (Back Danielsson and Jones 2020: p. 4, original emphasis). Put another way, this, and our earlier postcards, can be understood as assemblages of ongoing processes.

Zooming into the postcard, we find another autographic trace of this RTI image in its making. All RTI images naturally operate as 'metapictures' (Mitchell 1994) that embody a self-referential quality that triggers a metalevel discursive opportunity to consider what, when, where and how that specific technical image operates. The shiny sphere on the pedestal on which this huge metalithic sits is also reflecting on the making process from its side of the shoot. Relying on Mitchell's concept of metapictures, this RTI image is not merely an epistemological model, but an assemblage that allows us to observe observers and one that does not merely serve as an illustration to theory but one that pictures theory.

Remember that the metalithic on display is itself a material recursion, based on the virtual SfM photogrammetry taken of the physical lithic found in the chalk landscape of Wessex. The 'phygital nexus' (Dawson and Reilly 2019) through which we have consciously re(con)figured our (meta)lithic study via many strange loops has enabled our deliberately subversive art/archaeology intervention that simultaneously decomposes and exposes our processes of making and their dependencies, and thus also enables us to discard the shackles of the functionary. On the way, we have interlaced art and archaeological practice, cornstarch and silica, human and artificial intelligence, human and nonhuman cognition, as well as different scales and conceptions of time and chronology.

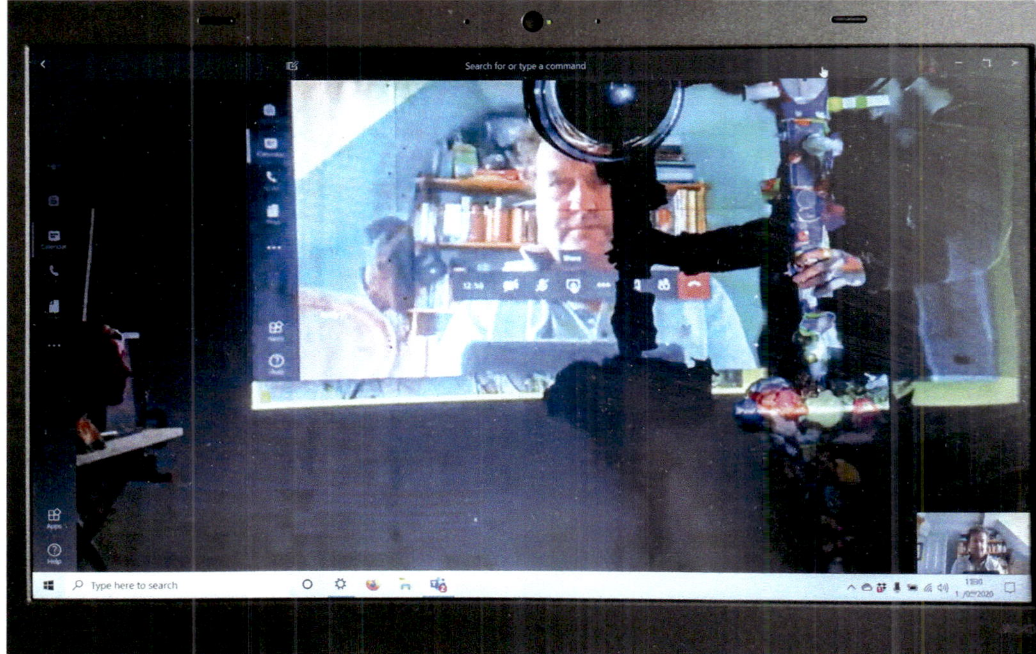

Postcard 12 'Spacetimemattering in a digital *mise en abyme*', recursive RTI image, 2021.
Image credit: Ian Dawson and Paul Reilly.

Postcard 12

> The human as data is wholly subsumed, but the human as code, and therefore performative, also persists as the ghost of work in a world of labour. (Cubitt 2014: p. 31)

Our final postcard is a personal reflection on our cyborgic art/archaeology practices and cognitive assemblages, and a small homage to the concept of recursion that helped lay the foundations of computers algorithms and, subsequently, robotic vision.

By convention, artefacts and works of art are foregrounded in photographs, paintings and images in general, while the maker and their modes and tools of making tend to slide into the background. The images are somehow supposed to speak for themselves. Dawson and Reilly decided to disrupt this convention by running the RTI process remotely, through the medium and format of a videoconference, in order to record, recursively, the recorders recording the subject. We call this technique *remote-RTI* (R-RTI). Dawson projected his side of the conference (showing Reilly in his office) onto his studio wall to provide the ambient lighting for this R-RTI session. We have come to regard the R-RTI technique as eminently pragmatic and useful. We have also learned, affirmatively, that '[w]hen objects join in networks and interact/intraact with human partners, the potential for surprises and unexpected results increases exponentially' (Hayles 2017: p. 84). In this R-RTI session Dawson negotiated the space and objects under the instruction of Reilly, who would grab screenshots of the session on his home computer. In this shot of his computer screen Reilly has captured a set of recursive images, or metapictures (Mitchell 1994), which dispute divisions between the analogue and the digital, and also create 'inadvertent images' (Geimer 2018), and this offers insights into the nature of the medium. Postcard 12 presents an example of what Douglas Hofstadter (1999, 2007) calls a 'strange loop' as seen from Reilly's particular vantage point on the proceedings. Implicit to Hofstadter's strange loops is the concept of infinity (∞). As Hofstadter (1994: p. 15) puts it, 'what else is a loop but a way of representing an endless process in a finite way'? The image of Reilly in his study which appears in the small window in the bottom right of his screen is also shown projected much larger on Dawson's studio wall. However, less obvious, but nevertheless still present, is another nested version of the image reflecting back off the mirrored dome on the rear wall. This is being (re)transmitted back to Reilly through the webcam on Dawson's side of the video-conference and back again to Dawson. Admittedly, this recursive metaimage occupies only a rapidly diminishing number of pixels on their return routes.

The paradoxical space of this postcard ensnares the human viewer in a trap laid out by the codification of perspectival images, yet it also 'provides a means for staging this capture and of playing it out in a reflexive mode' (Damisch 1994: p. 46). The strange loop here, created by the specific placement of the security mirror, recalls the mise en abymes of Jan van Eyck's (1434) *Arnolfini Wedding*, Robert Campin's (1438) *Heinrich von Werl Triptych* (Hockney 2006: pp. 82–5) and Edouard Manet's (1882) *Bar at the Folies-Bergère* (Foucault 1986). It also echoes the performative fugues of Johann Sebastian Bach, the printed recursions of staircases and waterfalls of Maurits Cornelis Escher's impossible drawings and, perhaps more interestingly here, the self-referential mathematical statements of Kurt Gödel's incompleteness theorem (Hofstadter [1979] 1999). Gödel's numerical theorem involved developing a coding scheme that enabled numbers to become statements not only about numbers, but also about the statements themselves. Ultimately, his theorem challenged the very logic of number systems and other formal axiomatic systems by proving that mathematical formulae could be shown to be true but could not be proven. Here, then, was a statement of the strange introspective loopiness of algorithmic recursion, loops that change themselves, something described by Charles Babbage in reference to his proposed mechanical general-purpose computer, or *analytical engine*, as capable of 'eating its own tail' (Hofstadter 1999: p. 25).

Looping back to Reilly's inadvertent, self-swallowing image, the apparition of the figure caught in the *mise en abyme* of the mirror and the webcams interrupts the illusionistic integrity of the representation, and creates what Joanne Zylinska identifies as both a 'nonhuman photograph' (Zylinska 2017) and an 'undigital photograph' (Zylinska 2020, 2021) rolled into one. Despite its classification, a *nonhuman* photograph actually includes a human element, which in this case is displaced and re-imag(in)ed by the reflection in the mirrors, by a non-machinic sleight of hand. The undigital photograph consists of the original image that was projected onto the wall and then modified by Dawson's superimposed figure and shadow. Both the 'person' and the shadow are agential elements acting upon the scene already captured by the webcam. In this specific alignment, the mirror reveals a heterotopia, a placeless place

> at once absolutely real, connected with all the space that surrounds it, and absolutely unreal, since in order to be perceived it has to pass through this virtual point which is over there. (Foucault 1986: p. 24)

In this postcard, the mirror *and* the mirrored spaces highlight this (dis)placement of mimetic representation, and the playful positions that Reilly and Dawson take exposes a self-enfolding commentary about what is happening while it is happening. Just as Gödel's incompleteness theorem loops to question coding, the recursive operations in this image collapse dimensional distinctions and fracture spatial representation in two, moving attention to the act that introduces these distinctions, and so bringing the 'composition of the map and the composition of the territory [to] effectively coincide' (Massumi 2014: p.25) as both sides of the mirror co-occur together.

Finally, we want to close using Paul Virilio's (1994) ironic concluding question in his book *The Vision Machine*: 'have you ever heard of a writer who writes for his pen...?' It lends us a parting reflection that even though our images are synthesised through layers of algorithms, they are not fully robotic, as they have been filtered through a conscious human decision-making medium.

References

Adkins, L. and Adkins, R. A. (1985) 'Neolithic Axes from Roman Sites in Britain', *Oxford Journal of Archaeology* 4(1): 69–76. Available at https://doi.org/10.1111/j.1468-0092.1985.tb00231.x (accessed 28 April 2022).

Back Danielsson, I.-M. and Jones, A. M. (2020) *Images in the Making: Art, Process, Archaeology*. Manchester: Manchester University Press

Bailey, D. (2017) 'Disarticulate – Repurpose – Disrupt: Art/Archaeology', *Cambridge Archaeological Journal* 27(4): 691–701. Available at https://doi.org/10.1017/S0959774317000713 (accessed 28 April 2022).

Bailey, D. (2018) 'Art/Archaeology: What Value Artistic–Archaeological Collaboration?', *Journal of Contemporary Archaeology* 4(2): 246–56. Available at https://doi.org/10.1558/jca.34116 (accessed 28 April 2022).

Barad, K. (2007) *Meeting the Universe Halfway: Quantum Physics and the Entanglement of Matter and Meaning*. Durham: Duke University Press.

Barad, K. (2014) 'Diffracting Diffraction: Cutting Together Apart', *Parallax* 20(3): 168–87. Available at https://doi.org/10.1080/13534645.2014.927623 (accessed 28 April 2022).

Barad, K. (2017) 'Troubling Time/s and Ecologies of Nothingness: Re-turning, Re-membering, and Facing the Incalculable', *New Formations* 92(92): 56–86. Available at https://doi.org/10.3898/NEWF:92.05.2017 (accessed 28 April 2022).

Barone, S., Paoli, A., Neri, P., Razionale, A. V., De Santis, M. L. and Mailland, F. (2018) 'Automatic Illustration of Lithics from 3d Scanned Models'., in *IOP Conference Series: Materials Science and Engineering* 364: 012017. Available at https://doi.org/10.1088/1757-899X/364/1/01201 (accessed 28 April 2022).

Bennett, J. (2010) *Vibrant Matter: A Political Ecology of Things*. Durham: Duke University Press.

Braidotti, R. (2013) *The Posthuman*. Cambridge: Polity Press.

Braidotti, R. (2019) *Posthuman Knowledge*. Cambridge: Polity Press.

Carusi, A., Sissel Hoel, A., Webmoor, T. and Woolgar, S. (eds) (2014) *Visualization in the Age of Computerization* (1st edition). London: Routledge.

CHI (n.d.) *Reflectance Transformation Imaging*. Cultural Heritage Imaging. Available at http://culturalheritageimaging.org/Technologies/RTI (accessed 28 April 2022).

Conneller, C. (2013) 'Deception and (Mis)Representation: Skeuomorphs, Materials and Form', in Alberti, B., Jones, A. M. and Pollard, J. (eds), *Archaeology After Interpretation*. Walnut Creek: Left Coast Press, pp. 119–33.

Cubitt, S. (2014) *The Practice of Light: A Genealogy of Visual Technologies from Prints to Pixels*. Leonardo Book Series. Cambridge, MA: MIT Press.

Damisch, H. (1994) *The Origin of Perspective*. Trans. J. Goodman. Cambridge, MA: MIT Press.

Dawson, I. (2021) 'Dirty RTI', in Back-Danielson, I-M. and Jones, A. (eds), *Images in the Making*. Manchester: Manchester University Press, pp. 51–64.

Dawson, I. and Minkin, L. (2014) 'Object Lessons: Copying and Reconstruction as a Teaching Strategy', *Art, Design and Communication in Higher Education* 13(1): 19–29.

Dawson, I. and Minkin, L. (2017) 'Grave Goods', in *Más allá del texto. Cultura digital y nuevas epistemologías*. San Andrés Cholula: Editorial Itaca, Universidad de las Américas Puebla Ex hacienda, pp. 205–21.

Dawson, I. and Reilly, P. (2019) 'Messy Assemblages, Residuality and Recursion within a Phygital Nexus', *Epoiesen: A Journal for Creative Engagement in History and Archaeology*. Available at https://doi.org/10.22215/epoiesen/2019.4 (accessed 28 April 2022).

Dawson, I., Jones, A. M., Minkin, L. and Reilly, P. (2021) *Diffracting Digital Images: Art, Archaeology and Cultural Heritage*. London: Routledge.

DeLanda, M. (2006) *A New Philosophy of Society: Assemblage Theory and Social Complexity*. London: Continuum.

Deleuze, G. and Guattari, F. (1987) *A Thousand Plateaus*. Minneapolis: University of Minnesota Press.

Devièse, T., Veall, M-A., Allen, R., Riesmeier, M., Cameron, J., Bonjean, D. and Higham, T. (2020) 'From Photogrammetry to Radiocarbon Dating; Investigating Hafting Adhesives on Stone Tools Using a Multi-Analytical Approach', *Journal of Archaeological Science: Reports* 34: 102664. Available at https://doi.org/10.1016/j.jasrep.2020.102664 (accessed 28 April 2022).

Dvořák, T. (2021) 'Eccentric Metrics in Visual Culture', in Dvořák, T. and Parikka, J. (eds), *Photography Off the Scale: Technologies and Theories of the Mass Image*. Edinburgh: Edinburgh University Press, pp. 41–60.

Edgeworth, M. (2015) 'From Spadework to Screenwork. New Forms of Archaeological Discovery in Digital Space', in Carusi, A., Hoel, A. S., Webmoor, T. and Woolgar, S. (eds), *Visualization in the Age of Computerization*. London: Routledge, pp. 40–58.

English Heritage (2018) *Multi-light Imaging Highlight-Reflectance Transformation Imaging (H-RTI) for Cultural Heritage*, V.2.0. London: English Heritage.

Farocki, H. (2004) 'Phantom Images', *Public* 29: 12–22.

Flusser, V. (2011) *Into the Universe of Technical Images*. Electronic Mediations 32. Minneapolis: University of Minnesota Press.

Foucault, M. (1986) 'Of Other Spaces', *Diacritics* 16: 22–7.

Gatt, H. (2019) *Combining Manual and Digital Archaeological Illustration Techniques in 3D*. Available at https://sketchfab.com/blogs/community/digital-and-man-ual-archaeological-illustration-techniques-in-3d (accessed 2 December 2020).

Gatys, L. A., Ecker, A. S. and Bethge, M. (2016) 'A Neural Algorithm of Artistic Style', in *Proceedings of the 2016 IEEE Conference on Computer Vision and Pattern Recognition*. Las Vegas: IEEE Computer Society, pp. 2414–23.

Geimer, P. (2018) *Inadvertent Images: A History of Photographic Apparitions*. Chicago: University of Chicago Press.

Giachetti, A., Ciortan, I., Daffara, C., Pintus, R. and Gobbetti, E. (2017) 'Multi-spectral RTI Analysis of Heterogeneous Artworks', in *GCH '17: Proceedings of the Eurographics Workshop on Graphics and Cultural Heritage, September 19–28, 2017*. Available at https://doi.org/10.2312/gch.20171288 (accessed 22 September 2023).

Gillespie, S. D. and Joyce, R. A. (2015) *Things in Motion: Object Itineraries in Anthropological Practice*. Santa Fe: SAR Press.

Haraway, D. (1991) 'A Cyborg Manifesto: Science, Technology, and Socialist-Feminism in the Late Twentieth Century', in *Simians, Cyborgs and Women: The Reinvention of Nature*. New York: Routledge, pp. 149–81.

Harrison, R. (2011) 'Surface Assemblages. Towards an Archaeology in and of the Present', *Archaeological Dialogues* 18(2): 141–61. Available at DOI:10.1017/S1380203811000195 (accessed 28 April 2022).

Hayles, K. (2017) *Unthought: The Power of the Cognitive Nonconscious*. Chicago: University of Chicago Press.

Heath, C. (2010) *First Thing Rotated*. Available at https://www.artarchaeologies.com/featuredwork_first_thing_rotated (accessed 28 April 2022).

Historic England (2017) *Photogrammetric Applications for Cultural Heritage. Guidance for Good Practice*. Swindon: Historic England.

Hockney, D. (2006) *Secret Knowledge: Rediscovering the Lost Techniques of the Old Masters* (new and expanded edition). London: Thames and Hudson.

Hofstadter, D. R. (1999 [1979]) *Gödel, Escher, Bach: An Eternal Golden Braid*. New York: Basic Books.

Hofstadter, D. R. (2007) *I Am a Strange Loop*. New York: Basic Books.

Holmes, O. W. (1859) 'The Stereoscope and the Stereograph', *The Atlantic*, June. Available at https://www.theatlantic.com/magazine/archive/1859/06/the-stereoscope-and-the-stereograph/303361 (accessed 28 April 2022).

Ingold, T. (2013) *Making: Anthropology, Archaeology, Art and Architecture*. London: Routledge.

Ingold, T. (2020) 'Commentary on Part I', in Back-Danielsson, I.-M. and Jones, A. M. (eds), *Images in the Making: Art, Process, Archaeology*. Manchester: Manchester University Press, pp. 65–70.

Jones, A. M. and Díaz-Guardamino, M. (2019) *Making a Mark: Image and Process in Neolithic Britain and Ireland*. Oxford: Oxbow Books.

Kittler, F. (2009) *Optical Media*. Cambridge: Polity.

Kotoula, Eleni (2016) 'Reflectance Transformation Imaging Beyond the Visible: Ultraviolet Reflected And Ultraviolet Induced Visible Fluorescence', in *CAA 2015: Keep the Revolution Going. Proceedings of the 43rd Annual Conference on CAA*. Oxford: Archaeopress, pp. 909–18.

Likavčan, L. and Heinicker, P. (2021) 'Planetary Diagrams: Towards an Autographic Theory of Climate Emergency', in Dvořák, T. and Parikka, J. (eds), *Photography Off the Scale: Technologies and Theories of the Mass Image*. Edinburgh: Edinburgh University Press, pp. 211–30.

Lord, J. W. (1993) *The Nature and Subsequent Uses of Flint, Vol. 1: The Basics of Lithic Technology*. Brandon: John Lord.

Manclossi, F., Rosen, S. A. and Boëda, E. (2019) 'From Stone to Metal: The Dynamics of Technological Change in the Decline of Chipped Stone Tool Production. A Case Study from the Southern Levant (5th–1st Millennia BCE)', *Journal of Archaeological Method and Theory* 26: 1276–326. Available at https://doi.org/10.1007/s10816-019-09412-2 (accessed 28 April 2022)

Massumi, B. (2014) *What Animals Tell Us About Politics*. Durham, NC: Duke University Press.

May, J. (2019) *Signal, Image, Architecture*. New York: Columbia University Press.

Miller, A. I. (2019) *AI Renaissance Machines: Inside the New World of Machine-Created Art, Literature, and Music*. Cambridge, MA: MIT Press.

Minkin, L. (2016) 'Out of Our Skins', *Journal of Visual Arts Practice* 15(2–3): 115–26.

Minkin, L. and Dawson, I. (2014) 'Object Lessons: Copying and Reconstruction as a Teaching Strategy', *Art, Design and Communication in Higher Education* 13(1): 19–29. Available at https://doi.org/10.1386/adch.13.1.19_1 (accessed 28 April 2022).

Mitchell, W. J. T. (1994) *Picture Theory: Essays on Verbal and Visual Representation*. Chicago: Chicago University Press.

Offenhuber, D. (2020) 'Data by Proxy – Material Traces as Autographic Visualizations', *IEEE Transactions on Visualization and Computer Graphics* 26(1): 98–108. Available at 10.1109/TVCG.2019.2934788 (accessed 28 April 2022).

Olivier, L. (2011) *The Dark Abyss of Time: Archaeology and Memory*. Trans. A. Greenspan. Walnut Creek: Altamira.

Parcak, S. (2009) *Satellite Remote Sensing for Archaeology*. London: Routledge.

Parcak, S. (2019) *Archaeology from Space: How the Future Shapes Our Past*. New York: Henry Holt.

Perry, S. (2019) 'The Enchantment of the Archaeological Record', *European Journal of Archaeology* 22(3): 354–71. Available at https://doi.org/10.1017/eaa.2019.24 (accessed 28 April 2022).

Raczynski-Henk, Y. (2017) *Drawing Lithic Artefacts*. Leiden: Sidestone Press.

Reilly, P. (2020) 'FlintFriday – Silica Alchemy I, II & III (Diffraction Images)'. Available https://www.artarchaeologies.com/featuredwork_reilly (accessed 25 August 2023).

Richstraka (1979) 'Partially Etched Silicon Dioxide via Nomarski DIC.jpg'. Wikipedia Commons. Available at https://doi.org/10.1558/jca.33150 (accessed 28 April 2022).

Siegesmund, R. and Kerry F. (2018) 'Interpreting Visual Information in Research: Tacit Knowledge and Nomadic Inquiry', in Hannes, K., Dierckx de Casterlé, B., Heylighen, A. and Truyen, F. (eds), *European Congress of Qualitative Inquiry Proceedings*. Leuven: NQRL, pp. 34–40.

Simonyan, K. and Zisserman, A. (2015) 'Very Deep Convolutional Networks for Large-Scale Image Recognition', in *International Conference on Learning Representations*. Available at https://arxiv.org/abs/1409.1556 (accessed 14 November 2020).

van Gijn, A. (2010) *Flint in Focus: Lithic Biographies in the Neolithic and Bronze Age*. Leiden: Sidestone Press.

Virilio, P. (1994) *The Vision Machine: Perspectives*, trans. J. Rose. Bloomington: Indiana University Press.

Wang, L., Wang, Z., Yang, X., et al. (2020) 'Photographic Style Transfer', *Visual Computer* 36: 317–31. Available at https://doi.org/10.1007/s00371-018-1609-4 (accessed 28 April 2022).

Zylinska, J. (2017) *Nonhuman Photography*. Cambridge, MA: MIT Press.

Zylinska, J. (2020) *AI Art: Machine Visions and Warped Dreams*. London: Open-humanities Press. Available at http://openhumanitiespress.org/books/titles/ai-art (accessed 28 April 2022).

Zylinska, J. (2021) 'Undigital Photography: Image Making Beyond Computation and AI', in Dvořák, T. and Parikka, J. (eds), *Photography Off the Scale: Technologies and Theories of the Mass Image*. Edinburgh: Edinburgh University Press, pp. 231–52.

13 Hi! I'm happy you're here!

Adham Faramawy

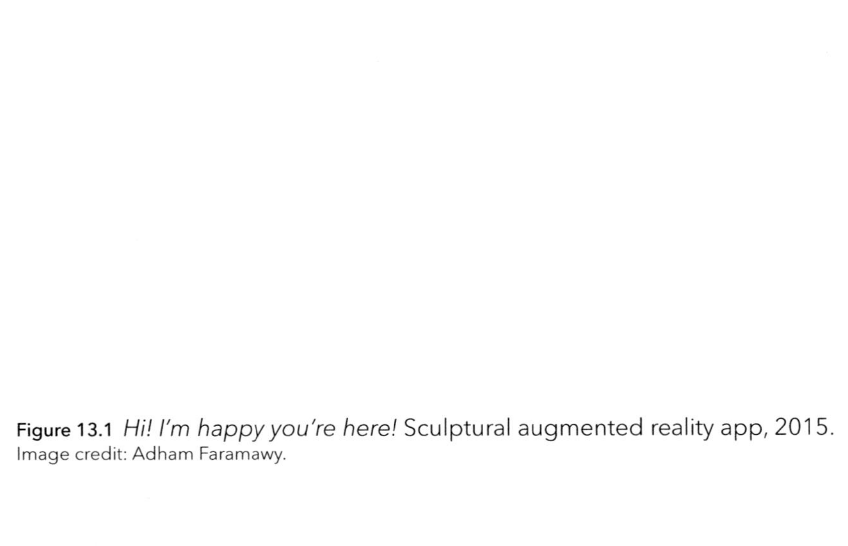

Figure 13.1 *Hi! I'm happy you're here!* Sculptural augmented reality app, 2015.
Image credit: Adham Faramawy.

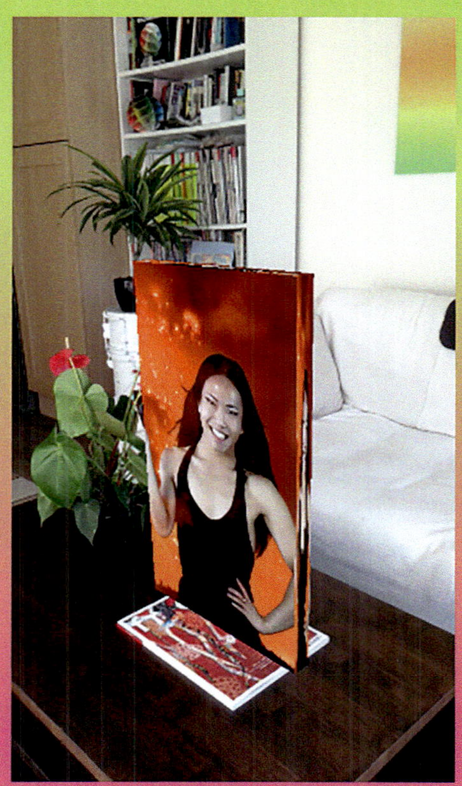

#HiImHappyYoureHere

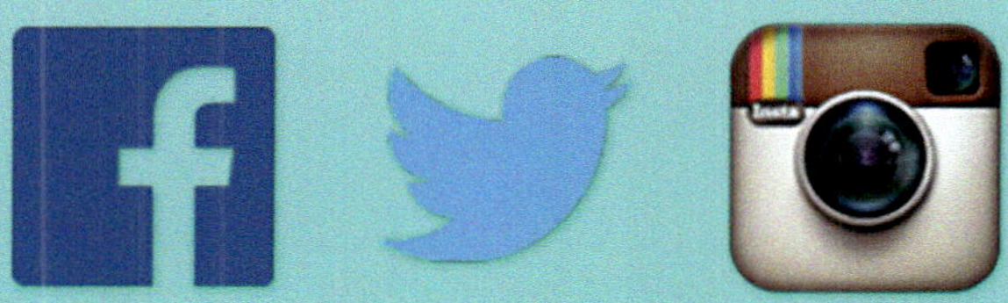

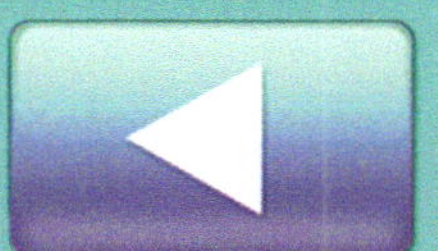

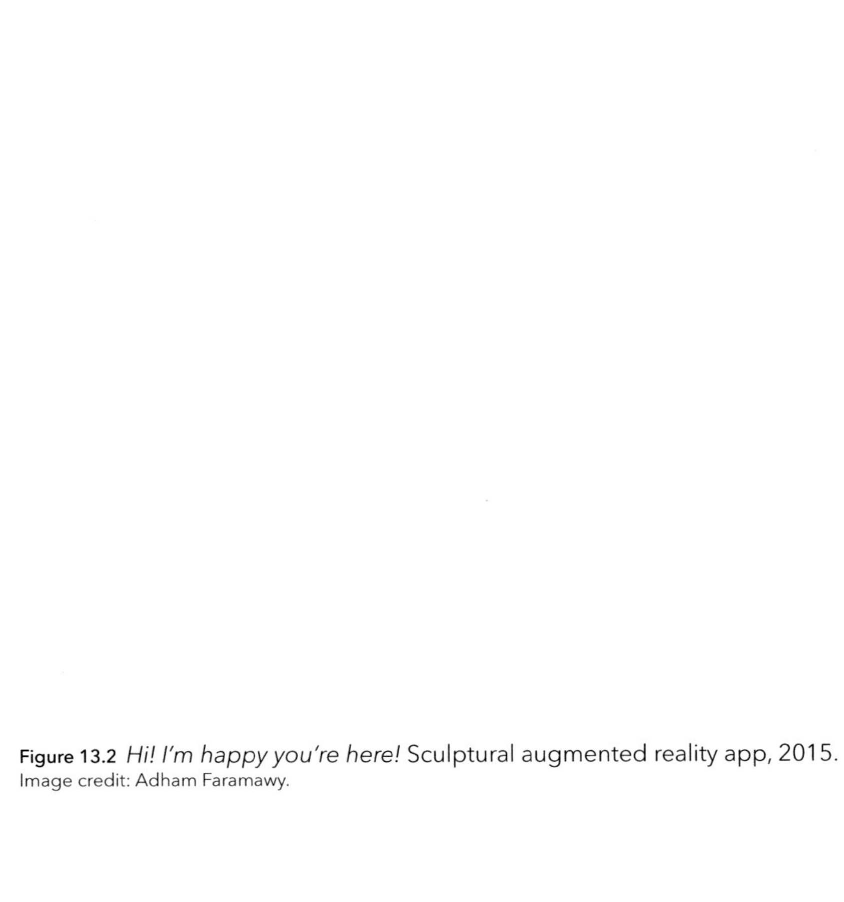

Figure 13.2 *Hi! I'm happy you're here!* Sculptural augmented reality app, 2015.
Image credit: Adham Faramawy.

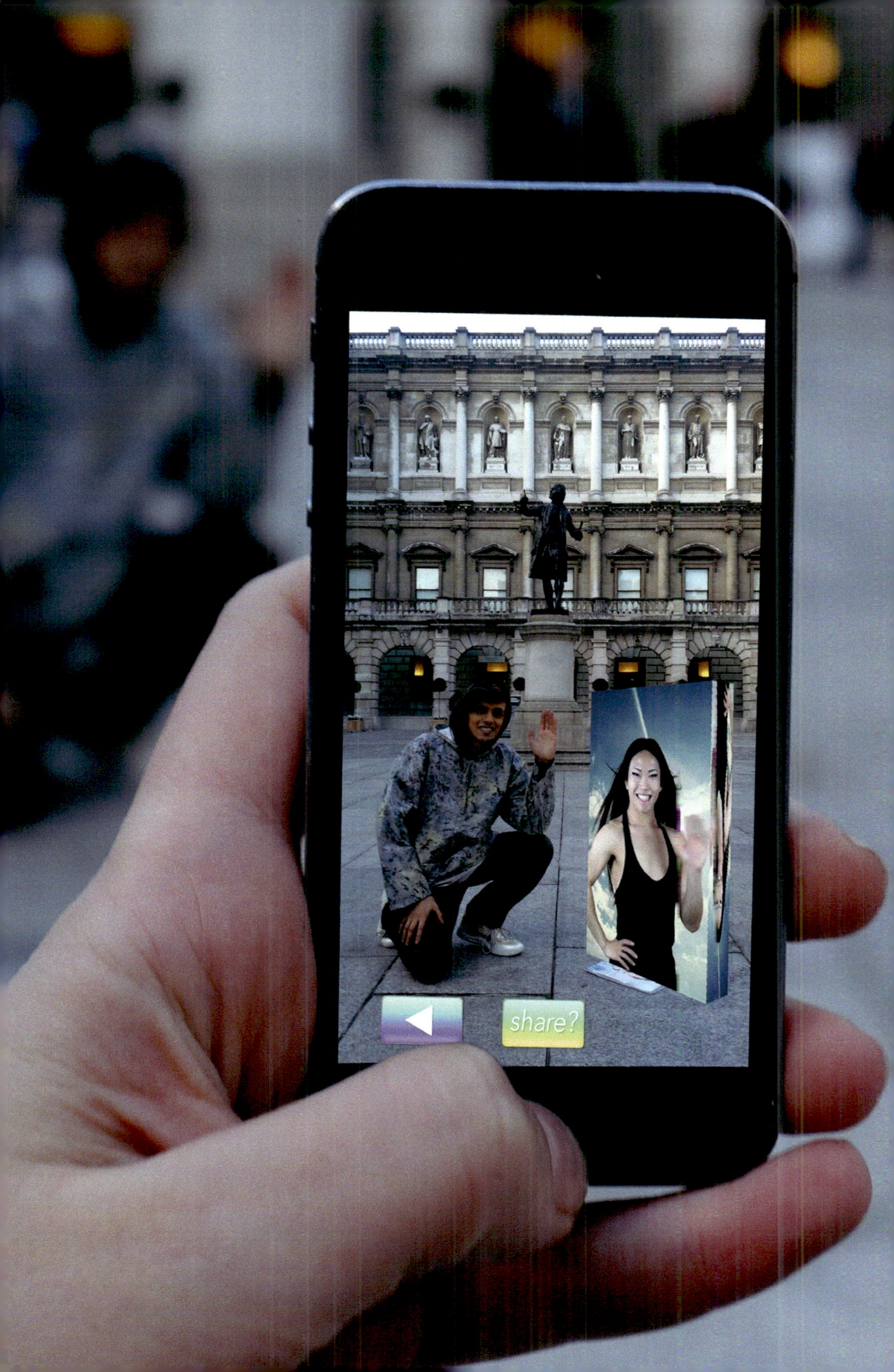

share?

Figure 13.3 *Hi! I'm happy you're here!* Sculptural augmented reality app, 2015. Image credit: Amelia Swan.

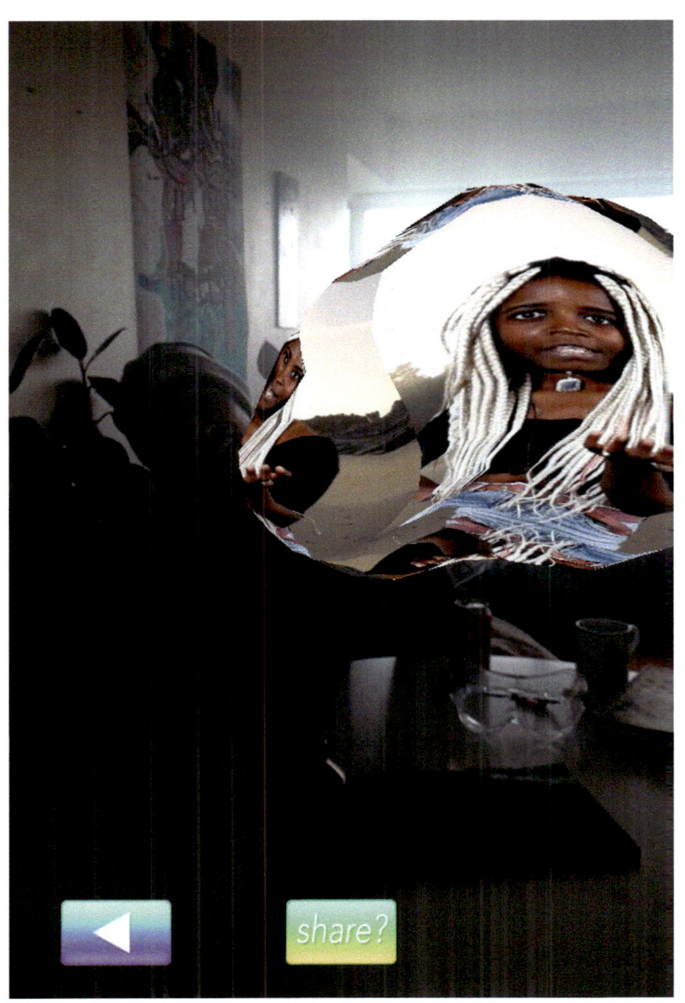

share?

Figure 13.4 *Hi! I'm happy you're here!* Sculptural augmented reality app, 2015.
Image credit: Leah Jennings.

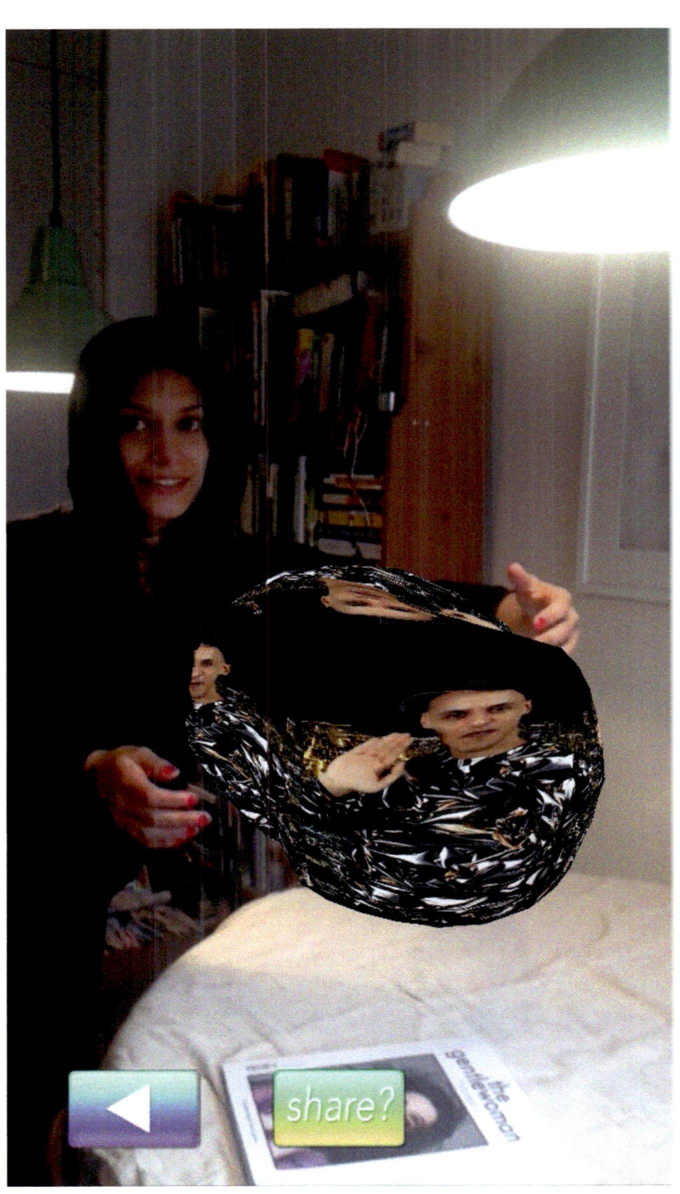

share?
the
gentlewoman

Figure 13.5 *Hi! I'm happy you're here!* Sculptural augmented reality app, 2015.
Image credit: Atiena Riollet.

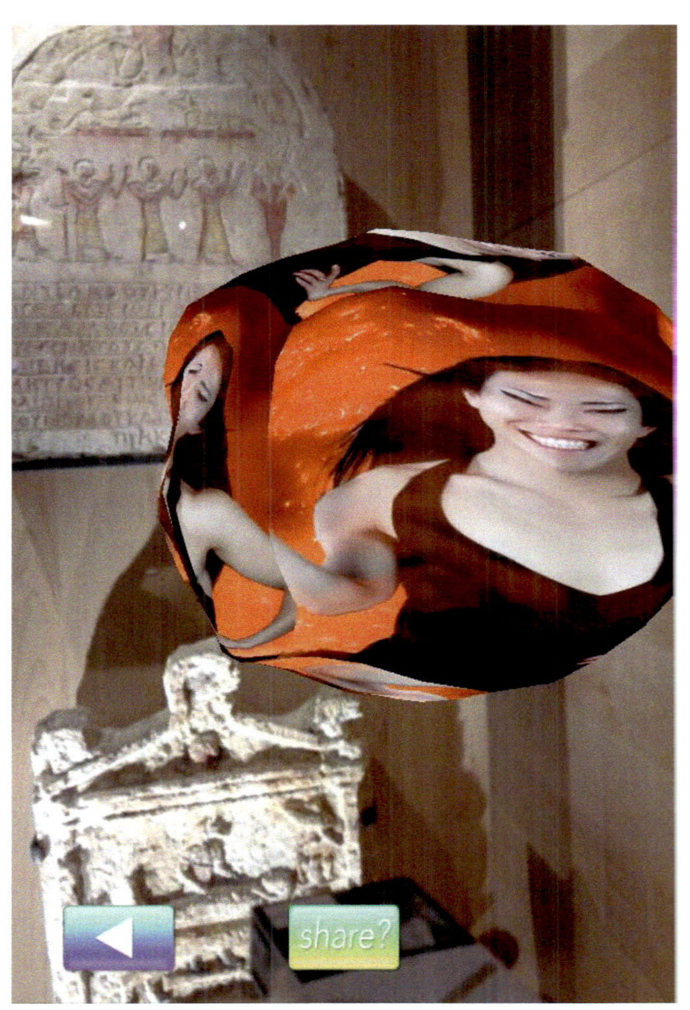
share?

Hi! I'm happy you're here!

Adham Faramawy

Sculptural augmented reality app, 2015
Performers: Le Fil, Laura Mireia and Bayly Shelton

The seed for this work was planted in conversations with my nephews. My family don't live in the UK anymore so for the last maybe ten years we've kept in touch via Skype. When my nephews were toddlers they lived in Sharjah and Dubai; now they live in Cairo. Most of our interaction has been telepresent, and initially they thought of me as a sort of game, an app that talks back and I sometimes, even now, find myself playing up to this; like, when they're talking about *Fortnight* for a bit too long, I might say, 'Okay, cool, hand me back to your mother', and I wondered what this shift in the performance of my embodiment might mean. Since the Covid pandemic this question has become more important for me because of the prevalence of video-streaming technology in my work, social and romantic life. Truly, what does it mean to perform yourself to the camera in these ways?

Hi! I'm happy you're here! was available from 2015 to 2018 on the App Store and Google Play for anyone to download and use for free. Upon opening the app, the user was asked to take a picture of a horizontal image. Once that image had been captured, it asked the user to step back, and an object appeared on the screen. This object was screen-like, and had a moving image embedded in its surface. The app allowed its user to circumnavigate the sculpture, to move about and capture screen-shots that could then be uploaded directly from the app to social media feeds, hashtagged to appear on my website.

I started to question what happens when the site of an embodied experience is located in the interface between the biological body and a device. With augmented reality, it was possible to produce objects that you couldn't touch. I wanted to push my work out of the gallery space and play with art historical etiquettes or protocols around the experience and viewership of sculpture, but also with the possibility of producing an object that can appear anywhere in multiples. I wanted to make a hyper-object that, in being shared as images, left a trace that in a way, co-opted its environment, the device it appears on and the interface with the user-viewer's body as part of the work.

Through the app, users were able to see themselves within multiple iterations of screen-selfies, interacting with objects that did not physically exist. The experience yielded a type of feedback loop, between robotic vision and virtual interfacing, evolving within the virtual screen-space, traversing to the physical and back again. The app drew users' attentions to systems of seeing, dissemination and potential surveillance and control through virtual platforms, asking, 'What might be the future of these kinds of augmented reality technologies, specifically the fallouts for visual perception, truth-telling (or false-truths), and the role of the user's body within the experience?'

I've been experimenting with materials, with movement, touch and the mediation of images. I know what it feels like to perform for the camera, to perform for someone seeing my image on a screen far away, but when I try to speak it, to relay the sensation, the words feel bitter to the tongue. It feels like I can only articulate this feeling of relating to bodies through screens by relating to the screen as a body and this feels like lack, like longing and like something unrequited. I think my relationship as a maker has been defined in relief to the contexts and environments I work within and the forms of complicity that can be produced in the making and the sharing. What does it mean as a person of colour to place my own image in commercial contexts, to, even in stealth, make my work available through the App Store and Google Play? My work exists in and supports problematic systems even in reaching out to find and destabilise their edges.

Every asset within the app, from the way users made the sculpture appear, to the embedded video of performers continually turning, smiling and waving, was meant to highlight their presence in the space as well as the idea that the physical presence of the sculpture was not separate to the viewer's body but rather in the interface between the user/viewer and their device. It was launched before the now widely used Pokémon Go and Snapchat filters made the use of augmented reality ubiquitous, a time when there was public and corporate funding available to produce artworks dealing and experimenting with these kinds of novel technologies.

I think that at the centre of this conversation and of my work more generally are investigations of complicity, anxiety and suspicion, and I wonder if this relates to how we think about vision in relation to nascent technologies. In the advent of new technologies that are broadening the scope of vision, I cannot and do not trust what I see. What kinds of instability are produced when recording and streaming technologies begin to integrate with my biological functions and senses? How do I continue to make meaning?

Hi! I'm happy you're here! was made possible with support by Arts Council England. It was made with technical help from Tom K. Kemp, Alex Chouls and Erin Ko. It was launched at 'Until Recently I Only Had A Voice', an academic symposium at the Royal Academy of Arts in London in 2015. The event was part of the David Lean public lecture series for the Royal Academy Schools and was organised by Adham Faramawy and Cécile B. Evans. The above text was written by Faramawy in response to questions posed by the editors; as the development of the app came out of a personal experience dealing with the disembodying effect of video phone calls, it felt necessary to present this text in the first person.

Farmamwy's practice encompasses moving image and multimedia components and engages with installation and print. Their practice has considered the role of technology and the body, and ways that technology relates to identity. Visual culture and the critical considerations of looking and seeing are also significant to their practice. Farmamwy's work from 2021 onwards considers interpersonal relationships, ideas surrounding maginalisation and cultural belonging.

Afterword.
Concluding Perception: Seeing and Seeming, Unseeing and Unseeming in the Fog

Esther Leslie

Robotic vision has often been our vision. We sometimes find ourselves looking into the eyes of robots – most likely the fictional clichéd ones of cinema and comic books, those ones that glow or shoot rays from themselves. Sooner or later, we will be gazing into the eyes of robots distributed in our daily life: customer service humanoids, bar tenders or border control robots, or the ones who have names (and even citizenship) already, such as Sophia, a social humanoid developed by Hong Kong-based Hanson Robotics, or Vyommitra, made by the Indian Space Research Organisation (ISRO) for the Gaganyaan mission. This involves an unmanned spacecraft, for which this legless humanoid, whose name translates from Sanskrit as Space Friend, can test out such functions as one day a human should undertake: monitor ambient heat radiation, use safety mechanisms and switches, receive and act on commands sent from ground stations, and respond, using bilingual speech. Relatives and descendants of these humanoids will likely populate our environments soon enough and will become familiar to us – their eyes may look like ours or like those of animals. Will we have solved thereby the shamefaced recognition of exploitation of that which serves us? Adorno (1997: p. 113) noted that there 'is nothing so expressive as the eyes of animals – especially apes – which seem objectively to mourn that they are not human'. The 'seem' is important here. It is not animals who mourn the difference, but we who mourn the fact that we are not human or humane enough for them or for each other, for we have it in ourselves to exploit animals, another part, along with us, of nature. Might the gaze into the eyes of robots alleviate this guilt? As Adorno noted to his colleague Max Horkheimer in a letter in 1956: 'Philosophy exists in order to redeem what you see in the look of an animal' (Adorno and Horkheimer 2011: p. 71). No redemption here required. The eyes look, but the gaze is not returned in a moral circuit. No nature has been abused in the making of this robot.

It is likely the case that, to date, few of us have had the experience of looking into the eyes of a robot. However, we have certainly had occasion to see *through* the eyes of robots, putting ourselves in their place, in order to see as they see. We might, for example, sometimes watch the reconstructions of LiDAR vision on little videos designed to bridge worlds of perception between humans and machines. These come in rainbow colours and are overlaid with rings and lines or dots in point clouds. We see diagrams of echolocation and sound waves. In addition to seeing as if a robot, we see the results that stem from machine vision – for example, when we see a reconstruction of the nano-scaled parts of the world – a cell, a single atom. This is assisted vision – not available to our eyes. We see through robotic vision what the world looks like at the scales imperceptible to our eyes when a scanning tunnelling microscope crosses a conducting surface with a sharp metal wire tip and brings into being – through non-optical means – an image of atoms produced by recording the vertical position needed to keep electrical current constant. We can see the pentacene molecule with its atoms and bonds and the blurry, red-orange glow from an array of atoms, captured by an electron microscope pixel array detector that incorporates 3D reconstruction algorithms, as they jiggle under heat. We see as the machine sees – or senses – and it becomes something seen for us and seeable by us.

Cinema has given us versions of how robots see, for example, first of all, in the 1976 film adaptation of Michael Crichton's *Westworld*. In this, the first 2D computer images to be seen on the commercial screen were images of a fugitive perceived as if through the optical systems of a gunslinger android, played by Yul Brynner. Creators John Whitney Jr and Gary Demos of Information International, Inc. turned some film stock, which is to say, something imprinted in clear detail on celluloid, into an imprecise, coarse pixel matrix by colour-separating each frame, scanning it and adding colours. It was then converted into rectangular blocks. Back then, robots, it would appear, in the fantasy of filmmakers, saw a clunky pixel world, with far less detail than ours. Since then, in cinematic confections, their visual systems have evolved or been developed to perceive in more detailed and information-rich ways. Any robot in a contemporary film would likely convey to the viewer perception of a high-resolution reality. It might also include aspects of non-human vision, such as points and lines and additional elements unfamiliar to human vision, including augmented-reality features. It may well also be annexed to various automated operative functions. These robots would see at least as well as the functional seeing systems that are more and more embedded in our world. These include the now well-established vision system products used in medical devices and pharmaceutical manufacturing and the production of cars, packaging, food, drink and electronics. The visual system automatically inspects, error-proofs and controls quality. Such systems are ever developing and a more recent example of an automated visual system is the retrospective facial recognition system adopted for use by the UK Metropolitan Police in October 2021. It scans and annotates historic images from CCTV, social media and other sources and so sees, one might say, into the past.

In earlier days, robotic or machinic visual systems relied on some sort of pre-programmed alertness to what to 'look out for' in a visual environment – based on rules for pattern matching or optical character recognition or the like. LiDAR uses object detection technologies through light and distance measuring. This substitutes for an optical system: light bounces off a surface and the time it takes to return to source is measured in order to map an environment for robots or autonomous vehicles. More sophisticated systems integrate self-developing machine learning and deep learning, whereby a robot can work out for itself what surrounds it and can then share that knowledge with others in its robotic community. Often machines see on our behalf, setting out to complete tasks we have defined quite precisely – we input what is to be perceived; the robot looks, on our command, for things we want or need them to see, detecting anomalies, clocking and logging individuals, reading barcodes, seeing through walls to find leaks. Sometimes, in a different way, we might come to see what it is that they are visualising or bringing into the world of vision, as an aesthetic gambit. It is not that we can see what they see – the visual productions are made for us to see and emerge from some kind of sensing converted into information. What is produced touches on the aesthetic always – all visuality has a philosophy of seeing encoded in it – but sometimes it explicitly engages with the question of what might we speculate about the seeing mechanisms of a robot – and how might it vibrate with our established aesthetic categories. An example would be where we see novel artworks made by artificial intelligence (AI), or, more memorably, the delirious visions of Google Deep Dream, which circulate across the internet as examples of what androids can make of a visual field, after its exposure to virtually all the digitised images that exist in the world. As if self-referentially, what they make of it in their automated seeing is a field of eyes looking back from everywhere.

We might also come to see how the world looks through new eyes that are and are not human, eyes that have started from scratch, such eyes as those that have used the most advanced science to return to the most rudimentary of visual systems. Something new has been occurring in the labs of late. In August 2021, eyes were grown in a laboratory on a fragment of brain tissue (Gabriel et al. 2021). Induced pluripotent stem cells, derived from skin cells and converted back into stem cells, were placed in culture that had all the conditions of an environment of a developing brain. Brain cell organoids – or models – the size of a pea, resulted. These miniature brains were then coaxed to develop basic eye structures, including optic cups, where the optic nerve meets the retina. Eyes grew in quite a large number of the pea-sized brains, in a process that took fifty days. Where it happened, two eyes grew, symmetrically at the front of the tiny brain. These eyes contained a lens and cornea tissue and a range of retinal cell types, and made between themselves neuronal networks that are able to sense light and convey informational signals to other parts of the brain. Eyes can be made, primitive sensory structures, that are now still rudimentary and promise to be of use in medical research into embryo development of congenital retinal disorders. But, of course, there is always an imagined future, into which these developments flow – and it is one in which these eyes become more sophisticated than human eyes.

Along with sight, it would seem, comes insight. And, so the speculators may muse, as they do with the brainwaves equivalent to those in pre-term babies now emanating in other cerebral organoids (Irving 2019), that through this developed capacity for vision, the organoids may develop self-awareness or consciousness. Were a computerised robot to merge with this biological feat, it could become a robot that saw in ways that were more akin to our mode of seeing. Such speculation is not unwarranted. Research is directed nowadays towards entities such as 'xenobots', derived from frog cells, 'a new class of artefact: a living, programmable organism', as the xenobots were described on first appearance in 2020 (Chandler 2020). Biology melds with AI – specifically the Deep Green supercomputer cluster at UVM's Vermont Advanced Computing Core – in order to trial, through simulation of combinations of cells and hundreds of thousands of different environmental conditions, endless possible behaviours. Selected from them, something is brought into being that possesses characteristics of life and can function in specifically desired ways. These might include the capacity, for ten days, to self-transport in linear or circular directions, using embryonic energy stores, in order to deliver drugs in the body, scrape out plaque from arteries or, perhaps, deal with waste or radioactivity in the oceans. These nanobots are programmable, but they also self-organise, including as a swarm, and mend themselves, if damage occurs. The second generation, in 2021 – whose lifespan has extended beyond ten days – grew into spheroids and some of the cells differentiated to produce cilia – these they use as legs to rapidly scuttle over a surface, whereas in the body they would have pushed out pathogens from the lungs and such like. In a frog embryo, cells cooperate to create a tadpole. Here, removed from that context, we see that cells can re-purpose their genetically encoded hardware, like cilia, for new functions such as locomotion. It is amazing that cells can spontaneously take on new roles and create new body plans and behaviours without long periods of evolutionary selection for those features (Tufts University 2021).

Other new capacities that are developed – or built in – include the ability to record, or at least a read/write capability to log a single bit of information, bringing into being 'molecular memory'. This is achieved using fluorescent reporter proteins that change colour under certain exposures. It would apparently not take much at this point to add eyes and a brain. Biological robots are with us, and what will they think when they see us? What sights from their tiny worlds will be communicated back for us? And will we be able to see through their new eyes? And what will their gaze demand of us?

And what will these new visions mean for our old sense and sensing of things? If we see these subvisible aspects of the world, things that are barred to our own vision systems, for whom is robotic vision a capacity? Is it now for us? Or is our seeing just one node in the system of bringing something into the world that only passes through us, but does not end with us? Some have argued that we live within a post-visual culture. For example, in his book 24/7, Jonathan Crary (2013: p. 47) made the case that to 'be preoccupied with the aesthetic properties of digital imagery ... is to evade the subordination of the image to a broad field of non-visual operations and requirements'. Image, that which speaks to vision, is degraded in favour of code, which has no visibility or no meaningful purchase on the realm of the visual. Digital code is invisible and exists only as 'performing' for Boris Groys (2008: p. 84). Alexander Galloway (2011: pp. 239, 244) contends that in the age of technological devices that are opaque, known only as sites of inputs and outputs, the task does not involve 'illuminating the black box by decoding it' but, rather, it is a matter of 'functionalizing the black box by programming it'. From these perspectives, and others, images under digitalised conditions are opaque in ways they have not been before. Once there might have been critical academic discussion of the dislocation between appearance and essence, as perceived, for example, by the dubious shiny surface of, say, the photographic image, in its role as proponent for the status quo and class relations as they exist, or cogent discussion of the manipulating frames of media imagery working to affirm contemporary mythologies. Now the visual systems work in the background and may be directly operative without passing through a human instance of appropriation into ideology: automatic facial recognition systems, assembly-line anomaly detection, or military-grade autonomous drones – lethal autonomous weapons systems (LAWS). The drones pick their own targets and kill autonomously from human input – reports (Kallenborn 2021) suggest that these may have been deployed for the first time in March 2020, in a skirmish in Libya. How might we describe these visioning events? Is the emphasis on how it is that robots 'see' and act? Or would we stress who does not see, and therefore succumbs to some sort of social blindness? Our seeing is not pushed to the fore here. Nor is it elsewhere. In the traditional zones where watching occurs – such as taking in screen-based media content on devices, or people-watching in cafes in the densely surveilled city centres – it is as if the watchers watch as a secondary effect of the primary purpose, which is to be watched. There are, so to say, always three of us in this relationship: subject, object, algorithm. Who is perceiving the world, when computers communicate with computers in the networked sensing of an Internet of Things? What can be seen for us through fog, in the fog of fog computing,[1] on the edges of edge computing, in realms of visuality unfamiliar to us because they are out of the orbit of human seeing, sensing, shaping?

Rather than post-visual, might we say that robotic vision may be provisional. That is to say, what is seen is just what is *seen for now*. This will change, as optical systems change. This involves both the how of seeing and the what of seeing – technically equipped humans see (or get machines to see for them) at ever smaller scales. To this extent, it is not only the case that robots see us, but it is we who become robotised in our seeing. We are programmed to perceive what targets itself at our vision, algorithmically calculated, optimised for vision, operationalised objects, such as Google Earth or Maps, people through filters and against backdrops, archives and scientific models colourised, AR and VR headsets, while our affective

---

1   The term 'fog computing' is often associated with the San Francisco-based company Cisco. It refers to a decentralised – close to the ground – computing infrastructure that takes advantage of the proliferation of computing devices. Data, computing, storage and applications are situated somewhere between the data source and the cloud. It promises improvements in efficiency as well as enhanced security and compliance. It is associated with the Internet of Things.

selves fall for people who, despite all appearances to the contrary, simply do not exist, as on the website This Person Does Not Exist (thispersondoesnotexist.com). Those figures are made by generative adversary networks, usually for malevolent purposes, such as making fake social media user profiles, in order to carry out catfishing and other social media-based crimes. These never-before-existing faces are generated out of an averaging of the characteristics of all the faces the network has ever been exposed to – or trained on – and then another neural network decides how plausible the face appears to be. The process bats back and forth between networks until it is deemed finished, which is to say, realistic enough to hoodwink a viewer.

We mere mortals are, apparently, conned by deepfakes. The fantasy is that robotic seeing will see so much more perfectly, objectively, capably than us fallible humans – and yet, events show us again and again that there is nothing easier to fool than a robot's vision, at the moment. At least, nothing is currently easier to fool than that vision system developed by Google in 2011, based on DNN classification systems and which began with the capacity to recognise cats in YouTube videos. From 2013 it was known that through the alteration of a few pixels, producing a doctored image known as an 'adversarial example', the AI could be fooled into thinking it observed something else. A self-driving vehicle races across an intersection because some plastic patches on a sign had fooled it into reading STOP as Speed Limit 45; a facial recognition system is thrown off by patterns on glasses or hats. Adversarial examples become adversarial attacks. The AI system known as CLIP can be thrown off by using words – an apple labelled as a pizza will be 'seen' as a pizza, because text was part of the training package. And then there are the inbuilt biases of various systems that make them see some things and not others – such as skin colour. Or that mean the neurons associated anything to do with the Middle East with terrorism or other inherited assumptions (Nkonde 2019). Plenty of the infinitely generatable faces on the Thispersondoesnotexist website have at their edges ghosted hands or indecipherable lumps of something fleshy looking or mismatched earrings – because the generative adversarial network (GAN) was just enough convinced by the assembled face object to let it pass. There is a subtler sign that these figures do not exist. Researchers from the State University of New York at Albany, the State University of New York at Buffalo and Keya Medical have noticed that images of faces produced using GANs tend to create pupils that are irregular, which is to say they are not as round as those in a human eye. It may be pleasing that the visual error is to be found in the visual system of the faked individual. Of course, once the error is perceived, some software tweak will come along to remediate it and so the game of deception continues (Guo et al. 2021).

It extends too, in ever more novel ways. In 2021, thispersondoesnotexist was joined by thiscatdoesnotexist. The historic entanglement of cats and the internet found a new articulation. At each refresh of the page, a new GAN-generated cat appears. More of these seem less convincing than the humans. The shapes of their heads seem off, disproportioned in some way, and their bodies dissolve oddly into fuzzy backgrounds, the fur blurry at the edges. The ears are often oversized, giving the cats a fox-like or owlish appearance. But the eyes always stare out – with their pupils ranging from slits to wide black holes. What does it mean to stare into these non-seeing eyes?

In this context, what does it mean to develop a critical image theory, when the image itself appears to have an altered ontology, or none at all? What frames this new imagery? Are we, as viewers, as seers, outside the frame that appears before us, or are we, instead, inside, within a seeming boundlessness of seeing, which is generated on the fly through the necessities of whatever world is being built before our eyes? The world created on the fly is something like the self-assembling world of open-world territories in gaming that appear as and when needed or once they are earnt – in combination with whatever processing power is available at the time. Have there ever been more conditions on what can be seen and by whom and when? And has there ever been so strong a focus on the optical, albeit one that is now accompanied in all regards by tactility, by the haptic? Walter Benjamin long ago spoke of a passage from the optical age to the tactile one. Film with its immersion within an architecture of cinema, photography with its proximity to the viewer (sometimes hand-held) are seen to supplement or replace an optical experience with a tactile one. Our image systems now, too, view in a tactile fashion, as a sensing mechanism feels images into being as it scans. Or these image systems see, automatically, and refer what has been seen to a database through which they rifle, just as an investigator rummages through files in a filing cabinet. Tactility, or the haptic, is a desirable condition in gaming, as the success of game systems such as Sony's PlayStation 5 testifies. Seeing is supplemented by haptic feedback, or, in other words, perception is also a type of feeling. In the haptic-enhanced version of Hideo Kojima's *Death Stranding*, every stone underfoot is sensed as a pressure, as the avatar crosses the landscape – that is to say, is felt on the hand which holds the vibrating controller, but also in some way, on the foot or body in general too, as part of an immersive experience. In *Returnal* the haptic feedback is part of the gameplay mechanics, allowing orientation – and so directing vision – in a 3D landscape, through buzzes deployed on different parts of the controller. We see and we feel. We feel as we see. Like robot vision, perhaps.

Tactility is a supplement to sight under real-world conditions when conditions of visibility are poor. We feel our way through the city when it is foggy. At this point, we replicate robotic 'seeing'. Our automatic detection systems for driving or parking feel their way through the city when it is clear and foggy. Now the city is always foggy – though not necessarily as a fog that can be perceived, though that too when the smog arrives, as it does ever more frequently in some parts of the world. The city is foggy, because it is tangled up by the sensing lines and communication networks of fog computing for the deployment of the Internet of Things. Fog computing is closer to the ground than the cloud and so it analyses the most time-sensitive data quickly, close to the source, making actions on the basis of what has been sensed occur rapidly – while it sifts data to send to the cloud for longer-term storage and further analysis. From this perspective, perhaps it is possible to say, also and in contradiction, that there is *only* critical image analysis – just that it is not always performed by humans. The robots are critics of the image – analysing, sifting, interpreting, classifying, ontologising. And should we wish to perform critical image analysis ourselves, in order to understand an image, we would have to penetrate the fog and find out where, when and by whom for what it came into being and what its production was tasked to do.

References

Adorno, T. W. (1997) *Aesthetic Theory*. Ed. G. Adorno. and R. Tiedemann trans. R. Hullot Kentor. London: Continuum.

Adorno, T. W. and Horkheimer, M. (2011) *Towards a New Manifesto*. Trans. R. Livingstone. London: Verso.

Chandler, S. (2020) *World's First Living Robot Invites New Opportunities and Risks*. Available at https://www.forbes.com/sites/simonchandler/2020/01/14/worlds-first-living- robot-invites-new-opportunities-and-risks/#379ef46c3caf (accessed 7 October 2021).

Crary, J. (2013) *24/7: Late Capitalism and the Ends of Sleep*. London: Verso.

Gabriel, E., et al. (2021) 'Human Brain Organoids Assemble Functionally Integrated Bilateral Optic Vesicles', *Cell Stem Cell*. Available at https://doi.org/10.1016/j.stem.2021.07.010 (accessed 18 October 2021).

Galloway, A. R. (2011) 'Black Box, Black Bloc', in Noys, B. (ed.), *Communization and Its Discontents: Contestation, Critique, and Contemporary Struggle*. Wiverhoe: Minor Compositions.

Groys, B. (2008) *Art Power*. Cambridge, MA: MIT Press.

Guo, H., Shu, H., Wang, X., Chang, M. and Lyu, S. (2021) 'Eyes Tell All: Irregular Pupil Shapes Reveal GAN-generated Faces'. Available at arxiv.org/abs/2109.00162 (accessed 18 October 2021).

Irving, M. (2019) 'Brain Waves Similar to Preterm Babies Detected in Lab-Grown Mini-brains'. Available at https://newatlas.com/biology/lab-grown-mini-brains-brainwaves-preterm-babies (accessed 7 October 2021).
Kallenborn, Z. (2021) 'Was a Flying Killer Robot Used in Libya? Quite Possibly'. Available at https://thebulletin.org/2021/05/was-a-flying-killer-robot-used-in-libya-quite-possibly (accessed 18 October 2021).
Nkonde, M. (2019) 'Automated Anti-Blackness: Facial Recognition in Brooklyn, New York', *Kennedy School Review* 20: 30–6.
Tufts University (2021) 'Scientists Create Next Gen Living Robots'. Available at https://www.sciencedaily.com/releases/2021/03/210331143050.htm (accessed 7 October 2021).

Index

workforce automation, 12, 29
Wozniak-O'Connor, V., 42, 43–4

xenobots, 326

Yingst, R.A., 188
You Will Obey (Mitton), 30–1

Zawieska, K., 36
Zlatev, J., 146, 148
Złotowski, J., 37, 42
zoomorphism, 42
Zuboff, S., 77
Zylinska, J., 5, 7, 269, 283, 303